Req 1303

£1 99

# Film Review
## 2001-2002

**James Cameron-Wilson** became a committed film buff when he moved to London at the age of 17. After a stint at the Webber Douglas Academy of Dramatic Art he joined *What's On In London* and took over from F Maurice Speed as cinema editor. Later, he edited the trade newspaper *Showbiz*, was commissioning editor for *Film Review*, was consultant for *The Movie Show* on BSkyB and a frequent presenter on the Radio 2 *Arts Programme*.

He is also author of the books *Hollywood: The New Generation*, *Young Hollywood*, *The Cinema of Robert De Niro* and *The Moviegoer's Quiz Book*. His film reviews are currently syndicated in *247* and the *What's On* magazines distributed in Birmingham, Manchester and Liverpool, and he has a regular column in *Film Review*, Britain's longest-running film magazine.

He has also reviewed for the BBC and Talk Radio and has written frequently for *The Times*, as well as contributing to *The Sunday Times*, *The Guardian* and *The Daily Telegraph*. On television he made over 100 appearances on *The Movie Show* both as critic and quiz master and has regularly popped up on CNN, Channel One and BBC Worldwide Television and was Britain's resident 'dial-a-film critic' for two years.

Besides the cinema, James Cameron-Wilson's academic interests include Cambodian wildlife, the mathematics of CD-ROMs and cellular reproduction, while his personal interests include his wife, ten-year-old daughter, dinner parties and reading.

Includes video releases and websites

# Film Review 2001-2002

JAMES CAMERON-WILSON

*Founding father: F. Maurice Speed*
*1911-1998*

Reynolds & Hearn Ltd
London

TO SCOT, FOR ALL YOUR INSPIRATION AND
ENCOURAGEMENT – AND THE BOOK-ENDS

# Acknowledgements

The author would like to proclaim his infinite gratitude
to the following,without whom this book would not
have been possible: David Aldridge,Charles Bacon,
Halle Berry, Ewen Brownrigg, Juliet Cameron-
Wilson, Ian Crane, Tim Dry, Pauline Dunham, Joel
Finler, Lizzie Frith, Marianne Gray, Marcus Hearn,
Adam Keen, Wendy Lloyd, Phil Matcham, Nigel
Mulock, Jonathan Rigby, Adrian Rigelsford, Scot
Woodward Myers, my mother, Daniel O'Brien,
Frances Palmer, Virginia Palmer, Sue Porter, Richard
Reynolds, Simon Rose, Mansel Stimpson and David
Nicholas Wilkinson. Till next year...

*Founding father:*
*F. Maurice Speed, 1911-1998*

First published in 2001 by
Reynolds & Hearn Ltd
61a Priory Road
Kew Gardens
Richmond
Surrey TW9 3DH

© 2001 James Cameron-Wilson

A CIP catalogue record for this book is available from the
British Library.

ISBN 1 903111 25 0

Designed by Paul Chamberlain.

Printed and bound in Great Britain by MPG Books Ltd,
Bodmin, Cornwall.

# Contents

**Right:** Audrey Tautou displays her life-enhancing charms in Jean-Pierre Jeunet's witty and inventive Amélie

# Introduction

The heart despairs. As Hollywood processed more generic swill than at any other time, so films like *The Mummy Returns*, *Lara Croft: Tomb Raider*, *Dr Dolittle 2* and *Scary Movie 2* reaped the commercial benefits. Anything remotely intelligent or different, such as *Almost Famous*, *Boiler Room*, *Memento*, *Nurse Betty*, *Wonder Boys* or *You Can Count on Me* was left in the marketing dust.

To judge by the last 12 months, what appealed to audiences most was hype, noise, digital effects and bodily functions. Even *Shrek*, a picture that managed to appeal to both audiences *and* critics, had all four staples by the bucketload. The hype, spearheaded by posters featuring the names of the voice artists in giant letters, started early in the year. The noise — produced by fire-breathing dragons, Lord Farquaad s guards and the like — was also present and accounted for. The computer animation, with its deep perspective and lifelike textures, was another huge leap in the field. And the bodily functions — an instant candle plucked straight from the ogre s auditory canal, not to mention the now mandatory flatulence — were also in

evidence. Still, it was all presented with considerable flair and subversive wit and appealed to both schoolchildren and opponents of the Disney monopoly. Indeed, the film s unforeseen prosperity — it is the second-highest grossing cartoon in history (after *The Lion King*) — elicited smug satisfaction within the industry, particularly at the expense of the Mouse House.

Still, there were exceptions to the box-office rule, the most surprising of which was the success of *Crouching Tiger, Hidden Dragon*. A co-production between the US, Taiwan and Hong Kong, the film was shot in Mandarin, was directed by the Taiwanese Ang Lee and starred the Hong Kong-born Chow Yun-Fat and Malaysian Michelle Yeoh. Movies with subtitles have never done well outside the large metropolitan areas of the US, yet *Crouching Tiger* bucked the trend. With its gravity-defying stunts and critical endorsement, it broke out of the elitist paddock of the foreign art-house and, aided by word-of-mouth, seeped into the multiplexes of the American heartland.

By the time the film had crawled its way up the box-office charts (when other titles were falling by the way-

side), *Crouching Tiger* was showing on 2,027 screens across the US. By July 2001 it had grossed a phenomenal $128 million in North America and over $210 million worldwide. While the secret of the film s success was the treatment of a popular genre with exemplary production values and creditable acting — thus serving the needs of both buff and critic — it is still remarkable that a subtitled film should do so well. As the English-American tongue continues to become the global lan-

guage of necessity, particularly with the spread of the internet, foreign cultures are losing out.

The irony is that any foreign film strong enough to break into either the British or US market has to be damned good by definition. Even so, the public at large seems little interested. Gone is the time when it was fashionable to catch the latest Bergman, Fellini or Truffaut, while today s most accomplished foreign filmmakers (think Lasse Hallstr m, Ang Lee and John

Woo) seem all too easily seduced by working in Hollywood.

So let me end on a note of optimism. After the success of *Delicatessen* and *The City of Lost Children*, Jean-Pierre Jeunet was lured to Tinseltown to direct *Alien Resurrection*. It took him almost five years to recover from the creative burn-out of that experience before returning to his native France to produce his best film to date. It s called *Am lie* and has more originality in any five minutes of its running time

than most mainstream films can boast in two hours. *Am lie* was an enormous success in France and let s hope that, by the time you read this, half the people who saw *Crouching Tiger* will have enjoyed its unique, life-enhancing charms. Contrary to popular opinion, foreign cinema has more to offer than jujitsu and chain sticks. It s a whole world out there.

**James Cameron-Wilson**
July 2001

*Right: Renée Zellweger (aka Mrs George Clooney) celebrates the box-office success of the UK's top movie,* Bridget Jones's Diary

***Below, clockwise from top left:***
Hannibal, *Bryan Singer directs* X-Men, Pearl Harbor, Snatch

# Top 20 UK Box-Office Hits

## July 2000 – June 2001

1. Bridget Jones's Diary
2. Gladiator
3. Chicken Run
4. The Mummy Returns
5. Hannibal
6. Shrek
7. Stuart Little
8. Mission: Impossible 2
9. Billy Elliot
10. What Women Want
11. X-Men
12. Meet the Parents
13. The Grinch
14. Cast Away
15. Dinosaur
16. What Lies Beneath
17. Charlie's Angels
18. Pearl Harbor
19. Snatch
20. Unbreakable

2. Brendan Fraser
3. Russell Crowe
4. Tom Cruise
5. Mel Gibson
6. Anthony Hopkins
7. Nicolas Cage
8. Tom Hanks
9. Robert De Niro
10. Jim Carrey

# Top 10 Box-Office Stars
## Star of the Year: Hugh Grant

Jumping to top position from fourth place last year, Hugh Grant continues to prove that his name really does mean something at the UK box-office. Of course, it helps that he keeps choosing scripts penned by Richard Curtis (*Four Weddings*, *Notting Hill*, *Bridget Jones*), but his good looks, self-effacing charm and high public profile also contribute to the must-see frenzy surrounding his films. Brendan Fraser continues to ride high on the success of the *Mummy* films, bringing a Harrison Ford-lite bravado to the screen, while Russell Crowe makes his first appearance on the chart thanks to *Gladiator* and *Proof of Life*. Meanwhile, Tom Cruise, Mel Gibson and Tom Hanks prove that they can do no wrong at the box-office, regardless of what subject they tackle. Few stars today – or at any other time, for that matter – can whip up a $425 million worldwide gross for a movie about a man stranded on a deserted island. Runners-up this year include Harrison Ford, Michelle Pfeiffer, Bruce Willis, Angelina Jolie, Cameron Diaz, Brad Pitt, Ben Affleck, George Clooney and Sandra Bullock.

# Releases of the Year

This section contains details of all the films released in Great Britain from 1 July 2000 to the end of June 2001 – the period covered by all the reference features in this book.

Leading actors are generally credited with the roles they played, followed by a summary of supporting players. Where an actor further down a cast list is of special interest then his/her role is generally credited as well.

For technical credits the normal abbreviations operate, and are as follows: Dir – for Director; Pro – for Producer; Ex Pro – for Executive Producer; Co-Pro – for Co-Producer; Assoc Pro – for Associate Producer; Line Pro – for Line Producer; Ph – for Cinematographer; Ed – for Editor; Pro Des – for Production Designer; and M – for composer.

Abbreviations for the names of film companies are also obvious when used, such as Fox for Twentieth Century Fox, and UIP for Universal International Pictures. The production company (or companies) is given first, the distribution company last.

Information at the foot of each entry is presented in the following order: running time/country of origin/year of production/date of British release/British certification.

*All films reviewed by James Cameron-Wilson unless otherwise specified.Additional contributors: Charles Bacon, Ewen Brownrigg, Tim Dry, Marianne Gray, Adam Keen, Wendy Lloyd, Scot Woodward Myers, Simon Rose and Mansel Stimpson*

## Star ratings
★★★★★ **Wonderful**
★★★★ **Very good**
★★★ **Good**
★★ **Mediocre**
★ **Insulting**

Ⓐ

## Abendland – Nightfall
★★★★★
Grossly underestimated, Fred Kelemen's portrayal of a dark night of the soul is a film for anyone who believes in cinema as a serious art form. Despite echoes of Tarkovsky and Godard, he creates his own despairing world in this story of a loving couple with conflicting views: he, unemployed, believes that he must leave her because he can only bring her down, while she is certain that their love alone can transform a world of squalor and misery. Kelemen combats what may well be his own pessimism by creating great art: haunting images, marvellous use of sound including songs, a compassion that makes you want to turn the brilliantly open ending into a positive one. The unnamed city setting is symbolic, giving universal relevance to the question we ultimately ask ourselves: will awareness of the greater horrors around them (loneliness, prostitution, child pornography) add to their defeatism, or help the man to reconsider and to embrace, if not too late, the love which is the only hope for both of them? [*Mansel Stimpson*]

● *Leni* Verena Jasch, *Anton* Wolfgang Michael, *the bell founder* Adolfo Assor, *Nina* Isa Hochgerner, *Paul* Urs Remond, *man in leather coat* Thomas Baumann, *with* Daniela Roquie-Magalhães, Rainer Kirchmann.
● *Dir, Screenplay* and *Ph* Fred Kelemen, *Pro* Alexander Ris, *Ex Pro* Jörg Rothe, *Pro Des* Ralf Küfner and Anette Kuhn, *Ed* Fred Kelemen, Anja Neraal and Nicola Undritz-Cope, *M* Rainer Kirchmann, *Costumes* Daniella Petrovics and Melanie Kutzke.

Mediopolis Berlin/Filmes do Tejo, Lisbon/WDR-Artificial Eye.
140 mins. Germany. 1999. Rel: 29 September 2000. Cert 18.

## About Adam ★½
Dublin; the present. Bored with the familiar male faces that attend the club where she sings, serial dater Lucy Owens is struck by the timidity of a handsome stranger, Adam. Asking him out on a date, Lucy is quickly won over by Adam's romantic gestures and, for the first time, feels the pangs of real love. However, Adam seems to have just as much in common with the rest of Lucy's family... Intended as a 'serious' romantic comedy with an urban edge and an amoral stance, *About Adam* is neither very funny nor thought-provoking. Being a lazy take on *Rashomon* with a dash of *Entertaining Mr Sloane*, the film's comic scenes verge on the silly (the normally poised Frances O'Connor overacts outrageously), while the conceit of Adam as an enigmatic seducer is both unexplored and unresolved. Ultimately, it is the viewer who is manipulated, but with no dramatic payoff it is an empty ride.

● *Adam* Stuart Townsend, *Laura Owens* Frances O'Connor, *Alice Owens* Charlotte Bradley, *Lucy Owens* Kate Hudson, *Peggy Owens* Rosaleen Linehan, *David Owens* Alan Maher, *Simon* Tommy Tiernan, *Martin* Brendan Dempsey, *Karen* Cathleen Bradley, *Professor McCormick* Roger Gregg.
● *Dir* and *Screenplay* Gerard Stembridge, *Pro* Anna Devlin and Marina Hughes, *Ex Pro* Harvey Weinstein, David M Thompson, David Aukin, Trea Leventhal and Rod Stoneman, *Line Pro* Mary Alleguen, *Ph* Bruno de Keyser, *Pro Des* Fiona Daly,

*Ed* Mary Finlay, *M* Adrian Johnston; songs performed by Kate Hudson, Rosaleen Linehan, The Fun Lovin' Criminals, Astrud Gilberto, and Peggy Lee, *Costumes* Eimear Ni Mhaoldomhnaigh.

Miramax HAL Films/BBC Films/Bord Scannán/Irish Film Board/Venus Prods-Metrodome.
97 mins. Ireland/UK/USA. 2000. Rel: 30 March 2001. Cert 15.

## The Adventures of Rocky and Bullwinkle ★¹/₂

Resigned to obscurity and re-runs, Rocky the flying squirrel and the dim-witted moose Bullwinkle find themselves back in demand when their arch enemies Boris Badenov and Natasha cross over into the 'real' world. When Boris and Natasha's Fearless Leader resolves to take over the US by submitting its populace to mind-numbing television, FBI agent Karen Sympathy must find a way to make Rocky and Bullwinkle three-dimensional... Dragging beloved icons of an earlier era into the cynicism of contemporary times – à la *The Brady Bunch Movie* and *Austin Powers* – is not only calculating but vaguely sinister. While there's some fun to be had at the expense of our own culture as viewed through more innocent eyes, it's now an old device done to death. And no amount of allusions to *Roger Rabbit* and Robert De Niro (Fearless Leader: 'Are you talkin' to me?'), silly sound effects and obscure in-jokes can disguise the ineptitude of this celebrity gruel which, in its attempt to appeal to both children and adults, entertains neither. FYI: Rocky and Bullwinkle first appeared in the ABCTV cartoon *Rocky and His Friends* on 19 November 1959. Then, in 1988, they appeared in the full-length, live-action feature *Boris and Natasha: The Movie.*

● *Natasha Fatale* Rene Russo, *Boris Badenov* Jason Alexander, *'Cappy' Von Trappment* Randy Quaid, *Martin* Kel Mitchell, *Lewis* Kenan Thompson, *Karen Sympathy* Piper Perabo, *Fearless Leader* Robert De Niro, *voice of Rocket J Squirrel* June Foray, *voice of Bullwinkle J Moose/narrator* Keith Scott, *President Signoff* James Rebhorn, *Judge Cameo* Whoopi Goldberg, *Minnie Mogul* Janeane Garofalo, *with* John Goodman, Billy Crystal, Carl Reiner, David Alan Grier, Johnathan Winters, Jon Polito, Norman Lloyd, Rod Biermann, Phil Proctor, Drena De Niro, Julia McAnuff, Steve Rankin.
● *Dir* Des McAnuff, *Pro* Jane Rosenthal and Robert De Niro, *Ex Pro* Tiffany Ward and David Nicksay, *Screenplay* Kenneth Lonergan, based on characters created by Jay Ward, *Ph* Mark Mothersbaugh, *Pro Des* Thomas Ackerman, *Ed* Gavin Bocquet, *M* Marlene Stewart, *Costumes* Dennis Virkler, *Animation* David Andrews.

Universal/Capella/KC Medien/Tribeca-Momentum Pictures.
92 mins. USA/Germany. 2000. Rel: 9 February 2001. Cert U.

## All the Pretty Horses ★★★

Texas/Mexico; 1949. When his mother sells off the family ranch, horse wrangler John Grady Cole decides to head for Mexico with his best friend, Lacey Rawlins, in order to live the life that he was born to... Like *Dancing With Wolves*, this is a big-sky, big-canvas movie and producer-director Billy Bob Thornton was right to bring it in at three hours-plus. Working from a deeply textured screenplay by Ted Tally, adapted from the National Book Award-winning novel by Cormac McCarthy, Thornton beautifully evokes the childhood friendship of John Grady and Lacey Rawlins, the atmosphere of post-war Texas and what it was like to live under the stars with just a horse for company. So where has the movie gone wrong? Don't blame Thornton, blame Miramax co-chairman Harvey Weinstein, who reportedly insisted that the director prune the movie down to its current running time of 117 minutes. The result is that, after we have settled in the saddle of John Grady's lyrical sojourn in Mexico, the film suddenly bolts off into miniseries territory, with the hurried courtship of John Grady and Alejandra reduced to a couple of moonlit clinches. We suddenly don't care what happens next – and a lot does happen, very suddenly. Wait for the Director's Cut; it might just be a masterpiece. FYI: The role of John Grady Cole was originally offered to Leonardo DiCaprio.

● *John Grady Cole* Matt Damon, *Lacey Rawlins* Henry Thomas, *Jimmy Blevins* Lucas Black, *Alejandra* Penélope Cruz, *Rocha* Ruben Blades, *Cole* Robert Patrick, *Judge* Bruce Dern, *J C Franklin* Sam Shepard, *Captain* Julio Oscar Mechoso, *Dona Alfonsa* Miriam Colon, *with* Angelina Torres, Elizabeth Ibarra, Lonnie Rodriguez, Daniel Lanois, Denes Lujan, Edwin Figueroa, Matthew E Montoya, Marc Miles.
● *Dir* Billy Bob Thornton, *Pro* Thornton and Robert Salerno, *Ex Pro* Sally Menke and Jonathan Gordon, *Co-Pro* Bruce Heller, *Screenplay* Ted Tally, *Ph* Barry Markowitz, *Pro Des* Clark Hunter, *Ed* Sally Menke, *M* Marty Stuart, Kristin Wilkinson and Larry Paxton, *Costumes* Doug Hall, *Sound* Stephen Hunter Flick and Peter A. Brown, *Stunts* Buddy Van Horn.

Miramax/Columbia-Columbia TriStar.
117 mins. USA. 2000. Rel: 25 May 2001. Cert 15.

## Almost Famous ★★★★¹/₂

San Diego/New York City; 1969-1973. Brought up by an unconventionally strict mother, 11-year-old William Miller only discovers rock music when his sister bequeaths her record collection to him just as she escapes the domestic fold. Enthralled by the new sound, Miller starts writing perceptive rock articles for a minor magazine called *Cream*. He is then hired by *Rolling Stone* to cover the national tour of Stillwater, an up-and-coming band. He is still only 15 and his mother is horrified, but it's the chance of a lifetime... An acutely observed, elegantly crafted and warmly affectionate valentine to the golden era of rock (The Stones, The Who, Led Zeppelin), *Almost Famous* is a movie for grown-ups who remember the excitement of buying their first Bob Dylan album. But, equally, it is about the glamour of drugs, sex, casual friendships and the whole seduction of the celebrity machine. Indeed, what Cameron Crowe's last film, *Jerry Maguire*, did for the victory of true love over greed ('Show me the money!', 'You complete me'), *Almost Famous* does for the triumph of integrity over exploitation. With extraordinarily charismatic performances from an exceptional cast (Crudup, McDormand, Hudson, Lee, Hoffman), a fabulous soundtrack (see credits) and wonderful dialogue, this is one for the archives. FYI: The part of Russell Hammond was written for Brad Pitt, but the actor backed off when he failed to click with the character.

● *Russell Hammond* Billy Crudup, *Elaine Miller* Frances McDormand, *Penny Lane/Lady Goodman* Kate Hudson, *Jeff Bebe* Jason Lee, *William Miller* Patrick Fugit, *Polexia Aphrodisia* Anna Paquin, *Sapphire* Fairuza Balk, *Dick Roswell* Noah Taylor, *Lester Bangs* Philip Seymour Hoffman, *Anita Miller* Zooey Deschanel, *young William Miller* Michael Angarano, *Ed Vallencourt* John Fedevich, *Leslie* Liz Stauber, *Jann Wenner* Eion Bailey, *Ben Fong-Torres* Terry Chen, Mark Kozelek, Olivia Rosewood, Jimmy Fallon, Bijou Phillips, Alice Marie Crowe, J J Cohen, Mark Pellington, Erin Foley, Peter Frampton, John Patrick Amedori, Nicole Spector.
● *Dir* and *Screenplay* Cameron Crowe, *Pro* Crowe and Ian Bryce, *Co-Pro* Lisa Stewart, *Ph* John Toll, *Art Dir* Clay A Griffith and Clayton R Hartley, *Ed* Joe Hutshing and Saar Klein, *M* Nancy Wilson; songs performed by The Chipmunks, Simon & Garfunkel, The Stooges, Black Sabbath, Yes, The Beach Boys, Stillwater, Rod Stewart, The Raspberries, The Allman Brothers Band, The Guess Who, Led Zeppelin, Neil Young, Deep Purple, Blodwyn Pig, MC5, David Bowie, Cat Stevens, Brenton Wood, The Who, Todd Rundgren, Jethro Tull, Joni Mitchell, Pete Droge, Little Feat, The Seeds, Lynyrd Skynyrd, Fleetwood Mac, Elton John, Steely Dan, Jim Hendrix, Clarence Carter, Free, Stevie Wonder, *Costumes* Betsy Heimann, *Visual effects* Ed Jones.

DreamWorks/Columbia Pictures/Vinyl Films-Columbia TriStar.
123 mins. USA. 2000. Rel: 9 February 2001. Cert 15.

## Along Came a Spider ★★★¹/₂

After failing to save his partner's life during an undercover police operation, serial killer expert Alex Cross has retired to a domestic life of self-recrimination. Then the daughter of an American senator is kidnapped and Cross, for reasons he cannot fathom, is baited by the kidnapper. But the most pressing ques-

tion on everybody's lips is why the girl was kidnapped in the first place... There are some pretty big holes in the logic of this follow-up to *Kiss the Girls*, but at least the characters behave like credible human beings. Again, Morgan Freeman casts his customary dignity over the proceedings and again is given uncommonly attractive company while he's at it (this time Monica Potter, replacing Ashley Judd). But it's Lee Tamahori's stylish, no-nonsense direction that keeps this hi-tech, frequently ingenious thriller more plausible and suspenseful than it deserves to be. One question, though. If Gary Soneji kidnapped Megan to get to Dimitri, why didn't he just kidnap Dimitri in the first place?

● *Alex Cross* Morgan Freeman, *Jezzie Flannagan* Monica Potter, *Gary Soneji/Jonathan Mercuzio* Michael Wincott, *Senator Hank Rose* Michael Moriarty, *Lauren Rose* Penelope Ann Miller, *Special Agent Oliver 'Ollie' McArthur* Dylan Baker, *Megan Rose* Mika Boorem, *Dimitri Starodubov* Anton Yelchin, *Agent Hickey* Kim Hawthorne, *FBI Special Agent Kyle Craig* Jay O Sanders, *Ben Devine* Billy Burke, *Vickie* Anna Maria Horsford, Scott Heindl, Christopher Shyer, Jill Teed, Ian Marsh, Samantha Ferris, Darryl Dillard.
● *Dir* Lee Tamahori, *Pro* David Brown and Joe Wizan, *Ex Pro* Morgan Freeman, *Co-Pro* Marty Hornstein, *Screenplay* Marc Moss and Lewis A Colick, based on the novel by James Patterson, *Ph* Matthew F Leonetti, *Pro Des* Ida Random, *Ed* Neil Travis, *M* Jerry Goldsmith, *Costumes* Sanja Milkovic Hays.

*Above: On the road again: rock stars and groupies find their music in Cameron Crowe's poetic, articulate and deeply personal* Almost Famous *(from Columbia TriStar)*

Paramount/David Brown/Phase 1 Prods/MFP Munich Film Partners-UIP.
103 mins. USA/Germany. 2001. Rel: 4 May 2001. Cert 15.

## American Movie ★★★½

Mark Borchardt, a 30-year-old native of Menomonee Falls, Wisconsin, and a father of three, dreams of becoming a professional movie director. Corralling the help of his friends, mother and even his kids, Borchardt pushes on relentlessly to complete his 30-minute slasher pic *Coven*. Admiring the genius of George A Romero and Tobe Hooper, he is something of a warped artist himself, whose indomitable spirit and aggressive nature actually gets things done. But it is the everyday characters who surround him – the inarticulate poor white trash of middle America – that makes this film so compelling, much like the *dramatis personae* of Terry Zwigoff's haunting documentary *Crumb*. Likewise, it is the small details that enliven Chris Smith's uneasy, comic portrait of frustration, like when Borchardt seduces his executive producer, his senile Uncle Bill, with talk of presenting him with a bottle of wine: `and what do you think of *that*?' A refreshing change from the hyped-up `making of' type movies about movies, *American Movie* is the *Blair Witch* of its genre. Even as the documentary (boasting far better production values than its subject) keeps a detached distance, one can hear the invisible laughter echoing in the face of its protagonist. Compulsive viewing.

● With Mark Borchardt (would-be filmmaker), Mike Schank, Uncle Bill, Monica Borchardt (Mark's mom), Cliff Borchardt (Mark's dad), Chris Borchardt (Mark's brother), Alex Borchardt (Mark's other brother), Ken Keen (friend), Joan Petrie (Mark's girlfriend).
● *Dir* and *Ph* Chris Smith, *Pro, Ph* and *Sound* Sarah Price, *Co-Pro* Jim McKay and Michael Stipe, *Ed* Smith, Barry Poltermann and Jun Diaz, *M* Mike Schank.

C-Hundred Film Corp/Bluemark Prods-Columbia TriStar.
105 mins. USA. 1999. Rel: 7 July 2000. Cert 15.

## Amores Perros ★★★★½

A long, sprawling, elliptical tapestry of life in Mexico City, *Amores Perros* is like a Latin-American saga from Robert Altman rewritten by Quentin Tarantino. With allusions to *Reservoir Dogs* and, structurally, *Pulp Fiction*, the film opens with a car chase, followed shortly afterwards by a horrific accident which serves as a narrative axis for the stories to come. The opening strand focuses on Octavio, a sweet but streetwise teenager who has become fed up with his older brother's abusive, criminal behaviour and so starts to woo his sister-in-law. Then there's Daniel Estrada, a well-to-do family man who is seeing a famous model on the side. And, at the opposite end of the social scale, El Chivo, an elderly, bearded down-and-out who har-

bours his own guilty secrets. But, besides the fatal car crash, what links these disparate characters is their love of their dogs, hence the film's title, translated as *Love's a Bitch*. With its energetic storytelling, vivid characterisation, layers of mystery and sudden outbursts of violence, *Amores Perros* is a compelling, shocking and darkly comic valentine to the madness of Mexico City which, in spite of its considerable length, is a constantly gripping work of cinema.

● *El Chivo* Emilio Echevarría, *Octavio* Gaël García Bernal, *Valeria Maya* Goya Toledo, *Daniel Estrada* Álvaro Guerrero, *Susana* Vanessa Bauche, *Luis Miranda Solares* Jorge Salinas, *Gustavo Miranda Garfias* Rodrigo Murray, *Ramiro* Marco Pérez, Adriana Barraza, Patricio Castillo, *Mamá de Susana* Dunia Saldívar.
● *Dir* and *Pro* Alejandro González Iñárritu, *Ex Pro* Martha Sosa Elizondo and Francisco González Compeán, *Screenplay* Guillermo Arriaga Jordán, *Ph* Rodrigo Prieto, *Pro Des* Brigitte Broch, *Ed* Luis Carballar, Alejandro González Iñárritu and Fernando Pérez, *M* Gustavo Santaolalla and Daniel Hidalgo; songs performed by Control Machete, Nacha Pop, Titán, Celia Cruz, Banda Espuela de Oro, The Hollies, Los del Garrote, and Fiebre, *Costumes* Gabriela Diaque, *Sound* Martín Hernández.

Altavista Films/Zeta Film-Optimum Releasing.
153 mins. Mexico. 2000. Rel: 18 May 2001. Cert 18.

## Another Life ★★

Manor Park, London/Ilford, Essex; 1913-1923. The spirited daughter of traditional middle class parents, Edith Graydon embraces the new liberalism imported from France. Then she marries her childhood sweetheart, Percy Thompson, and settles down to a conventional life. But she soon feels suffocated by the limitations imposed by her husband and is drawn to the charms of Freddie Bywaters, a P&O steward eight years her junior... The main problem with *Another Life* is that it feels like a period drama. Besides the constant clichés uttered by the cast, providing a sort of ABC of Edwardian-speak, the film's attention to period detail embalms the characters in a world of musty bric-a-brac and billboards for Tizer. Tragically, Edith Thompson was a very real and modern woman, and although Natasha Little manages to convey some of her fire and romanticism, we never feel that she is anything other than a character in a film. Worse, Nick Moran turns her long-suffering husband into a caricature (was Percy really such an insufferable prig?), while Ioan Gruffudd, as Bywaters, fails to provide the danger and sexual charisma that would make us believe him capable of adultery and murder.

● *Edith Jessie Thompson* Natasha Little, *Freddie Francis Bywaters* Ioan Gruffudd, *Percy Thompson* Nick Moran, *Ethel Graydon* Imelda Staunton, *Mr*

*Left: Microsoft in the head: Ryan Phillippe taps into a computer conspiracy in Peter Howitt's mildly gripping Antitrust (from Twentieth Century Fox)*

*Carlton* Tom Wilkinson, *Avis Graydon* Rachael Stirling, *Mrs Lester* Diana Coupland, *William* Michael Bertenshaw, *Newnie* Daniel Brocklebank, *Archie* Gyuri Sarossy, Elizabeth McKechnie, Judy Clifton, Simon Paris, Arthur Gerard, Michael Sheard, John Tordoff.

● *Dir* and *Screenplay* Philip Goodhew, *Pro* Angela Hart, *Ex Pro* Danny Passi, Alexander Harakis, Fabio Chino Quaradeghini, Gary Smith and Chris Craib, *Line Pro* Simon Hardy, *Ph* Simon Archer, *Pro Des* James Merifield, *Ed* Jamie Trevill, *M* James McConnel, *Costumes* Stephanie Collie.

Winchester Films/Lucida Film Investments/Arts Council of England/Boxer Films/Alibi Pictures/National Lottery-Winchester Film.
101 mins. UK. 2000. Rel: 15 June 2001. Cert 15.

## Antitrust ★★★

The future is bright and the future is digital conversion. On the verge of launching his own garage-based digital 'start-up' operation, techno whiz kid Milo Hoffman is headhunted by the billionaire computer magnate Gary Winston. Winston is primed to initiate his own dream vision, Synapse, which will be able to link every computer, telephone, TV and radio from one digital source. He just needs Milo to fine-tune the system... The latest upgrade in a sequence of movies that includes *Sneakers*, *Hackers* and *Enemy of the State*, this *Parallax View*-lite zeros in on Bill Gates for its kill. Set in and around a Pacific Northwest computer campus and featuring a nerdy, bespectacled 40-ish software tsar, *Antitrust* comports itself like a poison pen letter to Microsoft.

However, much like a new edition of Microsoftware, the film's ideas and possibilities are very exciting but quickly become mundane. Once again Ryan Phillippe proves that he is the most insipid 25-year-old in Hollywood, leaving the acting to a confidant and passionate Tim Robbins (deliciously underplaying the menace of an overgrown schoolboy) as Bill Gates, er, Gary Winston. The imaginative production design also deserves a mention, making this a fun if only mildly gripping thriller.

● *Milo Hoffman* Ryan Phillippe, *Lisa Calighan* Rachael Leigh Cook, *Alice Poulson/Rebecca Paul* Claire Forlani, *Gary Winston* Tim Robbins, *Bob Shrot* Douglas McFerran, *Lyle Barton* Richard Roundtree, *Larry Banks* Tygh Runyan, *Teddy Chin* Yee Jee Tso, *Brian Bissel* Nate Dushku, *Phil Grimes* Ned Bellamy, *Redmond* Tyler Labine, *Stinky* Jonathon Young, Scott Bellis, David Lovgren, Zahf Hajee, Ed Beechner, Elizabeth Carol Savenkoff, Miguel de Icaza, Scott McNealy, *homeless man* Peter Howitt.

● *Dir* Peter Howitt, *Pro* Nick Wechsler, Keith Addis and David Nicksay, *Ex Pro* David Hoberman, Ashok Amritraj, C O Erickson and Julia Chasman, *Screenplay* Howard Franklin, *Ph* John Bailey, *Pro Des* Catherine Hardwicke, *Ed* Zach Staenberg, *M* Don Davis; songs performed by Marcy Playground, Supergrass, Stereophonics, Joe Strummer and Mescaleros, Elliott Smith, David Bowie, Bill Conti, Dandy Warhols, Massive Attack, and Everclear, *Costumes* Maya Mani.

MGM/Hyde Park Entertainment/Industry Entertainment-Fox.
109 mins. USA. 2000. Rel: 4 May 2001. Cert 12.

## The Art of War ★¹/₂

Hong Kong/New York; the very near future. When ultra-secret agent Neil Shaw uncovers a Chinese plot to sabotage the United Nations, he finds himself the scapegoat for a high-level murder. However, as Shaw doesn't even officially exist, he can expect scant protection from his employers... You'll find little art in this, unless your idea of spiritual creativity is the reproduction of video game heroics superimposed onto a live-action canvas. This is one of those films in which the characters merely exist to serve the mechanics of a formulaic plot. Yet while initially convoluted and confusing, the storyline quickly becomes overly familiar as the usual suspects jump along the dotted line to diminishing returns. Illogical, hackneyed and far-fetched, *The Art of War* is a B-movie with A-movie pretensions.

● *Neil Shaw* Wesley Snipes, *Eleanor Hooks* Anne Archer, *Franklin Capella* Maury Chaykin, *Julia Fang* Marie Matiko, *David Chan* Cary-Hiroyuki Tagawa, *Bly* Michael Biehn, *UN Secretary General Douglas Thomas* Donald Sutherland, *Novak* Liliana Komorowska, *Ambassador Wu* James Hong, *Ray* Paul Hopkins, Glen Chin Ying-Ming, Ron Yuan, Bonnie Mak, Uni Park, Erin Selby.
● *Dir* Christian Duguay, *Pro* Nicolas Clermont, *Ex Pro* Elie Samaha, Dan Halsted and Wesley Snipes, *Co-Pro* Richard Lalonde, *Screenplay* Wayne Beach and Simon Davis Barry, *Ph* Pierre Gill, *Pro Des* Anne Pritchard, *Ed* Michel Arcand, *M* Normand Corbeil, *Costumes* Odette Gadoury.

Morgan Creek/Franchise Pictures/Amen Ra Films/ Filmline International/Canadian Film or Video Production Tax Credit-Warner. 117 mins. Canada/USA. 2000. Rel: 8 December 2000. Cert 18.

## Audition ★★★★

Tokyo; the present. Seven years after the death of his wife, video producer Shigeharu Aoyama is persuaded by his teenage son to bring some romance back into his life. So, at the suggestion of a colleague, Shigeharu holds an open audition disguised as a casting session for a new movie. There he meets Asami Yamasaki, a shy and gentle beauty who fits his bill for the perfect bride... It's hard to get a grip on *Audition*, but it's certainly one of a kind. At first a poignant drama, then a gentle comedy and next, possibly, a romance, it climaxes on a note so visceral that it's almost pornographic in its sadism. Director Miike Takashi is certainly a talent to watch, while Eihi Shiina is unforgettable as the timid, poised and ravishingly beautiful personification of misguided vengeance. The most profoundly disturbing film since Michael Haneke's *Funny Games* (1997), Takashi's seventh feature will kick you in the gut and then start playing with your mind. But remember this: 'Words create lies – pain can be trusted.'

● *Shigeharu Aoyama* Ryo Ishibashi, *Asami Yamasaki* Eihi Shiina, *Shigehiko Aoyama* Tetsu Sawaki, *Yasuhisa Yoshikawa* Jun Kunimura, *Ryôko Aoyama* Miyuki Matsuda.
● *Dir* Miike Takashi, *Pro* Akemi Suyama and Satoshi Fukushima, *Ex Pro* Toyoyuki Yokohama, *Screenplay* Daisuki Tengan, from the novel by Ryu Murakami, *Ph* Hideo Yamakami, *Pro Des* Tatsuo Ozeki, *Ed* Yusushi Shimamura, *M* Koji Endo, *Costumes* Tomoe Kumagai.

Omega Project/Creators Co./AFDF Korea/Body Sonic/ Filmface-Metro Tartan. 115 mins. Japan/South Korea. 1999. Rel: 16 March 2001. Cert 18.

## Autumn in New York ★★¹/₂

Will Keane is successful, wealthy, utterly charming and absurdly good-looking for a man of 48. He is also a cad and a womaniser, a black mark his friends and colleagues accept with a begrudging forbearance. Then Will homes in on the 22-year-old Charlotte Fielding, the beautiful daughter of a late friend. Will knows the relationship can't last, but Charlotte hopes that it will last at least until her premature death from a malignant tumour... If one had to suffer through two hours of a doomed romance between a middle-aged Lothario and a young gamine, one could do a lot worse than watch Richard Gere and Winona Ryder at it. While Ms Ryder continues her mutual love affair with the camera, at 29 she still looks too young to play a 22-year-old. More dispiriting still is the casting of Gere as a man who, at 48, looks amazing for his age – Gere is actually 51. But then this is a film of beautiful surfaces and is maybe too enthralled by its own imagery, whether it be the first kiss between Will and Charlotte followed by a flight of doves or just the way Gere grates his parmesan. Like a porcelain vase, the film is lovely to look at but hollow inside.

● *Will Keane* Richard Gere, *Charlotte Fielding* Winona Ryder, *Dolores* Elaine Stritch, *John* Anthony LaPaglia, *Sarah* Sherry Stringfield, *Dr Sibley* Mary Beth Hurt, *Lynn* Jill Hennessy, *Lisa Tyler* Vera Farmiga, *Simon* Sam Trammell, *Shannon* Kali Rocha, *with* J K Simmons, Steve Randazzo, Ranjit Chowdhry, Audrey Quock, Ted Koch, Bill Raymond, Earl Carroll.
● *Dir* Joan Chen, *Pro* Tom Rosenberg, Gary Lucchesi and Amy Robinson, *Ex Pro* Ted Tannebaum and Ron Bozman, *Screenplay* Allison Burnett, *Ph* Changwei Gu, *Pro Des* Mark Friedberg, *Ed* Ruby Yang, *M* Gabriel Yared, *Costumes* Carol Oditz.

MGM/Lakeshore-Columbia TriStar. 106 mins. USA. 2000. Rel: 15 June 2001. Cert 15.

**Left:** *Elizabeth Hurley proves that the Devil has all the best curves in Harold Ramis's hilarious* Bedazzled *(from Twentieth Century Fox)*

## Bamboozled ★★

Forever weighing weighing his satire down with in-yer-face melodrama, writer-director Spike Lee now turns to the representation of blacks in the mass media. Here, he casts Damon Wayans as Pierre Delacroix, a Harvard-educated TV writer who is asked to come up with a ratings winner. Delving into the past, Delacroix revives the tradition of the minstrel extravaganza as a slap-in-the-face to racist America. However, the all-dancing, all-singing *Mantan: The New Millennium Minstrel Show* becomes an enormous hit… Lee did a lot of research for this film and there are some astonishing insights into the way blacks have been depicted in recent cultural history. It's a shame, then, that the director over-eggs his pudding, completely loses his focus and runs riot (for well over two hours) with his radical concept. FYI: The title is taken from the Malcolm X speech in which the nationalist leader declared, 'You've been led astray, led amok, you've been bamboozled.' [*Ewen Brownrigg*]

● *Pierre Delacroix* Damon Wayans, *Manray/Mantan* Savion Glover, *Sloan Hopkins* Jada Pinkett-Smith, *Womack/Sleep 'N' Eat* Tommy Davidson, *Dunwitty* Michael Rapaport, *Honeycutt* Thomas Jefferson Byrd, *Junebug* Paul Mooney, Sarah Jones, Gillian Iliana Waters, Susan Batson, DJ Scratch, Jason Bernard, *and as themselves* Imhotep Gary Byrd, Johnnie L Cochran Jr, Rev Al Sharpton, Mira Sorvino and Matthew Modine.
● *Dir* and *Screenplay* Spike Lee, *Pro* Jon Kilik and Spike Lee, *Assoc Pro* Kisha Imani Cameron, *Ph* Ellen Kuras, *Pro Des* Victor Kempster, *Ed* Sam Pollard, *M* Terence Blanchard; songs performed by Stevie Wonder, Prince, Profyle, Angie Stone, The Maumaus, Erykah Badu, The Roots, Gerald Levert, Common, Bruce Hornsby etc, *Costumes* Ruth E Carter, *Choreography* Savion Glover.

New Line Cinema/40 Acres and a Mule Filmworks-Entertainment.
136 mins. USA. 2000. Rel: 6 April 2001. Cert 15.

## Beau Travail ★½

In the peace and quiet of the former French colony of Djibouti, East Africa, Sergeant-Major Galoup takes an irrational dislike to Gilles Sentain, a new recruit under his command. When the newcomer establishes his heroism in the course of an irregular accident, his officer's hatred merely intensifies… Ostensibly an adaptation of Herman Melville's *Billy Budd*, this is the sort of minimalist cinema that gives minimalist cinema a bad name. Subjected to endless shots of men ironing, cutting up vegetables and lying on beds, one craves the sight of Gary Cooper vaulting a sand dune. With no character development and the only two action scenes so thrown away as to be subliminal, *Beau Travail* can only possibly appeal to pacifists looking for an excuse to ridicule the Foreign Legion.

● *Sergeant-Major Galoup* Denis Lavant, *Bruno Forestier* Michel Subor, *Gilles Sentain* Grégoire Colin, *young woman* Marta Tafesse Kassa.
● *Dir* Claire Denis, *Pro* Jérôme Minet, *Screenplay* Denis and Jean-Pol Fargeau, *Ph* Agnès Godard, *Pro Des* Arnaud de Moléron, *Ed* Nelly Quettier, *M* Eran Tzur; Benjamin Britten, *Costumes* Judy Shrewsbury.

Pathé Television/SM Films/La sept ARTE, etc-Artificial Eye. 93 mins. France. 1998. Rel: 14 July 2000. Cert 15.

## Beautiful Creatures ★★★

Glasgow; the present. Following a horrendous row with her brutish boyfriend, Tony, Dorothy decides to flee Glasgow for London. However, just as she's about to board the bus, her constant companion, a white Alsatian called Pluto, runs off. Seconds later, Dorothy comes across a woman being throttled by a drunk, so she picks up a bar of scaffolding and knocks him out. Together, the women cart the unconscious man back to Dorothy's high-rise apartment (which has been ransacked by Tony) and plan their next move... An ingeniously tooled thriller with an undercurrent of scabrous humour, *Beautiful Creatures* scores top marks for artful plotting. It's also exceptionally well acted by the four principals, with the men in particular (Glen and Norton) turning in tightly coiled displays of male aggression. One could argue that the film fails to present a single sympathetic male character, but then this stylish cross between *Thelma & Louise* and *Shallow Grave* doesn't pretend to be *Brigadoon*. It's just a shame that the climax is so contrived.

● *Petula Peploe* Rachel Weisz, *Dorothy* Susan Lynch, *Tony* Iain Glen, *Ronnie McMinn* Maurice Roëves, *Det Inspector George Hepburn* Alex Norton, *Brian McMinn* Tom Mannion, *with* Jake D'Arcy, Robin Laing, Pauline Lynch, John Murtagh, Stewart Preston, Ron Donachie, Ellie Haddington, Paul Higgins and *Pluto, the Alsatian* Storm.
● *Dir* Bill Eagles, *Pro* Alan J Wands and Simon Donald, *Screenplay* Donald, *Ph* James Welland, *Pro Des* Andy Harris, *Ed* Jon Gregory, *M* Murray Gold; songs performed by Dean Martin, B15 Project, Sandie Shaw, Helen Shapiro, Texas, Gladys Knight & The Pips, and The Getaway People, *Costumes* Trisha Biggar.

DNA Films/Universal/National Lottery/Arts Council of England-UIP. 88 mins. UK. 2000. Rel: 19 January 2001. Cert 18.

## Bedazzled ★★★★

San Francisco; the present. Elliot Richards is the ultimate loser, the sort of well-meaning milksop who's ignored by men and invisible to girls. Then, when his second encounter in four years with the lovely Alison Gardner backfires, he vows that he 'would give any-thing to have that woman.' Enter the Devil in a stunning red dress, offering him seven wishes in exchange for his soul... From the opening credit sequence which slyly exposes the ambiguity of the entire human race, *Bedazzled* hits the ground running. Energetically directed from a terrific script (updated from the 1967 British comedy of the same name), this is farce that doesn't let up. Indeed, from the initial meeting between Brendan Fraser and Elizabeth Hurley (he: 'You're *hot*!', she: 'You have *no* idea') to the crowd-pleasing climax, the film keeps its balls – and invention – spinning. And while Ms Hurley is inspired casting as the Princess of Darkness, it is Fraser who constantly amazes, whether playing a 7'6" basketball jock or a gay aesthete. Great fun.

● *Elliot Richards* Brendan Fraser, *The Devil* Elizabeth Hurley, *Alison Gardner/Nicole* Frances O'Connor, *Carol* Miriam Shor, *Dan* Orlando Jones, *Bob* Paul Adelstein, *Jerry/Lance* Toby Huss, *John Wilkes Booth* Julian Firth, *with* Gabriel Casseus, Brian Doyle-Murray, Aaron Lustig, Roger Hammond, Suzanne Herrington, Paul Simon.
● *Dir* Harold Ramis, *Pro* Ramis and Trevor Albert, *Ex Pro* Neil Machlis, *Co-Pro* Suzanne Herrington, *Screenplay* Ramis, Larry Gelbart and Peter Tolan, *Ph* Bill Pope, *Pro Des* Rick Heinrichs, *Ed* Craig P Herring, *M* David Newman; songs performed by Johnnie Taylor, Banana Oil, Tone Loc, Apollo Four Forty, Gary Schreiner, Gipsy Kings, Brendan Fraser, Meeks, Gary Glitter, 2 Unlimited, Tulku, Sister Hazel, Prozzäk, *Costumes* Deena Appel, *Visual effects* Richard Edlund, *Sound* Sandy Berman.

Fox/Regency Enterprises/Taurus Film-Fox. 93 mins. USA. 2000. Rel: 10 November 2000. Cert 12.

## Before Night Falls ★★¹/₂

Winner of the Grand Jury Prize at the 2000 Venice Film Festival, this biography of the Cuban writer Reinaldo Arenas is a disjointed and uneven affair, not unlike the cinematic equivalent of a Gauguin painting. Like painter-turned-director Julian Schnabel's previous film, *Basquiat*, it is a rough-and-ready hotch-potch of styles that charts the tragic trajectory of a tortured artist. For the black painter Jean Michel Basquiat it was a descent into drugs and delusions of grandeur, for Arenas it is irrational persecution for his homosexuality and writing. Just by dint of being an artist, Arenas is branded a 'counter-revolutionary' by Castro's Communist regime and is subjected to no end of demeaning punishments, while his books, smuggled out of the country, become best-sellers overseas. As Arenas, Javier Bardem affects a hunched demeanour countered by a sheepish grin, a performance which won the Spanish actor accolades from the National Board of Review and the National Society of Film Critics, as well as an Oscar nomina-

**Left:** Northern exposure: Gary Lewis in Stephen Daldry's funny, moving and generally outstanding Billy Elliot (from UIP)

tion. As in *Basquiat*, there are somewhat distracting cameos from major stars, with Sean Penn as a gold-toothed Cuban peasant and Johnny Depp as a drag queen with a bounteous rectum (don't ask). Schnabel may have captured the soul of Arenas, but he has framed it in a remarkably poorly made film.

● *Reinaldo Arenas* Javier Bardem, *Lázaro Gómez Carriles* Olivier Martinez, *Pepé Malas* Andrea Di Stefano, *Lt Victor/Bon Bon* Johnny Depp, *Cuco Sanchez* Sean Penn, *Heberto Zorilla Ochoa* Michael Wincott, *Reinaldo's mother* Olatz López Garmendia, *teenage Reinaldo* Vito Maria Schnabel, *Fina Zorilla Ochoa* Najwa Nimri, *Virgilio Piñera* Hector Babenco, *Juan Abrau* John Ortiz, *with* Santiago Magill, Alfredo Villa, Maurice Compte, Vincent Laresca, Pedro Armendáriz, Cy Schnabel, Olmo Schnabel, Jerzy Skolimowski, Lola Schnabel, Stella Schnabel, Jack Schnabel, Esther Schnabel.
● *Dir* Julian Schnabel, *Pro* Jon Kilik, *Ex Pro* Schnabel and Olatz López Garmendia, *Screenplay* Schnabel, Cunningham O'Keefe and Lázaro Gómez Carriles, *Ph* Xavier Pérez Grobet and Guillermo Rosas, *Pro Des* Salvador Parra, *Ed* Michael Berenbaum, *M* Carter Burwell, Lou Reed and Laurie Anderson; Mahler, Morricone, *Costumes* Mariestela Fernández.

Grandview Pictures-Fox.
135 mins. USA. 2000. Rel: 15 June 2001. Cert 18.

## Best in Show ★★

As extensive preparations are made in Philadelphia for the annual Mayflower Kennel Club Dog Show, across the US various contestants and their human custodians ready themselves for the big event. Tensions run high... Dog owners being such easy prey for comic ridicule and the mockumentary such a tired format now, *Best in Show* is no Crufts winner. On the whole, the film's eccentric caricatures are a wearisome lot, although there's a sprinkling of price-less cameos further down the cast list: Larry Miller as a bloodthirsty suicide negotiator, Jim Piddock a straight-faced, *very* believable commentator and Hiro Kanagawa a helpful if irritated pet shop owner. The dogs themselves look good but exhibit none of the personality of their guardians.

● *Meg Swan* Parker Posey, *Hamilton Swan* Michael Hitchcock, *Cookie Fleck* Catherine O'Hara, *Gerry Fleck* Eugene Levy, *Dr Theodore W Millbank III* Bob Balaban, *Harlan Pepper* Christopher Guest, *Stefan Vanderhoof* Michael McKean, *Scott Donlan* John Michael Higgins, *Leslie Ward Cabot* Patrick Cranshaw, *Sherri Ann Cabot* Jennifer Coolidge, *Graham Chissolm* Don Lake, *Christy Cummings* Jane Lynch, *Buck Laughlin* Fred Willard, *Trevor Beckwith* Jim Piddock, *Dr Chuck Nelken* Jay Brazeau, *hotel manager* Ed Begley Jr, *pet shop owner* Hiro Kanagawa, *with* Lewis Arquette, Will Sasso, Linda Kash, Larry Miller, Cody Gregg, Malcolm Stewart, Carmen Aguirre, Don S Davis.
● *Dir* Christopher Guest, *Pro* Karen Murphy, *Ex Pro* Gordon Mark, *Screenplay* Guest and Eugene Levy, *Ph* Roberto Schaefer, *Pro Des* Joseph T Garrity, *Ed* Robert Leighton, *M* Jeffrey C J Vanston, *Costumes* Monique Prudhomme.

Castle Rock-Warner.
90 mins. USA. 2000. Rel: 9 March 2001. Cert 12.

## Billy Elliot ★★★★½

Durham; 1984. Billy Elliot, 11, is not like other boys growing up in the oppressed, male-orientated, cash-strapped north of England. The son and younger brother of striking miners, Billy is tough, but he also has a soft spot for Fred Astaire and an affection for his late mother's piano. When he surreptitiously switches boxing classes for ballet, he finds a natural talent for dance. However, he knows that his father would sooner beat him senseless than see his son indulge in something fit only for `nancy' boys... Anchored by a strong story and blessed with a miraculous performance from newcomer Jamie Bell (who, like Billy, kept his enthusiasm for dance from his classmates), *Billy Elliot* mixes its gritty realism and earthy humour with some stylistic flourishes to potent effect. Yet it is the detail that is so enriching: the way Billy flicks a stick like Fred Astaire cocking a cane, the almost subliminal presence of riot police, and the later confusion of Billy's father (wonderfully played by Gary Lewis). All in all, then, this is an outstanding directorial debut for Stephen Daldry, former director of London's Royal Court Theatre. Previously known as *Dancer*.

● *Mrs Wilkinson* Julie Walters, *Dad* Gary Lewis, *Billy Elliot* Jamie Bell, *Grandma* Jean Heywood, *Tony Elliot* Jamie Draven, *Michael* Stuart Wells, *Mr Braithwaite* Billy Fane, *Debbie* Nicola Blackwell, *Mr Wilkinson* Colin MacLachlan, *Sheila Briggs* Charlie Hardwick, *Principal* Patrick Malahide, *with* Mike Elliot, Carol McGuigan, Joe Renton, Janine Birkett, Barbara Leigh-Hunt, Imogen Claire, Adam Cooper.
● *Dir* Stephen Daldry, *Pro* Greg Brenman and Jon Finn, *Ex Pro* Natascha Wharton, Charles Brand, Tessa Ross and David M Thompson, *Line Pro* Tori Parry, *Screenplay* Lee Hall, *Ph* Brian Tufano, *Pro Des* Maria Djurkovic, *Ed* John Wilson, *M* Stephen Warbeck; songs performed by Fred Astaire, T-Rex, The Clash, The Jam, Eagle-Eye Cherry etc, *Costumes* Stewart Meacham, *Choreographer* Peter Darling.

Working Title/BBC Films/Arts Council of England/Tiger Aspect Pictures/National Lottery-UIP.
110 mins. UK. 2000. Rel: 29 September 2000. Cert 15.

## Black and White ★★

Of course, nothing is really black and white in this world and the boundaries are changing even faster on the culturally fluctuating streets of New York City. Here, the blonde offspring from a rich middle class family mixes with black gangstaz and hip-hop artists, a brazen homosexual is married to a heterosexual filmmaker and a scrupulous basketball player is corrupted by a member of the NYPD. In a world that has let them down, a cross-section of American society struggles to latch onto a new identity, rejecting the roots that have formed them... Mounting an ensemble drama on the scale of *Shorts Cuts* and *Magnolia*, writer-director James Toback has amassed a wonderfully eclectic cast. However, lacking the stylistic finesse of an Altman or Anderson, he fails to sustain any sense of dramatic momentum. Instead, by opting for a *cinéma vérité* approach – utilising video and a hand-held camera – Toback has created a documentary immediacy that captures some choice moments, particularly an unguarded reaction from Mike Tyson (playing himself) and some unrestrained sexual activity. But for the most part, Toback's raw, undisciplined experiment rambles on unchecked and, like the director's previous films, leaves one with a feeling of weariness and disenchantment.

● *Scotty* Scott Caan, *Terry* Robert Downey Jr, *Sheila King* Stacy Edwards, *Raven* Gaby Hoffmann, *Dean* Allan Houston, *Kim* Kim Matulova, *Billy King* Joe Pantoliano, *Charlie* Bijou Phillips, *Rich Bower* Power, *Cigar* Raekwon, *Greta* Claudia Schiffer, *Will King* William Lee Scott, *Sam Donager* Brooke Shields, *Det Mark Clear* Ben Stiller, *Marty King* Eddie Kaye Thomas, *himself* Mike Tyson, *himself* George Wayne, *Wren* Elijah Wood, *Arnie Tishman* James Toback, *with* Kidada Jones, Jared Leto, Marla Maples, Method Man, Brett Ratner, Sticky Fingaz, Fredro Starr, Thaddaeus Birkett, Frank Pesce, Chuck Zito, Frank Adonis.
● *Dir* and *Screenplay* James Toback, *Pro* Michael Mailer, Daniel Bigel and Ron Rotholz, *Ex Pro* Hooman Majd, Edward R. Pressman, Mark Burg and Oren Koules, *Assoc Pro* Alinur Velidedeoglu and Power, *Line Pro* Jennifer Roth, *Ph* David Ferrara, *Pro Des* Anne Ross, *Ed* Myron Kerstein, *M* American Cream Team and Oli `Power' Grant; J S Bach, Shostakovich, Vivaldi; songs performed by The Stylistics, Superb, Raekwon, Mobb Deep, Rhyme Recka, Chip Banks, Björk, Luther Vandross, Method Man, Redman, The Jaguars, Isaac Hayes, Aretha Franklin, Bob Marley & The Wailers, Baby Thad, Canibus, LV etc, *Costumes* Jacki Roach.

Screen Gems/Palm Pictures-Columbia TriStar.
99 mins. USA. 1999. Rel: 10 November 2000. Cert 18.

## Blackboards – Takhté Siah ★★★★

Though somewhat hard-going, this film impresses because it is so deeply felt. It is the work of the young Iranian filmmaker Samira Makhmalbaf who gave us *The Apple* and, like that film, it combines realism with symbolic elements. Here, we follow the experiences of two teachers, each carrying a blackboard, as they seek students in the mountainous area near the Iran/Iraq border. One encounters youths transporting contraband goods to the border, and the other, becoming a guide to elderly nomads attempting to return home, finds among them a young mother who becomes his wife. However, the film offers less a story than a situation: if the theme of education is shared with the accessible *Not One Less*, the portrayal of people at the mercy of fate and with military hostilities always threatening to erupt is almost Beckettian. A demanding but courageous film well photographed. [*Mansel Stimpson*]

● *Saïd* Saïd Mohamadi, *Halalheh* Behnaz Jafari, *Reeboir* Bahman Ghobadi, *Ribvar* Rafat Moradi, Mohamad Karim Rahmaty, Rasol Mohamadi.
● *Dir* Samira Makhmalbaf, *Pro* Mohsen Makhmalbaf and Marco Muller, *Ex Pro* Mohamad Ahmadi, *Screenplay* Mohsen Makhmalbaf and Samira Makhmalbaf, *Ph* Ebrahim Ghafori, *Ed* Mohsen Makhmalbaf, *M* Mohamad Reza Darvishi.

Makhmalbaf Film/Fabrica Cinema/Radiotelevisione Italiana/T-Mark-Artificial Eye.
85 mins. Iran/Italy. 2000. Rel: 29 December 2000. Cert PG.

### Bless the Child ★★¹/₂

New York City; the present. When her kid sister drops off a baby at her apartment, nurse Maggie O'Connor raises the child as her own. Diagnosed as mildly autistic, the girl, Cody, begins to show signs of unusual powers and at the age of six is reclaimed by her biological mother. Maggie smells a rat (in fact, she sees thousands) and fights to win the child back. However, there are greater forces than she who want the girl for their own nefarious ends... As far as films about Satanic possession go, *Bless the Child* has some good ideas, but just as many pilfered ones (including a line lifted straight out of *The Usual Suspects*). With clumps of duff dialogue and far too many 'in-the-nick-of-time' clichés, the film is piloted at a decent clip and Kim Basinger gives it a strong sympathetic centre. And the fleeting presence of rats and demons – as if glimpsed by the imagination – are quite effective. Oh, and Christina Ricci has a terrific death scene.

● *Maggie O'Connor* Kim Basinger, *John Travis* Jimmy Smits, *Eric Stark* Rufus Sewell, *Reverend Grissom* Ian Holm, *Jenna O'Connor* Angela Bettis, *Cheri* Christina Ricci, *Cody* Holliston Coleman, *Sister Rosa* Lumi Cavazos, *Bugatti* Michael Gaston, *Stuart* Eugene Lipinski, *Dahnya* Dimitra Arlys, *Maria* Anne Betancourt, *with* Helen Stenborg, Dan Warry-Smith, Elisabeth Rosen, Tony Del Rio, Vincent Corazza, Gary Hudson, Nicolas Marti Salgado, Yan Birch, Wanda Lee Evans, Neville Edwards.
● *Dir* Chuck Russell, *Pro* Mace Neufeld, *Ex Pro* Robert Rehme, Lis Kern and Bruce Davey, *Screenplay* Tom Rickman and Clifford Green & Ellen Green, from the novel by Cathy Cash Spellman, *Ph* Peter Menzies Jr., *Pro Des* Carol Spier, *Ed* Alan Heim, *M* Christopher Young, *Costumes* Denise Cronenberg.

Icon/Paramount-Icon.
110 mins. USA. 2000. Rel: 5 January 2001. Cert 15.

*Left: Her beautiful laundry: Kim Basinger in Chuck Russell's rather clichéd but occasionally effective* Bless the Child *(from Icon)*

### Blow ★★★

Brought up in New England on the bread line, George Jung swears that he will never fall into the same trap as his hard-working, hardbitten father. So when he discovers the commercial potential of marijuana, George decides to become America's first self-made drug-dealing millionaire... A true American tragedy, *Blow* is a fascinating portrait of greed that is ultimately undone by its ambitious scope. Unlike *Traffic*, which exposed the many facets of the drug trade in a story covering a matter of months, *Blow* attempts to condense George Jung's entire life into just over two hours. While director Ted Demme keeps things moving at a brisk pace, aided by fast cutting, contemporary songs and explanatory captions, the film loses its credibility when the grey hairs, liver spots and latex start taking over. With his gaunt countenance and chiselled cheekbones, Depp looks ludicrous with a padded midriff, while it seems odd to cast Rachel Griffiths as his mother. Good actress that she is, Griffiths never seems old enough to be the matriarchal Jung – but then in real life she is five years Depp's junior. However, this is an ongoing problem for Demme, whose last film, *Life*, saw Eddie Murphy and Martin Lawrence age 67 years. FYI: George Jung's beloved daughter Kristina, who still refuses to visit her father in prison, makes a brief appearance as a clerk in the film.

● *George Jung* Johnny Depp, *Mirtha Jung* Penélope Cruz, *Barbara Buckley* Franka Potente, *Ermine Jung* Rachel Griffiths, *Derek Foreal* Paul Reubens, *Fred Jung* Ray Liotta, *Diego Delgado* Jordi Molla, *Pablo Escobar* Cliff Curtis, *Kevin Dulli* Max Perlich, *Tuna* Ethan Suplee, *young Kristina Jung* Emma Roberts, *Kristina Jung* James King, *Jack Stevens* Charles Noland, *with* Miguel Sandoval, Kevin Gage, Tony Amendola, Jesse James, Emma Roberts, Bobcat

*Right: Drug honey: Johnny Depp hangs out with Penélope Cruz in Ted Demme's periodically fascinating but ultimately over-ambitious* Blow *(from Entertainment)*

Goldthwait, Nigel Perez, Michael Tucci, Dan Ferro, Monet Mazur, Lola Glaudini, Jennifer Gimenez, *Archie Zigmond* Edward Demme, Daniel Escobar, *clerk* Kristina Jung, *detective #2* Richard LaGravenese.
● *Dir* Ted Demme, *Pro* Demme, Joel Stillerman and Denis Leary, *Ex Pro* Georgia Kacandes and Michael de Luca, *Screenplay* David McKenna and Nick Cassavetes, *Ph* Ellen Kuras, *Pro Des* Michael Hanan, *Ed* Kevin Tent, *M* Graeme Revell; songs performed by The Rolling Stones, the Hollywood Flames, Money Mark, Booker T & the MGs, Link Wray, Birds & Brass, Faces, The Hottest Mariachi in Mexico, Louis Armstrong, Cream, Manfred Mann's Earth Band, Tito Puento & His Orchestra, KC & the Sunshine Band, J Girls, Lynyrd Skynyrd, Bob Dylan, Nikka Costa etc, *Costumes* Mark Bridges, *Johnny Depp's make-up design* Kevin Yagher.

New Line Cinema/Spanky Pictures/Apostle-Entertainment.
123 mins. USA. 2001. Rel: 25 May 2001. Cert 18.

## Blow Dry ★¹/₂

An inconspicuous town nestled in the Yorkshire hills, Keighley is about to become host to the British Hairdressing Championships. And so a parade of outrageous types spill into the quiet streets while local barber Phil Allen looks on in disgust. But, in the hairdressing world, Allen used to be something of a legend himself... With a keen eye on the American market and a lazy eye for genuine human interaction, *Blow Dry* is a calculated, patronising and predictable comedy with nary a snip of credibility. Saddled with stock stereotypes, an indifferent turn from Alan Rickman and a mawkishly contrived subplot, this just isn't funny nor remotely believable. Worse, 22-year-old American

heartthrob Josh Hartnett (*Halloween H20*, *Pearl Harbor*) is plonked down into the proceedings as Rickman's son, with an accent bearing little relation to anything mortal. With actors of the calibre of Rachel Griffiths and Bill Nighy tragically wasted and the writer of *The Full Monty* slacking, *Blow Dry* is more than a disappointment. Besides, the same subject was treated with considerably more wit, ingenuity and flair in last year's *The Big Tease*. Previously known as *Never Better*.

● *Phil Allen* Alan Rickman, *Shelley Allen* Natasha Richardson, *Sandra* Rachel Griffiths, *Christina Robertson* Rachael Leigh Cook, *Brian Allen* Josh Hartnett, *Ray Robertson* Bill Nighy, *Jasmine* Heidi Klum, *Louis* Hugh Bonneville, *Tony, mayor of Keighley* Warren Clarke, *Daisy* Rosemary Harris, *Noah Thwaite* David Bradley, *Saul Thwaite* Ben Crompton, *Margaret Thwaite* Ann Rye, *Vincent* Peter McDonald, *with* Ray Emmet Brown, Mark Benton, Gordon Langford-Rowe, Peter Kay, Elizabeth Woodcock, Willie Ross, Paul Copley, Oliver Ford Davies, Janet Henfrey, Christopher Biggins.
● *Dir* Paddy Breathnach, *Pro* Ruth Jackson, William Horberg and David Rubin, *Ex Pro* Sydney Pollack, Guy East and Nigel Sinclair, *Screenplay* Simon Beaufoy, *Ph* Cían de Buitléar, *Pro Des* Sophie Becher, *Ed* Tony Lawson, *M* Patrick Doyle; songs performed by Hoi Polloi, Roger Whittaker, Jackie Wilson, Kid Creole and the Coconuts, Climax Blues Band, Highliners, Bill Withers and Skip Scarborough, Billy Ocean, Rachel Griffiths etc, *Costumes* Rosie Hackett, *Hair/makeup design* Jenny Shircore.

Intermedia Films/Miramax/West Eleven Films/Mirage Enterprises/IMF-Buena Vista.
90 mins. Germany/UK/USA. 2000. Rel: 30 March 2001. Cert 15.

## Bodywork ★'/₂

London; the present. Talk about a half-baked idea. A personality-arrested idiot (played by a charmless Hans Matheson) is duped over a dodgy Jaguar deal and ends up being framed for a prostitute's murder. One thing leads to another and, improbably, the idiot is always in the wrong place at the wrong time, becoming a fugitive from the law. Not only is Matheson very bad (uncharismatic, unfunny, unbelievable) but his character does things like walk down the street in his underpants and answer the front door with a saucepan on his head (*why*?). Too much, however, remains unanswered in this raw and uneven thing that doesn't know whether it wants to be a farce, a black comedy or a nasty thriller.

● *Virgil Guppy* Hans Matheson, *Tiffany Shades* Charlotte Coleman, *Fiona Money* Beth Winslet, *Alex Gordon* Peter Ferdinando, *Billy Hunch* Clive Russell, *Poppy Fields* Lynda Bellingham, *Pamela Lee* Rachel de Thame, *David Leer* Michael Attwell, *Buddy Leer* Peter Moreton, *Boss Torrie* Jeremy Clyde, *with* Simon Gregor, Jordan Maxwell, Grahame Fox, Frank Mills, Velibor Topic, Rachel Colover, Stewart Harwood, Jane Bertish, Willie Ross, Roger Frost, Alan Jones.
● *Dir* and *Screenplay* Gareth Rhys Jones, *Pro* Richard McGill, *Ex Pro* Simon Decker, *Ph* Thomas Wuthrich, *Pro Des* Jeremy Bear, *Ed* Susan Spivey and Tariq Anwar, *M* Srdjan Kurpjel and Black Tooth, *Costumes* Diane Holmes and Jayne Gregory.

Wolfmoon Film-Guerilla Films.
93 mins. UK. 1998. Rel: 20 October 2000. Cert 18.

## Boesman & Lena ★★

Boesman and Lena have fallen on hard times. Eking out a pitiful living on the mud flats outside Cape Town, they sell empty bottles for money and build temporary shelters out of branches, sacking and rusting metal. Then a Xhosa tribesman joins them and Boesman unleashes years of institutionalised racism upon the old stranger's head... Adapted from Athol Fugard's 1970 play by the dramatist's life-long friend John Berry, *Boesman & Lena* makes few concessions to the cinema. Essentially a two-hander in a single setting, the film is ineffably dull and theatrical, which no amount of shouting and ranting from Danny Glover and Angela Bassett can salvage. Intriguingly, both actors are far more convincing in the film's brief, wordless flashbacks. FYI: John Berry died just a few days before completing post-production.

● *Boesman* Danny Glover, *Lena* Angela Bassett, *old African* Willie Jonah, *with* Graham Weir, Anton Stoltz.
● *Dir* and *Screenplay* John Berry, *Pro* François Ivernel and Pierre Rissient, *Co-Pro* Jeremy Nathan and John Stodel, *Line Pro* Nina Heyns, *Ph* Alain Choquart, *Pro Des* Max Berto, *Ed* Claudine Bouche and Jeanne Moutard, *M* Wally Badarou, *Costumes* Diana Cilliers, *Sound* Emmanuel Augeard.

Pathé Image/Primedia Pictures/Canal Plus/La Sept Arte- Pathé.
88 mins. France/South Africa. 1999. Rel: 20 April 2001. Cert 12.

## Book of Shadows: Blair Witch 2 ★★★

How on earth do you make a sequel to something that was such a one-off phenomenon – something that was, in fact, a faux-documentary? Well, *Book of Shadows* is not so much a sequel as a sly commentary on the success of the first film. It both acknowledges its predecessor as a sham and as a source of considerable annoyance to the residents of Burkittsville, Maryland, whose backyard has become a circus for thrill-seeking tourists. And so five fans of *Blair Witch* arrive in the Black Hills to experience for themselves those demonic woods. Armed with the latest technology, Jeff, Kim, Stephen, Tristen and good witch Erica bed down for the night only to wake up next morning to find all their belongings and equipment trashed – all, that is, except for the tapes with the evidence of what happened while they slept. Beating a hasty retreat, the unhappy campers discover that five hours of the previous night are inexplicably unaccounted for on the videos. Then they notice that they all have mysterious marks on their skin which are getting bigger by the hour... An ingenious twist on the original blockbuster, *Book of Shadows* is a genuinely scary examination of the cult of notoriety and of the serious damage done by collective delusion. It's a shame, then, that the film's final act fails to live up to its earlier promise, as the campers turn on themselves without the sense to realise that there really *is* something evil lurking in Burkittsville.

● *Kim* Kim Director, *Jeffrey* Jeffrey Donovan, *Erica* Erica Leerhsen, *Tristen* Tristen Skyler, *Stephen* Stephen Barker Turner, *with* Kurt Loder, Chuck Scarborough, Bruce Reed, Joe Berlinger, Sara Phillips, Lauren Hulsey, Raynor Scheine, Kennen Sisco.
● *Dir* Joe Berlinger, *Pro* Bill Carraro, *Ex Pro* Daniel Myrick and Eduardo Sanchez, *Screenplay* Berlinger and Dick Beebe, *Ph* Nancy Schreiber, *Pro Des* Vince Peranio, *Ed* Sarah Flack, *M* Carter Burwell; songs performed by Marilyn Manson, Sunshine, Julie Reeves, UPO, Elastica, Queens of the Stone Age, Rob Zombie, godhead, Project 86, Death in Vegas, Poe, At the Drive-In etc, *Costumes* Melissa Toth.

Artisan Entertainment-Momentum Pictures.
90 mins. USA. 2000. Rel: 27 October 2000. Cert 15.

## Born Romantic ★★¹⁄₂

London; today. Various characters on a losing wicket romantically intersect at the salsa club El Corazon and its nearby taxi service, Kismet Cabs... While continuing the ensemble format and romantic theme of his first film, *This Year's Love*, writer-director David Kane has this time fashioned an English variation of an Alan Rudolph vehicle, complete with the latter's fondness for eccentric characters, patchwork narrative and jazzy score. However, besides Adrian Lester's levelheaded taxi driver – who acts as the film's conscience – Kane has failed to provide any really sympathetic or credible characters and too often resorts to caricature (Catherine McCormack's morbid and ditzy Jocelyn being a particular grotesque). Had we believed more in these sad sacks, then we may have cared for them at least a little. Filmed in and around Hoxton, Clerkenwell, Shoreditch and Hackney.

● *Frankie* Craig Ferguson, *second driver* Ian Hart, *Maureen 'Mo' Docherty* Jane Horrocks, *Jimmy Shearsmith* Adrian Lester, *Jocelyn Joy* Catherine McCormack, *Eddie O'Rourke* Jimi Mistry, *Fergus Greer* David Morrissey, *Eleanor* Olivia Williams, *Barney* Kenneth Cranham, *first driver* John Thomson, *Ray* Paddy Considine, *Carolanne* Hermione Norris, *Suzy* Sally Phillips, *Libby* Jessica Stevenson, *Wayne* Martin Savage, *Maria* Louise Delamere, *with* José Ordoñez Fernandes De Souza, Tony Maudsley, Mel Raido, Martin Savage, Ashley Walters, Simon Boswell (*on guitar*).
● *Dir* and *Screenplay* David Kane, *Pro* Michele Camarda, *Ex Pro* David M Thompson, Alistair MacLean-Clark and Melvyn Singer, *Line Pro* Sally French, *Ph* Robert Alazraki, *Pro Des* Sarah Greenwood, *Ed* Michael Parker, *M* Simon Boswell; songs performed by Craig Ferguson, Jane Horrocks and Dean Martin, Pigforce, DLG, The Fania All-Stars, Cheo Feliciano, Tito Puente, Ruben Gonzalez, Nina Miranda, Morcheeba, Elvis Crespo, Robby Salanis, Ricky Martin, Shiver etc, *Costumes* Jill Taylor, *Choreography* José Ordoñez Fernandes De Souza.

BBC Films/Harvest Pictures/Kismet Film-Optimum Releasing.
96 mins. UK. 2000. Rel: 9 March 2001. Cert 15.

## Bounce ★★¹⁄₂

When Buddy Amaral, an arrogant advertising agent, sees the chance for a one-night stand, he gives up his seat on a plane to fellow passenger Greg Janello. But when the plane he was meant to be on crashes, he sets about finding the widow of the man who took his ticket. As it happens, the said widow, Abby, is a smart and lovely woman whom Buddy immediately falls for. But how can he tell her that it should have been him on that fateful flight? ... You can only string an audience along so far. With the rails of the plot laid down so calculatingly, we know that Buddy will have to tell Abby his terrible secret. Yet Buddy and Abby's romance is allowed to blossom away, while, for his silence, Buddy remains an insufferable jerk. For the second outing from the director of the witty and offbeat *The Opposite of Sex*, this *Random Hearts*-lite is a major disappointment. Manipulative to a fault, it is only partially redeemed by another glowing turn from Gwyneth Paltrow and a canny supporting one from Johnny Galecki as the obligatory gay sidekick.

● *Buddy Amaral* Ben Affleck, *Abby Janello* Gwyneth Paltrow, *Jim Weller* Joe Morton, *Mimi* Natasha Henstridge *Greg Janello* Tony Goldwyn, *Janice Guerrero* Jennifer Grey, *Ron Wachter* Edward Edwards, *Scott Janello* Alex D Linz, *Joey Janello* David Dorfman, *Seth* Johnny Galecki, *Donna Heisen* Caroline Aaron, *with* Lisa Carpenter Prewitt, Juan Garcia, Mary Ellen Lyon, Thea Mann, Sam Robards and (*uncredited*) *Prosecuting Attorney Mandel* David Paymer.
● *Dir* and *Screenplay* Don Roos, *Pro* Steve Golin and Michael Besman, *Ex Pro* Bob Weinstein, Harvey Weinstein, Bob Osher and Meryl Poster, *Ph* Robert Elswit, *Pro Des* David Wasco, *Ed* David Codron, *M* Mychael Danna; songs performed by Smokey Robinson & The Miracles, The Drifters, Zap Mama, Beth Orton, Gingersol, Dido and Massive Attack, *Costumes* Peter Mitchell and Giorgio Armani.

Miramax-Buena Vista.
106 mins. USA. 2000. Rel: 19 January 2001. Cert 12.

## Bread and Roses ★★★¹⁄₂

Having illegally entered Los Angeles from Mexico City and escaped a near-rape from a coyote (an immigrant trafficker), Maya moves in with her sister Rosa. Desperate for work, Maya joins Rosa as a cleaner at an enormous office block where she is forced to donate her first month's salary to her boss. Conditions are bad, but Maya is happy to be working. Then a charismatic activist from the 'Justice For Janitors' campaign goads her to fight for her right to benefits and more pay... Once again taking everyday, recognisably human characters and plunging them into an extraordinary context, Ken Loach has made the most engrossing film about cleaners ever to hit a cinema screen. Utilising natural light and a hand-held camera, and coaxing passionate and naturalistic performances from his cast, Loach creates a sense of documentary-like immediacy that feeds the humanitarian message of his film. Besides unearthing an aspect of Los Angeles seldom caught by the movie camera, *Bread and Roses* is enriched by a fiery, spontaneous turn from the Mexican actress Pilar Padilla in her first film role. Inspired by real events.

**Left:** *Making a clean sweep: Adrien Brody (centre) fights for the rights of immigrant janitors in Ken Loach's engrossing and passionate* Bread and Roses *(from FilmFour)*

● *Maya* Pilar Padilla, *Sam* Adrien Brody, *Rosa* Elpidia Carrillo, *Bert* Jack McGee, *Simone* Monica Rivas, *Berta* Maria Orellana, *Ella* Beverly Reynolds, *Marina* Elena Antonenko, *Ruben* Alonso Chavez, *Teresa* Estela Maeda, *Perez* George Lopez, Frank Davila, Lillian Hurst, Mayron Payes, Julian Orea, Javier Torres, Blake Clark, Pepe Serna, Tom Gilroy, *and (as themselves)* Vanessa Angel, William Atherton, Lara Belmont, Benicio Del Toro, Oded Fehr, Stuart Gordon, Chris Penn, Ron Perlman, Tim Roth, Robin Tunney, Samuel West, Stephanie Zimbalist.
● *Dir* Ken Loach, *Pro* Rebecca O'Brien, *Ex Pro* Ulrich Felsberg, *Screenplay* Paul Laverty, *Ph* Barry Ackroyd, *Pro Des* Martin Johnson, *Ed* Jonathan Morris, *M* James Fenton, *Costumes* Michelle Michel.

Parallax Pictures/Road Movies/Tornasol/Alta Films/British Screen/BskyB/BAC Films/La Sept Cinéma/Recorded Picture Company, etc-Film Four. 110 mins. UK/Germany/Spain/France/Italy. 2000. Rel: 27 April 2001. Cert 15.

## Breakfast of Champions ★

Midland City, USA; today. Dwayne Hoover is more than just a successful car salesman, he is a local icon, a savvy businessman whose platitudinous hype has turned him into a messiah for a material-istically drip-fed America. Just then, the town's first arts festival decides to honour an obscure sci-fi writer, Kilgore Trout, whose skewed vision of the universe has an unsettling and dangerous effect on Hoover... Alan Rudolph had wanted to make a film of Kurt Vonnegut Jr's 1973 satire before he had

even directed his first film, *Welcome to LA*, in 1977. But what might have seemed courageous, perceptive and outrageous back then is no longer so. Other than having the opportunity of seeing Nick Nolte in a see-through red dress, Glenne Headly in her undies and Bruce Willis in his worst performance yet, there's little to recommend this over-directed farce. OK, so consumerism sucks and it makes mad-men of us all. Next?

● *Dwayne Hoover* Bruce Willis, *Kilgore Trout* Albert Finney, *Harry LeSabre* Nick Nolte, *Celia Hoover* Barbara Hershey, *Francine Pefko* Glenne Headly, *Bunny Hoover* Lukas Haas, *Wayne Hoobler* Omar Epps, *Grace Le Sabre* Vicki Lewis, *Fred T. Barry* Buck Henry, *Eliot Rosewater/Gilbert* Ken Campell, *Bill Bailey* Jake Johannsen, *Moe* Will Patton, *Maria Maritimo* Alison Eastwood, *Eli* Michael Clarke Duncan, *Lottie* Dawn Didawick, *with* Chip Zien, Owen Wilson, Shawnee Smith, Michael Jai White, Keith Joe Dick, Kurt Vonnegut Jr, William Nagel, Alexa Robbins, Tom Robbins, Raymond O'Connor, Tisha Sterling, Matt Callahan, Doug Hamblin, *Scout Willis* Scout LaRue Willis, Denise Simone.
● *Dir* and *Screenplay* Alan Rudolph, *Pro* David Blocker and David Willis, *Assoc Pro* Sandra Tomita, *Ph* Elliot Davis, *Pro Des* Nina Ruscio, *Ed* Suzy Elmiger, *M* Mark Isham; songs performed by Martin Denny, The Ink Spots, Arthur Lyman, and Lukas Haas, *Costumes* Rudy Dillon.

Sugar Creek/Hollywood Pictures/Summit Entertainment/ Flying Heart Films-Warner. 110 mins. USA. 1999. Rel: 14 July 2000. Cert 15.

**Right:** 'Now, is that 28 or 29 I've smoked today?': Renée Zellweger in Sharon Maguire's funny and enormously popular Bridget Jones's Diary (from UIP)

## Bridget Jones's Diary ★★★

London; the present. Thirtysomething, single and nine stone and three pounds, Bridget Jones is developing a crush on her boss, the stylish and gorgeous Daniel Cleaver. There's also Mark Darcy, of course, an old family friend, but in spite of his romantic looks he is bit of a stuffed shirt. However, Bridget, who works in publishing and has an arse the size of Brazil, is not very successful in love, a predicament hardly helped by her verbal incontinence... As to be expected from a screenplay by the original author Helen Fielding, Richard Curtis (*Four Weddings, Bean, Notting Hill*) and the veteran playwright and scenarist Andrew Davies, *Bridget Jones's Diary* is very slick and very funny. There is also something rather mechanical about it, with too many familiar stereotypes and not enough real life to make Bridget's pathetic existence ring true. But there are some wonderful performances, particularly from Hugh Grant and Colin Firth, who perfectly embody Bridget's attractive suitors and their ambiguous agendas. Renée Zellweger, however, who piled on over 15 pounds and a fluctuating English accent for the role of Bridget, never really mines the comic potential of the material. FYI: First-time director Sharon Maguire was the original model for Bridget Jones's girlfriend Shazza, played by Sally Phillips in the film, while Richard Curtis is a former lover of Fielding's.

● *Bridget Jones* Renée Zellweger, *Daniel Cleaver* Hugh Grant, *Mark Darcy* Colin Firth, *Colin Jones, Bridget's dad* Jim Broadbent, *Pam Jones, Bridget's mum* Gemma Jones, *Geoffrey Alconbury* James Faulkner, *Mr Fitzherbert* Paul Brooke, *Perpetua* Felicity Montague, *Jude* Shirley Henderson, *Shazza* Sally Phillips, *Tom* James Callis, *Natasha* Embeth Davidtz, *Julian* Patrick Barlow, *Lara* Lisa Barbuscia, *Richard Finch* Neil Pearson, *with* Celia Imrie, Charmian May, Gareth Marks, John Clegg, Salman Rushdie, Matthew Bates, Jeffrey Archer, Honor Blackman, Joan Blackman, Claire Skinner, Donald Douglas.
● *Dir* Sharon Maguire, *Pro* Tim Bevan, Eric Fellner and Jonathan Cavendish, *Ex Pro* Helen Fielding, *Co-Pro* Debra Hayward and Liza Chasin, *Screenplay* Fielding, Andrew Davies and Richard Curtis, *Ph* Stuart Dryburgh, *Pro Des* Gemma Jackson, *Ed* Martin Walsh, *M* Patrick Doyle; songs performed by Gabrielle, Aretha Franklin, Geri Halliwell, Robbie Williams, Chaka Khan, Pretenders, Sheryl Crow, Shelby Lynne, Dina Carroll, Andy Williams, Rosey, Diana Ross & Marvin Gaye, Alisha's Attic, Jamie O'Neal, Artful Dodger & Robbie Craig with Craig David, and Aaron Soul, *Costumes* Rachael Fleming, *Voice coach* Barbara Berkery.

Universal/Canal Plus/Miramax/Working Title-UIP. 105 mins. UK/USA/France. 2001. Rel: 13 April 2001. Cert 15.

## Bring It On ★★¹/₂

San Diego, California; today. For Torrance Shipman, cheerleading is not only a way of life, it *is* her life. So when she's elected captain of the Rancho Carne High School cheerleading squad her world is made complete. It is then that she discovers that the routines she's inherited are rip-offs – and the national cheerleading championships are only five weeks away... Know this: cheerleading is a serious business. And *Bring It On* takes cheerleading very seriously. Of course, it's hard to share the film's gravity for its subject, and the sub-*Clueless* dialogue (`she puts the itch into bitch') doesn't help. But

**Left:** 'Who do we appreciate? Kirsten Dunst!' The girls get into their stride in Peyton Reed's peppy, zippy Bring It On (from Entertainment)

the actors bring enormous pep to their roles and, while Kirsten Dunst has become typecast as a wholesome overachiever (*Drop Dead Gorgeous*, *The Virgin Suicides*), she could be the next generation's Gwyneth Paltrow. However, it's Eliza Dushku – as an initially reluctant recruit – who supplies the film's best performance (and its only edge). And the combination of crisp photography and snappy editing further helps to wear down the barriers of cynicism. Previously known as *Cheer Fever*.

● *Torrance Shipman* Kirsten Dunst, *Isis* Gabrielle Union, *Missy Pantone* Eliza Dushku, *Cliff Pantone* Jesse Bradford, *Christine Shipman* Sherry Hursey, *Bruce Shipman* Holmes Osborne, *Courtney Egbert* Clare Kramer, *Whitney Dow* Nicole Bilderback, *Jan* Nathan West, *Les* Huntley Ritter, *Sparky Polastri* Ian Roberts, *Aaron* Richard Hillman, *Lava* Shamari Fears, *Justin Shipman* Cody McMains, *Pauletta* Aloma Wright, *with* Lindsay Sloane, Tsianina Joelson, Rini Bell, Natina Reed, Brandi Williams, Bianca Kajlich.
● *Dir* Peyton Reed, *Pro* Marc Abraham and Thomas A Bliss, *Ex Pro* Armyan Bernstein, Max Wong, Caitlin Scanlon and Paddy Cullen, *Co-Pro* Patricia Wolff and Jessica Bendinger, *Screenplay* Bendinger, *Ph* Shawn Maurer, *Pro Des* Sharon Lomofsky, *Ed* Larry Bock, *M* Christophe Beck; Tchaikovsky; songs performed by Mest, Sum 41, Atomic Kitten, Blaque, Jungle Brothers, BIS, sister2sister, 2 Unlimited, Daphne & Celeste, Sweets, Mark Bryan, 95 South, Sons of Poseidon, Zebrahead, Sygnature, 2 Live Crew, Kinsu, P.Y.T., B*witched, Da Beat Bros, Joey Fatone Jr etc, *Costumes* Mary Jane Fort, *Choreography* Ann Fletcher.

Universal/Beacon Pictures-Entertainment.
98 mins. USA. 2000. Rel: 20 October 2000. Cert 12.

## The Broken Hearts Club ★★★★

West Hollywood, Los Angeles; the present. The centre of a close-knit coterie of gay men in their late twenties, Dennis suddenly decides he wants more out of life than casual sex and frivolous badinage. But he has become so entrenched in a certain gay-orientated lifestyle that 'getting out' could be as difficult as it was to 'come out'... As Dennis and his friends sit around complaining about the representation of homosexuals in American cinema (the Aids victim, the gay confidant, etc), they seem little aware that they are occupying the centre of a thriving new genre. Of course, most of these films – *Love! Valour! Compassion!*, *Billy's Hollywood Screen Kiss*, etc – have hardly gone mainstream. However, *The Broken Hearts Club*, a witty, calculatingly gay take on *Steel Magnolias*, is a film that should appeal to any mildly tolerant demographic with a sense of humour and a compassionate bone or two. Perceptive, energetic, extremely well acted and above all very funny, *The Broken Hearts Club* is not only a hugely entertaining film but an education for non-gay audiences.

● *Benji* Zach Braff, *Cole* Dean Cain, *Kevin* Andrew Keegan, *Leslie* Nia Long, *Jack* John Mahoney, *Anne* Mary McCormack, *Howie* Matt McGrath, *Dennis* Timothy Olyphant, *Taylor* Billy Porter, *Marshall* Justin Theroux, *Patrick* Ben Weber, *purple guy* Robert Arce, *Kip Rogers* Michael Bergin, *Betty* Jennifer Coolidge, *catcher* Kerr Smith, *with* Chris Payne Gilbert, John Brandon, Diane McBain, Chris Wiehl, Chris Kane, Chris Weitz, Matt Reid.
● *Dir* and *Screenplay* Greg Berlanti, *Pro* Mickey Liddell and Joseph Middleton, *Line Pro* Connie Dolph, *Co-Pro* Julie Plec and Sam Irvin, *Ph* Paul

Elliott, *Pro Des* Charlie Daboub, *Ed* Todd Busch, *M* Christopher Beck; songs performed by The Miracles, Georgio Moroder, Shannon, Barry Harris, Kim English, GTS, Kym Mazelle and Mary Beth Maziars, *Costumes* Mas Kondo, *Swing* Krit (Pon) Fagtongpun.

Banner Entertainment-Columbia TriStar.
95 mins. USA. 2000. Rel: 11 May 2001. Cert 15.

## Brother ★¹/₂

The technical skill displayed here prevents Takeshi Kitano's *Brother* from being insulting on all levels. Nevertheless, any film offering two hours of indiscriminate slaughter accompanied by minimal plot and characterisation is an insult to good taste (or perhaps it's worse, for this movie is posited on the notion that this violence will give pleasure to the audience). The director plays a yakuza who, seeking out his half-brother in LA, becomes caught up in conflicts involving rival drug dealers, their suppliers and the Mafia, with never a policeman in sight. The film also features an Afro-American (Omar Epps) who is recognised by this dealer in death as his soul brother and who comes to love and respect him in return. Kitano's most unpleasant work since *Violent Cop*, it's very well made and totally repugnant. [*Mansel Stimpson*]

● *Yamamoto* Beat Takeshi, *Denny* Omar Epps, *Ken* Claude Maki, *Shirase* Masaya Kato, *Harada* Ren Ohsugi, *Kato* Susumu Terajima, *Susimoto* James Shigeta, *with* Royale Watkins, Lombardo Boyar, Ryo Ishibashi, Tetsuya Watari, Kool Mo Dee, Tatyana Ali, Tuesday Night.
● *Dir* and *Screenplay* Takeshi Kitano, *Pro* Masayuki Mori and Jeremy Thomas, *Ph* Katsumi Yanagijima, *Pro Des* Norihiro Isoda, *Ed* Takeshi Kitano and Yoshinori Ota, *M* Joe Hisaishi, *Costumes* Yohji Yamamoto.

Recorded Picture Company/Office Kitano/FilmFour/BAC Films-FilmFour.
113 mins. Japan/UK/USA/France. 2000. Rel: 23 March 2001. Cert 18.

## But I'm a Cheerleader ★★

Because she's vegetarian, admires Georgia O'Keefe and dislikes kissing her boyfriend, Megan Bloomfield is presumed to be a lesbian by her family and is sent off to a rehab centre for gays (of which, apparently, there are more than 200 in the US). A model and willing student at True Directions, Megan is paired with the rebellious `Graham' and finds herself gradually falling in love… A camp satire of homophobia, Jamie Babbit's debut feature misses its target by a mile as it pays homage to John Waters and succumbs to some rather obvious (and repetitious) slapstick. There are some nice performances from Natasha Lyonne and the constantly underrated Clea DuVall, and a surprising turn from RuPaul (who sports a T-shirt with the legend `Straight is Great'), but the film just isn't as funny as it thinks it is.

● *Megan Bloomfield* Natasha Lyonne, *Graham Eaton* Clea DuVall, *Dolph* Dante Basco, *Mike* RuPaul Charles, *Rock* Eddie Cibrian, *Peter Bloomfield* Bud Cort, *Hilary* Melanie Lynskey, *Lloyd* Wesley Mann, *Joel* Joel Michaely, *Mary J. Brown* Cathy Moriarty, *Nancy Bloomfield, Megan's mom* Mink Stole, *Andre* Douglas Spain, *Clayton* Kip Pardue, *Jan* Katrina Phillips, *Kimberly* Michelle Williams, *with* Ione Skye, Katharine Towne, Richard Moll, Julie Delpy.
● *Dir* Jamie Babbit, *Pro* Andrea Sperling and Leanna Creel, *Ex Pro* Michael Burns, Marc Butan, Peter Locke and Donald Kushner, *Screenplay* Brian Wayne Peterson, *Ph* Jules Labarthe, *Pro Des* Rachel Kamerman, *Ed* Cecily Rhett, *M* Pat Irwin; songs performed by April March, Dressy Bessy, Sissy Bar, Saint Etienne, Summer's Eve, Wanda Jackson, Go Sailor, RuPaul, Lois etc, *Costumes* Alix Friedberg.

Franchise Pictures/Ignite Entertainment/Kushner-Locke/HKM Films-Metrodome.
89 mins. USA. 1999. Rel: 9 March 2001. Cert 15.

## Butterfly's Tongue – La Lengua de las Mariposas ★★★★¹/₂

Traditional filmmaking of a thoroughly reliable kind, José Luis Cuerda's childhood study is set in rural Spain in the mid-thirties. It centres on eight-year-old Moncho (Lozano) and portrays the beneficial influence on him of an elderly teacher (the well-cast Fernán-Gómez). The film also encompasses adolescent love, a family secret and the sexual discoveries common to rites of passage movies, all as part of its portrait of a community. Two thirds of the way through, however, the film becomes something more substantial. It may not quite equal Louis Malle's *Au Revoir, Les Enfants*, but the increasingly disturbing build-up of pressures foreshadowing the Spanish Civil War and the revelation that not even young Moncho can remain unaffected by them lead to a conclusion all the more powerful for making no concessions to popular appeal. [*Mansel Stimpson*]

● *Don Gregorio* Fernando Fernán-Gómez, *Moncho* Manuel Lozano, *Rosa* Uxía Blanco, *Ramón* Gonzalo Uriarte, *Andrés* Alexis de Los Santos, *O'Lis* Guillermo Toledo, Tamar Novas, Elena Fernández, Jesús Castejón, Roberto Vidal
● *Dir* José Luis Cuerda, *Ex Pro* Cuerda and Fernando Bovaira, *Screenplay* Rafael Azcona, based on *La Lengua de las Mariposas*, *Carmiña* and *Un Saxo en a niebla*, from the book *¿Qué me quieres amor?* by Manuel Rivas, *Ph* Javier Salmones, *Pro Des* Josep Rosell, *Ed* Nacho Ruiz Capillas, *M* Alejandro Amenábar, *Costumes* Sonia Grande.

Sogtel/Canal Plus, etc-Metrodome.
95 mins. Spain. 1998. Rel: 28 July 2000. Cert 15.

## Captain Corelli's Mandolin ★★★

Argostoli, Cephallonia, Ionian Islands; 1940-1947. An island in the Ionian Sea, Cephallonia is inhabited by goats and madmen and has been half forgotten by the world. Then, during the Second World War, Cephallonia is occupied by Italian forces and Captain Antonio Corelli comes to stay with Dr Iannis, the proud doctor of the village of Argostoli. At first viewed as a hostile enemy, Corelli, a mandolin-playing soldier with a passion for life and music – and for Iannis' daughter, Pelagia – is gradually accepted into the fabric of the island... The epic, complex story of a tragic community, Louis de Bernières' publishing phenomenon was bound to be adapted to the screen. The fact that Miramax have decided to turn the novel into a chocolate box romance is irrelevant. What is sad is that the island of Cephallonia has lost its sense of place. The Iannis house has no other function than as a platform for the characters' drama (where, for instance, does Pelagia sleep?), while the island itself has been transformed into a mythical Paradise. Even this would be OK if the story's structure hadn't been so disjointed. Nevertheless, the film has a number of incidental pleasures, including a magnificent performance from John Hurt as the wise and dignified Dr Iannis, some glorious cinematography and, of course, the wonderful mandolin playing of Corelli.

● *Captain Antonio Corelli* Nicolas Cage, *Pelagia* Penélope Cruz, *Dr Iannis* John Hurt, *Mandras* Christian Bale, *Captain Gunter Weber* David Morrissey, *Drosoula* Irene Papas, *Eleni, Pelagia's friend* Viki Maragaki, *the younger Lemoni* Joanna-Daria Adraktas, *the older Lemoni* Ira Tavlaridis, *with* Gerasimos Skiadaresis, Aspasia Kralli, Michalis Giannatos, George Kotanidis, Piero Maggiò, Vincenzo Ricotta, Patrick Malahide.
● *Dir* John Madden, *Pro* Tim Bevan, Eric Fellner, Kevin Loader and Mark Huffam, *Co-Pro* Jane Frazer and Debra Hayward, *Screenplay* Shawn Slovo, based on the novel by Louis de Bernières, *Ph* John Toll, *Pro Des* Jim Clay, *Ed* Mick Audsley, *M* Stephen Warbeck, *Costumes* Alexandra Byrne, *Dialect coach* Joan Washington.

Universal/Canal Plus/Miramax/Working Title/Free Range Films-UIP.
140 mins. USA/France/UK. 2001. Rel: 4 May 2001. Cert 15.

## The Captive – La Captive ★★★

Proust's literary masterpiece is so vast that it's no surprise to find that this free modernisation of one section of it at no point duplicates either *Swann In Love* or *Time Regained*. *The Captive* centres on

**Above:** Penélope Cruz is disappointed that Nicolas Cage forgot the chocolates with the caramel crème centres – in John Madden's disjointed and glutinous Captain Corelli's Mandolin (from UIP)

Simon (Merhar) and his intense desire for Ariane (the striking Sylvie Testud), which leads him into obsessive jealousy over any affairs, real or imagined, she may be having. There's psychological truth in the way that Simon's need for control and exclusivity makes him determined to know everything about the woman he loves (a male need which renders him vulnerable to fearful speculation about lesbianism and Ariane's possible involvement in it). Chantal Akerman's film possesses style and precision, but her total lack of sympathy for Simon keeps us distanced and the film ends in needless obscurity. Thought provoking, but also taxing. [*Mansel Stimpson*]

● *Simon* Stanislas Merhar, *Ariane* Sylvie Testud, *Andrée* Olivia Bonamy, *Françoise* Liliane Rovere, *grandmother* Françoise Bertin, *Léa* Aurore Clement, *with* Vanessa Larré, Samuel Tasinaje, Anna Mouglalis.

● *Dir* Chantal Akerman, *Pro* Paulo Branco, *Screenplay* Akerman and Erik de Kuyper, inspired by Marcel Proust's *La Prisonnière*, *Ph* Sabine Lancelin, *Pro Des* Antoine Beau, *Ed* Claire Atherton, *M* Rachmaninov, Schubert, Mozart, *Costumes* Nathalie Du Roscoät.

Gemini Films/Arte France Cinema/Paradise Films/Canal Plus/CNC/Gimages 3-Artificial Eye.
118 mins. France/Belgium. 2000. Rel: 27 April 2001. Cert 15.

## Caravan
*See Himalaya*

## Cast Away ★★★★
Federal Express trouble-shooter Chuck Noland lives by the clock and is proud of the fact. In Moscow, he commandeers a child's bike to make a delivery on time, an act he regards as a testament to his integrity. He believes in keeping promises: to his employer, his clients, his girlfriend Kelly. When he's asked to supervise a shipment over the Christmas holiday, he pledges to Kelly that he will be back in time for New Year's Eve. But he never figured that his plane would go down in the Pacific... This is a great story with a huge message with a major star directed by a master technician. From the opening scene in which a FedEx package makes its way from Tennessee to Moscow, to the closing question mark, *Cast Away* exerts a powerful spell. Hanks invests extraordinary energy into his performance and lost 55 pounds in an eight-month hiatus between the shooting of the first and second part of the movie. There's also a sensational plane crash (up there with *Alive* and *Fearless*), some glorious cinematography and a surprising lack of mawkishness. The movie is long, but then it really needs to be.

● *Chuck Noland* Tom Hanks, *Kelly Frears* Helen Hunt, *Stan* Nick Searcy, *Bettina Peterson* Lari White, *Jerry Lovett* Chris Noth, *with* Jenifer Lewis, Geoffrey Blake, Peter Von Berg, Semion Sudarikov, Michael Forest, Viveka Davis, Nan Martin, Anne Bellamy, Dennis Letts, Elden Henson, Vin Martin, Garret Davis, Jay Acovone, Fred Smith.
● *Dir* Robert Zemeckis, *Pro* Zemeckis, Steve Starkey, Tom Hanks and Jack Rapke, *Ex Pro* Joan Bradshaw, *Screenplay* William Broyles Jr, *Ph* Don Burgess, *Pro Des* Rick Carter, *Ed* Arthur Schmidt, *M* Alan Silvestri; songs performed by Elvis Presley, Chuck Berry, Charles Brown and Vince Guaraldi, *Costumes* Joanna Johnston, *Visual effects* Ken Ralston, *Sound* Randy Thom, *weight loss advisor* Dr Paul McAuley.

DreamWorks/Fox/Imagemovers/Playtone-UIP.
144 mins. USA. 2000. Rel: 12 January 2001. Cert 12.

## Cecil B. Demented ★★
Hollywood goddess Honey Whitlock is in Baltimore for the premiere of her new film, *Some Kind of Happiness*. But no sooner has she stepped onto the stage of the Senator Theatre, than she is abducted at gunpoint by renegade director Cecil B Demented. He and his motley crew of underground filmmakers then force her to star in their own anarchic, zero-budgeted feature... John Waters, who's now 54, still trades on his reputation as the Pope of Trash/Prince of Puke and is still producing provocative ideas. Here, in this outrageous attack on mainstream cinema, he chucks out dialogue like, 'We're horny – but the film comes first,' and punctuates the horizon with cinema marquees offering such treasures as *Patch Adams – The Director's Cut*. However, this is a one-joke film with one-note stereotypes and after half an hour it all becomes very tedious.

● *Honey Whitlock* Melanie Griffith, *Sinclair Stevens* aka *Cecil B Demented* Stephen Dorff, *Cherish* Alicia Witt, *Lyle* Adrian Grenier, *Lewis* Larry Gilliard Jr, *Raven* Maggie Gyllenhaal, *Rodney* Jack Noseworthy, *Petie* Mike Shannon, *Dinah* Harriet Dodge, *Chardonnay* Zenzele Uzoma, *Fidget* Eric M Barry, *Pam* Erika Lynn Rupli, *Mrs. Mallory* Mink Stole, *Fidget's mother* Patty Hearst, *Libby* Ricki Lake, *with* Roseanne, Eric Roberts, Ray Felton, Peter Gil, John Waters.
● *Dir* and *Screenplay* John Waters, *Pro* John Fielder, Joe Caracciolo Jr and Mark Tarlov, *Ex Pro* Anthony DeLorenzo and Fred Bernstein, *Assoc Pro* Pat Moran, *Ph* Robert Stevens, *Pro Des* Vincent Peranio, *Ed* Jeffrey Wolf, *M* Zoë Poledouris and Basil Poledouris; songs performed by Moby, The Locust, Teflon the Bull, Meatjack, The Sex-O-Rama Band, Liberace etc, *Costumes* Van Smith.

Artisan Entertainment/Canal Plus/Polar Entertainment-Momentum Pictures.
88 mins. USA/France. 2000. Rel: 8 December 2000. Cert 18.

## The Cell ★★★
In a small chamber within the bowels of a research institute, a psychologist attempts to make contact with a comatose boy through the wonders of 'synaptic transfer'. By literally entering her patient's mindscape, Catherine Deane hopes to bring the boy back to consciousness. While she is actually dealing in an untried science, Catherine is the only hope for FBI agent Peter Novak, who needs to pinpoint the whereabouts of the latest victim of a comatose serial killer... On one level, *The Cell* is a unique and shattering piece of cinema. However, its obscure scientific methodology and sci-fi antecedents (*Coma*, *Dreamscape*, *The Lawnmower Man*) merely cloak something far more disturbing. Another variation of

*Seven* and *The Silence of the Lambs*, the film dresses up its depravity with breathtaking theatrical effects, digital technology and the presence of vultures, snakes, bugs and spiders. But while attempting to justify its agenda through some psychobabble about the innocent boy trapped within the monstrous man, it cannot disguise either its blood lust or its misogyny. Think of the darkest science fiction of, say, Robin Cook reinvented by H R Giger (or indeed Salvador Dalí), and you'd be on the right track. FYI: First-time director Tarsem Singh, who was educated in a Himalayan boarding school, has won numerous awards for his commercials and music videos.

● *Catherine Deane* Jennifer Lopez, *Peter Novak* Vince Vaughn, *Carl Stargher* Vincent D'Onofrio, *Dr Miriam Kent* Marianne Jean-Baptiste, *Gordon Ramsey* Jake Weber, *Henry West* Dylan Baker, *Julia Hickson* Tara Subkoff, *Dr Cooperman* Gerry Becker, *Edward Baines* Colton James, *Dr Reid* Pruitt Taylor Vince, *with* James Gammon, Dean Norris, Musetta Vander, Patrick Bauchau, Catherine Sutherland, Lauri Johnson, John Cothran Jr, Jack Conley, Jake Thomas, Gareth Williams, Glenda Chism, *Valentine the dog* Tim.
● *Dir* Tarsem Singh, *Pro* Julio Caro and Eric McLeod, *Ex Pro* Donna Langley and Carolyn Manetti, *Co-Pro* Mark Protosevich and Stephen J Ross, *Screenplay* Protosevich, *Ph* Paul Laufer, *Pro Des* Tom Foden, *Ed* Paul Rubell and Robert Duffy, *M* Howard Shore, *Costumes* Eiko Ishioka and April Napier, *Visual effects* Kevin Tod Haug.

New Line Cinema/Caro-McLeod/Radical Media-Entertainment.
107 mins. USA. 2000. Rel: 15 September 2000. Cert 18.

## Centre Stage ★★

New York; the present. A number of ballet students from various backgrounds fight their own personal demons as they strive to compete in a year-end performance that could launch their careers... With its contemporary stereotypes and stock situations, this dated amalgam of *Fame* and *The Turning Point* does boast some marvellous dance sequences, but stops in its tracks whenever the music gives way to yet more teenage angst. Director Nicholas Hytner (*The Madness of King George*) does manage to expose the pain and perspiration involved in competitive dance but fails to provide a credible canvas for his characters to bleed on. [*Ewen Brownrigg*]

● *Jody* Amanda Schull, *Eva* Zoë Saldana, *Maureen* Susan May Pratt, *Jonathan Reeves* Peter Gallagher, *Nancy* Debra Monk, *Juliette* Donna Murphy, *Cooper* Ethan Stiefel, *Charlie* Sascha Radetsky, *Sergei* Ilia Kulik, *Jim* Eion Bailey, *Erik* Shakiem Evans.
● *Dir* Nicholas Hytner, *Pro* Laurence Mark, *Co-Pro*

**Above:** *A mind of her own: Jennifer Lopez in cerebral mode in Tarsem Singh's disturbing, visually astonishing* The Cell *(from Entertainment)*

Caroline Baron, *Screenplay* Carol Heikkinen, *Ph* Geoffrey Simpson, *Pro Des* David Gropman, *Ed* Tariq Anwar, *M* George Fenton; Tchaikovsky; songs performed by Mandy Moore, International Five, Ashley Ballard, PYT, Thunderbugs, Cyrena, Jamiroquai, Red Hot Chilli Peppers, Elvis Crespo and Gizelle D'Cole, Michael Jackson, and Ruff Endz, *Costumes* Ruth Myers, *Choreography* Susan Stroman and Christopher Wheeldon.

Columbia-Columbia TriStar.
113 mins. USA. 2000. Rel: 16 February 2001. Cert 12.

## Charlie's Angels ★

Beautiful, bright and highly skilled in the martial arts, Natalie, Dylan and Alex are crack agents employed by Charles Townsend Associates, a hi-tech private detective outfit. When they are hired to

*Above: Three's a clown: Lucy Liu, Cameron Diaz and Drew Barrymore in McG's silly, brainless Charlie's Angels (from Columbia TriStar)*

recover a state-of-the-art voice-recognition security system, the girls discover that they have been set up by somebody determined to wipe out Charlie himself... A high-concept fiasco with a low IQ, this update of the 1976-81 TV series is a cacophonous insult to its audiences' intelligence. With pilfered stunts from other movies (*Mission: Impossible*), borrowed music cues (*Mission: Impossible*, James Bond) and inane cultural references (when the girls appear in kimonos, The Vapors' `Turning Japanese' pops up on the soundtrack), *Charlie's Angels* is an adolescent, undisciplined mishmash of recycled ephemera. And the giggling ineptitude of its protagonists makes little sense as they manage to survive insurmountable odds with barely a bruise between them. Miss Marple would be horrified.

● *Natalie* Cameron Diaz, *Dylan* Drew Barrymore, *Alex* Lucy Liu, *John Bosley* Bill Murray, *Eric Knox* Sam Rockwell, *Roger Corwin* Tim Curry, *Vivian Wood* Kelly Lynch, *Thin Man* Crispin Glover, *Jason* Matt LeBlanc, *Mr Jones* LL Cool J, *Chad* Tom Green, *Pete* Luke Wilson, *Pasqual* Sean Whalen, *with* Tim Dunaway, Alex Trebek, Mark Ryan, Melissa McCarthy, Ned Bellamy, Andrew Wilson, *voice of Charlie* John Forsythe.

● *Dir* McG (Joseph McGinty Nichol), *Pro* Leonard Goldberg, Drew Barrymore and Nancy Juvonen, *Ex Pro* Betty Thomas, Jenno Topping and Joseph M. Caracciolo, *Screenplay* Ryan Rowe & Ed Solomon and John August, *Ph* Russell Carpenter, *Pro Des* J. Michael Riva, *Ed* Wayne Wahrman and Peter Teschner, *M* Edward Shearmur; songs performed by Korn, Mötley Crüe, Wham!, The Flying Lizards, Joan Jett & The Blackhearts, Apollo Four Forty, Juice Newton, Tavares, Enigma, The Vapors, Destiny's Child, Deee-Lite, Prodigy, Aerosmith, Nomad, Heart, Spandau Ballet, Leo Sayer, Digital Underground, Caviar, Sir Mix-A-Lot, Marvin Gaye, Jan Hammer, Looking Glass, Lunatic Calm, Hednoize, Blur, Michael Jackson, Fatboy Slim, Rod Stewart, Blink 182, *Costumes* Joseph G. Aulisi.

Columbia Pictures/Leonard Goldberg/Flower Films/Tall Trees Prods-Columbia TriStar.
98 mins. USA. 2000. Rel: 24 November 2000. Cert 15.

## Cherry Falls ★¹/₂

Cherry Falls, Virginia (where else?); the present. When the chaste students of George Washington High find out that a psycho killer is targeting the local

**Left:** Brittany points out the waiter who confused the order for cherry coke – in Geoffrey Wright's ludicrous Cherry Falls (from Entertainment)

virgins, they quickly abandon the high moral ground. But before the cherries pop, some more cherries fall... This may be virgin territory for Australian director Geoffrey Wright (of *Romper Stomper* notoriety), but he's pulling the same rabbits out of old hats. Note: 1) Frightened girl in darkened library should not retreat *backwards* down a corridor; 2) Unarmed boy in the woods at night should *not* approach a car whose owner he cannot identify; 3) Casting directors should *not* hire Michael Biehn when they are looking for credibility. And so on. As it happens, *Cherry Falls* is meant to be a satire, but its tone is so straight that it plays like a bad slasher pic (which, for all its protestations, it is). After *Scream* it's hard to take these things seriously, particularly an entry that adheres to the conventions of the genre so slavishly.

● *Jody Marken* Brittany Murphy, *Sheriff Brent Marken* Michael Biehn, *Kenny Ascott* Gabriel Mann, *Leonard Marliston* Jay Mohr, *Marge Marken* Candy Clark, *Deputy Mina* Amanda Anka, *Principal Tom Sisler* Joe Inscoe, *Sandy* Natalie Ramsey, *Mark* Douglas Spain, *Rod Harper* Jesse Bradford, *Ben* Michael Weston, *Timmy* Keram Malicki-Sanchez, *Special Agent Bronhill* Mark Joy, *with* Bre Blair, Kristen Miller, Joannah Portman, Vicki Davis.
● *Dir* Geoffrey Wright, *Pro* Marshall Persinger and Eli Selden, *Ex Pro* Scott Shiffman and Julie Silverman Yorn, *Co-Ex Pro* Ken Selden and Joyce Schweickert, *Screenplay* Ken Selden, *Ph* Anthony B Richmond, *Pro Des* Marek Dobrowolski, *Ed* John F. Link, *M* Walter Werzowa, *Costumes* Louise Frogley, *Sound* Harry Cohen and Steve Williams.

October Films/Rogue Pictures/Industry Entertainment/ Fresh Produce Company-Entertainment.
91 mins. USA. 1999. Rel: 25 August 2000. Cert 15.

## Children of Heaven ★★★★

Art and popular appeal go hand in hand in this Iranian film about a poor family. When the father attempts to find work with his young son in attendance, Majid Majidi achieves both an echo of De Sica's classic *Bicycle Thieves* and a compelling sequence of his own. But the main emphasis is on the boy, first his efforts to hide the loss of a pair of shoes by sharing with his sister, and then his attempt to redeem himself by winning a long distance running race. The sterner critics, disliking the fact that the finale recalls *Chariots of Fire*, were over harsh on a sincere, affecting film almost as good as its successor, *The Colour of Paradise*. The climax may push a bit too hard, but, humorous and touching by turn, the film is powered by its strong human sympathies. [*Mansel Stimpson*]

● Mohammed Amir Naji, Fereshte Sarabandi, Karnal Mirkarimi, Amir Farrokh Hashemian.
● *Dir* and *Screenplay* Majid Majidi, *Pro* Mohammed Sared Seyedzadeh, *Ph* Parviz Malekzaade, *Ed* Hassan Hassandoost. *No other credits available.*

Institute for the Intellectual Development of Children and Young Adults-Miramax.
86 mins. Iran. 1997. Rel: 7 July 2000. No Cert.

*Above: All because the lady loves…: Juliette Binoche sets things aright in Lasse Hallström's sophisticated and delicate* Chocolat *(from Buena Vista)*

## The Children of the Century

*See Les Enfants du siècle*

## Chocolat ★★★★

The village of Lansquenet, France, has pretty much remained unchanged for centuries. Wedded to tradition and the church, the populace is preparing for Lent when a mysterious woman and her young daughter arrive to take up the lease on a dilapidated patisserie. There, the woman, Vianne Rocher, opens a chocolaterie and starts tempting the locals with tastes beyond their wildest dreams… Much like the bewitching confectionery that Vianne serves up in her shop, *Chocolat* is a sophisticated, delicate truffle with a decidedly sweet tooth. Beautifully shot (in the French region of Burgundy), magically scored and impeccably acted by a particularly strong cast (with Judi Dench once again stealing every scene she is in),

*Chocolat* is a delight from the word go. A fairy tale that addresses very pertinent issues (tolerance, humanity, forgiveness), this is one film that makes a virtue of its originality.

● *Vianne Rocher* Juliette Binoche, *Armande Voizin* Judi Dench, *Comte De Reynaud* Alfred Molina, *Josephine Muscat* Lena Olin, *Roux* Johnny Depp, *Caroline Clairmont* Carrie-Anne Moss, *Guillaume Blerot* John Wood, *Madame Audel* Leslie Caron, *Luc Clairmont* Aurelien Parent Kocnig, *Yvette Marceau* Elizabeth Commelin, *Alphonse Marceau* Ron Cook, *Pere Henri* Hugh O'Conor, *Serge Muscat* Peter Stormare, *Anouk Rocher* Victoire Thivisol, *with* Antonio Gil-Martinez, Helene Cardona, Arnaud Adam, *Charly the Dog* Sally.
● *Dir* Lasse Hallström, *Pro* David Brown, Kit Golden and Leslie Holleran, *Ex Pro* Bob Weinstein, Harvey Weinstein, Meryl Poster and Alan C Blomquist, *Co-Pro* Mark Cooper, *Co-Ex Pro* Michelle Raimo, *Screenplay* Robert Nelson Jacobs, from the novel by Joanne Harris, *Ph* Roger Pratt, *Pro Des* David Gropman, *Ed* Andrew Mondshein, *M* Rachel Portman, *Costumes* Renée Ehrlich Kalfus, *Chocolate expert* Walter Bienz.

Miramax-Buena Vista.
121 mins. USA. 2000. Rel: 2 March 2001. Cert 12.

## Chopper ★★★¹/₂

Australia; 1978-1991. Convicted for a bungled kidnapping attempt, Mark 'Chopper' Read kills his first man in the maximum security wing of Melbourne's Pentridge Prison. Released eight years later, Chopper enters the real world and resolves to build on his growing reputation as a ruthless thug… Part-social commentary, part-black comedy, *Chopper* hacks out its own unique genre as a semi-fictionalised portrait of Australia's most notorious killer after Ned Kelly. At times displaying an almost documentary-like realism, the film attempts to explain how a common criminal becomes intoxicated by his own notoriety. But while doing this, it also takes enormous pleasure in poking fun at more serious pictures like *Henry: Portrait of a Serial Killer*. However, all this would have been for nought were it not for Eric Bana's extraordinary performance. Actually suggested by Chopper himself, stand-up comic Bana manages to be both sympathetic and frightening, honourable and despicable, changing in the course of 13 years from a slim, clean-cut con to a bloated, metal-dentured monster, a man governed by unpredictable outbursts of rage tempered by moments of abject apology.

● *Mark 'Chopper' Brandon Read* Eric Bana, *Jimmy Loughnan* Simon Lyndon, *Keithy George* David Field, *Bluey* Dan Wyllie, *Det Downie* Bill Young, *Neville*

*Bartos* Vince Colosimo, *Keith Read* Kenny Graham, *Tanya* Kate Beahan, *with* Gary Waddell, Caleb Duff, Hilton Henderson, Fred Barker, Brian Mannix, Robert Rabiah, Serge Liistro, Pam Western, Peter Hardy, Skye Wansey, David Paterson.
● *Dir* and *Screenplay* Andrew Dominik, based on the books of Mark Brandon Read, *Pro* Michele Bennett, *Ex Pro* Al Clark and Martin Fabinyi, *Co-Pro* Michael Gudinski, *Ph* Kevin Hayward and Geoffrey Hall, *Pro Des* Paddy Reardon, *Ed* Ken Sallows, *M* Mick Harvey; songs performed by Frankie Laine, Chain, Rose Tattoo, The Saints, The Loved Ones etc, *Costumes* Terry Ryan, *Sound* Frank Lipson, *2nd unit director* Rowan Woods.

Pariah Films/Australian Film Finance Corp./Mushroom Pictures/Film Victoria-Metrodome.
94 mins. Australia. 2000. Rel: 24 November 2000. Cert 18.

## Chuck and Buck ★★★★

A brilliantly original work, this tale cleverly twists our expectations. Buck (played impressively by the film's writer Mike White) pursues his former childhood friend Chuck to Los Angeles. At once a comic and disturbing figure, Buck's persistent interference with Chuck at work and in his relationship with his girl-friend brings to mind newspaper reports of sinister stalkers. But then we realise that, retarded as he seems to be, Buck's determination to get Chuck to acknowl-edge the sexual bond which existed between them in their childhood is justified. We suddenly see that it's Chuck, in denial about his homosexuality, who is the more truly immature. Although presumably not intending it, the film is unfortunately capable of being read as a work which equates homosexuality with the inability to outgrow an infantile state. Nevertheless, it's powerful, intriguing and not with-out humour. A film to see and discuss. [*Mansel Stimpson*]

● *Buck O'Brien* Mike White, *Charlie 'Chuck' Sitter* Chris Weitz, *Beverly* Lupe Ontiveros, *Carlyn* Beth Colt, *Sam* Paul Weitz, *Jamila* Maya Rudolph, *with* Mary Wigmore, Paul Sand, Gino Buccola, Annette Murphy, Tony Maxwell, Vince Duffy, Chuy Chávez.
● *Dir* Miguel Arteta, *Pro* Matthew Greenfield, *Ex Pro* Jason Kliot and Joana Vicente, *Co-Ex Pro* Thomas Brown and Charles J Rusbasan, *Co-Pro* Scott M Cort and Beth Colt, *Screenplay* Mike White, *Ph* Chuy Chávez, *Pro Des* Renée Davenport, *Ed* Jeff Betancourt, *M* Joey Waronker, Tony Maxwell and Smokey Hormel, *Costumes* Elaine Montalvo, *Sound* Ann Scibelli.

Artisan Entertainment/Blow Up Pictures/Flan De Coco-Metrodome.
95 mins. USA. 2000. Rel: 10 November 2000. Cert 15.

## The Claim ★★★

Sierra Nevada, California; 1867. A town built on the spoils of the Gold Rush, Kingdom Come is ruled with a rod of iron by Daniel Dillon, an Irish immi-grant. Then the arrival of a surveyor and his men from the Central Pacific Railroad brings new blood to the community. But it is the appearance of Dillon's wife and daughter, whom he had sold for gold many years earlier, that really sets the cat among the pigeons... Transplanting Thomas Hardy's *The Mayor of Casterbridge* to 1860s California, Michael Winterbottom has found himself a suitably visceral and pictorial canvas for his cinematic prowess. From the blizzard-stung mountains of the Sierra Nevada to the minimalist interiors and cruelly naked complex-ions of the cast, *The Claim* is a visual treat. It also boasts complex characters, whose moral shading shifts with the evolution of the story, as well as a strong narrative. Even so, due to a stylistic preva-lence, the characters never seem entirely real, as if fixed in an old, sepia-tinted photograph. Nevertheless, this is a riveting, albeit emotionally unengaging, examination of a fascinating period of American history. Filmed in Alberta and Colorado. Previously known as *Kingdom Come*.

● *Dalglish* Wes Bentley, *Lucia* Milla Jovovich, *Elena Dillon* Nastassja Kinski, *Daniel Dillon* Peter Mullan, *Hope Dillon* Sarah Polley, *Bellinger* Julian Richings, *Sweetley* Sean McGinley, *Annie* Shirley Henderson, *with* Marie Brassard, Bill Chesterman, Artur Ciastkowski, Duncan Fraser, Kate Hennig, Tom McCamus.
● *Dir* Michael Winterbottom, *Pro* Andrew Eaton, *Ex Pro* Martin Katz, Alexis Lloyd, Andrea Calderwood, David M Thompson and Mark Shivas, *Line Pro* Anita Overland, *Co-Pro* Douglas Berquist, *Screenplay* Frank Cottrell Boyce, *Ph* Alwin Kuchler, *Pro Des* Mark Tildesley, *Ed* Trevor Waite, *M* Michael Nyman, *Costumes* Joanne Hansen.

United Artists/Revolution Films/DB Entertainment/Grosvenor Park Prods/Arts Council of England/Canal Plus/Alliance Atlantis/National Lottery/BBC Films-Pathé.
120 mins. UK/Canada/France. 2000. Rel: 2 February 2000. Cert 15.

## The Closer You Get ★★★★

In the village of Kilvara, one of the more isolated cor-ners of County Donegal, the men folk are bemoaning the lack of romance and sex in their lives. So they place an ad in *The Miami Herald* extolling the virtues of their picturesque village, inviting fit, sporty and beautiful women – 'ideally between the ages of 20 and 21' – to their annual St Martha's Day dance. And so, in a frenzy of anticipation, the men embark on improving their health and appearance... Full of charm and brimming with priceless moments of incidental humour, this wryly wrought, offbeat human comedy joins the ranks of *Hear My Song* and *Waking Ned* as a slice of feel-good Irish whimsy. From the array of expertly judged performances (is Ian Hart Britain's most undervalued actor?) to an uplifting score from Rachel Portman (her best in aeons), this is pure joy. Incidentally, the story was inspired by a real incident in Barcelona in which a group of Spanish men advertised for brides.

● *Kiernan O'Donnagh* Ian Hart, *Ian O'Donnagh* Sean McGinley, *Kate* Niamh Cusack, *Mary* Ruth McCabe, *Pat* Ewan Stewart, *Sean* Sean McDonagh, *Siobhan* Cathleen Bradley, *Ollie* Pat Shortt, *Ella* Deborah Barnett, *Father Hubert Mallone* Risteard Cooper, *Dollie* Maureen O'Brien, *with* Pat Laffan, Frank Laverty, Britta Smith, Patricia Martin, Doreen Keough, Pauline Hutton, Nuala O'Neill, Dessie Gallagher, Joan Sheehy, Michael McDougall, Nora Keneghan.
● *Dir* Aileen Ritchie, *Pro* Uberto Pasolini, *Co-Pro* Polly Leys and Mark Huffam, *Screenplay* William Ivory, from a story by Herbie Wave, *Ph* Robert Alazraki, *Pro Des* Tom McCullagh, *Ed* Sue Wyatt, *M* Rachel Portman; songs performed by The Saw Doctors, Edwyn Collins, Touch & Go, The Proclaimers, Ricky Valance, The Real Thing, Louis Armstrong, Jackie Wilson, Mae McKenna and John Parricelli, etc, *Costumes* Kathy Strachan.

Fox Searchlight/Redwave/Irish Film Industry-Fox.
92 mins. USA/UK/Ireland. 1999. Rel: 8 September 2000. Cert 12.

## Code Unknown – Code inconnu Récit incomplet de divers voyages ★★★

Paris; the present. An urban mosaic of contemporary alienation, *Code Unknown* is a far cry from Michael Haneke's last two films released here, *Benny's Video* and *Funny Games*, both of which were extremely disturbing contemplations of violence. Here, Haneke takes a number of disparate characters and haphazardly eavesdrops on their lives as they struggle to communicate in a society that denies us our right to individuality. Thus, a deaf child desperately tries to convey an acted 'emotion' to her classmates. A young black teacher is arrested for reprimanding a teenager after the latter has humiliated a beggar. An actress attempts to discover the identity of the writer of an SOS pushed through her letter box. And so on... *Code Unknown* (subtitled *Incomplete Tales of Several Journeys*) is perceptive, intelligent and daring but structurally lazy. Opening in London a week after *Amores Perros* [qv], a similarly turbulent portrait of a major city in social crisis (Mexico City in lieu of Paris), Haneke's cinematic essay does leave one yearning for a stronger narrative.

● *Anne Laurent* Juliette Binoche, *Georges* Thierry Neuvic, *the farmer* Sepp Bierbichler, *Jean* Alexandre Hamidi, *Aminate* Hélène Diarra, *Amadou* Ona Lu Yenke, *the father* Djibril Kouyate, *Salimata* Guessi Diakite-Goumdo, *Maria* Luminita Gheorghiu, *the director* Didier Flamand, *with* Crenguta Hariton Stoica, Bob Niculescu, Bruno Todeschni, Paulus Manker, Walide Afkir, Arsinée Khanjian, Nathalie Richard, Féodor Atkine.
● *Dir* and *Screenplay* Michael Haneke, *Pro* Marin Karmitz and Alain Sarde, *Line Pro* Yvon Crenn, *Ph* Jürgen Jürges, *Ed* Andreas Prochaska, Karin Hartusch and Nadinee Muse, *M* Giba Gonçalves, *Costumes* Françoise Clavel, *war photos* Luc Delahaye.
Arte France Cinema/France 2 Cinema/Bavaria Film/ZDF/Romanian Culture Ministry/Filmex Romania/Canal Plus/Eurimages/Procirep-Artificial Eye.
117 mins. France/Germany/Romania. 2000. Rel: 25 May 2001. Cert 15.

## The Colour of Paradise – Ranghe-khoda ★★★★¹/₂

Although eight-year-old Mohammad has been blind from birth, his perception of his surroundings is remarkable. However, his widowed father, a self-pitying coal worker, seems oblivious to the beauty of the mountainous region in which they live. In fact, Mohammad's father is planning to abandon his son so that he can get on with his own colourless life... Seldom does one film produce so many remarkable images: the blind boy awkwardly climbing a tree to reinstate a baby bird to its nest, a train of peasant girls carrying trees as if sporting a new line in verdant overcoats, an old woman scooping up a stranded fish and carrying it to deeper water... Yet in spite of the visual power of the film's palette, it is the presence of the young and genuinely blind Mohsen Ramezani that really distinguishes Majidi's poetic and wonderfully poignant film. The Iranian title translates as *The Colour of God*. FYI: Majid Majidi previously directed *Children of Heaven* [qv], the only Iranian feature to receive an Oscar nomination for best foreign-language film.

● *Mohammad* Mohsen Ramezani, *Hasham, Mohammad's father* Hossein Mahjub, *Granndmother* Salameh Feyzi, *Hanyeh, Mohammad's sister* Elham Shafifi, *Bahareh, Mohammad's other sister* Farahnaz Safari, *blind centre teacher* Mohammad Rahamaney, *with* Zahra Mizani, Kamal Mirkarimi, Morteza Fatemi.
● *Dir* and *Screenplay* Majid Majidi, *Pro* Mehdi Mahabadi, Ali Ghaem Maghami and Mohsen Sarab, *Ex Pro* Mehdi Karimi, *Ph* Hashem Attar, *Pro Des* Masood Madadi, *Ed* Hassan Hassandoost, *M* Ali Reza Kohandairi, *Costumes* Asghar Negadeimani.

Varahonar-Optimum Releasing.
90 mins. Iran. 1999. Rel: 4 August 2000. Cert PG.

## Confessions of a Trick Baby ★¹/₂

Crystal is a frumpy thief with an eating disorder. Cyclona is a scrawny lesbian who likes to chop people up. The only thing they have in common is the prison cell they share, a place for ritual masturbation and vomiting. Then the girls escape, head for Mexico and leave behind them a trail of death and destruction... A trashy, revisionist take on *Hansel and Gretel*, *Trick Baby* is so bad that it's almost watchable. With a fixation on vomiting, blood and profane language, it only periodically aspires to the exploitational heights of, say, *The Toxic Avenger*. Part of the problem is that Natasha Lyonne and Maria Celedonio are no Susan Sarandon and Geena Davis, while the characters they play possess no redeeming qualities whatsoever. The fact is, writer-director Matthew Bright just can't direct actors (Vincent Gallo, as the witch, turns in his weakest performance), although he delivers the occasional moment of self-mocking humour (as the witch is pushed into her oven, Crystal snaps, 'Roast in peace!').

● *Crystal/White Girl* Natasha Lyonne, *Cyclona/Angela* Maria Celedonio, *Sister Gomez* Vincent Gallo, *Mr Butz* David Alan Grier, *Det Crefilo* Bob Dawson, *Det Dollar* Jennifer Griffin, *Judge Kaltenbrenner* John Landis, *drifter* Michael T Weiss, *Mrs Wilson* April Telek, *Flacco* Max Perlich, *Blanca* Kendall Saunders, *Mousy* Nicole Parker Smith, *with* Richard Henderey, Pat Waldron, Tom Heaton, Julia Ocenas.
● *Dir* and *Screenplay* Matthew Bright, *Pro* Brad Wyman, *Ex Pro* Peter Locke, Donald Kushner, Samuel Hadida and Victor Hadida, *Assoc Pro* Natasha Lyonne, *Ph* Joel Ransom, *Pro Des* Joel Ransom, *Ed* Suzanne Hines, *M* Kennard Ramsey, *Costumes* Katia Stano.

Kusher Locke Co./Davis Film/Muse/Brad Wyman-Metro Tartan.
97 mins. USA/France/Canada. 1999. Rel: 24 November 2000. Cert 18.

## The Contender ★★★★★

The very near future; Washington DC. When the American president decides to nominate a woman, Laine Hanson, to be his second-in-command, her past comes under public scrutiny. However, Hanson refuses to deny that she was privy to a sexual indiscretion at university, insisting that her past and her personal life have no bearing on her professional integrity. Then incriminating photographs of her involved in a three-way sex act are released on the Internet... In spite of a mild tendency towards old-fashioned histrionics (underlined by a somewhat over-enthusiastic score), *The Contender* refuses to pander to cliché or trite cop-outs. Yet it's hard to recall when a film last brought politics so vividly to life. As it is, writer-director Rod Lurie (erstwhile film critic for *Empire* and *Premiere*) serves up some smashing dialogue, peppering his fast-paced scenario with sly references to recent American history (Chapperquiddick, Clinton's moral digression in the Oval Office). Lurie has also cooked up a magnificent banquet of meaty characters, providing the likes of Gary Oldman, Joan Allen, Jeff Bridges and Sam Elliott with the opportunity to deliver award-winning-calibre performances. It's a great story, too, stylishly executed, and one that manages to be hard-hitting, pertinent and surprisingly soul-stirring.

● *Shelly Runyon* Gary Oldman, *Laine Billings Hanson* Joan Allen, *President Jackson Evans* Jeff Bridges, *Reginald Webster* Christian Slater, *Jack Hathaway* William Petersen, *Oscar Billings* Philip Baker Hall, *Jerry Toliver* Saul Rubinek, *Kermit Newman* Sam Elliott, *Cynthia Lee* Mariel Hemingway, *Lewis Hollis* Mike Binder, *William Hanson* Robin Thomas, *Paige Willomina* Kathryn Morris, *Fiona Hathaway* Kristen Shaw, *Makerowitz* Douglas Urbanski, *with* Noah Fryrear, Angelica Torn, Joe Taylor, Tony Booth, Michael Kennedy, Larry King, Ric Young.
● *Dir* and *Screenplay* Rod Lurie, *Pro* Marc Frydman, Douglas Urbanski, Willi Baer and James Spies, *Ex Pro* Dr Rainer Bienger, Gary Oldman and Maurice Leblond, *Co-Pro* Scott Shiffman and Steve Loglisci, *Ph* Denis Maloney, *Pro Des* Alexander Hammond, *Ed* Michael Jablow, *M* Larry Groupe; Mozart, Chopin; songs performed by Jeff Bridges and Kim Carnes, Julianna Raye, *Costumes* Matthew Jacobsen, *Sound* Stephen Hunter Flick.

DreamWorks/Cinerenta/Cinecontender/Battleground/SE8 Group-Icon.
126 mins. USA/UK/Germany. 2000. Rel: 20 April 2001. Cert 15.

## Coyote Ugly ★★

Big Bad New York; today. Yearning to fulfil her dream as a songwriter, 21-year-old Violet Sanford finally shrugs off her ties to her widowed father and heads for New York. However, she hadn't realised what a tough business the music industry was to crack and ends up getting work at the eponymous saloon where the girls are expected to do more than just pour drinks... A calculated cross between *Cocktail* and *Flashdance* – with a dash of *Saturday Night Fever* – *Coyote Ugly* is not so much a movie, more a piece of ruthless packaging. But in an age when even the word slick is becoming undervalued, this cheesy by-the-numbers saga of the small-town girl finding her feet in the big city is too loosely developed to stick. Piper Perabo, a Spanish omelette of Julia Roberts, Carly Simon and Lauren Hutton, overreacts to everybody and everything like Bambi on a caffeine high, while even the editing is sloppy. The film does display some energy and the babes are gorgeous, but is that enough?

● *Violet Sanford* Piper Perabo, *Lil* Maria Bello, *Rachel* Bridget Moynahan, *Zoe* Tyra Banks, *Kevin O'Donnell* Adam Garcia, *Bill Sanford* John Goodman, *Gloria* Melanie Lynskey, *Cammie* Izabella Miko, *Lou* Del Pentecost, *Danny* Michael Weston, *herself* LeAnn Rimes, *with* Jeremy Rowley, Bud Cort, Victor Argo, Frank Medrano, Diane Hudock, Tara McLean, Ken Campbell, Jack McGee, *photographer* Michael Bay.
● *Dir* David McNally, *Pro* Jerry Bruckheimer and Chad Oman, *Ex Pro* Mike Stenson and Scott Gardenhour, *Screenplay* Gina Wendkos, *Ph* Amir Mokri, *Pro Des* Jon Hutman, *Ed* William Goldenberg, *M* Trevor Horn; songs performed by Sugar Ray, LeAnn Rimes, Snap, Def Leppard, Lenny Kravitz, Rare Blend, Third Eye Blind, INXS, Anastacia, Blondie, Pigeonhed, Joe Strummer and The Mescaleros, Kid Rock, The Stray Cats, Unwritten Law, Billy Idol, Don Henley, The Miracles, Elvis Presley etc, *Costumes* Marlene Stewart, *Choreographer* Travis Payne.

Touchstone Pictures/Jerry Bruckheimer Films–Buena Vista.
101 mins. USA. 2000. Rel: 20 October 2000. Cert 12.

## The Criminal ★★★

In spite of the presence of so many concurrent British crime thrillers, *The Criminal* starts exceedingly promisingly. Steven Mackintosh – sexy, dangerous, working class – is talking straight to camera about the ills of dance music, recalling the cocky voiceover of *Trainspotting*, *Lock, Stock...*, even *A Clockwork Orange*. We then realise that our hero is a little drunk and rambling on to some upper-crust crumpet in a late-night bar. Yet in spite of his fumbled attempts at smooth seduction, the girl goes back to his flat anyway – but doesn't last for long. Changing tack dramatically with a punch in the face – sustained by both the protagonist and the viewer – the film introduces us to Inspector Walker, a brutal and aggressive cop beautifully realised by Bernard Hill. There's also excellent support from Holly Aird as Hill's partner, a slick soundtrack from The Music Sculptors and some starkly atmospheric photography of rainy, nocturnal London. First-timer Julian Simpson is definitely a talent to watch – as stylist, writer of dialogue and a director of actors – but after a sublime first half, *The Criminal* unravels rapidly, ending up as a silly, convoluted and highly unsatisfactory contrivance.

● *'J'* Steven Mackintosh, *Sarah Reid/Sarah Maitland* Natasha Little, *Inspector Walker* Bernard Hill, *Det*

*Peter Hume* Eddie Izzard, *Det Rebecca White* Holly Aird, *Mason Reid* Yvan Attal, *Harris* Andrew Tiernan, *Noble* Barry Stearn, *Grace* Jana Carpenter, *Jonny* Daniel Brocklebank, *Clive* Norman Lovett, *Lucy* Lisa Jacobs, *Mr Thomas* Timothy Bateson, *with* Justin Shevlin, Abigail Blackmore, Matthew Blackmore, Ingrid Bradley, Lisa Jacobs.
● *Dir* and *Screenplay* Julian Simpson, *Pro* Chris Johnson, Mark Aarons and David Chapman, *Ex Pro* H Michael Heuser, Dan Genetti and Suzette Newman, *Line Pro* Paul Sarony, *Ph* Nic Morris, *Pro Des* Martyn John, *Ed* Aarons, *M* The Music Sculptors, *Costumes* Rosie Hackett.

Palm Pictures/Storm Entertainment/The Christopher Johnson Co-DownTown.
99 mins. UK/USA. 1999. Rel: 12 January 2001. Cert 15.

## The Crimson Rivers ★★★

A corpse with its hands cut off and its eyes gouged out is found strung 150-feet up a mountainside. Legendary vice cop Pierre Niémans is brought in from Paris to investigate and discovers a tight-knit community at the beck-and-call of an elite, self-governing university. Meanwhile, 60 miles away, another singularly unconventional cop is looking into the desecration of a mausoleum by skinheads... A huge hit in its native France, *The Crimson Rivers* offers spectacular vistas of the French Alps, two of the country's most charismatic screen presences (Reno and Cassel) and enough morbid pathology to keep Thomas Harris transfixed. The story is also rather gripping, particularly as it slyly draws Reno's impatient, world-weary Niémans and Cassel's unconventional, hot-headed Kerkerian into the same grisly case. However, no sooner have Niémans and Kerkerian teamed up beyond the halfway mark, than this dark, edgy thriller switches into a buddy-buddy movie of the Joel Silver school, complete with a ludicrous, far-fetched ending.

● *Pierre Niémans* Jean Reno, *Max Kerkerian* Vincent Cassel, *Fanny Ferreira/Judith Hérault* Nadia Fares, *Sister Andrée* Dominique Sanda, *Captain Dahmane* Karim Belkhadra, *Dr Bernard Chernezé* Jean-Pierre Cassel, *the dean* Didier Flamand, *with* Laurent Lafitte, Robert Gendreu, Christophe Bernard, Nicky Naude, Tonio Descanvelle, Olivier Rousset, Françoise Loreau.
● *Dir* Mathieu Kassovitz, *Pro* Alain Goldman, *Line Pro* Jerôme Chaloux, *Screenplay* Kassovitz and Jean-Christophe Grangé, based on the novel *Red Blood Rivers* by Grangé, *Ph* Thierry Arbogast, *Pro Des* Thierry Flamand, *Ed* Maryline Monthieux, *M* Bruno Coulais, *Sound* Vincent Tully and Cyril Holtz, *Snow and rain* Christophe Messaoudi, *Corpses* Jean-Christophe Spadaccini and Denis Gastou.

Gaumont/Legende Entreprises/TF1 Films/Canal Plus-Columbia TriStar.
105 mins. France. 2000. Rel: 8 June 2001. Cert 15.

## Crouching Tiger, Hidden Dragon – Wo Hu Zang Long ★★★★

Early 19th century; China. When the legendary warrior Li Mu Bai decides to entrust his 400-year-old sword, The Green Destiny, to a notable in Peking, it is stolen by a masked, and extraordinarily dextrous, thief. Resolved to win back the sword, Li's lifelong friend and female warrior Yu Shu Lien helps Li to uncover the identity of the thief, who turns out to be a spiteful and extremely beautiful young woman, Jen. Li offers to teach Jen the Wudan creed of fighting, but she rejects his offer, believing herself to be the greatest warrior of all... Having explored 18th century English society, 1970s New England amorality and the American Civil War, Taiwanese director Ang Lee now turns his attention to the martial arts. And art he brings to this extremely complex, sweeping tale of honour, revenge and destiny, as if David Lean had been unleashed on South-East Asia. From the arresting interiors to scenes set in Peking, the desert, mountains and bamboo forests, the film strikes a visually distinctive chord. Lee is also responsible for introducing the finest acting ever to grace such a genre piece, his performers bringing a profound dignity to many of the film's quieter scenes. But it is the gravity-defying, perspective-bending stunts that won this film its reputation, although much of the weightless combat might seem more at home in *Apollo 13*.

● *Li Mu Bai* Chow Yun-Fat, *Yu Shu Lien* Michelle Yeoh, *Jen* Zhang ZiYi, *Lo* Chang Chen, *Sir Te* Lung Sihung, *Jade Fox* Cheng Pei Pei, *Governor Yu* Li Fa Zeng, *with* Gao Xian, Hai Yan, Wang Deming, Li Li, Li Kai, Feng Jian Hua.
● *Dir* Ang Lee, *Pro* Bill Kong, Hsu Li King and Ang Lee, *Ex Pro* James Schamus and David Linde, *Co-Pro* Zheng Quan Gang and Dong Ping, *Screenplay* Schamus, Wang Hui Ling and Tsai Kuo Jung, from the fourth part of a five-part novel by Wang Du Lu, *Ph* Peter Pau, *Pro Des* and *Costumes* Tim Yip, *Ed* Tim Squyres, *M* Tan Dun; cello solos performed by Yo-Yo Ma, *Choreography* Yuen Wo Ping.

Sony Pictures Classics/Columbia Pictures/Film Production Asia/Good Machine International/Edko Films/Zoom Hunt/ China Film Coproduction Corp, etc-Columbia TriStar.
120 mins. China/Taiwan/USA. 2000. Rel: 5 January 2001. Cert 12.

**Left:** *Martial art? Michelle Yeoh kicks some serious butt in Ang Lee's profound, epic, sweeping, visually distinctive* Crouching Tiger, Hidden Dragon *(from Columbia TriStar)*

## Damnation – Kárhozat ★

In a rain-swept area of industrial Hungary, Karrer, a self-pitying barfly, attempts to resurrect an affair he once had with a married chanteuse... You have to admire anything called *Damnation* although, unlike Stephen King's *Misery*, this really does live up to its name. After an interminable opening in which the camera lingers on a string of cable cars carrying coal, the film treats us to a series of grainy establishing shots (in black-and-white, no less) of a depressed corner of Hungary where very little happens. With no apparent irony, the film's message would appear to be that life is a terrible waste of time. This may be art (a moot point) but it certainly isn't cinema.

● *Karrer* Miklós B Szekely, *the singer* Vali Kerekes, *cloakroom attendant* Hédi Temessy, *Sebestyen* György Cserhalmi, *Willarsky* Gyula Pauer.
● *Dir* Béla Tarr, *Pro* József Marx, *Screenplay* Tarr and László Krasznahorkai, *Ph* Gábor Medvigy, *Pro Des* and *Costumes* Gyula Pauer, *Ed* Ágnes Hranitzky, *M* Mihály Vig.

Magyar Filmintézet/MOKÉP/Magyar Televizió-Artificial Eye. 120 mins. Hungary. 1988. Rel: 30 March 2001. Cert 15.

## Dancer In the Dark ★★★★★

Washington State; 1964. Afraid that her ten-year-old son will inherit her congenital blindness, Selma, a Czech immigrant, spends increasingly longer hours at her factory to save up for a corrective operation. However, Selma escapes the oppression of her life by imagining herself in spectacular musical songs, the rhythm of the machinery taking on the sound of a mechanical orchestra... Imagine this: a musical filmed in Cinemascope with seven choreographed dance sequences utilising up to a hundred cameras. But this being a film from Lars von Trier (*Breaking the Waves, The Idiots*), *Dancer in the Dark* is no ordinary musical. The story of a young woman going blind, it is as heartbreaking as it is resolutely fresh and original in its execution. Shot on video in Sweden with a remarkably eclectic cast (an Icelandic pop star, a French legend, an Oscar-winning American etc), the film is an attempt to recreate the emotional intensity of opera in the 19th century. Calling on a correlative artifice that distinguished that genre, von Trier has achieved his aim through the strength of his story, an almost documentary-like feel in the telling (aided by hand-held camerawork) and an extraordinarily touching performance from Björk. FYI: Initially, the singer resisted the temptation to star, but von Trier insisted (over the course of a year), arguing that the music and songs which Björk had composed should be a natural and plausible extension of the main character.

● *Selma Jezková* Björk, *Kathy* Catherine Deneuve, *Bill* David Morse, *Jeff* Peter Stormare, *Oldrich Novy* Joel Grey, *Samuel, the director* Vincent Paterson, *Linda* Cara Seymour, *Norman* Jean-Marc Barr, *Gene Jezková* Vladica Kostic, *Brenda* Siobhan Fallon, *district attorney* Zeljko Ivanek, *judge* Reathel Bean, *Dr Porkorny* Udo Kier, *new defence counsel* Luke Reilly, *with* Jens Albinus, Stellan Skarsgard.
● *Dir* and *Screenplay* Lars von Trier, *Pro* Vibeke Windeløv, *Ex Pro* Peter Aalbæk Jensen, *Ph* Robby Muller, *Pro Des* Karl Juliusson, *Ed* Molly Malene Stensgaard and François Gédigier, *M* Björk; *lyrics* by von Trier and Sjón Sigurdsson; songs performed by Björk, Catherine Deneuve, Peter Stormare, David Morse, Cara Seymour, Joel Grey, Siobhan Fallon, *Costumes* Manon Rasmussen, *Choreography* Vincent Paterson, *Sound* Per Streit.

Zentropa Entertainment/S4 Trust Film/Svenska Film/ Väst/ Liberator/Pain Unlimited/What Else?/Icelandic Film Corporation/SVT Drama/Arte Germany/FilmFour/ Angel Scandinavia/Canal Plus/Danish Film Institute/ Swedish Film Institute/Norwegian Film Institute/ Icelandic Film Institute/Finnish Film Foundation/Nordic Film/ Eurimages, etc-Film Four. 140 mins. Denmark/France/Sweden/Italy/Germany/ Norway/Netherlands/Iceland/Finland/UK/ USA. 2000. Rel: 15 September 2000. Cert 15.

## Dark Days ★★★

The story of how British filmmaker Marc Singer went to New York, spent two years with homeless people living in a tunnel and earned their collaboration in making a feature-length documentary about their situation could have provided effective dramatic shaping for this comment on the destitute. But, instead, Singer opts for an hour or so of comments by these outcasts (mainly males) without adding any commentary or outside observation, and the only development comes late on when the authorities eject them. The sense of community achieved by these survivors is brought out and the film is certainly committed, but it calls out for a TV presentation followed by a discussion of the issues involved. The black-and-white photography evokes the tradition of those American photographers whose pictures of the deprived have used art to create potent social criticism. [*Mansel Stimpson*]

● With Ralph S, Henry, Dee, Esteban, Atoulio, Tommy, Cathy, Brian, Joe, Bernard, Tito, Ozzy, Jasmine, Rick Rubell, Mike Harris etc.
● *Dir, Pro* and *Ph* Marc Singer, *Ex Pro* Paolo Seganti, Randall Mesdon, Morton Swinsky and Gordon Paul, *Co-Pro* Ben Freedman, *Ed* Melissa Neidich, *M* DJ Shadow.

Picture Farm/The Sundance Channel-Optimum Releasing. 82 mins. USA. 2000. Rel: 9 March 2001. Cert 15.

**Left:** *Olivier Assayas explores love, family and pottery in his intelligent and insightful* Les Destinées Sentimentales *(from Pathé)*

## Dead Babies ★

Appleseed Rectory, the Home Counties, England; the near future. A group of twentysomething misfits get together for a weekend of sex and drugs in the company of three visiting Americans. However, the Bacchanalian free-for-all is marred by the presence of an extremely sick practical joker... Black comedy? Theatre of Cruelty? Cinema of the Absurd? Whatever one chooses to label this full-bodied adaptation of Martin Amis' second novel (published in 1975), it is still a nihilistic tale about a group of grotesque caricatures. A sort of *Peter's Friends* on acid, it has something to offend everyone, being a cruel, homophobic, misanthropic attack on human dignity. It's disquieting to think that anybody could actually find this funny, although it is meant to be. Footnote: Andy Nyman, who plays the overweight, vertically challenged, severely flatulent, under-endowed, halitosic and spotty Keith Whitehead, must get some kind of award for delivering the year's most ego-punishing performance.

● *Quentin* Paul Bettany, *Lucy* Katy Carmichael, *Roxanne* Hayley Carr, *Giles Colstream* Charlie Condou, *Celia* Alexandra Gilbreath, *Marvell* William Marsh, *Skip* Kris Marshall, *Keith Whitehead* Andy Nyman, *Andy* Cristian Solimeno, *Diana* Olivia Williams, *with* Elaine Ives-Cameron, Denzil Kilvington, Chris Power, Jonathon Magnanti.
● *Dir* and *Screenplay* William Marsh, *Pro* Richard Holmes and Neil Peplow, *Ex Pro* Ben Hilton, *Ph* Daniel Cohen, *Pro Des* Mark Tanner, *Ed* Eddie Hamilton, *M* Mark 'Meat Katie' Pember and Marvin Beaver, *Costumes* Ralph Holes.

Gruber Films/Civilian Content/Outer Edge Films/ European Script Fund-Redbus.
101 mins. UK. 2000. Rel: 26 February 2001. Cert 18.

## Les Destinées Sentimentales
★★★★¹/₂

Long but engrossing, this family saga is marvellously cast, even in non-speaking roles, as writer-director Olivier Assayas demonstrates that insight and intelligence can give fresh life to what might have been a conventional French period tale covering the years from 1900 to 1930. Central here is Jean (Berling), who is summoned back to France to take over his family's pottery business after some years in Switzerland with his second wife, Pauline. Few films have so clear-sightedly investigated the changing bond between a couple over a period of time, while Isabelle Huppert is compelling as the discarded former spouse. A scene of homage to Bergman's *Fanny and Alexander* goes awry, but the misjudgments are minor and the film is admirable in its social observation as well as in its presentation of a wide range of believable characters. [*Mansel Stimpson*]

● *Pauline* Emmanuelle Béart, *Jean Barnery* Charles Berling, *Nathalie* Isabelle Huppert, *Philippe Pommerel* Olivier Perrier, *Julie Desca* Dominique Reymond, *with* André Marcon, Alexandra London, Julie Depardieu, Rémi Martin, Georges Wilson.
● *Dir* Olivier Assayas, *Pro* Bruno Pesery, *Screenplay* Assayas and Jacques Fieschi, *Ph* Éric Gautier, *Pro Des* Katia Wyszkop, *Ed* Luc Barnier, *M* Guillaume Lekeu, *Costumes* Anaïs Romand.

Arena Films/TF1 Films/Canal Plus, etc-Pathé.
180 mins. France/Switzerland. 2000. Rel: 8 December
2000. Cert 12.

## Digimon – The Movie ★★¹/₂

Originating from the popular Animé television
show, Digimon are 'digital monsters' who can
change shape and possess great destructive power.
Comprised of three segments (each gleaned from
longer Japanese episodes), the film, in its first chap-
ter, introduces one of the terminally cute creatures to
its young owners, henceforth referred to as the
Digidestined. Part two finds them combating an evil
Digimon who's infiltrated the Internet and is wreak-
ing havoc in major cities. Part three has them uniting again to defeat a corrupt Digimon infected by a
computer virus. While poor animation and incomprehensible editing often makes viewing tedious for
adults, the story genuinely emphasises the value of
teamwork. Invoking topical computer and internet
references reminds adults that the world is indeed
changing and that kids can have a profound influence on it. A contemporary soundtrack featuring the
Barenaked Ladies, Fatboy Slim, Mighty Mighty
Bosstones and Smashmouth is an added bonus. [*Scot
Woodward Myers*]

● Voices: *Kari* Lara Jill Miller, *Tai* Joshua Seth, *Red
Greymon* Bob Papenbrook, *Parrotmon* David Lodge,
*with* Dorothy Elias-Fahn, Michael Sorich, Peggy
O'Neal, Jeff Nimoy, Bob Buchholz.
● *Dir* Mamoru Hosada and Shigeyasu Yamauchi,
*Pro* Hiromi Seki and Terri-Lei O'Malley, *Ex Pro* Tan
Takaiwa, *Screenplay* Reiko Yoshida, *English adapta-
tion* Jeff Nimoy and Bob Buchholz, *Ed* Douglas
Purgason and Gary A Friedman, *M* Udi Harpaz and
Amotz Plessner, *Animation* Takaaki Yamashita,
Hisashi Nakayama and Masahiro Aizawa

Fox Kids/Saban Entertainment/Toei Animation Co.-Fox.
88 mins. Japan/USA. 1999/2000. Rel: 16 February 2001.
Cert PG.

## Dinosaur ★★★★★

Earth; the late Cretaceous Period, 65 million years
ago. Adopted by a family of lemurs, the orphaned
iguanodon Aladar more than pulls his weight when
the earth is devastated by a deadly meteor shower...
Dollar-per-minute the most expensive film ever
made (the budget being in the $150-$200m
region), *Dinosaur* is an astonishing breakthrough in
computer animation. Seamlessly blending its pre-
historic characters against spectacular backdrops
filmed in California, Australia, Hawaii, Florida,
Venezuela and Western Samoa, the film creates a
wondrous new world that enraptures the imagination. From the treacherous freewheeling journey of

an iguanodon egg and a fiery detonation of an aster-
oid to an epic dinosaur march across the desert and
various attacks from roaring carnotaurs, the film is
a marvel of spectacle. It's hard to imagine animation
getting any more realistic than this – the cartoonish
features of the characters are actually a relief – while
the absence of all-singing, all-dancing critters is a
blessing (Elton John and Phil Collins were otherwise engaged). However, the story's similarity to the
plot of *The Land Before Time*, *Tarzan* and even *Red
River* is a shame.

● Voices: *Plio* Alfre Woodard, *Yar* Ossie Davis, *Zini*
Max Casella, *Suri* Hayden Panettiere, *Aladar* D.B.
Sweeney, *Kron* Samuel E Wright, *Bruton* Peter
Siragusa, *Neera* Julianna Margulies, *Baylene* Joan
Plowright, *Eema* Della Reese.
● *Dir* Ralph Zondag and Eric Leighton, *Pro* Pam
Marsden, *Co-Pro* Baker Bloodworth, *Screenplay* John
Harrison and Robert Nelson Jacobs, based on 'an
original screenplay' by Walon Green, *Pro Des* Walter
P Martishius, *Ed* H Lee Peterson, *M* James Newton
Howard, *Visual effects* Neil Krepela, *Sound*
Christopher Boyes.

Walt Disney Pictures-Buena Vista.
82 mins. USA. 2000. Rel: 13 October 2000. Cert PG.

## The Dish ★★★★

In July of 1969 a small backwater in New South
Wales, Australia, becomes a central cog in the
Apollo 11 mission to the moon. In the middle of a
sheep paddock, a 1000-ton satellite dish is in prime
position to track the spaceship's progress – and to
relay Neil Armstrong's legendary TV footage to the
rest of the world. So it's a shame, then, that Mitch
forget to prime the fuel line to the back-up genera-
tor... Only Australia could produce a movie about a
satellite dish and make it wonderful. Yet it's the very
combination of recognisable human beings caught
up in such a historical moment that makes this
sweet, funny and revelatory film so appealing.
Beautifully photographed and peppered with
moments of incidental humour, *The Dish* draws on
the offbeat comedy of the director's previous feature, *The Castle*, and then places it into this extraordinary historical context. As the 'dishmaster,' Sam
Neill is particularly good, providing an anchor of
confident laid-back authority in a sea of eccentricity. Based on a true story.

● *Cliff Buxton* Sam Neill, *Ross 'Mitch' Mitchell*
Kevin Harrington, *Glenn Latham* Tom Long, *Al
Burnett* Patrick Warburton, *May 'Masie' McIntyre*
Genevieve Mooy, *Rudi Kellerman* Tayler Kane, *Prime
Minister* Bille Brown, *Mayor Bob McIntyre* Roy
Billing, *Len Purvis* Andrew S Gilbert, *Marie McIntyre*
Lenka Kripac, *Keith Morrison* Matthew Moore,

*Left:* In space no one can see you screw up: Sam Neill and colleagues admire the sky in Rob Sitch's sweet and funny The Dish (from Icon)

*Janine* Eliza Szonert, *US Ambassador* John McMartin, *Billy McIntyre* Carl Snell, *with* Roz Hammond, Naomi Wright, Kerry Walker, Frank Bennett, Charles 'Bud' Tingwell, Colette Mann.
● *Dir* Rob Sitch, *Pro* Sitch, Santo Cilauro, Tom Gleisner, Jane Kennedy and Michael Hirsh, *Line Pro* Debra Choate, *Screenplay* Sitch, Cilauro, Gleisner and Kennedy, *Ph* Graeme Wood, *Pro Des* Carrie Kennedy, *Ed* Jill Bilcock, *M* Edmund Choi; songs

performed by Tina Arena, Russell Morris, Frank Bennett, The Loved Ones, Herb Alpert & The Tijuana Brass, Bert Kaempfert and His Orchestra, Mason Williams, Blood Sweat & Tears, The Moody Blues, The Youngbloods, Thunderclap Newman, Steppenwolf etc, *Costumes* Kitty Stuckey.

Working Dog-Icon.
101 mins. Australia. 2000. Rel: 11 May 2001. Cert 12.

## Disney's The Kid ★★

In two days' time, image consultant Russell Duritz will be 40, yet he still lives alone, doesn't own a dog and has never got his pilot's licence. However, he is professionally fulfilled, extremely rich and has a beautiful girlfriend. But is it enough? And who is that irritating kid who calls himself Rusty Duritz and shares the same birthmark and scar as Russell? Got goose bumps already? I hope not. Trust Disney to take a crass American concept like 'the inner child' and then market it as a cinematic reality. Cloying, corny and painfully over-scored, *The Kid* is not even original, taking an idea used by Peter Ustinov in his play *Photo Finish*. Also, for a film about a man and a boy, it's ironic that the three most interesting characters are all women – Russell's spirited girlfriend (the lovely Emily Mortimer), his sarcastic secretary (Lily Tomlin on top form) and the garrulous TV presenter he meets on a plane (the always wonderful Jean Smart).

● *Russell Duritz* Bruce Willis, *Rusty Duritz* Spencer Breslin, *Amy* Emily Mortimer, *Janet* Lily Tomlin, *Deirdre Lafever* Jean Smart, *Kenny* Chi McBride, *Sam Duritz* Daniel Von Bargen, *Dr Alexander* Dana Ivey, *with* Susan Dalian, Stanley Anderson, Juanita Moore, Esther Scott, Larry King, Stuart Scott, Rich Eisen, Harold Greene, Matthew Perry.
● *Dir* Jon Turteltaub, *Pro* Turteltaub, Christina Steinberg and Hunt Lowry, *Ex Pro* Arnold Rifkin and David Willis, *Screenplay* Audrey Wells, *Ph* Peter Menzies, *Pro Des* Garreth Stover, *Ed* Peter Honess and David Rennie, *M* Marc Shaiman; songs performed by Kevon Edmonds, The 5th Dimension, Robert Cornford, Jackie Wilson, *Costumes* Gloria Gresham.

Walt Disney Pictures/Junction Entertainment-Buena Vista. 104 mins. USA. 2000. Rel: 10 November 2000. Cert PG.

## Down to Earth ★¹/₂

New York; today. Lance Barton is an aspiring comic who is only funny off-stage. Still, his loyal agent Whitney Daniels has secured him a spot in an Amateur Night Contest at the Apollo. Then, due to a celestial cock-up, Lance is killed in a road accident and demands the rest of his life back. So, with a little tweaking of destiny, Lance is given his pick of fresh corpses to inhabit until the books can be squared... The cinema being the visual medium that it is, it is hard to expect an audience to strain its imagination just because Chris Rock wants to play all the parts. A stand-up comic with two Emmys and two Grammys to his name, Rock has been at his best on film in supporting roles speaking other people's lines (indeed, he had the best line in Kevin Smith's *Dogma*). But here we are expected to believe him as an overweight, 53-year-old white man – and with Rick Baker's magical make-up nowhere in sight! And another thing, there's no difference between the bad jokes Lance tells and the good ones.

● *Lance Barton* Chris Rock, *Sontee Jenkins* Regina King, *Cisco* Mark Addy, *Mr Keyes* Eugene Levy, *Whitney Daniels* Frankie Faison, *Winston Sklar* Greg Germann, *Mrs Wellington* Jennifer Coolidge, *Mr King* Chazz Palminteri, *Wanda* Wanda Sykes, *Phil Quon* John Cho, *with* Mario Joyner, Bryetta Calloway, Martha Chaves, Brian Rhodes.
● *Dir* Chris Weitz and Paul Weitz, *Pro* Sean Daniel, Michael Rotenberg and James Jacks, *Ex Pro* Chris Rock and Barry Berg, *Screenplay* Chris Rock, Lance Crouther, Ali Le Roi and Louis CK, based on the film *Heaven Can Wait*, scripted by Elaine May and Warren Beatty, itself based on the play by Harry Segall, *Ph* Richard Crudo, *Pro Des* Paul Peters, *Ed* Priscilla Nedd Friendly, *M* Jamshied Sharifi; songs performed by Lauryn Hill, Eric Carmen, Bone Thugs-n Harmony, Sevendust, Snoop Doggy Dogg, KC & the Sunshine Band, DMX, Jordan Brown, Mystikal, Monica, Sticky Fingaz and Eminem etc, *Costumes* DeBrae Little.

Paramount/Village Roadshow/NPV Entertainment/ Alphaville 3 Arts Entertainment-UIP. 86 mins. USA/Australia/Germany. 2001. Rel: 8 June 2001. Cert 12.

## Dr Seuss' How the Grinch Stole Christmas

*See The Grinch*

## Dracula 2001 ★★★

London/New Orleans; the present. Marcus and his gang of sophisticated thieves haven't a clue what's in the closely guarded vault of Carfax Antiquities in London – but they know that it must be priceless. Having broken through the elaborate security defences, the gang finds little of value other than a silver coffin. Unable to open it then and there, they take the coffin on their private jet back to America. Then, as the plane approaches the mainland, Count Dracula rises from his 100-year sleep... One year after he last appeared on the cinema screen in the 1999 *Pumpkin Hill* (as played by Ralph P Martin), Dracula is given a new historical context (as a reincarnation of Judas!) and a sexual makeover in this entertaining update. Making the most of new technology welded onto the latest teenage cynicism, *Dracula 2001* manages to poke fun at itself while scaring up some genuine thrills. There are also some priceless lines (Jonny Lee Miller, while dispensing with a vampire: 'Never, *ever* fuck with an antiques dealer!') and, for horror buffs, plenty of knowing allusions. And while the Count can no longer find fresh virgins, at least his female prey work at a Virgin Megastore. US title: *Dracula 2000*.

● *Simon Shepherd* Jonny Lee Miller, *Mary Heller* Justine Waddell, *Dracula* Gerard Butler, *Lucy*

*Left: Blood in the bayou: Gerard Butler looks for the employees of Richard Branson in Patrick Lussier's funny, scary Dracula 2001 (from Buena Vista)*

Colleen Ann Fitzpatrick, *Solina* Jennifer Esposito, *Nightshade* Danny Masterson, *Valerie Sharp* Jeri Ryan, *Eddie* Lochlyn Munro, *Trick* Sean Patrick Thomas, *Marcus* Omar Epps, *Abraham Van Helsing* Christopher Plummer, *Dax* Tig Fong, *with* Tony Munch, Shane West, Nathan Fillion, Jonathan Whittaker, Karon Briscoe.
● *Dir* and *Ed* Patrick Lussier, *Pro* Joel Soisson and W K Border, *Ex Pro* Wes Craven, Marianne Maddalena, Bob Weinstein, Harvey Weinstein and Andrew Rona, *Screenplay* Soisson, from a story by Soisson and Lussier, *Ph* Peter Pau, *Pro Des* Carol Spier and Peter Devaney Flanagan, *M* Marco Beltrami; songs performed by Powerman 5000, Monster Magnet, Godhead with Marilyn Manson, Endo, Half Cooked, Slayer, Disturbed, Pantera, The Oslo, Saliva, Flybanger, Taproot etc, *Costumes* Denise Cronenberg, *Visual effects* Erik Henry, *Makeup effects* Gary J Tunnicliffe, *Sound* Steve Boeddeker.

Miramax/Dimension Films/Neo Art/Logic-Buena Vista. 88 mins. USA. 2000. Rel: 15 June 2001. Cert 15.

## Dude, Where's My Car? ★

Jesse and Chester wake up to find their refrigerator filled with pudding, their girlfriends mad at them and Jesse's car missing. The dumb and dumber duo then stumble into one bizarre situation after another while searching for the car. Not only do they end up owing money to a transvestite stripper, but they encounter a mini van full of cultists (amiably led by America's *Queer as Folk* star Hal Sparks) and two rival factions of aliens trying to find the 'continuum transfunctioner'... Despite an unending deluge of sophomoric

pranks, there's simply not enough pot in the world to elicit a giggle from the Gen X stoners this film alternately parodies and glorifies. I don't know when I've last seen a movie this tortuously unfunny. [*Scot Woodward Myers*]

● *Jesse* Ashton Kutcher, *Chester* Seann William Scott, *Wanda* Jennifer Garner, *Wilma* Marla Sokoloff, *Nelson* David Herman, *Christie Boner* Kristy Swanson, *Zoltan* Hal Sparks, *with* Turtle, Keone Young, John Toles-Bey, Fabio, Brent Spiner, Dominic Capone.
● *Dir* Danny Leiner, *Pro* Wayne Rice, Broderick Johnson, Andrew Kosove and Gil Netter, *Co-Pro* Nancy Paloian-Breznikar, *Screenplay* Philip Stark, *Ph* Robert Stevens, *Pro Des* Charles Breen, *M* David Kitay; songs performed by Dangerman, Grand Theft Auto, Blur, Harvey Danger, Ween, Terry Wilson, Hot Chocolate, Size 14, Spy, Freestylers, Young MC, Good Charlotte, Zebrahead, Ladysmith Black Mambazo, SILT etc, *Costumes* Pamela Withers.

Fox-Fox. 83 mins. USA. 2000. Rel: 9 February 2001. Cert 15.

## Duets ★★★¹/₂

At various points across the American mainland, six characters hear of a karaoke competition in Omaha, Nebraska, and head there in the hope of scooping the $5000 grand prize. But there are complications: middle-aged hustler Ricky Dean meets up with his daughter for the first time, unhinged salesman Todd Woods discovers that his partner is an escaped convict and idealistic cab driver Billy gets landed with a ball-busting harridan... Having proved that she can do accents,

play a boy and win an Oscar, Gwyneth Paltrow now shows what a fabulous singer she is. But this is an ensemble piece (directed by Gwyneth's dad), which gathers dramatic momentum as we get to know the characters, like a concerto building to a crescendo. However, it is the songs that really distinguish this likeable road musical, although Paul Giamatti's central performance as a salesman who turns against homogenised America (much like Michael Douglas in *Falling Down*) is a gem of comic pathos. For the record, Gwyneth's three songs here are 'Bette Davis Eyes', 'Cruisin'' and 'Just My Imagination'.

● *Suzi Loomis* Maria Bello, *Reggie Kane* Andre Braugher, *Todd Woods* Paul Giamatti, *Ricky Dean* Huey Lewis, *Liv* Gwyneth Paltrow, *Billy Hannon* Scott Speedman, *Harriet Cahagan* Marian Seldes, *Candy Woods* Kiersten Warren, *Arlene* Angelina Phillips, *Blair* Angie Dickinson, *Ronny Jackson* Lochlyn Munro, *with* Carol Alexander, Steve Oatway, Erika von Tagen, Keegan Tracy, Candus Churchill, Larry Dutton.
● *Dir* Bruce Paltrow, *Pro* Paltrow, Kevin Jones and John Byrum, *Ex Pro* Lee R Mayes, Neil Canton, Tony Ludwig and Alan Riche, *Screenplay* Byrum, *Ph* Paul Sarossy, *Pro Des* Sharon Seymour, *Ed* Jerry Greenberg, *M* David Newman; songs performed by Lochlyn Munro, Marty Lewis, Huey Lewis, Larry Klein, Edgar Winter, Paul Giamatti, Wall of Voodoo, Arnold McCuller, Gary Glitter, Gwyneth Paltrow, John Pinette, Kenneth 'Babyface' Edmonds etc, *Costumes* Mary Claire Hannan.

Hollywood Pictures/Seven Arts Pictures/Beacon Pictures-Icon. 114 mins. USA. 2000. Rel: 17 November 2000. Cert 15.

## Dungeons & Dragons ★★★

Magicians are the ruling class in the land of Izmer and Profion is the most powerful of them all. He's determined to acquire the Rod of Savrille, a relic that will grant him power over red dragons and enable him to defeat the young, more egalitarian Empress Savina. The flies in his ointment are a ramshackle team of adventurers including young mage Marina, a pair of thieves named Ridley and Snails, a boisterous dwarf and a slinky elf. Together they brave magic, clever traps and the deliciously evil henchman, Damodar, to thwart Profion's scheme... Based on the fantasy role-playing game that has obsessed many a high school and college student since the early 1980s, *Dungeons & Dragons* took director Courtney Solomon ten years to bring to the big screen. Moments of shockingly bad acting are interspersed with dazzling images and inspired effects, culminating in a grand battle between dragon armies. [*Scot Woodward Myers*]

● *Ridley Freeborn* Justin Whalin, *Snails* Marlon Wayans, *Marina Pretensa* Zoe McLellan, *Empress Savina* Thora Birch, *Norda* Kristen Wilson, *Xilus* Richard O'Brien, *Halvarth* Tom Baker, *Damodar* Bruce Payne, *Archmage Profion* Jeremy Irons, *Azmath* Robert Miano, *with* Tomas Havrlik, Edward Jewesbury, Matthew O'Toole, David O'Kelly, Kia Jam, Robert Henny.
● *Dir* Courtney Solomon, *Pro* Kia Jam and Tom Hammel, *Ex Pro* Joel Silver, Allan Zeman and Nelson Leong, *Co-Pro* Steve Richards and Ann Flagella, *Screenplay* Topper Lilien and Carroll Cartwright, *Ph* Doug Milsome, *Pro Des* Bryce Perrin, *Ed* Caroline Ross, *M* Justin Caine Burnett, *Costumes* Barbara Lane.

New Line Cinema/Sweetpea Entertainment-Entertainment. 108 mins. 2000. USA. Rel: 16 February 2001. Cert 12.

## East-West – Est-Ouest ★★★¹/₂

Russia; 1946-1957. Shortly after the Second World War, over four million expatriated Russians – POWs, emigrants and soldiers who fought for their country's freedom – were invited by Stalin to return to their beloved motherland. But, once there, they were summarily executed, tortured and/or deported to far-flung corners of the empire.

For, in his supreme wisdom, Stalin believed that his people stranded beyond the Iron Curtain had been tainted by the Western evil. Alexeï Golovin, his young French wife, Marie, and their son, Sérioja, are some of the lucky ones: they are crammed into a house along with four other families. Marie immediately craves to return to Paris, but her passport is destroyed. Meanwhile, her husband takes to the bed of a female neighbour... A vivid and dramatic recreation of a little-known passage of Russian history, *East-West* is another ambitious drama from the director of the Oscar-winning *Indochine*. And thanks to an exceptionally strong story, a sweeping score from Patrick Doyle and powerfully internal performances from Bonnaire and Menchikov, the film grips the attention from the word go. It does go on a bit, but the final, dramatic payoff is certainly worth the wait.

● *Marie Golovin* Sandrine Bonnaire, *Alexeï Golovin* Oleg Menchikov, *Sacha* Sergueï Bodrov Jr., *Gabrielle Develay* Catherine Deneuve, *7-year-old Sérioja Golovin* Ruben Tapiero, *14-year-old Sérioja Golovin* Erwan Baynaud, *Pirogov* Grigori Manoukov, *Olga* Tatiana Doguileva, *Colonel Boïko* Bogdan Stupka, *with* Meglena Karalambova, Atanass Atanassov, Tania Massalitinova, René Féret.
● *Dir* Régis Wargnier, *Pro* Yves Marmion, *Line Pro* Gérard Crosnier and Andreï Belous, *Screenplay* Wargnier, Roustam Ibraguimbekov, Sergueï Bodrov and Louis Gardel, *Ph* Laurent Dailland, *Ed* Hervé Schneid, *Pro Des* Vladimir Svetozarov and Alexeï Levtchenko, *M* Patrick Doyle, *Costumes* Pierre-Yves Gayraud.

UGC YM/France 3 Cinéma/NTV Profit/Gala Films/Mate Prods/Eurimages/Sofinergie 5/Canal Plus, etc-Gala Film. 125 mins. France/Russia/Bulgaria/Spain. 1999. Rel: 24 November 2000. Cert 12.

## Elephant Juice ★★

London; today. Seven professional Londoners, variously involved with each other, have dinner and decide to find their friend Billy a partner. However, the path of true love runs far from smooth and as Billy embarks on an affair with an American waitress, his friends find their own relationships very much in transition… If you mouth the words 'elephant juice' it looks like you're saying 'I love you,' a pertinent metaphor for the lip service writer Amy Jenkins pays her characters here. Best known for scripting the highly successful TV series *This Life*, Jenkins fails to flesh out her cinematic equivalents

in the time allotted. Some of the acting is good enough, but the characters fail to spring to life. [*Ewen Brownrigg*]

● *Jules* Emmanuelle Béart, *Billy* Sean Gallagher, *Will* Daniel LaPaine, *Frank* Mark Strong, *Daphne* Daniela Nardini, *Dodie* Kimberly Williams, *Graham* Lennie James, *George* Lee Williams, *Kathy* Kate Gartside, *Aileen* Rebecca Palmer, *Rock* James Thornton, *with* Sabra Williams, Sharon Bower, Evelyn Doggart, Rob Jarvis.
● *Dir* Sam Miller, *Pro* Miller, Amy Jenkins and Sheila Fraser Milne, *Ex Pro* David Aukin, Trea Hoving and Colin Leventhal, *Assoc Pro* Allon Reich, *Screenplay* Amy Jenkins, from an idea by Jenkins and Miller, *Ph* Adrian Wild, *Pro Des* Grant Hicks, *Ed* Elen Pierce Lewis, *M* Tim Atack; songs performed by Terry Callier, Manic Street Preachers, Chet Baker, Wire, Rinocerose, Locksmith, Vegas Soul, Henry Mancini, Superstar etc, *Costumes* Jill Taylor.

Miramax Films/Film Four/HAL Films-Metrodome. 88 mins. UK/USA. 1999. Rel: 22 September 2000. Cert 18.

## The Emperor and the Assassin – Jing Ke Ci Qin Wang ★★★★

In the third century BC, Ying Zheng, the king of Qin, resolves to unify the seven states of China under his own rule. However, to counter the censure of other nations, he plots a reasonable motive for each incursion. Thus, at the suggestion of Lady Zhao, his childhood sweetheart, he agrees to risk an assassination attempt from the neighbouring kingdom of Yan. But the contracted killer, the noble Jing Ke, has sworn off murder in favour of peddling sandals. Meanwhile, Zheng marshals his omnipotent army for a ruthless attack... In spite of its huge scope and multi-national investment, Chen Kaige's historical epic is a largely character-driven drama. But, with characters that would not seem out of place in a Shakespearean tragedy, Chen is playing with a full deck. Furthermore, the director has managed to fashion the film's most powerful moments from its quietest scenes, as a repertoire of smiles and stares lay a minefield of emo-

*Above: Back in the USSR: Sandrine Bonnaire and Oleg Menchikov in Régis Wargnier's vivid and dramatic* East-West *(from Gala)*

tional trip wires. Still, the battle sequences are truly spectacular even if they appear surprisingly truncated (Chen re-cut the film four times). An intelligent, invigorating history lesson that is all the more powerful for constantly counteracting audience expectations.

● *Lady Zhao* Gong Li, *Jing Ke* Zhang Fengyi, *Ying Zheng* Li Xuejian, *Dan, Prince of Yan* Sun Zhou, *General Fan Yuqi* Lu Xiaohe, *Marquis Changxin* Wang Zhiwen, *Lu Buwei* Chen Kaige, *Queen Mother* Gu Yongfei, Zhao Benshan, Ding Haifeng, *blind girl* Zhou Xun.
● *Dir* Chen Kaige, *Pro* Han Sanping, Shirley Kao and Satoru Iseki, *Ex Pro* Chen Kaige, Tsuguhiko Kadokawa and Hiromitsu Furukawa, *Assoc Pro* Philip Lee and Sunmin Park, *Line Pro* Zhang Xia and Bai Yu, *Screenplay* Wang Peigong and Chen Kaige, *Ph* Zhao Fei, *Pro Des* Tu Juhua, *Ed* Zhao Xinxia, *M* Zhao Jiping, *Costumes* Mo Xiaomin.

Shin Corporation/Canal Plus/New Wave Co/Beijing Film Studio/NDF/China Film-Columbia TriStar.
161 mins. Japan/China/France. 1999. Rel: 21 July 2000. Cert 12.

## The Emperor's New Groove ★★★¹/₂

A long time ago in a faraway land, Kuzco, the emperor of an enormous realm, ruled with a rod of irony and a really bad attitude. Then, when he relieves his chief advisor of her post, she plots to kill him, a ruse that backfires when Kuzco is turned into a llama. Carted off to a far-flung corner of his empire, Kuzco is now at the mercy of a good-natured peasant, whose village the emperor had planned to turn into a summer resort… An irreverent and comic surprise, *The Emperor's New Groove* differs from standard Disney animation in that it is crudely drawn but very funny. With a splendid vocal reading from David Spade as the film's anti-hero and some comic invention worthy of Tom & Jerry, it is as adult-friendly as it is prime slapstick for kids. Thus magic spells and a pesky squirrel vie with contemporary jargon and jokes at the expense of sexual ambiguity. A mere slip of a film (compared to the artistic and moral complexity of, say, *Pocahontas*), it is briskly paced and extremely entertaining. Previously known as *Kingdom of the Sun*.

● Voices: *Kuzco* David Spade, *Pacha* John Goodman, *Yzma* Eartha Kitt, *Kronk* Patrick Warburton, *Chicha* Wendie Malick, *Chaca* Kellyann Kelso, *Tipo* Eli Russell Linnetz, *with* John Fielder, Miriam Flynn, Jess Harnell, Sherry Lynn, Steve Susskind.
● *Dir* Mark Dindal, *Pro* Randy Fullmer, *Ex Pro* Don Hahn, *Assoc Pro* Patricia Hicks, *Screenplay* David Reynolds, from a story by Dindal and Chris Williams, *Pro Des* Paul Felix, *Art* Colin Stimpson, *Ed* Pamela Ziegenhagen-Shefland, *M* John Debney; songs: *M* Sting and David Hartley; *lyrics*: Sting, 'Perfect World' sung by Tom Jones, 'My Funny Friend and Me' sung by Sting, *Sound* Tim Chau.

Walt Disney Pictures-Buena Vista.
78 mins. USA. 2000. Rel: 16 February 2001. Cert U.

## Enemy at the Gates ★★★¹/₂

September 1942-February 1943; Stalingrad, Russia. Not so much a city as a symbol of Russia's might, Stalingrad is being systematically demolished by the Germans. With the Russian forces shot to shreds by the enemy in front and by their own officers from behind, Soviet morale is all but wiped out. Then a shepherd from the Urals becomes a reluctant hero when his marksmanship gradually depletes the ranks of high-ranking Nazi officers… They don't make films like this any more and certainly not on this budget (north of £60 million by some estimates). A sweeping, visually stunning war movie in which the Russians are played by English actors and the Nazi villain by an American, *Enemy at the Gates* recalls the sort of violent, culturally displaced programmers dished out in the 1960s. However, that decade produced nothing like the spectacle shown here which, with the aid of computer imagery, shows Stalingrad as a smoking, rubble-strewn conurbation stretching as far as the eye can see. But it's the strength of the central story (culled from a number of historical sources) and the vivid characterisations that make this drama so watchable. FYI: At the time of writing, *Enemy at the Gates* goes down in history as the most expensive European film ever made.

● *Vassili Zaitsev* Jude Law, *Danilov* Joseph Fiennes, *Tania* Rachel Weisz, *Nikita Sergeyevich Khrushchev* Bob Hoskins, *Major Konig* Ed Harris, *Koulikov* Ron Perlman, *Mother Filipov* Eva Mattes, *Sacha* Gabriel Marshall-Thomson, *General Paulus* Matthias Habich, *Volody* Ivan Shvedoff, *with* Sophie Rois, Mario Bandi, Mikhail Matveev.
● *Dir* Jean-Jacques Annaud, *Pro* Annaud and John D. Schofield, *Ex Pro* Alain Godard and Alisa Tager, *Ph* Robert Fraisse, *Pro Des* Wolf Kroeger, *Ed* Noelle Boisson and Humphrey Dixon, *M* James Horner, *Costumes* Janty Yates, *Visual effects* Peter Chiang.

Mandalay Pictures/KC Medien/MP Film Management/Repérage-Pathé.
145 mins. Germany/UK/Ireland. Rel: 16 March 2001. Cert 15.

## Les Enfants du siècle – The Children of the Century ★¹/₂

Paris; 1832-1835. As George Sand (aka Amandine Lucie Dupin), at 29, gains notoriety for her forthright writing, the 23-year-old Alfred de Musset is dubbed 'the most gifted poet and writer of his generation.' Both disillusioned by love, Sand and de Musset become fast friends and quickly evolve into the talk of Paris. Then they consummate their relationship and take a fateful sojourn to Italy… As revealed in the witty and entertaining film *Impromptu* (1989), George Sand was an extraordinary woman and is a wonderful vehicle for a film. However, this thunderingly heavy-going melodrama does her little justice. The problem, pedestrian direction and poor structure aside, is that Diane Kurys' 'romance' is little more than a series of artfully composed clinches and tiresome tantrums. Quite what Sand, with all her intelligence, beauty and vitality, saw in de Musset is a mystery. Irrational, volatile, petulant, vicious, weak, self-centred, violent, childish, destructive and self-pitying, de Musset is a terrible character and is done no favours by Benoît Magimel's shrill and uncharismatic interpretation.

● *George Sand* Juliette Binoche, *Alfred de Musset* Benoît Magimel, *Dr Pietro Pagello* Stefano Dionisi, *François Buloz* Robin Renucci, *Aimée d'Alton* Isabelle Carré, *Gustave Planche* Patrick Chesnais, *Marie Dorval* Karin Viard, *Paull de Musset* Olivier Foubert, *Mme de Musset* Marie-France Mignal, *with* Arnaud Giovaninetti, Denis Podalydes, Michel Robin, Yacha Kurys.
● *Dir* Diane Kurys, *Pro* Kurys and Alain Sarde, *Ex Pro* Robert Benmussa, *Assoc Pro* Christine Gozlan, *Co-Pro* Robert Benmussa, *Screenplay* Kurys, Francois Olivier Rousseau and Murray Head, *Ph* Vilko Filac, *Pro Des* Bernard Vezat, *Ed* Joële Van Effenterre, *M* Luis Bacalov; Bruckner, Schumann, Bellini, Liszt, *Costumes* Christian Lacroix.

Alain Sarde/Alexandre Films/France 2 Cinéma/Canal Plus/ Studio Images 5/FilmFour-Film Four.
108 mins. France/UK. 1999. Rel: 6 April 2001. Cert 15.

## The Escort ★★¹/₂

Pierre is in London ostensibly to carry out research for his new novel. Tricked into buying a girl a drink, he is beaten up by a bouncer and left on the street, where he is found by the flash and confidant Tom. Befriended and taken in by the latter, Pierre gradually finds his feet and embarks on a new career as a male escort... A French actor not known for his looks, Daniel Auteuil is not an obvious choice to play a male escort in London. But then Pierre is written as a 45-year-old Frenchman who rediscovers his vanity and so it should all make perfect sense. Unfortunately, though, it doesn't, in spite of the director's attempt at fly-on-the-wall realism, unusual locations and some restless, hand-held camerawork. In spite of this and the strength of the central premise – a middle-aged man searching for the lie that will unlock his fantasies – *The Escort* ends up being sleazy, unconvincing and incoherent.

● *Pierre* Daniel Auteuil, *Tom* Stuart Townsend, *Kim* Liz Walker, *Gem* Noah Taylor, *Jessica* Frances Barber, *Patricia* Claire Skinner, *Catherine* Béatrice Agenin, *Patricia's husband* Peter Mullan, *Harry* Kriss Dosanjh, *Sue* Alice Evans, *Maureen* Susan Porrett, *with* Keith Allen, Ben Whishaw, Barbara Flynn, Anastasia Hille, Sarah-Jane Potts, Amanda Ryan, Heathcote Williams, Peter Hugo-Daly, Tam Dean Burn, Mar Sodupe, Suzanne Burden.

● *Dir* Michel Blanc, *Pro* Claude Berri, *Ex Pro* Annabel Karouby and Pierre Grunstein, *Co-Pro* Timothy Burrill, *Assoc Pro* Romain Bremond, *Line Pro* Sally French, *Screenplay* Blanc and Nick Love, from an idea by Hanif Kureishi, *Ph* Barry Ackroyd, *Pro Des* Gary Williamson, *Ed* Maryline Monthieux, *M* Barry Adamson, *Costumes* Ralph Holes.

Claude Berri/Pathé/Renn Prods/France 3 Cinéma/Canal Plus- Pathé.
106 mins. France/UK. 1999. Rel: 8 December 2000. Cert 18.

## Essex Boys ★★★

Essex, England; today. When local gangster Jason Locke is released from prison, young cabby Billy Reynolds is assigned to be his chauffeur. Soon, Billy is making more money in a single night than he used to collect for a week's work. He's also seduced by the glamour of the underworld but gets in over his head when Locke sets about settling some old scores… One of the better gangland thrillers to emerge from Britain this year, *Essex Boys* benefits from some fine performances (particularly from Charlie Creed-Miles) and by uncluttered direction. Inspired by a 'single true event,' the film is to be commended for not glamorising its subject, and for presenting it in a very real light, aided by excellent location work. If only the genre's clichés hadn't been quite so abundant. [*Charles Bacon*]

● *Jason Locke* Sean Bean, *Lisa Locke* Alex Kingston, *Billy Reynolds* Charlie Creed-Miles, *John Dyke* Tom Wilkinson, *Peter Chase* Larry Lamb, *Suzy Welch* Holly Davidson, *Henry Hobbs* Terence Rigby, *Nicole* Amelia Lowdell, *with* Gareth Milne, Gary Love.
● *Dir* Terry Winsor, *Pro* Jeff Pope, *Ex Pro* Pippa Cross, *Line Pro* Paul Frift, *Screenplay* Pope and Winsor, *Ph* John Daly, *Pro Des* Chris Edwards, *Ed* Edward Mansell, *M* Colin Towns, *Costumes* Sarah Lubel, *Special effects* Graham Longhurst.

Granada Film-Pathé.
102 mins. UK. 1999. Rel: 14 July 2000. Cert 18.

## An Everlasting Piece ★★★¹/₂

Belfast; the 1980s. From its witty title to its whimsical, poignant charm, this Irish tale from Barry Levinson was virtually thrown away by its distributor on both sides of the Atlantic. The 'piece' in question is not a typo but a toupée, a magnificent crown flogged to bald men by a pair of eccentric barbers. One Catholic and the other Protestant, Colm and George meet in a psychiatric hospital and start up their own company called Piece People. However, their trade comes under moral scrutiny when Colm gets an offer from the IRA for 30 wigs, while his girlfriend, Bronagh, arranges a lucrative deal with the British army, a large number of whose soldiers are losing their hair due to stress under fire. A novel look at The Troubles, *An Everlasting Piece* could easily haven fallen foul of some heavy-handed moralising, but thankfully Levinson provides a light, deft touch, while screenwriter Barry McEvoy (the son of a hairpiece salesman in real life) turns in an irresistible performance as Colm. [*Ewen Brownrigg*]

● *Colm O'Neill* Barry McEvoy, *George* Brian F O'Byrne, *Bronagh* Anna Friel, *Gerty* Pauline McLynn, *Mrs O'Neill* Ruth McCabe, *Mickey* Laurence Kinlan, *Scalper* Billy Connolly, *Mr Black* Des McAleer, *with* Colum Convey, Ian Cregg, David Pearse.
● *Dir* Barry Levinson, *Pro* Levinson, Mark Johnson, Louis Digiaimo, Jerome O'Connor and Paula Weinstein, *Ex Pro* Patrick McCormick, *Co-Pro* Morgan O'Sullivan and James Flynn, and Tiffany Daniel and Louis Digiaimo Jr, *Screenplay* Barry McEvoy, *Ph* Seamus Deasy, *Pro Des* Nathan Crowley, *Ed* Stu Linder, *M* Hans Zimmer; songs performed by Talking Heads, The Bothy Band, Queen and David Bowie, Billy Valentine, The Clancy Brothers, Van Morrison, *Costumes* Joan Bergin.

DreamWorks/Columbia/Bayahibe Films/Baltimore/Spring Creek/Irish Film Industry-Columbia TriStar.
102 mins. USA/Ireland. 2000. Rel: 23 March 2001. Cert 15.

## Evolution ★★★★

In a quiet backwater of Arizona, a meteorite crashes to earth, leaving a giant crater in the ground. Extracting a portion of rock from the site, Ira Kane and Harry Block, two local college professors, discover that organisms from the meteor are growing at an alarming rate. Indeed, the simple alien life forms are, in a matter of days, evolving into complex and potentially dangerous creatures... A small-scale *Independence Day* with the accent on laughs, *Evolution* is an amiable comedy from the director of *Ghostbusters* and its sequel. And, once again, Ivan Reitman recognises the importance of comic chemistry, eliciting priceless performances from his cast, in particular a dry-as-toast delivery from David Duchovny (an actor who, after this and *Return to Me*, is shaping up to be one of the most accomplished light comedians of his day). It's also a credit to the scriptwriters that, in spite of the gross appearance of the aliens in the film, the basic biology seems to make sense. Great fun.

● *Dr Ira Kane* David Duchovny, *Harry Block* Orlando Jones, *Wayne* Seann William Scott, *Allison Reid* Julianne Moore, *General Russell Woodman* Ted Levine, *Deke* Ethan Suplee, *Nadine* Katharine Towne, *Danny* Michael Ray Bower, *Flemming* Ty Burrell, *Barry Cartwright* Gregory Itzin, *Governor Lewis* Dan Aykroyd, *with* Pat Kilbane, Ashley Clark, Michelle Wolff, Sarah Silverman, Richard Moll, Wayne Duvall, Michael Chapman, Miriam Flynn, Lee Garlington.
● *Dir* Ivan Reitman, *Pro* Reitman, Daniel Goldberg and Joe Medjuck, *Ex Pro* Tom Pollock, Jeff Apple, David Rodgers and (uncredited) Steven Spielberg, *Assoc*

*Pro* Sheldon Kahn, Kenneth Schwenker and Ronell Venter, *Co-Pro* Paul Deason, *Screenplay* David Diamond, David Weissman and Don Jakoby, *Ph* Michael Chapman, *Pro Des* J Michael Riva, *Ed* Sheldon Kahn and Wendy Greene Bricmont, *M* John Powell; songs performed by Powerman 5000, Self, Buckcherry, Patty Larkin, Samantha Mumba, Brassy, Wild Cherry, *Costumes* Aggie Guerard Rodgers, *Visual effects* Phil Tippett, *Evolutionary consultant* Mark Shelley.

DreamWorks/Columbia/The Montecito Picture Company-Columbia TriStar.
102 mins. USA. 2001. Rel: 22 June 2001. Cert PG.

## Exit Wounds ★★★

Steven Seagal plays rebellious cop Orin Boyd who is assigned to the worst precinct in the city. After $5 million in heroin goes missing from the precinct's property vault, Boyd teams up with local crime boss Latrell Walker (rap star DMX) to expose a ring of drug traffickers working with dirty cops. Of course, Boyd manages to expose the corruption of the system and kicks a lot of ass along the way... Seagal and DMX do an adequate job in their brooding roles, but Tom Arnold and Anthony Anderson steal every scene. Arnold plays a talk-show host who meets Boyd in his anger management class (a funny enough concept in itself) and Anderson plays Walker's fast-talking right-hand man. In addition, Jill Hennessy is magnetic as police commander Annette Mulcahy. So, Seagal's finally learned that his wooden acting can't carry an entire film. Surrounded by strong actors and excellent characters, *Exit Wounds* lifts itself well beyond the usual Seagal/Joel Silver fare. [*Scot Woodward Myers*]

● *Orin Boyd* Steven Seagal, *Latrell Walker* DMX, *George Clark* Isaiah Washington, *TK* Anthony Anderson, *Strutt* Michael Jai White, *Hinges* Bill Duke, *Annette Mulcahy* Jill Hennessy, *Henry Wayne* Tom Arnold, *Montini* David Vadim, *Useldinger* Matthew G Taylor, *with* Eva Mendes, Paolo Mastropietro, Shane Daly.
● *Dir* Andrzej Bartkowiak, *Pro* Joel Silver and Dan Cracchiolo, *Ex Pro* Bruce Berman, *Co-Pro* John M. Eckert and Ernest Johnson, *Screenplay* Ed Horowitz and Richard D'Ovidio, based on the novel by John Westermann, *Ph* Glen MacPherson, *Pro Des* Paul Denham Austerberry, *Ed* Derek G Brechin, *M* Jeff Rona and Damon 'Grease' Blackman; songs performed by Funkmaster Flex, Fun Lovin' Criminals, DMX, James Brown, Tank, Drag-On and Aja, Trick Daddy, Moby, Ideal, Outsiderz 4 Life etc, *Costumes* Jennifer Bryan, *Martial arts choreography* Dion Lam.

Warner/Village Roadshow/NPV/Silver Pictures-Warner.
101 mins. USA/Australia. 2001. Rel: 27 April 2001. Cert 18.

## Extension du Domaine de la Lutte
*See Whatever*

**Left:** Nicolas Cage shows off his sartorial shortcomings in Brett Ratner's contrived, manipulative and derivative The Family Man (from Entertainment)

## Faithless ★★★★¹/₂

This is a major addition to the oeuvre of Ingmar Bergman, notwithstanding that his screenplay is directed by Liv Ullmann (her best work to date in this capacity). In its power and ability to involve, it far surpasses such studies of matrimonial discord as *Scenes From a Marriage* (1971). Bergman has drawn on his own life for this remorseful but sharp dissection of the consequences of a wife's infidelity. With wife (Lena Endre), husband (Thomas Hanzon), and lover (Krister Henriksson) all viewed with an understanding that never softens the implied criticism but avoids mere blame, it can be said that the couple's young daughter is the only innocent victim. Despite a few structural weaknesses, this long film is immensely impressive. An added fascination comes from the framework whereby, in a deliberately stylised present, the wife appears to a writer named Bergman to tell her tale in ultra-realistic mode. You can see her interlocutor as the lover grown old or as Ingmar Bergman himself and, in an outstanding cast, it's Erland Josephson, whose eyes suggest a man reliving what he is being told, who steals the film. Remarkable. [*Mansel Stimpson*]

● *Marianne Vogler* Lena Endre, *Bergman* Erland Josephson, *David* Krister Henriksson, *Markus* Thomas Hanzon, *Isabelle* Michelle Gylemo, *Margareta* Juni Dahr, *Martin Goldman* Philip Zanden, *Petra Holst* Therese Brunnander, *Anna Berg* Marie Richardson.
● *Dir* Liv Ullmann, *Pro* Kaj Larsen, *Ex Pro* Maria Curman, *Screenplay* Ingmar Bergman, *Ph* Jörgen Persson, *Pro Des* Göran Wassberg, *Ed* Sylvia Ingemarsson, *M* various, *Costumes* Inger Elvira Pehrsson.

SVT Drama/Swedish Filminstitute/Nordisk Film and TV Fund, etc-Metro Tartan.
154 mins. Sweden/Norway/Finland. 2000. Rel: 9 February 2001. Cert 15.

## The Family Man ★★

Jack Campbell is the king of his universe, a man who loves his job as an investment banker, his luxury Manhattan penthouse and the easy, beautiful women who come with the territory. Then he gets a phone call from a girlfriend he stood up 13 years earlier, and the next morning – Christmas – he wakes up in her bed. As it happens, he has also turned into her husband and is the father of her two children... An update of *It's a Wonderful Life* without the charm, *The Family Man* is contrived, manipulative and derivative. With Bruce *Pulp Fiction* Willis finding his inner child in *Disney's The Kid* and now Nicolas *Leaving Las Vegas* Cage transformed into a doe-eyed daddio, the treacle is running thick in Hollywood these days. Can Michael *Wonder Boys* Douglas be far behind? And remember, changing diapers and taking out the trash is more fun (that is, more *fulfilling*) than driving around in a Ferrari and having sex with supermodels.

● *Jack Campbell* Nicolas Cage, *Kate Reynolds* Téa Leoni, *Arnie* Jeremy Piven, *Alan Mintz* Saul Rubinek, *Cash* Don Cheadle, *Lassiter* Josef Sommer, *Annie* Mackenzie Vega, *John* Jake Milkovich and Ryan Milkovich, *Evelyn Thompson* Lisa Thornhill, *Big Ed* Harve Presnell, *Adelle* Mary Beth Hurt, *Paula* Amber Valletta, *Bill* Tom McGowan, *Frank, the security man* Daniel Whitner, *with* Francine York, Ruth Williamson, John O'Donahue, Gianni Russo, Robert Downey Snr, *Lucy the dog* Ellis.
● *Dir* Brett Ratner, *Pro* Marc Abraham, Zvi Howard Rosenman, Tony Ludwig and Alan Riche, *Ex Pro* Armyan Bernstein, Thomas A Bliss and Andrew Z Davis, *Screenplay* David Diamond and David Weissman, *Ph* Dante Spinotti, *Pro Des* Kristi Zea, *Ed* Mark Helfrich, *M* Danny Elfman; Verdi, Rossini; songs performed by Burl Ives, Lena Horne, Johnny

Mathis, The Mills Brothers, The Rolling Stones, Raffi, Chris Isaak, Daniel May, Henry Mancini, Elvis Costello, Mr Big, Nicolas Cage ('La La Means I Love You'), Blue Magic, Seal, Morcheeba etc, *Costumes* Betsy Heimann, *Special effects* John Richardson.

Universal Pictures/Beacon Pictures/Riche/Ludwig-Zvi Howard Rosenman/Saturn-Entertainment.
126 mins. USA. 2000. Rel: 22 December 2000. Cert 12.

## La Fidélité ★★

Like Leos Carax's *Pola X*, this is a pretentious and self-indulgent movie of excessive length offering a free modernisation of a classic French novel (in this case, *La Princesse de Clèves*). Writer-director Andrzej Zulawski created it for his partner Sophie Marceau. She plays a photographer in Paris who, working for a scandal sheet, starts an affair with an older man (Pascal Greggory), an editor of probity in the publishing business. Although drawn to a fellow photographer and rival, she marries the editor and resists the younger man's advances. In contrast to her promiscuous past, she now insists on fidelity but there's tragedy ahead. The film is very well photographed and fast-moving, but its humour and drama clash until both elements are submerged in a ludicrous climax. The narrative may not be obscure, but it's improbable and devoid of any clear ultimate purpose. For the record, the fact that the film is so explicit sexually but was awarded a lower certificate than '18' provided early confirmation of a new stance on sex scenes by the British Board of Film Classification. [*Mansel Stimpson*]

● *Clélia* Sophie Marceau, *Clève* Pascal Greggory, *Nemo* Guillaume Canet, *Lucien Mac Roi* Michel Subor, *Clélia's mother* Magali Noël, *Diane* Edith Scob, *with* Manuel Lelievre, Aurelien Recoing, Jean-Charles Dumay.
● *Dir* and *Screenplay* Andrzej Zulawski, *Pro* Paulo Branco, *Ph* Patrick Blossier, *Pro Des* Jean Vincent Puzos, *Ed* Marie-Sophie Dubus, *M* Andrzej Korzynski, *Costumes* Caroline de Vivaise.

Gemini Films/France 3 Cinéma/Spider Films/Madragoa Films/Canal Plus-Artificial Eye.
166 mins. France. 2000. Rel: 1 December 2000. Cert 15.

## 15 Minutes ★★★

New York City; today. 'I love America,' sneers Czech sociopath Emil Slovak, 'nobody is responsible for what they do.' Feigning insanity, Emil cuts up a few bodies while his dumb Russian sidekick records the murders on video. Emil and Oleg have come to America to make their fortune and they know the legal loopholes and what sells. Meanwhile, publicity-hungry news anchor Robert Hawkins is looking for his next kill ('If it bleeds, it leads') – and so a match is made in media Heaven... John Herzfeld, who

directed the wry, offbeat *2 Days in the Valley*, now straps on his Oliver Stone hat to direct this over-the-top, in-yer-face assault on the media. Tipping the viewer off from the word go (the villains have obviously watched too many third-rate videos), the film careens from broad satire to action melodrama with the subtlety of a pile-driver. On the downside, Robert De Niro (as a media-savvy cop) pulls his customary faces and the subject is just so stale (anybody see *Network* 25 years ago?). To its advantage, Edward Burns is nicely understated as the reluctant hero (an arson investigator who never watches TV), while Marinelli and Robinson provide a pulse-racing, percussive score. Visceral, entertaining and very silly.

● *Eddie Flemming* Robert De Niro, *Jordy Warsaw* Edward Burns, *Robert Hawkins* Kelsey Grammer, *Leon Jackson* Avery Brooks, *Nicolette 'Nicky' Karas* Melina Kanakaredes, *Emil Slovak* Karel Roden, *Oleg Razgul* Oleg Taktarov, *Daphne Handlova* Vera Farmiga, *Captain Duffy* James Handy, *Rose Hearn* Charlize Theron, *Cassandra* Kim Cattrall, *mugger* David Alan Grier, *with* John DiResta, Darius McCrary, Bruce Cutler, Vladimir Mashkov, Arina Gasanova, Noelle Evans, Mindy Marin, Paul Herman, Roseanne, Peter Arnett, Barry Primus.
● *Dir* and *Screenplay* John Herzfeld, *Pro* Nick Wechsler and Keith Addis, and David Blocker and John Herzfeld, *Ex Pro* Claire Rudnick Polstein, *Ph* Jean Yves Escoffier, *Pro Des* Mayne Berke, *Ed* Steven Cohen, *M* Anthony Marinelli and J. Peter Robinson; songs performed by Rinocerose, Crazy Russian Folk 'n' Roll Band Limpop, Ballistic Mystic, Gus Gus, David Gray, Maxim and Skin, God Lives Underwater, Johann Langlie, *Costumes* April Ferry, *Casting* Mindy Marin.

New Line Cinema/Industry Entertainment/New Redemption/Tribeca-Entertainment.
121 mins. USA. 2001. Rel: 23 March 2001. Cert 18.

## Finding Forrester ★★★★★

New York City; today. Sixteen-year-old Jamal Wallace loves reading and writing. However, he keeps his passion secret so as to retain a modicum of street credibility with his friends. He is also a fine basketball player, a talent that lands him a prime place at an elite Manhattan prep school. Meanwhile, he strikes up an unlikely friendship with a neighbourhood recluse, a grey-haired misanthrope who takes a surprising interest in Jamal's writing... Expanding on the theme of the anomalous prodigy he developed with his outstanding *Good Will Hunting*, director Gus Van Sant has fashioned another stirring, articulate drama. Served by an informed and intelligent script by radio broadcaster Mike Rich, Van Sant has fine-tuned a marvellous performance from the non-professional, 16-year-old Rob

Brown and has accommodated one of the meatiest and most unexpected turns from Sean Connery in the autumn of the latter's career. Rich with insight and quotable lines ('You write your first draft with your heart; you write your second with your head'), *Finding Forrester* has as much to say about writing and education as it does about the art of living life to the full. This is a mature, surprising and fully satisfying film that just about escapes any ghosts of sentimentality. PS. Any similarities between William Forrester and J D Salinger are entirely intentional.

● *William Forrester* Sean Connery, *Professor Robert Crawford* F Murray Abraham, *Claire Spence* Anna Paquin, *Terrell* Busta Rhymes, *Jamal Wallace* Rob Brown, *Dr Spence* Michael Nouri, *Ms Joyce* April Grace, *Coleridge* Michael Pitt, *Matthews* Richard Easton, *Massie* Glenn Fitzgerald, *Damon* Zane Copeland Jr, *with* James 'Fly' Williams III, Stephanie Berry, Damany Mathis, Damien Lee, Tom Kearns, Matt Malloy, Jimmy Bobbitt, Sophia Wu, and (*uncredited*) Matt Damon.
● *Dir* Gus Van Sant, *Pro* Laurence Mark, Sean Connery and Rhonda Tollefson, *Ex Pro* Dany Wolf and Jonathan King, *Screenplay* Mike Rich, *Ph* Harris Savides, *Pro Des* Jane Musky, *Ed* Valdis Oskarsdottir, *M* Bill Frisell; songs performed by Jimmy Bobbitt, Miles Davis etc, *Costumes* Ann Roth.

Columbia/Fountainbridge Films/Government of Ontario-Columbia TriStar.
137 mins. USA/Canada. 2000. Rel: 23 February 2001. Cert 12.

## Flamenco ★★★★★

Art illuminates art in Carlos Saura's finest musical film since *Blood Wedding*. His unique blend of elements (a theatrically styled performance in a single setting unites with brilliant cinematic technique utilising camera positions, colour changes and editing) is here applied to create a truly historic cultural document. There's no story, simply a series of songs and dances as great artists are recorded by the camera for posterity. They exemplify the range of flamenco and its gut qualities. Not even the foolish decision to leave the lyrics un-subtitled on the British print can hide the fact that this is a masterpiece. The ending, as the music fades and the sounds of everyday life reassert themselves, is one of the most perfectly judged conclusions in film history. The great photography is by Vittorio Storaro and the film's release here is belated – it was made in 1995. A classic. [*Mansel Stimpson*]

● With Joaquín Cortés, Mario Maya, Matilde Coral, Enrique Morente, Jose Menesses, Paco de Lucía, Manolo Sanlucar, Lole y Manuel, Farruco, Farruquito, José Mercé.
● *Dir* and *Screenplay* Carlos Saura, *Pro* Juan Lebrón,

*Ex Pro* José López Rodero, *Ph* Vittorio Storaro, *Pro Des* Rafael Palmero, *Ed* Pablo del Amo, *M* various, *M Dir* Isidro Muñoz, *Costumes* Rafael Palmero.

Juan Lebrón Prods/RTVA Radio Televisión de Andalucía/Sogepaq/Canal Plus, etc-Metrodome. 102 mins. Spain. 1995. Rel: 7 July 2000. Cert U.

**Above:** *Neanderthal ham: Kristen Johnston and Mark Addy grin and bear it in Brian Levant's mindless* The Flintstones in Viva Rock Vegas *(from UIP)*

## Flawless ★★¹/₂

New York's Lower East Side; the present. Retired security guard Walt Koontz is a strict conservative and something of a hero in his neighbourhood. However, now that he lives in a run-down motel he is forced to suffer the close proximity of an overweight and rambunctious drag queen. Then, following a stroke that leaves him partially paralysed, Walt is encouraged to take up singing lessons as part of his rehabilitation. Refusing to leave his apartment, he reluctantly takes up lessons with the 'faggot' he has openly scorned... You have to hand it to De Niro – he'll try just about anything. Yet even this claustrophobic, low-budget character piece has his signature stamped all over it. This, then, is De Niro in *Awakenings* mode and one can't get away from the fact that he's acting his little socks off. Far better, however, is Philip Seymour Hoffman, who's forgiven for acting – he is playing a drag queen, after all. But the best performances come from players further down the cast list, particularly Daphne Rubin-Vega as the tango dancer who accepts Walt for who he is. Even so, the film's manipulative conceit is so relentless that the quiet, affecting moments are lost in the overall scheme. And the melodramatic climax is so cack-handed it's laughable.

● *Walt Koontz* Robert De Niro, *Rusty Zimmerman* Philip Seymour Hoffman, *Leonard Wilcox* Barry

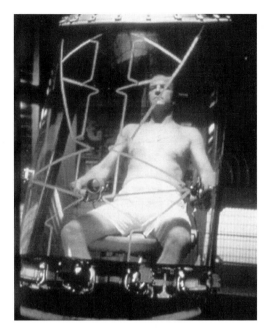

*Right:* Christopher Lambert tries out a new line in retro-futuristic furniture in Geoff Murphy's 'truly awful' Fortress 2: Re-entry (from Columbia TriStar)

Miller, *Tommy Walsh* Skipp Sudduth, *Amazing Grace* Nashom Benjamin, *Pago* Rory Cochrane, *Raymond Camacho* Vincent Laresca, *Dr Nirmala* Madhur Jaffrey, *Cha Cha* Wilson Jermaine Heredia, *Tia* Daphne Rubin-Vega, *Amber* Karina Arroyave, *Karen* Wanda De Jesus, *Mr Z* Luis Saguar, *with* John Enos, Mina Bern, Shiek Madhur-Bey, Chris Bauer, Scott Allen Cooper, Jude Ciccolella, Mark Margolis, Bruce Roberts, Mitchell Lichtenstein.
● *Dir* and *Screenplay* Joel Schumacher, *Pro* Schumacher and Jane Rosenthal, *Ex Pro* Neil Machlis, *Co-Pro* Caroline Baron and Amy Sayres, *Ph* Declan Quinn, *Pro Des* Jan Roelfs, *Ed* Mark Stevens, *M* Bruce Roberts; songs performed by Bruce Roberts, Nashom Benjamin, Rory Cochrane, Nelson Eddy, Taylor Dayne, *Costumes* Daniel Orlandi.

MGM/Tribeca-Optimum Releasing.
111 mins. USA. 1999. Rel: 24 November 2000. Cert 15.

## The Flintstones in Viva Rock Vegas ★¹/₂

Bedrock; the Stone Age. Prior to their days of marital harmony, Fred Flintstone and Barney Rubble are just a couple of awkward guys in search of female companionship. But when Fred hooks up with `caveless' girl Wilma Slaghoople, infatuation is quickly followed by the realisation that she is way out of his league. And with conniving playboy Chip Rockefeller zeroing in for her hand in marriage, how can poor Fred hope to compete? … Seldom has so much money and talent been squandered on such unmitigated rubbish. From the mindless miscasting of Stephen Baldwin as the diminutive and mild-mannered Barney to the slew of obvious gags, the film is an insult to Neanderthal man. And how many puns on `rock' and

'stone' can an audience take? Only Jane Krakowski, as a spirited and wide-eyed Betty, actually looks like she wants to be in the film.

● *Fred Flintstone* Mark Addy, *Barney Rubble* Stephen Baldwin, *Wilma Slaghoople* Kristen Johnston, *Betty O'Shale* Jane Krakowski, *Chip Rockefeller* Thomas Gibson, *Pearl Slaghoople* Joan Collins, *Gazoo/Mick Jagged* Alan Cumming, *Colonel Slagpoole* Harvey Korman, *with* Alex Meneses, John Taylor, Tony Longo, Taylor Negron, Jack McGee, Duan Davis.
● *Dir* Brian Levant, *Pro* Bruce Cohen, *Ex Pro* William Hanna, Joseph Barbera and Dennis E Jones, *Co-Pro* Bart Brown, *Screenplay* Deborah Kaplan, Harry Elfont, Jim Cash & Jack Epps Jr, *Ph* Jamie Anderson, *Pro Des* Christopher Burian-Mohr, *Ed* Kent Beyda, *M* David Newman; songs performed by Ann-Margret, Mark Addy, Nick Lowe and His Cowboy Outfit, New Radicals, *Costumes* Robert Turturice, *Creature effects* Jim Henson's Creature Shop.

Universal/Hanna-Barbera/Amblin Entertainment-UIP.
91 mins. USA. 2000. Rel: 28 July 2000. Cert PG.

## Fortress 2: Re-entry ★

The USA; ten years later. Having escaped from the maximum security prison of the first film, John Brennick is betrayed by a renegade and ends up back in stir. But this time the slammer's in outer space and the prisoners are fitted with implants directly monitored by the guards. A bit of a problem, then, for Brennick, who is determined to re-join his family… A low-budget, bromidic quickie, *Fortress 2* is hampered by cheap production values, over-acting and an indolent performance from Christopher Lambert who looks as if he's cryogenically sealed from the rest of the film. Truly awful. [*Charles Bacon*]

● *John Brennick* Christopher Lambert, *Susan Mendenall* Pam Grier, *Peter Teller* Patrick Malahide, *Elena Rivera* Liz May-Brice, *Stanley Nussbaum* Willie Garson, *Marcus Jackson* Anthony C Hall, *Max Polk* Nick Brimble, *Sato* Yuji Okumoto, *Nestor* David Roberson, *with* Beth Toussaint, Fredric Lane, Carl Chase, John Flock.
● *Dir* Geoff Murphy, *Pro* John Flock, *Ex Pro* Romain Schroeder, *Line Pro* Tom Reeve, *Screenplay* Flock and Peter Doyle II, from a story by Steven Feinberg & Troy Neighbors, *Ph* Hiro Narita, *Pro Des* Simon Bowles, *Ed* James R Symons, *M* Christopher Franke, *Costumes* Cynthia Dumont, *Special effects* Kent Estep.

Gower Prods/Carousel Picture Co.-Columbia TriStar.
92 mins. USA/Luxembourg. 1999. Rel: 21 July 2000. Cert 15.

## Gendernauts ★★

A documentary that lifts the lid on the closeted world of transgender, *Gendernauts* begs more questions than it answers. Set entirely within a bizarre subculture of San Francisco (aka Queer Mecca), the film parades its cast of transsexuals, hermaphrodites and drag royalty like the contestants of a freak show pageant. Fewer talking heads and more straightforward information would have added considerable interest to what is without doubt a fascinating subject.

● With Sandy Stone, Susan Stryker, Texas Tomboy, Annie Sprinkle, Max Valerio, Jordy Jones, Joan Jett Blakk, Sister Roma, Queer David, Mo B Dick, Tornado, Pearl Harbour, Elvis Herselvis etc. Narrator: Monika Treut.
● *Dir, Pro* and *Screenplay* Monika Treut, *Ph* Elfi Mikesch, *Ed* Eric Schefter, *M* Georg Kajanus.

Hyena Films/WDR/ARTE-Millivres Multimedia. 84 mins. Germany. 1999. Rel: 15 September 2000. No Cert.

## Get Over It ★★★★

Berke and Allison have been dating for 16 months and three days, so when Allison jilts him, Berke's world falls apart. In a bid to get her back, he joins the school's musical production of *A Midsummer Night's Rockin Eve*, but he can't hold a tune together any better than his love life. So he takes musical tuition from Kelly, his best mate's little sister... Judged by the standards of teenage romantic comedy, *Get Over It* is at the top of its class. Taking certain thematic elements of *A Midsummer Night's Dream* and harnessing them to a traditional boy-loses-girl scenario, the film twists its inevitable narrative arc in a number of engaging ways. There are a slew of likeable performances, an upbeat soundtrack and a hysterical turn from Martin Short as the musical drama coach ('Bill Shakespeare is a wonderful poet, but Burt Bacharach he ain't'). In fact, it's hard to believe that scenarist R Lee Fleming Jr previously brought us the anodyne teen hit *She's All That*. But then sophomore director Tommy O'Haver displays a wonderfully deft touch, as he did with his inspired debut feature *Billy's Hollywood Screen Kiss*.

● *Kelly* Kirsten Dunst, *Berke Landers* Ben Foster, *Allison* Melissa Sagemiller, *Dennis* Sisqó, *Striker* Shane West, *Felix* Colin Hanks, *Beverly Landers* Swoosie Kurtz, *Frank Landers* Ed Begley Jr, *Dr Desmond Forrest-Oates* Martin Short, *Maggie* Zoë Saldana, *Basin* Mila Kunis, *Mistress Moira* Carmen Electra, *Little Steve* Dov Tiefenbach, *Dora Lynn Tisdale* Kylie Bax, *Jessica* Jeanie Calleja, *with* Vitamin C, Coolio, Christopher Jacot, Park Bench, Daniel Enright, Andrew McGillivray, Megan Fahlenboch, Jonathan Whittaker, 'Love Matters' director Tommy O'Haver.
● *Dir* Tommy O'Haver, *Pro* Michael Burns, Marc

**Above:** *Scouse Hunt: Neil Fitzmaurice and Dominic Carter in Jim Doyle's amiable and amusing going off, big time (from Entertainment)*

Butan and Paul Feldsher, *Ex Pro* Jeremy Kramer and Jill Sobel Messick, *Co-Pro* Richard Hull, Leanna Creel and Louise Rosner, *Screenplay* R. Lee Fleming Jr, *Ph* Maryse Alberti, *Pro Des* Robin Standefer, *Ed* Jeff Betancourt, *M* Steve Bartek; songs performed by Shorty 101, Fatboy Slim, Basement Jaxx, American Hi-Fi, Mikaila, Elvis Costello and the Attractions, Badly Drawn Boy, Caviar, Captain & Tennille, Kirsten Dunst, The Wondermints, Splitsville, Resident Filters, Touch and Go, Mr Natural, *Costumes* Mary Jane Fort.

Miramax/Ignite Entertainment/Morpheus-Momentum Pictutres. 86 mins. USA. 2001. Rel: 8 June 2001. Cert 12.

## The Gift ★★★

Annie Wilson, a widow with three small sons, has the gift of clairvoyance. However, in the sleepy town of Brixton, Georgia, only the disturbed and disenchanted seek her services, helping her get by with small donations. Then, when the daughter of a local bigwig goes missing, the police reluctantly call on Annie to assist them with their investigations... Although *The Gift* is essentially a generic thriller from a generic filmmaker (*The Evil Dead*, *Darkman*), it is easy to see why such an outstanding cast was attracted to it. Two years ago Sam Raimi directed the gripping and evocative *A Simple Plan*, while the screenwriters, Billy Bob Thornton and Tom Epperson, previously collaborated on the critically acclaimed *One False Move* and *A Family Thing*. And how could the Australian-born Cate Blanchett resist playing a Southern clairvoyant, perennial studmuffin Keanu Reeves an abusive husband and Giovanni Ribisi a psychotic car mechanic? All these are great roles and, thankfully, the actors don't overplay their hand. Indeed, it's not until way past the halfway mark that the film starts behaving like a mechanical whodunit.

● *Annie Wilson* Cate Blanchett, *Buddy Cole* Giovanni Ribisi, *Donnie Barksdale* Keanu Reeves, *Jessica King* Katie Holmes, *Wayne Collins* Greg Kinnear, *Valerie Barksdale* Hilary Swank, *Gerald Weems* Michael Jeter, *Linda* Kim Dickens, *David Duncan* Gary Cole, *Annie's granny* Rosemary Harris, *Sheriff Pearl Johnson* J K Simmons, *Kenneth King* Chelcie Ross, *Mike Wilson* Lynnsee Provence, *Tommy Lee Ballard* Danny Elfman, *with* John Beasley, Hunter McGilvray, Nathan Lewis, Benjamin Peacock, Alex Lee.
● *Dir* Sam Raimi, *Pro* James Jacks, Tom Rosenberg and Gary Lucchesi, *Ex Pro* Sean Daniel, Ted Tannebaum, Gregory Goodman and Rob Tapert, *Screenplay* Billy Bob Thornton and Tom Epperson, *Ph* Jamie Anderson, *Pro Des* Neil Spisak, *Ed* Arthur Coburn and Bob Murawski, *M* Christopher Young; songs performed by Lee Hazlewood and The Souvenirs, *Costumes* Julie Weiss.

Lakeshore Entertainment/Paramount Classics/Alphaville-Redbus.
112 mins. USA. 2000. Rel: 2 March 2001. Cert 15.

## Ginger Snaps ★★★¹/₂

Bailey Downs, Ontario, Canada; the present. Self-styled outcasts Ginger and Brigitte Fitzgerald have never fitted in at school, an institution they refer to as a 'hormonal toilet'. They are far more interested in the phenomenon of suicide, an obsession they even carry into their academic work. Then, following her first period and an encounter with a nocturnal 'beast', Ginger starts behaving *really* oddly... If you can imagine *Heathers* welded onto *I Was a Teenage Werewolf*, then you may have some idea what to expect from this fiercely original, funny and gruesome lycanthropic romp. Smartly balancing some straight-faced humour with genuine ickiness (dog lovers beware), *Ginger Snaps* reveals a real talent in Canadian filmmaker John Fawcett (whose first film, *The Boys Club*, nabbed five Genie nominations). Likewise, the 22-year-old Emily Perkins as the 15-year-old Brigitte (recalling a pretty, female Marilyn Manson) is a real find. Only the final 15 minutes, featuring a highly implausible 'creature', let the side down. Favourite line: 'Girls, I told you – no more death in the house' (delivered by Mimi Rogers as the sisters' determinedly cheery mother).

● *Brigitte Fitzgerald* Emily Perkins, *Ginger Fitzgerald* Katharine Isabelle, *Sam* Kris Lemche, *Pamela Fitzgerald* Mimi Rogers, *Jason* Jesse Moss, *Trina Sinclair* Danielle Hampton, *Henry Fitzgerald* John Bourgeois, *Mr Wayne* Peter Keleghan, *with* Christopher Redman, Jimmy MacInnis, Lindsey Leese, *Creature/Gingerwolf* Nick Nolan.
● *Dir* John Fawcett, *Pro* Steve Hoban and Karen Lee Hall, *Ex Pro* Noah Segal, Alicia Reilly-Larson and Daniel Lyon, *Assoc Pro* Tina Goldlist, *Screenplay* Karen Walton, from a story by Walton and Fawcett, *Ph* Thom

Best, *Pro Des* Todd Cherniawsky, *Ed* Brett Sullivan, *M* Michael Shields, *Costumes* Lea Carlson, *Make-up* and *Creature effects* Paul Jones, *Sound* David McCallum.

Copper Heart Entertainment/Walter Pictures/TVA Int./ Lions Gate/Telefilm Canada/Movie Network-Optimum Releasing.
104 mins. Canada. 2000. Rel: 29 June 2001. Cert 18.

## Girlfight ★★¹/₂

Diana Guzman has a lot to be angry about. Brought up on the poverty line in the housing projects of Brooklyn, she is reared by a father blind to her needs, while her mother took her own life years ago. Now 18, Diana is in her last year at high school and discovers an unexpected outlet – in the ring at the local boxing club... As a portrait of alienated youth in contemporary New York, *Girlfight* reveals an authentic and fresh voice in first-time director Karyn Kusama, herself a former boxer. Kusama, who won the best director prize at the 2000 Sundance Festival, is particularly adept at writing economic and believable dialogue and has coaxed an arresting performance from non-professional Michelle Rodriguez, who resembles a young Ice Cube (with a dash of Brando). However, the film is less inspiring as a dramatic work, its boxing sequences proving particularly weak in a genre noted for its built-in excitement, while the ending is all too inevitable. Incidentally, *Girlfight* is an interesting reversal of the British *Billy Elliott* [qv], in which a boy, also against his father's wishes, ducks out of boxing lessons in order to take up ballet.

● *Diana Guzman* Michelle Rodriguez, *Hector* Jaime Tirelli, *Sandro Guzman* Paul Calderon, *Adrian* Santiago Douglas, *Marisol* Elisa Bocanegra, *Cal* Herb Lovelle, *Tiny Guzman* Ray Santiago, *science teacher* John Sayles, *Veronica* Shannon Walker Williams, *with* Alicia Ashley, Thomas Barbour, Louis Guss, Victor Sierra.
● *Dir* and *Screenplay* Karyn Kusama, *Pro* Sarah Green, Martha Griffin and Maggie Renzi, *Ex Pro* John Sayles, Jonathan Sehring and Caroline Kaplan, *Ph* Patrick Cady, *Pro Des* Stephen Beatrice, *Ed* Plummy Tucker, *M* Theodore Shapiro, *Costumes* Luca Mosca and Marco Cattoretti.

The Independent Film Channel/Green/Renzi-Columbia TriStar.
112 mins. USA. 2000. Rel: 20 April 2001. Cert 15.

## going off, big time ★★★

Liverpool; today. Following his raid on a pub that fatally backfires, criminal hotshot Mark Clayton hides out at the home of his solicitor, Stacey Bannerman. There he begins to tell her his life story, from his days in prison, his befriending of a veteran crook and then, on the outside, his formation of a protection racket... A kind of *Gangster No. 1*-lite, this debut feature from

*Left: Cracked surfaces: Jeremy Northam and Uma Thurman in James Ivory's visually sumptuous if somewhat laboured The Golden Bowl (from Buena Vista)*

director Jim Doyle and scripter-star Neil Fitzmaurice is actually an amiable and amusing addition to the postmodern British gangster genre. While the second half doesn't exactly live up to the first, there are a number of choice moments throughout. Bernard Hill turns in another classic performance as the seen-it-all hard man, while the scene in which four cops lap up Ecstasy-spiced ice cream is a hoot. [*Charles Bacon*]

● *Mark Clayton* Neil Fitzmaurice, *Ozzi Shepherd* Dominic Carter, *Paul* Nick Lamont, *Charlie* Nick Moss, *John* Vinnie Adams, *Stacey Bannerman* Sarah Alexander, *Murray* Bernard Hill, *Flipper* Peter Kay, with Huggy Leaver, Del Henney, Jimmy Gallagher, Stan Boardman, Sidney Livingstone, Cerys Griffiths.
● *Dir* Jim Doyle, *Pro* Ian Brody, *Co-Pro* Jonny Boston, *Assoc Pro* Tony Fitzmaurice and Richard Cave, *Line Pro* Amanda Nally, *Screenplay* Neil Fitzmaurice, *Ph* Damian Bromley, *Pro Des* David Butterworth, *Ed* Julian Day, *M* Andy Roberts, *Costumes* Monica Aslanian.

KT Films/Entertainment/Catalysm/SpinOff-Entertainment.
87 mins. UK. 2000. Rel: 3 November 2000. Cert 18.

## The Golden Bowl ★★★

England/Italy; 1903-1909. Searching for a wedding present for his fiancée Maggie, the Italian Prince Amerigo accompanies his friend Charlotte to an antique shop in Bloomsbury. There they find a beautiful and elegant crystal bowl decorated in gold, but Amerigo rejects it due to an invisible flaw. Ironically, Amerigo's own marriage comes to reflect the discarded antique as he and Charlotte continue the affair they started in Rome... In spite of his ubiquity on screen, Henry James has proved to be a problem for filmmakers, both with his complex interior dialogues and absence of cinematic action. However, this is a bold stab at the writer's greatest – if most demanding – work, with a fine turn from Nick Nolte as the noble and insightful billionaire Adam Verver and with predictably magnificent production values and locations. Notwithstanding, director Ivory does tend to labour the subtext, sometimes to a laughable degree, and Anjelica Huston's accent appears to have a life of its own (New England? Mississippi?). Filmed in Italy and in England at Burleigh House, Helmingham Hall, Belvoir Castle and Syon Park. Favourite scene: in which apparently 'live' waxworks eavesdrop on Amerigo and Charlotte.

● *Adam Verver* Nick Nolte, *Charlotte Stant* Uma Thurman, *Fanny Assingham* Anjelica Huston, *Prince Amerigo* Jeremy Northam, *Maggie Verver* Kate Beckinsale, *Colonel Bob Assingham* James Fox, *Lady Castledean* Madeleine Potter, *Jarvis, the shopkeeper* Peter Eyre, *Lord Castledean* Nicholas Day, *Mr Blint* Robin Hart, *lecturer* Nickolas Grace, with Daniel Byam Shaw, Francesco Giuffrida, Marta Paola Richeldi, Anthony Bevan, Neville Phillips, Paul Bradley, Lucy Freeman, Phillip Tabor.
● *Dir* James Ivory, *Pro* Ismail Merchant, *Ex Pro* Paul Bradley and Richard Hawley, *Screenplay* Ruth Prawer Jhabvala, *Ph* Tony Pierce Roberts, *Pro Des* Andrew Sanders, *Ed* John David Allen, *M* Richard Robbins, *Costumes* John Bright, *Choreography* Karole Armitage, *Hair* Carol Hemming.

Merchant Ivory Productions/TF1 International/Miramax-Buena Vista.
126 mins. UK/France/USA. 2000. Rel: 3 November 2000. Cert 12.

## Gone in 60 Seconds ★★¹/₂

In his time, Randall 'Memphis' Raines was responsible for 47 per cent of the car thefts in his area. Now he's retired, teaches children stockcar racing and wants nothing to do with the life that left so many of his friends dead or in prison. Then his little brother ends up in an unholy mess and in order to save his life Memphis is ordered to steal 50 cars in three days... The original *Gone in 60 Seconds*, made in 1974 by junkyard dealer H B Halicki (who was killed while making the sequel), largely substituted plot for car crashes (total bodycount: 90). Here, the accent is still very much on the hardware, with a 1967 Shelby Mustang dubbed Eleanor stealing the acting honours in spite of a top-of-the-line cast. This is a shame, as the likes of Cage, Jolie, Ribisi and Duvall deserve more meat on their chassis. But, as popcorn movies go, this one certainly has a tiger in its tank and the stunts are suitably awesome (with Cage doing most of his own driving). However, some incoherent plotting and a lot of muffled dialogue take away from the adrenaline rush.

● *Randall 'Memphis' Raines* Nicolas Cage, *Sara 'Sway' Wayland* Angelina Jolie, *Kip Raines* Giovanni Ribisi, *Detective Roland Castlebeck* Delroy Lindo, *Atley Jackson* Will Patton, *Raymond Calitri* Christopher Eccleston, *Donny Astricky* Chi McBride, *Otto Halliwell* Robert Duvall, *Toby* William Lee Scott, *Tumbler* Scott Caan, *Freb* James Duval, *The Sphinx* Vinnie Jones, *Detective Drycoff* Timothy Olyphant, *Helen Raines* Grace Zabriskie, *Junie* Frances Fisher, *with* T J Cross, Dean Rader Duvall, Billy Devlin, Arye Gross, Scott Rosenberg, Tyler Patton, Carmen Argenziano, John Carroll Lynch, Trevor Goddard, Master P, Ken Jenkins.
● *Dir* Dominic Sena, *Pro* Jerry Bruckheimer and Mike Stenson, *Ex Pro* Jonathan Hensleigh, Chad Oman, Barry Waldman, Denise Shakarian Halicki, Robert Stone & Webster Stone, *Screenplay* Scott Rosenberg, *Ph* Paul Cameron, *Pro Des* Jeff Mann, *Ed* Tom Muldoon and Chris Lebenzon, *M* Trevor Rabin; songs performed by Moby, Crystal Method, Gomez, Johnny Cash, Groove Armada, A3, War, BT, Apollo Four Forty, Ice Cube, Method Man and Redman, The Chemical Brothers, DMX, Jane's Addiction, Caviar, George Thorogood and The Destroyers, The Cult etc, *Costumes* Marlene Stewart, *Special effects* Mike Meinardus, *Stunt coordinator* Chuck Picerni Jr, *Picture car coordinator* Michael D Antunez.

Touchstone Pictures/Jerry Bruckheimer Films-Buena Vista International.
118 mins. USA. 2000. Rel: 4 August 2000. Cert 15.

## Goodbye Charlie Bright ★★★★

Charlie, Justin, Damien, Frankie and Tommy have grown up on the council estates of South London and petty crime has always been a part of their lives. Then, when Tommy leaves for the army and Frankie gets his girlfriend pregnant, Charlie realises that it's time to move on. However, his best friend, Justin, seems locked into his old ways and it's becoming increasingly hard to justify his irresponsible behaviour... Yet another slice-of-life tale from the council estates of Britain, *Goodbye Charlie Bright* can place itself alongside *Trainspotting* and *Human Traffic* as one of the more successful descents into the nihilism of British youth. Distinguished by winning turns from an excellent young cast (with his disarming grin and rakish charm, Roland Manookian should go far), the film is a stylish, energetic but authentic look at what it means to be born and raised with few prospects for a fulfilling life. An excellent soundtrack (see credits) and some unexpected moments of humour and compassionate insight further add to what is one of the most surprisingly good British films of the year. Previously known as *Strong Boys*.

● *Charlie* Paul Nicholls, *Justin* Roland Manookian, *Hector* Richard Driscoll, *Francis* Danny Dyer, *Tony Immaculate* Jamie Foreman, *Dad* David Thewlis, *Eddie* Phil Daniels, *Blondie* Dani Behr, *Damien* Alexis Rodney, *Tommy's dad* Frank Harper, *Tommy* Sid Mitchell, *Julie* Nicola Stapleton, *Duke* Brian Jordan, *Charlie's mum* Kate Buffery, *with* Lucy Bowen, Tameka Empson, Sian Welsh, Susanna Page, Edna Doré, *Julie's mum* Kathleen Stapleton, Eve Bland.
● *Dir* Nick Love, *Pro* Charles Steel and Lisa Bryer, *Ex Pro* David Forrest, Beau Rogers and Cyril Mégret, *Co-Pro* Suzanne Warren, Stephen Cleary and Simon Channing-Williams, *Assoc Pro* Kiki Miyake, *Screenplay* Love and Dominic Eames, *Ph* Tony Imi, *Pro Des* Eve Stewart, *Ed* Patrick Moore, *M* Ivor Guest; Mozart; songs performed by Robbie Williams and Kylie Minogue, Craig David, Lady Spirit and In the House, Leona Williams, McCormick Bros, Love Connection, Moby, Lynden David Hall, Monk & Canatella, Leftfield, Oasis etc, *Costumes* Ffion Elinor.

Flashpoint/Bonaparte Films/Cowboy Films/Imagine Films-Metrodome.
87 mins. UK. 2000. Rel: 11 May 2001. Cert 18.

## Gossip ★★

Derrick, Cathy and Travis are college roommates who start and then track the dissemination of a rumour as a sociological experiment. Even more quickly than they expected, the bit of gossip flies out of control and their lives inevitably follow. Cathy tries to right the situation only to find herself thwarted by Machiavellian ringleader Derrick. Brilliantly artistic but naïve Travis seems innocently drawn along for the ride. But are any of them so innocent? ... This 'after school special' blown up to big screen proportions actually has a lot going for it. But stylish design and able performances can't quite overcome both a plot and a director who seem to run out of steam by the denouement. Still, as a cautionary tale of just how easy it is to destroy people's lives, it remains effective. This is what happens when kids have too much time and money on their hands. [*Scot Woodward Myers*]

● *Derrick Webb* James Marsden, *Cathy Jones* Lena Headey, *Travis* Norman Reedus, *Naomi Preston* Kate Hudson, *Sheila* Marisa Coughlan, *Det Kelly* Sharon Lawrence, *Professor Goodwin* Eric Bogosian, *Det Curtis* Edward James Olmos, *Beau Edson* Joshua Jackson, *Rebecca Lewis* Stephanie Mills, *with* Kwok Wing Leung, Poe, Raven Dauda, Kristin Booth, Elizabeth Guber, Charles Guggenheim, Marion Guggenheim.
● *Dir* Davis Guggenheim, *Pro* Jeffrey Silver and Bobby Newmyer, *Ex Pro* Joel Schumacher and Bruce Berman, *Co-Pro* John M Eckert, *Assoc Pro* Susan E Novick, *Screenplay* Gregory Poirier and Theresa Rebeck, *Ph* Andrzej Bartkowiak, *Pro Des* David Nichols, *Ed* Jay Cassidy, *M* Graeme Revell; songs performed by Poe, Morcheeba, God Lives Underwater, Tinstar, Hednoize, Dusty Springfield, Richard Butler, The Folk Implosion, Curve, James Marsden, Tonic etc, *Costumes* Louise Mingenbach.

Warner/Village Roadshow/NPV Entertainment-Warner. 90 mins. USA/Australia. 2000. Rel: 25 August 2000. Cert 15.

## Le Goût des autres – The Taste of Others ★★★★

In its unpretentious way this quintessentially French comedy takes in pathos and suffering to create a fully fledged view of life. At its heart is the story of a factory owner (Bacri) who, married to a woman who forces her taste on him, expands his horizons when he falls for an actress (Alvaro) who is hoping for a child before it becomes too late. Her artistic circle is contrasted with his background, while further comparisons bring in two employees, the factory owner's regular chauffeur and his temporary bodyguard, and their relationships. Various threads thus intertwine, often humorously but also providing some astute comments on social and class distinctions. Agnès Jaoui, who also appears as one of a highly impressive cast, makes an assured directorial debut here. With so many characters the narrative could on occasion be advantageously clearer and the ending is less subtle than the rest, but these are minor weaknesses in a highly civilised film. [*Mansel Stimpson*]

● *Clara Devaux* Annie Alvaro, *Jean-Pierre Castella* Jean-Pierre Bacri, *Béatrice* Brigitte Catillon, *Bruno Deschamps* Alain Shabat, *Benoît* Raphael Defour, *Weber* Xavier de Guillebon, *Manie* Agnès Jaoui, *Franck Moreno* Gérard Lanvin, *Valérie* Anne Le Ny, *Angélique* Christiane Millet, *Antoine* Wladimir Yordanoff, *Castella's father* Robert Bacri.
● *Dir* Agnès Jaoui, *Pro* Christian Bérard and Charles Gassot, *Ex Pro* Jacques Hinstin, *Screenplay* Jaoui and Jean-Pierre Bacri, *Ph* Laurent Dailland, *Pro Des* François Emmanuelli, *Ed* Hervé de Luze, *M* Mozart, Mendelssohn, George Handel, Verdi, Harold Purcell, Schubert etc, *Costumes* Jackie Stephens-Budin.

Telema/Les Films A4/France 2 Cinema/Canal Plus-Pathé. 112 mins. France. 2000. Rel: 25 May 2001. Cert 15.

## Goya in Bordeaux – Goya en Burdeos ★★

In self-imposed exile in Bordeaux, the great Spanish painter Francisco de Goya, now in his eighties and completely deaf, ruminates on his life... Employing a similar narrative device as Raul Ruiz used for his film on Marcel Proust, *Time Regained* – the bedridden artist consumed by fragmentary memories of his past – Carlos Saura jettisons fluidity for theatrical trickery. Opening with an awkward transformation in which the entrails of a bull are replaced by the magnificent features of the great Spanish actor Francisco Rabal, the film exhibits early promise but soon gets mired in the director's self-conscious artifice. Thus, with its stage lighting effects, back-lit screens and simultaneous appearance of the old and young Goya, the exercise is not so much a film as a theatrical indulgence. To be sure, there are some interesting ideas at work here – the filmmaker drawing a correlation between cinema and art – but it makes for wearisome viewing.

● *Francisco José de Goya y Lucientes* Francisco Rabal, *The Duchess of Alba* Maribel Verdú, *Goya as a young man* José Coronado, *Leocadia* Eulalia Ramón, *Rosarito, Leocadia's daughter* Dafné Fernández, *José de la Cruz* Emilio Gutiérrez Caba.
● *Dir* and *Screenplay* Carlos Saura, *Pro* Andrés Vicente Gómez, *Co-Pro* Fulvio Lucisano, *Ph* Vittorio Storaro, *Pro Des* Pierre-Louis Thévenet, *Ed* Julia Juaniz, *M* Roque Baños, *Costumes* Pedro Moreno.

Andrés Vicente Gómez/Lolafilms, SA/RAI, etc-Downtown Pictures. 104 mins. Spain/Italy. 1999. Rel: 29 September 2000. Cert 15.

## Grey Owl ★★¹/₂

Elk River/Lake Abitibi/Ajawaan Lake, Ontario/Saskatchewan, Canada; 1934-36. A trapper and occasional guide, Grey Owl (or He Who Flies By Night) is a man who prefers his own company and is most at home in the remote wilderness of Canada. But the publication of a series of his articles on the life of the Native American Indian and the distraction of an attractive and loving woman are about to change Grey Owl's life forever... The problem with slow-burning passions is that by the time you get to light the fire you can lose sight of the firewood. Richard Attenborough has harboured a desire to bring the true story of Grey Owl to the screen for 63 years and while it remains an interesting concept, the film itself is dull. Besides wooden turns from Pierce Brosnan and Annie Galipeau and a stilted structure that seems to slip through time, *Grey Owl* has little narrative momentum until its belated dramatic pay-off. Well meaning, to be sure, but not very exciting. Filmed substantially in Quebec.

● *Archie Grey Owl* Pierce Brosnan, *Anahareo* aka *Pony* Annie Galipeau, *Ned White Bear* Nathaniel Arcand,

**Right:** *How Hollywood Degraded Dr Seuss: Jim Carrey manfully attempts to salvage Ron Howard's cringeingly awful* The Grinch *(from UIP)*

get), while the six-year-old Taylor Momsen cast as Cindy Lou Who is, to put it charitably, no Mara Wilson. The original was designed to help teach children to read – the film will teach them to stick to their books. US title: *Dr Seuss' How the Grinch Stole Christmas.*

● *The Grinch* Jim Carrey, *May Who* Jeffrey Tambor, *Martha May Whovier* Christine Baranski, *Lou Lou Who* Bill Irwin, *Betty Lou Who* Molly Shannon, *Cindy Lou Who* Taylor Momsen, *Max* Kelley, *with* Jeremy Howard, T J Thyne, Lacey Kohl, Nadja Pionilla, Jim Meskimen, Clint Howard, Rance Howard, Deep Roy, Mindy Sterling, Gavin Grazer, Walter Franks, Verne J Troyer, Bryce Howard, *voice of Max the Dog* Frank Welker; *narrator* Anthony Hopkins.
● *Dir* Ron Howard, *Pro* Howard and Brian Grazer, *Ex Pro* Todd Hallowell, *Assoc Pro* Aldric La'auli Porter, Louis Velis, David Womark and Linda Fields-Hill, *Screenplay* Jeffrey Price and Peter S Seaman, *Ph* Don Peterman, *Pro Des* Michael Corenblith, *Ed* Dan Hanley and Mike Hill, *M* James Horner; songs performed by Faith Hill, Taylor Momsen, Barenaked Ladies, Kriste Collins, Smash Mouth, I found god, eels, Jim Carrey, Ben Folds etc, *Costumes* Rita Ryack, *Dermatologist* Dr Gary Lask.

Universal/Imagine Entertainment-UIP.
105 mins. USA. 2000. Rel: 1 December 2000. Cert PG.

## Groove ★★¹/₂

Following in the wake of the British *Human Traffic* and *Sorted*, this is yet another low-budget exploration of the clubbing phenomenon and recreational drugs. Set in the underground rave scene of San Francisco and featuring a cast of likeable unknowns, Greg Harrison's debut film as director is atmospheric, energetic and well-acted, which is more than his dialogue deserves. And, on a moral note, *Groove* could come in for some major criticism for its celebration of Ecstasy and other illegal substances. So please take the 18 certificate seriously. [*Charles Bacon*]

● *Harmony Stitts* Mackenzie Firgens, *Leyla Heydel* Lola Glaudini, *David Turner* Hamish Linklater, *Colin Turner* Denny Kirkwood, *Beth Anderson* Rachel True, *Ernie Townsend* Steve Van Wormer, *Anthony Mitchell* Vince Riverside, *with* Ari Gold, Angelo Spizziri, Nick Offerman, John Digweed.
● *Dir, Screenplay* and *Ed* Greg Harrison, *Pro* Danielle Renfrew, *Ex Pro* Jeff Southard, *Ph* Matthew Irving, *Pro Des* Chris Ferreira, *M* various; songs performed by Symbiosis, John Digweed, Mixmaster Morris, Jonah Sharp, The Hardkiss Brothers, Octave One, WishFM, Ming + FS, DJ Garth, N'Dea Davenport, DJ Polywog, Lew Baldwin, Christian Smith, LIFT, DJ Baggadonuts, Jondi & Spesh, DJ caliban, Bandwidth etc, *Costumes* Kei Hashinoguchi, *Sound* Andrea Gard.

415 Prods-Columbia TriStar.
84 mins. USA. 2000. Rel: 15 December 2000. Cert 18.

*Harry Champlin* Vlasta Vrana, *Jim Wood* David Fox, *Walter Perry* Charles Powell, *Ada Belaney* Stephanie Cole, *Carrie Belaney* Renée Asherson, *Cyrus Finney* Stewart Bick, *Jim Bernard* Graham Greene, *with* John Dunn-Hill, Saginaw Grant, Jimmy Herman, Jacques Lussier, Floyd Crow Westerman, Seann Gallagher.
● *Dir* Richard Attenborough, *Pro* Jake Eberts and Claude Léger, *Ex Pro* Barr Potter and Lenny Young, *Co-Pro* Diana Hawkins and Josette Perrotta, *Screenplay* William Nicholson, *Ph* Roger Pratt, *Pro Des* Anthony Pratt, *Ed* Lesley Walker, *M* George Fenton and David Lawson, *Costumes* Renée April, *beaver specialist* Bill Carrick.

Largo Entertainment/Transfilm/Beaver Prods-Fox.
118 mins. UK/Canada. 1998. Rel: 3 November 2000. Cert PG.

## The Grinch ★¹/₂

Every Who down in Who-ville liked Christmas a lot. But the Grinch, who lived just north of Who-ville, did NOT! And so the hairy green outcast sets about ruining Christmas for his friendly little neighbours... It's a tall order to translate any beloved classic to the screen, but Dr Seuss' *How the Grinch Stole Christmas* would seem to be a particularly challenging mission. On the one hand, Ron Howard and his creative team have done a miraculous job in recreating the fantastical world of Who-ville. They were also wise to choose Jim Carrey to play the hideously splenetic Grinch (one would hate to think what any other actor would have made of the role – say, Robin Williams?). However, the original text allows for little expansion, and for the film to introduce a whole section on The Grinch's childhood is a disastrous miscalculation. The Whos themselves are a tiresome and ugly race of humanoid dolts (who deserve everything they

**Left:** *Music to her ears: Iben Hjejle keeps John Cusack guessing in Stephen Frears' marvellously witty* High Fidelity *(from Buena Vista)*

### Hamlet ★★★

Hotel Elsinore, New York; the present. Following the death of the president of the Denmark Corporation, the magnate's wife marries his brother in unseemly haste. Her son, Hamlet, visited by the ghost of his father, suspects murder most foul... Coming just four years after Kenneth Branagh's film and ten years after Franco Zeffirelli's, Michael Almereyda's transposition of Shakespeare's longest and most famous play to contemporary New York can at best be described as an academic exercise. Jettisoning over half the text ('Alas, poor Yorick' indeed!), Almereyda has lost the poetry and emotional power of the play, although his visually luxuriant palette of technological imagery finds an arresting symbiosis with the elegance of the dialogue. Forsooth, with its cannonade of neon graphics it doth resemble a pageant of product placement. Still, who can resist the prospect of Bill Murray giving voice to Polonius? FYI: This is actually the *44th* screen version of *Hamlet*.

● *Hamlet* Ethan Hawke, *Claudius* Kyle MacLachlan, *Gertrude* Diane Venora, *Laertes* Liev Schreiber, *Ophelia* Julia Stiles, *Polonius* Bill Murray, *Horatio* Karl Geary, *Rosencrantz* Steve Zahn, *Guildenstern* Dechen Thurman, *ghost of Hamlet's father* Sam Shepard, *Marcella* Paula Malcomson, *gravedigger* Jeffrey Wright, *Osric* Paul Bartel, *Fortinbras* Casey Affleck, *priest* Robert Thurman, *flight captain* Tim Blake Nelson, *with* John Martin, Bernadette Jurkowski, Robin MacNeil.
● *Dir* and *Adaptation* Michael Almereyda, *Pro* Andrew Fierberg and Amy Hobby, *Ex Pro* Jason Blum and John Sloss, *Line Pro* Callum Greene, *Ph* John de Borman, *Pro Des* Gideon Ponte, *Ed* Kristina Boden, *M* Carter Burwell, *Costumes* Luca Mosca and Marco Cattoretti.

Miramax/Double A Films-FilmFour.
111 mins. USA. 2000. Rel: 15 December 2000. Cert 12.

### Hannibal ★★★¹/₂

Following a botched stakeout ending in the death of five people, FBI agent Clarice Sterling has become the disgrace of her department. However, the revelation that the notorious cannibal Hannibal Lecter is now at large somewhere in Europe might just lead to Clarice's redemption... *Hannibal* is an extremely handsome film, as one would expect from a director of Ridley Scott's credentials. Nevertheless, it hardly approaches the filmmaker's finest work (*Alien, Blade Runner, Thelma & Louise, Gladiator*). Scott has resolutely refused to make a sequel until now, but with Anthony Hopkins returning to the role that earned him his stellar stripes (and an Oscar) and with a script by David Mamet and Steven Zaillian, it's easy to see how Scott was tempted. Yet in spite of its charismatic protagonist and several powerful moments, *Hannibal* is no better a thriller than many of the *Seven* school and is guilty of far too many longueurs. As Clarice Starling, Julianne Moore is an able replacement for Jodie Foster and there's a wonderful turn from Gary Oldman as the horrendously disfigured Mason Verger, whose explanation for his self-inflicted mutilation – 'It seemed like a good idea at the time' – brings a welcome whiff of black humour. But the film really belongs to Hopkins, whose mix of high civility and animal brutality proves to be a wonderfully compelling cocktail. Yet moments of extreme sadism will put off many mainstream viewers who managed to stomach even the more disturbing aspects of *The Silence of the Lambs*.

● *Dr Hannibal Lecter* Anthony Hopkins, *Clarice Starling* Julianne Moore, *Paul Krendler* Ray Liotta, *Barney* Frankie R Faison, *Inspector Rinaldo Pazzi* Giancarlo Giannini, *Allegra Pazzi* Francesca Neri, *Mason Verger* Gary Oldman, *Dr Cordell Doemling* Zeljko Ivanek, *Evelda Drumgo* Hazelle Goodman, *FBI Agent Pearsall* David Andrews, *Gnocco* Enrico Lo Verso, *Carlo* Ivano Marescotti, *Officer Bolton* Terry Serpico, *Agent Benetti* Andrea Piedimonte, *with* Francis Guinan, Mark Margolis, Fabrizio Gifuni, Ennio Coltorti, Alex Corrado, Marco Greco, Boyd Kestner, Peter Shaw, Don McManus, Ted Koch, Bruce MacVittie, Giannina Facio, Judie Aronson.
● *Dir* Ridley Scott, *Pro* Scott, Dino De Laurentiis and Martha De Laurentiis, *Ex Pro* Branko Lustig, *Line Pro* Lucio Trentini, *Screenplay* David Mamet and Steven Zaillian, from the novel by Thomas Harris, *Ph* John Mathieson, *Pro Des* Norris Spencer, *Ed* Pietro Scalia, *M* Hans Zimmer, *Costumes* Janty Yates, *Make-up* Keith Vanderlaan, Greg Cannom and Wes Wofford.

Universal/MGM/Dino De Laurentiis/Scott Free-UIP.
132 mins. USA. 2001. Rel: 16 February 2001. Cert 18.

## Harry, He's Here To Help – Harry, un ami qui vous veut du bien ★★★★★

Michel and Claire Pape are driving through the French countryside on a hot, clammy afternoon. With no air conditioning and three extremely irritable young daughters in tow, their trip is becoming increasingly intolerable. Then, at a rest stop, Michel bumps into Harry, an old school friend he cannot even remember. Calm, friendly and insistent, Harry suggests that he and his girlfriend, Plum, follow the Papes to their summer retreat. There, Harry quickly sets about putting Michel's life to rights... Like all good scenarios, Dominik Moll's is deceptively simple. By building up his narrative with subtle flecks of detail and flashes of humour, the filmmaker draws the viewer into his narrative web with confident ease. Furthermore, he has fashioned entirely believable characters and has trapped them in a story that constantly takes one by surprise, both in its ordinariness and eccentricity. And by constantly moving the emotional boundaries – are we meant to laugh, cry or shudder? – he has created the most satisfying and creepy European thriller since the Franco-Dutch *The Vanishing* in 1988. A masterclass of cinema and one that has the intelligence to let its actors breathe.

● *Michel Pape* Laurent Lucas, *Harry Balestrero* Sergi Lopez, *Claire Pape* Mathilde Seigner, *Plum* Sophie Guillemin, *Michel's mother* Liliane Rovere, *Michel's*

*father* Dominique Rozan, *Eric* Michel Fau, *with* Victoire De Koster, Laurie Caminita, Lorena Caminita.
● *Dir* Dominik Moll, *Pro* Michel Saint-Jean, *Screenplay* Moll and Gilles Marchand, *Ph* Matthieu Poirot-Delpech, *Pro Des* Michel Barthélémy, *Ed* Yannick Kergoat, *M* David Sinclair Whitaker, *Costumes* Virginie Montel.

Diaphona Films/M6 Films/Canal Plus/Sofinergie 5-Artificial Eye.
117 mins. France. 2000. Rel: 10 November 2000. Cert 15.

## High Fidelity ★★★¹/₂

Rob Gordon is a relatively well-adjusted, well-educated kind of guy. He's read *The Unbearable Lightness of Being* and *Love in the Time of Cholera*, even if he did prefer Johnny Cash's autobiography. He now runs an elitist record shop in the wrong part of Chicago, an outlet specialising in deleted singles by The Smiths and all things vinyl. Rob also makes top-ten lists of things, mainly musical, but also romantic. And Laura, his girlfriend, has just walked out – but is she going to make his top-five of all-time heartbreakers? So, does Rob need a life or what? … Although a blatant Americanisation of Nick Hornby's London-set novel, the author's passionate interest in music and the romantic condition is suitably universal. Here, John Cusack rehashes his role as the off-kilter, contrary dreamer, a sort of development-arrested male Shirley Valentine or postmodern Alfie, who talks to the camera and shares his most intimate neuroses. Unfortunately, *High Fidelity* never gets beyond being anything than an anecdotal screen diary, but Rob's marvellously witty commentary, the eclectic soundtrack (see credits) and the array of warmly observed characters make this a sure bet for cult status.

● *Rob Gordon* John Cusack, *Laura* Iben Hjejle, *Dick* Todd Louiso, *Barry* Jack Black, *Marie De Salle* Lisa Bonet, *Charlie* Catherine Zeta-Jones, *Liz* Joan Cusack, *Ian* Tim Robbins, *Alison* Shannon Stillo, *Penny* Joelle Carter, *Caroline* Natasha Gregson Wagner, *Sarah* Lili Taylor, *Anaugh* Sara Gilbert, *Rob's mom* Margaret Travolta, *minister* Dick Cusack, *himself* Bruce Springsteen, *with* Chris Rehmann, Ben Carr, Laura Whyte, Jill Peterson, K K Dodds, Susie Cusack.
● *Dir* Stephen Frears, *Pro* Tim Bevan and Rudd Simmons, *Ex Pro* Mike Newell, Alan Greenspan and Liza Chasin, *Co-Pro* John Cusack, *D V Devincentis* and Steve Pink, *Screenplay* Devincentis, Pink and Cusack, and Scott Rosenberg, *Ph* Seamus McGarvey, *Pro Des* David Chapman and Therese Deprez, *Ed* Mick Audsley, *M* Howard Shore; songs performed by The Thirteenth Floor Elevators, Elton John, Joan Jett & The Blackhearts, Katrina and the Waves, Liz Phair, Bruce Springsteen, Smog, Goldie, Barry White, Love, Plush, The Chemical Brothers, The Velvet Underground, Aretha Franklin, Stiff Little Fingers, Queen, Al Green, Elvis Costello & the Attractions,

*Left:* Tunnelvision: Keira Knightley, Thora Birch, Desmond Harrington and Laurence Fox in Nick Hamm's pedestrian The Hole *(from Pathé)*

Bob Dylan, Grand Funk Railroad, De La Soul, Harry Nilsson, Eric B and Rakim, Fishbone, Stereolab, The Kinks, High Llamas, Jackie Wilson, Stevie Wonder etc, etc, *Costumes* Laura Cunningham Bauer.

Touchstone Pictures/Working Title/Dogstar Films/New Crime Prods-Buena Vista.
113 mins. USA/UK. 2000. Rel: 21 July 2000. Cert. 15.

## Hímalaya ★★★★

Dolpo, Northwest Nepal; today. Returning from a mountain trek, herdsman Karma informs the village chief that his son has died in an accident. Believing this to be a lie, the chief opposes his peers and decides to lead the next yak caravan himself, in spite of the dangers and his great age. However, Karma, determined to be the next chief, sets off early without him, ignoring the caution of the gods... Watching this extraordinary film, it's hard to know whether it is set in the present or a thousand years ago. As it is, it is a drama re-enacted from real events, with the tribal chief Thilen Lhondup playing his own character (renamed Tinlé). The French director Eric Valli, who has lived in Nepal since 1983, wanted to preserve on film the culture of the Nepalese villagers who had become his friends and so crafted this very contemporary tale. Illuminating the magnificent faces of his largely non-professional cast and capturing the magnificent mountainscapes that frame them, Valli has created an authentic and sensual piece of humanistic cinema. Bruno Coulais' evocative, sweeping music (which won the 1999 Cesar) is another plus. Also known as *Caravan*. FYI: The Indian actress Lhapka Tsamchoe previously played a character called Péma in *Seven Years in Tibet*.

● *Tinlé* Thilen Lhondup, *Péma* Lhapka Tsamchoe, *Karma* Gurgon Kyap, *Norbu* Karma Tensing Nyima Lama, *Passang* Karma Wangiel, *Jampa* Jampa Kalsang Tamang, *with* Tsering Dorjee, Labrang Tundup, Pemba Bika, Karma Chewang, Karma Tensing.
● *Dir* Eric Valli, *Pro* Jacques Perrin and Christopher Barratier, *Ex Pro* Jean Trégomain, *Screenplay* Valli, Perrin, Olivier Dazart, Jean-Claude Guillerbaud, Louis Gardel and Nathalie Azoulai, *Ph* Eric Guichard and Jean-Paul Meurisse, *Pro Des* Jérome Krowicki and Tenzin Norbu Lama, *Ed* Marie-Josèphe Yoyotte, *M* Bruno Coulais, *Costumes* and *accessories* Karma Tundung Gurung and Michel Debats.

Galatée Films/France 2 Cinéma/Bac Films/Antelope (UK)/National Studios Ltd (Nepal)/Canal Plus/European Script Fund, etc-Momentum Pictures.
108 mins. France/Switzerland/Nepal/UK. 1999. Rel: 18 August 2000. Cert PG.

## The Hole ★★

Emerging bloodied and traumatised from a mysterious and sinister ordeal, 16-year-old public school girl Liz Dunn is the police's only link with the truth. But can psychologist Philippa Horwood unlock the teenager's mind before prime suspect Martin Taylor is released from police custody? … Essentially a straightforward whodunit, *The Hole* is dressed up, contorted and manipulated into something entirely more interesting, thus unduly raising the viewer's expectations. This would have been fine were we given anything other than stock characters with shallow agendas stuck in a fairly uninteresting set-up. Thrillers set in claustrophobic surroundings are the hardest to pull off well, and in

*Right:* *Transparent virtues: Kevin Bacon hoodwinks Elisabeth Shue in Paul Verhoeven's entertaining if silly* Hollow Man *(from Columbia TriStar)*

spite of a first-rate English accent from Thora Birch (*Alaska, American Beauty*) and some handsome production values, *The Hole* delivers less than it promises.

● *Liz Dunn* Thora Birch, *Frankie* Keira Knightley, *Mike* Desmond Harrington, *Geoff* Laurence Fox, *Martin Taylor* Daniel Brocklebank, *Dr Philippa Horwood* Embeth Davidtz, *DCS Tom Howard* Steven Waddington, *Daisy* Emma Griffiths Malin, *Mrs Dunn* Gemma Craven, *with* Gemma Powell, Anastasia Hille, Kelly Hunter, Claire Fox.
● *Dir* Nick Hamm, *Pro* Lisa Bryer, Jeremy Bolt and Pippa Cross, *Ex Pro* François Ivernel and Andrea Calderwood, *Co-Pro* Suzanne Warren, *Assoc Pro* Rebecca Hodgson, *Screenplay* Ben Court and Caroline Ip, *Ph* Denis Crossan, *Pro Des* Eve Stewart, *Ed* Niven Howie, *M* Clint Mansell; songs performed by Architects, Grand Theft Audio, Dusted, Rico Capuano, Porn Kings, Rae + Christian, *Costumes* Verity Hawkes, *Sound* Paul Davies, *Voice coach* Mel Churcher.

Pathé Pictures/Film Council/Canal Plus/Cowboy Films/Granada Film/National Film Lottery- Pathé. 102 mins. UK/France. 2001. Rel: 20 April 2001. Cert 15.

## Hollow Man ★★¹/₂

Washington DC; the present. Having successfully reduced a dog and gorilla to an invisible state – and reversed the process – brilliant scientist Sebastian Caine uses his breakthrough serum on himself. But when his transparent body fails to regain its visibility, Caine's mind and morals go on the blink... Bearing in mind that the notion of an invisible man is pretty absurd to begin with, Andrew Marlowe's script and the cutting

edge effects go some way in making sense of it. So, how do you see an invisible man? With thermal glasses, of course. So, how do you hide from thermal glasses? Easy – you surround yourself with steam. Notwithstanding, the possibilities hinted at in the film's first half are never really exploited (besides the manipulation of a naked breast by an invisible hand), while in the second the film resorts to the sort of silliness where once-brilliant scientists start behaving like hysterical morons in yet another *Ten Little Indians* scenario. *Memoirs of an Invisible Man* (1992) was so much better.

● *Linda McKay* Elisabeth Shue, *Sebastian Caine* Kevin Bacon, *Matthew Kensington* Josh Brolin, *Sarah Kennedy* Kim Dickens, *Carter Abbey* Greg Grunberg, *Frank Chase* Joey Slotnick, *Janice Walton* Mary Randle, *Dr Kramer* William Devane, *Sebastian's neighbour* Rhona Mitra, *with* Pablo Espinosa, Margot Rose, J. Patrick McCormack.
● *Dir* Paul Verhoeven, *Pro* Alan Marshall and Douglas Wick, *Ex Pro* Marion Rosenberg, *Co-Pro* Stacy Lumbrezer, *Screenplay* Andrew M Marlowe, from a story by Marlowe and Gary Scott Thompson, *Ph* Jost Vacano, *Pro Des* Allan Cameron, *Ed* Mark Goldblatt, *M* Jerry Goldsmith, *Costumes* Ellen Mirojnick, *Visual effects* Scott E Anderson.

Columbia Pictures-Columbia TriStar. 112 mins. USA. 2000. Rel: 29 September 2000. Cert 18.

## Hotel Splendide ★★★¹/₂

There is very little splendid about this dilapidated lodging-cum-health spa stuck on a remote island off the British Isles. Formerly run by the matriarchal Mrs

Blanche, the hotel serves up a regular diet of indigestible food and colonic irrigation. Then the chef's ex-girlfriend, Kath, a former employee in the kitchen, returns and has a surprisingly salutary effect on the establishment, the staff and the few remaining residents… A splendidly British variation of *Delicatessen* with a strong whiff of the Coen brothers, *Hotel Splendide* is a bold and original black satire that deserved to find a larger audience than it did. Marking the feature debut of the music video/commercials director Terence Gross, the film showcases some delicious performances from a suitably eccentric cast, with Stephen Tompkinson surpassing himself as the Splendide's sleazy manager. However, it's Katrin Cartlidge, as the resident 'treatment' specialist, who gives the film a poignancy and credibility that cuts through the comedy with an unnerving pungency. [*Charles Bacon*]

● *Kath* Toni Collette, *Ronald Blanche* Daniel Craig, *Cora Blanche* Katrin Cartlidge, *Dezmond Blanche* Stephen Tompkinson, *Stanley Smith* Hugh O'Conor, *Lorna Bull* Helen McCrory, *Morton Blanche* Peter Vaughan, *Sergei Gorgomov* Joerg Stadler, *with* Clare Cathcart, John Boswall, Toby Jones, *the image/voice of Mrs Blanche* Imogen Claire.
● *Dir* and *Screenplay* Terence Gross, *Pro* Ildiko Kemeny, *Ex Pro* Robert Buckler, *Ph* Gyula Pados, *Pro Des* Alison Dominitz, *Ed* Michael Ellis, *M* Mark Tschanz, *Costumes* Michelle Pernetta.

FilmFour/TOC Films/Renegade Films/Decameron Films/European Production Fund, etc-FilmFour.
98 mins. UK/France. 1999. Rel: 22 September 2000. Cert 15.

## The House of Mirth ★★★¹/₂

New York; 1905-7. A woman of fine social education and moral principle, Lily Bart has reached her thirties without a husband to support her accustomed lifestyle. Resisting the temptation to marry for money, she yearns for the love of the personable lawyer Lawrence Selden, but neither see a future in their union. Then Lily is tricked into a foolhardy investment and falls prey to the unforgiving hypocrisy of the society she depends on… The English director Terence Davies (*Distant Voices Still Lives*, *The Neon Bible*), in comparing Jane Austen to the American novelist Edith Wharton, notes, 'With Wharton the gloves are off and there's blood on the walls.' Be that as it may, there is no visible gore in this articulate and precise adaptation of Wharton's 1905 work, although there's plenty of teeth in the barbed pleasantries. As Davies methodically tears off the layers of artifice that bound New York society at the turn of the century, the gloves are most definitely discarded. And while budgetary constraints force a claustrophobic mood onto the drama (which, as it happens, is not at all inappropriate), one longs for the occasional street scene to set a note of period perspective. But this is an interior piece, and the words speak volumes, delivered with loaded deliberation by a first-rate cast (as the duplicitous Bertha Dorset, Laura Linney is particularly memorable).

● *Lily Bart* Gillian Anderson, *Lawrence Selden* Eric Stoltz, *Gus Trenor* Dan Aykroyd, *Bertha Dorset* Laura Linney, *Sim Rosedale* Anthony LaPaglia, *Carry Fisher* Elizabeth McGovern, *Mrs Peniston* Eleanor Bron, *Grace Stepney* Jodhi May, *George Dorset* Terry Kinney, *Judy Trenor* Penny Downie, *Percy Gryce* Pearce Quigley, *Mrs Haffen* Mary MacLeod, *Jack Stepney* Paul Venables, *Gwen Stepney* Serena Gordon, *with* Helen Coker, Trevor Martin, Kate Wooldridge, Ralph Riach, Brian Pettifer, Lesley Harcourt, Pamela Dwyer, Lorelei King, Linda Marlowe, Roy Sampson, Clare Higgins.
● *Dir* and *Screenplay* Terence Davies, *Pro* Olivia Stewart, *Ex Pro* Bob Last and Pippa Cross, *Co-Pro* Alan J Wands, *Ph* Remi Adefarasin, *Pro Des* Don Taylor, *Ed* Michael Parker, *M* various, *Costumes* Monica Howe.

Three Rivers/Granada Film/Arts Council of England/FilmFour/Scottish Arts Council/Showtime/Glasgow Film Fund-Film Four.
140 mins. UK/USA. 2000. Rel: 13 October 2000. Cert PG.

## L'Humanité – Humanity ★★¹/₂

No rating system can adequately contend with a film like this. Bruno Dumont's ambitious follow-up to *La Vie de Jésus* makes us feel that only Scope images will suffice for cinema. This is great filmmaking, and the non-professional cast impress as far as their roles permit. Nevertheless, as we observe a cop, the woman he dotes on and her lover, our belief is sabotaged by many improbabilities, including the least convincing investigation of a girl's rape ever screened, and by Dumont's wilful refusal to make his narrative clear despite taking 148 minutes to tell his story. Dumont has himself declared that he doesn't mind whether or not the audience pick out the one detail in the last shot crucial to the plot. The sexual frankness is carried over from his previous film, but stupidity, pretentiousness and true cinematic brilliance have rarely met as here. [*Mansel Stimpson*]

● *Pharaon De Winter* Emmanuel Schotté, *Domino* Séverine Caneele, *Joseph* Philippe Tullier, *Commandant* Ghislain Ghesquiére, *Eliane, Pharaon's mother* Ginette Allègre, *with* Daniel Leroux, Daniel Pétillon, Robert Bunzi.
● *Dir* and *Screenplay* Bruno Dumont, *Pro* Jean Bréhat and Rachid Bouchareb, *Ph* Yves Cape, *Ed* Guy Lecorne, *M* Richard Cuvillier, *Costumes* Nathalie Raoul.

3B Prods/ARTE France Cinéma/CRRAV/CNC/Canal Plus-Artificial Eye.
148 mins. France. 1999. Rel: 8 September 2000. Cert 18.

## I Could Read the Sky ★★★★

Recalling the work of the late Margaret Tait, Nichola Bruce's debut film combines the poetic and the everyday as an elderly Irishman living in England (Dermot Healy) looks back on his life. Derived from a photographic novel, it achieves a fluidity of images which is truly cinematic, while the style adopted evokes the work of Samuel Beckett. Much of the time words are heard in the form of a monologue, but music also plays a great part in this film, and it's one of the factors which ensure that this is a work deeply rooted in Irish culture. The manner may verge on the *avant-garde*, but the themes – childhood memories, the loneliness of an immigrant who feels displaced, recollections of love lost – are sufficiently potent to reach the hearts of any audience prepared to attune to its wavelength. [*Mansel Stimpson*]

● *the old man* Dermot Healy, *Maggie* Maria Doyle Kennedy, *Francie* Brendan Coyle, *PJ* Stephen Rea, *Kate Creevy* Lisa O'Reilly, *Uncle Rosco* Sezso, *young Eileen* Rachael Pilkington, *with* Aidan O'Toole, Jimmy McCreevy, Geraldine Fitzgerald.
● *Dir* and *Screenplay* Nichola Bruce, from the book by Timothy O'Grady and Steve Pyke, *Pro* Janine Marmot, *Co-Pro* Nicholas O'Neill, *Ph* Seamus McGarvey and Owen McPolin, *Pro Des* Jane Bruce, *Ed* Catherine Creed and (on line) Trevor Smith, *M* Iarla O'Lionáird, *Costumes* Helen Kane, *Sound* Joakim Sundström.

The Arts Council of England/Bord Scannán na hÉireann/ Irish Film Board/Channel 4/BFI/Real World Records/ Gemini Films/National Lottery, etc-Artificial Eye.
86 mins. UK/Ireland/France. 1999. Rel: 27 October 2000. Cert 15.

## The In Crowd ★

South Carolina; the present. When Adrien Williams is released from psychiatric hospital, she is given a job at an exclusive beach-side resort on condition that she doesn't drink, take drugs or wander out of the area. Then she is befriended by Brittany Foster, a rich, spoilt member of the club with a sinister agenda. Murder and lesbianism quickly follow… The sort of stuff best suited to a 4.00 am slot on Channel 5, *The In Crowd* is clearly out of its empty mind. Tedious, ineptly acted and ludicrously plotted, it disappoints on even the basic level it aspires to. [*Ewen Brownrigg*]

● *Brittany Foster* Susan Ward, *Adrien Williams* Lori Heuring, *Matt Curtis* Matthew Settle, *Bobby* Nathan Bexton, *Dr Amanda Giles* Tess Harper, *Kelly* Laurie Fortier, *Joanne* Kim Murphy, *Andy* Jay R. Ferguson, *Wayne* A.J. Buckley, *Morgan* Katharine Towne, *Dr Henry Thompson* Daniel Hugh Kelly, *with* Charlie Finn, Ethan Erickson, Erinn Bartlett, Peter Mackenzie, Taylor Negron.
● *Dir* Mary Lambert, *Pro* James G Robinson, *Ex Pro* Jonathan A Zimbert and Michael Rachmil,

*Screenplay* Mark Gibson and Philip Halprin, *Ph* Tom Priestley, *Pro Des* John D Kretschmer, *Ed* Pasquale Buba, *M* Jeff Rona; songs performed by Andrea Parker, Pilfers, Scott Spock, Jimmie's Chicken Shack, Vachik, Makana, Nero Zero, Methods of Mayhem, The Hippos, Miari, Tracy Bonham etc, *Costumes* Jennifer L Bryan.

Morgan Creek-Warner.
105 mins. USA. 2000. Rel: 1 June 2001. Cert 12.

## In the Mood For Love ★★★¹/₂

Hong Kong; 1962. Having moved into adjacent apartments on the same day, a married newspaper editor and the wife of a travelling businessman find that their respective partners share a shocking secret... A sort of Oriental *Brief Encounter*, *In the Mood for Love* is another affected exercise in style over emotion from Wong Kar-Wai, the director of *Days of Being Wild*, *Chungking Express* and *Happy Together*. But while one might defend the endeavour as an art film, one should not forget that art, surely, is a means to support, celebrate and enhance emotion, at the very least to provoke a reaction in the viewer. However, Wong seems determined to distance his audience by placing his protagonists in a stylistic cage. At its best, this is a mood piece, a contemplation of what might have been, to be tasted – rather than consumed or analysed – for its melancholy piquancy.

● *Su Li-Zhen* Maggie Cheung, *Chow Mo-Wan* Tony Leung, *Mrs Suen* Rebecca Pan, *Mr Ho* Lai Chen, *Ah-Ping* Siu Ping-Iam, *the Amah* Chin Chi-Ang.
● *Dir*, *Pro* and *Screenplay* Wong Kar-Wai, *Ex Pro* Chan Ye-cheng, *Assoc Pro* Jacky Pang Yee-wah, *Ph* Christopher Doyle and Mark Li Pingbing, *Pro Des* and *Ed* William Chang, *M* Michael Galasso.

Block 2 Pictures/Paradis Films/Jet Tone Films-Metro Tartan.
98 mins. Hong Kong/France. 2000. Rel: 27 October 2000. Cert PG.

## In Too Deep ★★★¹/₂

A story about an undercover cop getting 'in too deep' is hardly breaking new ground. What makes this stand out is one of the finest ethnic casts ever assembled for a film. Omar Epps is positively chameleonic as Detective Jeff Cole, who returns to his ghetto roots to put away a powerful drug lord (project 'God' father Dwayne Gittens, impressively played by LL Cool J). Sheathed in all-too-plausible street cred as hustler J Reid, Cole spends years getting close to God in order to destroy his Cincinnati empire. Playing J Reid inexorably corrupts good guy Cole despite efforts by his boss (Tucci) and girlfriend Myra. *In Too Deep* doesn't flinch from showing the devastating effect that seemingly philanthropic drug lords really have on their brothers in the 'hood.

**Left:** *Auf Wiedersehen, Mein Kinder: Mark Jonathan Harris's deeply felt, Oscar-winning documentary* Into the Arms of Strangers *(from Warner)*

While it may be that, visually, the film is sometimes a little too slick, director Michael Rymer weaves a compelling tale of urban life. [*Scot Woodward Myers*]

● *Jeff Cole/J Reid* Omar Epps, *Dwayne Gittens/God* LL Cool J, *Myra* Nia Long, *Preston D'Ambrosio* Stanley Tucci, *Breezy T* Hill Harper, *Daniel Connelly* Jake Weber, *Wesley* Richard Brooks, *Rick Scott* David Patrick Kelly, *Det Angela Wilson* Pam Grier, *Pam* Veronica Webb, *Dr Bratton* Ron Canada, *with* Robert LaSardo, Gano Grills, Ivonne Coll, Don Harvey, Jermaine Dupri, Guillermo Díaz, Sticky Fingaz, Victor Rivers, Angel Torres.
● *Dir* Michael Rymer, *Pro* Paul Aaron and Michael Henry Brown, *Screenplay* Michael Henry Brown and Paul Aaron, *Ex Pro* Don Carmody, Jeremy Kramer, Amy Slotnick, Bob Weinstein and Harvey Weinstein, *Ph* Ellery Ryan, *Pro Des* Dan Leigh, *Ed* Dany Cooper, *M* Christopher Young; songs performed by Mobb Deep and Lil' Kim, Nas & Nature, Ali Vegas, R. Kelly, Trick Daddy, Capone-N-Noreaga and The Lox, Method Man & Redman, Domino, Imajin, 50 Cent, E-Day, Miles Davis, Jill Scott, Donny Hathaway, Jagged Edge, *Costumes* Shawn Barton.

Dimension Films/Suntaur Entertainment-Metrodome. 97 mins. USA. 1999. Rel: 14 July 2000. Cert 18.

## Inbetweeners ★

It's a new term at the University of Great Britain and first-year student David is about to discover the wonders and pitfalls of campus life... Shot for £30,000 on a digital camera, *Inbetweeners* not only looks awful but is devoid of wit, originality and invention. Intended as an exposé of university life in contemporary Britain, this first feature from Darren Paul Fisher manages to be dull, contrived and totally out of touch with its subject. [*Ewen Brownrigg*]

● *David Marshall* Finlay Robertson, *Nicole Miles* Kate Loustau, *Steph Thornhill* Lynn Edmonstone, *Jack Easterford* Toby Walton, *Cassie Sanderson* Sarah Vandenbergh, *with* Kate Kennedy, Jane Peachey, Gary Fannin, Mark Paterson, Andrew Legge.
● *Dir, Pro* and *Screenplay* Darren Paul Fisher, *Ex Pro* Anil Dave, John Hair, Marion Gaskin and James Grant Media Ltd, *Assoc Pro* Sue Kennedy, *Ph* Matthew Woolf, *Pro Des* Henry Davis, *Ed* Fisher, Kerrie Campbell and Allan Williams, *M* Nick Senior; songs performed by 187, A. Fernbach, Bellatrix, Body Electric, D-Day, Johnny, Rick Astley, Triplexl, Toffee etc, *Costumes* Angela Egan and Suzannah Harman.

Britpack Film-Winstone. 90 mins. UK. 2001. Rel: 18 May 2001. Cert 15.

## Into the Arms of Strangers ★★★★¹/₂

Finely judged and deeply felt, this documentary feature by Mark Jonathan Harris is a valuable historical document. Unlike most recent films linked to the Holocaust, this one offers much unfamiliar material by telling of Jewish children separated from their parents who sent them to England in 1938 and 1939 to escape the menace of Nazi Germany (the film's subtitle is *Stories of the Kindertransport*). It features recent interviews with those involved intercut with historical footage, and it's support-

*Right:* Leap of Faith:
Jordana Brewster in
Adam Brooks's
unconvincing and
over-complicated
The Invisible Circus
(from Entertainment)

ed by an admirably discreet commentary perfectly delivered by Dame Judi Dench. A little long at 117 minutes and not quite as moving as 1998's *The Last Days*, the film survives such minor quibbles to be an extremely welcome and touching record, one which in passing provides a telling reflection of English life in that era. Winner of the Oscar for Best Documentary Feature. [*Mansel Stimpson*]

● With Lorraine Allard, Lory Cahn, Hedy Epstein, Kurt Fuchel, Alexander Gordon, Eva Hayman, Jack Hellman, Bertha Leverton, Ursula Rosenfeld, Inge Sadan, Lore Segal etc. *Narrator* Judi Dench.
● *Dir* and *Screenplay* Mark Jonathan Harris, *Pro* Deborah Oppenheimer, *Line Pro* Lou Fusaro, *Ph* Don Lenzer, *Ed* Kate Amend, *M* Lee Holdridge, *Sound* Gary Rydstrom, *Researcher* Corrinne Collett.

Warner/Sabine Films-Warner.
117 mins. USA. 2000. Rel: 24 November 2000. Cert PG.

## The Invisible Circus ★★

San Francisco/Paris/Berlin/Portugal; 1976-1970. Feeling disconnected from the bourgeois world around her, Phoebe decides to embark on a pilgrimage to Europe before starting university in the autumn. Six years earlier her older sister, Faith, had died under mysterious circumstances in Portugal. Before she can move on with her own life, Phoebe is determined to solve the mystery of her sister's death… In spite of tenable performances from Brewster and Diaz, Adam Brooks' political mystery lacks both cohesion and conviction. It also over-reaches itself in its complex structure, leading to confusion and, ultimately, disinterest in the viewer. [*Charles Bacon*]

● *Phoebe O'Connor* Jordana Brewster, *Wolf* Christopher Eccleston, *Faith O'Connor* Cameron Diaz, *Gail O'Connor* Blythe Danner, *Gene* Patrick Bergin, *young Phoebe* Camilla Belle, *Claire* Isabelle Pasco, *Eric* Moritz Bleibtreu.
● *Dir* and *Screenplay* Adam Brooks, based on the book by Jennifer Egan, *Pro* Julia Wechsler and Nick Wechsler, *Ex Pro* Tim van Rellim, *Ph* Henry Braham, *Pro Des* Robin Standefer, *Ed* Elizabeth Kling, *M* Nick Laird-Clowes, *Costumes* Donna Zakowska.

Fine Line Features/Industry Entertainment-Entertainment.
93 mins. USA. 2000. Rel: 23 February 2001. Cert 15.

## It Was an Accident ★★¹/₂

Walthamstow, East London; today. Nicky Burkett is basically a trustworthy, good-natured bloke who has just served four years in the slammer for what, he insists, `was an accident.' Now he's determined to go straight, get a job and make amends with his girlfriend, the daughter of a local copper. But the crime-infested streets of London and a series of further accidents suck our hapless hero into an escalating vortex of transgression… A loose adaptation of Jeremy Cameron's novel, this umpteenth British crime comedy makes up in colourful dialogue and plot twists what it lacks in style and credibility. Indeed, one can't help thinking that in the hands of another director all this could have been a lot funnier and more convincing. It's certainly sad to see the lovely Thandie Newton in what must be her most stilted performance to date, although Chiwetel Ejiofor (*Greenwich Mean Time*) makes a sympathetic and engaging leading man. Incidentally, this is the *sixth* film released in Britain in 2000 to feature violence against cows (following *Three Kings*, *Lake Placid*, *Battlefield Earth*, *Me, Myself & Irene* and *O Brother, Where Art Thou?*).

● *Nicky Burkett* Chiwetel Ejiofor, *Mickey Cousins* Max Beesley, *Fitch* James Bolam, *Kelly* Nicola Stapleton, *Holdsworth* Neil Dudgeon, *George Hurlock* Hugh Quarshie, *Noreen Hurlock* Thandie Newton, *Sharon Burkett* Jacqueline Williams, *Rameez* Sidh Solanki, *Jimmy Foley* Cavan Clerkin, *Dean Longmuire* Fraser Ayres, *Danny Burkett* Louis-Rae Beadle, *with* Roy Paul Chowdhry, Jeff Innocen, Rhydian Jai-Persaud, Jeff Mirza, Alan Hireson, Saikat Ahamed, Tej Patel, Evelyn Doggart, Norby West.
● *Dir* Metin Hüseyin, *Pro* Paul Goodman, *Ex Pro* Alexis Lloyd, Andrea Calderwood and David Barron, *Assoc Pro* and *Screenplay* Ol Parker, *Ph* Guy Dufaux, *Pro Des* Joseph Bennett, *Ed* Annie Kocur, *M* Courtney Pine, *Costumes* Susannah Buxton.

Pathé Pictures/Arts Council of England/Canal Plus/Litmus/National Lottery-Pathé.
101 mins. UK. 2000. Rel: 27 October 2000. Cert 18.

## Jesus' Son ★★

Known only as Fuckhead, a young man ambles his way across America in the early 1970s experimenting with a variety of illegal substances (uppers, downers, magic mushrooms, heroin, you name it). Along the way he hooks up with various misfits who hardly arrest his downward spiral, until, eventually, he finds an unlikely redemption... An adaptation of the collected short stories of Denis Johnson, *Jesus' Son* sits uneasily as a film. Uncertain in tone and alternately smug and pointless and disjointed and tasteless, it succeeds only in parts. For instance, there is a brilliantly surreal sequence in which Fuckhead and fellow hospital orderly Georgie – both high on drugs – encounter a patient with a hunting knife embedded in his eye. And as Billy's on-again, off-again girlfriend, Samantha Morton brings genuine passion and confusion to her role as a heroin addict. But these are slim pickings in a film that plays on its weirdness for effect and ends up going nowhere.

● *Fuckhead* Billy Crudup, *Michelle* Samantha Morton, *Mira* Holly Hunter, *Bill* Dennis Hopper, *Wayne* Denis Leary, *Georgie* Jack Black, *John Smith* Will Patton, *Dr Shanis* Greg Germann, *Richard* Steve Buck, with Robert Michael Kelly, Torben Brooks, Ben Shenkman, Scott Oster, Elizabeth Cuthrell, Denis Johnson, David Urrutia.
● *Dir* Alison Maclean, *Pro* Lydia Dean Pilcher, Elizabeth Cuthrell and David Urrutia, *Ex Pro* Steven Tuttleman, *Co-Pro* Margot Bridger, *Assoc Pro* Oren Moverman, *Screenplay* Cuthrell, Urrutia and Moverman, *Ph* Adam Kimmel, *Pro Des* David Doernberg, *Ed* Geraldine Peroni and Stuart Levy, *M* Joe Henry; songs performed by Dick Dale & His Del-Tones, Camphor, Paul Revere and The Raiders, Wilco, Bob Dylan, Neil Young, Booker T and the MGs, Joe Henry, Dorothy Moore, The Kendalls etc, *Costumes* Kasia Walicka Maimone, *Visual effects* Jeffrey Cox.

Alliance Atlantis/Lions Gate/Evenstar Films-Alliance Releasing.
108 mins. USA/Canada. 1999. Rel: 7 July 2000. Cert 18.

## Judy Berlin ★★★½

Writer-director Eric Mendelsohn weaves a poignant tale of lives in desperate need of greater meaning. Barbara Barrie plays Sue Berlin, a lonely teacher enjoying a flirtation with her married principal Arthur Gold. Her daughter Judy (Edie Falco) is an aspiring actress who strikes up her own relationship with Arthur's son, down-and-out director wannabe, David Gold. While these two couples pursue their respective relationships, we're treated to Madeline Kahn's wonderful final film role as Arthur's manic wife Alice, who both touches and frustrates us as she struggles to cope with the fact that Arthur no longer loves her. The characters are achingly real and made all the more so by the surreal environment of the movie: the drama unfolds during an extended solar eclipse with the whole story shot in black and white. How better to highlight the shades of grey that permeate these middle-class lives in their suburban distress? [*Scot Woodward Myers*]

● *Sue Berlin* Barbara Barrie, *Arthur Gold* Bob Dishy, *Judy Berlin* Edie Falco, *Maddie* Carlin Glynn, *David Gold* Aaron Harnick, *Dolores Engler* Bette Henritze, *Alice Gold* Madeline Kahn, *Marie* Julie Kavner, *Bea* Anne Meara, with Novella Nelson, Peter Appel, Marcia DeBonis, Glenn Fitzgerald, Marcus Giamatti.
● *Dir, Screenplay* and *Ed* Eric Mendelsohn, *Pro* Rocco Caruso, *Line Pro* Lisa Kolasa, *Ph* Jeffrey Seckendorf, *Pro Des* Charlie Kulsziski, *M* Michael Nicholas; Mozart, *Costumes* Sue Gandy.

Caruso/Mendelsohn/Sundance Institute-Blue Light.
94 mins. USA. 1998. Rel: 8 December 2000. Cert 15.

## julien donkey-boy ★½

New Jersey; today. Julien works at a school for the blind, his sister is pregnant by an unknown man and their father wears a gas mask around the house while talking utter nonsense. Of course, they're all completely mad... While a film starring *Trainspotting*'s Ewen Bremner, Oscar nominee Chloë Sevigny, German director Werner Herzog and an armless dwarf has some curiosity value, *julien donkey-boy* is to be approached with caution. An experimental and often visually indecipherable contemplation on schizophrenia (the film is dedicated to the director's schizophrenic uncle), *julien donkey-boy* is like a dysfunctional home movie (it is, after all, shot without a script using a hand-held digital camera). To be fair, schizophrenia is a terrible affliction – and we're lucky that there are so few films about it. But is it art?

● *Julien* Ewen Bremner, *Pearl* Chloë Sevigny, *father* Werner Herzog, *Chris* Evan Neumann, *Grandma* Joyce Kobylak, *Chrissy* Chrissy Kobylak, *neighbour* Alvin Law, *pond boy* Brian Frisk, with Miriam Martinez, Virginia Reath, Ricky Ashley, Punky.
● *Dir* and *Screenplay* Harmony Korine, *Pro* Scott Macaulay, Cary Woods and Robin O'Hara, *Line Pro* Jim Czarnecki, *Ph* Anthony Dod Mantle, *Ed* Valdis Oskarsdottir, *M* various; Dvorak, Strauss etc.

Independent Pictures/Forensic/391-Metro Tartan.
99 mins. USA. 1999. Rel: 29 September 2000. Cert 15.

## Kadosh – Sacred ★★★★

Mea Shearim, Jerusalem; the present. In spite of ten years of marital happiness, Orthodox Jewish couple Meir and Rivka have not managed to produce an heir. With the Torah maintaining that a woman's sole duty is to raise children, Rivka is becoming the laughing stock of her community. Meanwhile, her sister Malka is lined up to marry Yossef, an obnoxiously devout scholar. But Malka loves the handsome Yaakov and is determined not to fall into the same trap as her sister... Completing his trilogy of films focusing on three major Israeli cities (following *Devarim* and *Yom Yom*, which, respectively, were set in Tel Aviv and Haifa), Amos Gitaï has fashioned a fascinating insight into the closeted world of the Orthodox Jewish community. With a minimum of narrative tricks, Gitaï has introduced his camera into this arcane world with an almost voyeuristic detachment. Coaxing extraordinary performances from his two leading actresses, the director has created a work of enormous authenticity and nuance that drives home its message –the unbending chauvinism of traditional Jewish law – with a subtlety that creeps up on the viewer with surprising impact.

● *Rivka* Yaël Abecassis, *Meir* Yoram Hattab, *Malka* Meital Barda, *Yossef* Uri Ran Klauzner, *Rav Shimon* Yussef Abu Warda, *Yaakov* Sami Hori, *Elisheva* Lea Koenig, *with* Rivka Michaeli, Samuel Calderon, David Cohen, Orian Zacay, Amos Gitaï.
● *Dir* Amos Gitaï, *Pro* Gitaï and Michel Propper, *Ex Pro* Laurent Truchot and Shuky Fridman, *Assoc Pro* Roberto Cicutto and Laurent Thiry, *Screenplay* Gitaï, Eliette Abecassis and Jacky Cukier, *Ph* Renato Berta, *Pro Des* Miguel Markin, *Ed* Monica Coleman and Kobi Netanel, *M* Philippe Eidel, *Costumes* Laura Dinulasco.

Agav Hafakot/M.P. Prods/Canal Plus/Mikado Film/RAI/Telad/Procirep-Downtown.
116 mins. Israel/France/Italy. 1999. Rel: 21 July 2000. Cert 15.

## Keeping the Faith ★★★

New York's Upper West Side; today. Long before Jacob Schram became a successful rabbi and Brian Finn a popular Roman Catholic priest, they were childhood friends inseparable from their soul mate, Anna Reilly. But when Anna left with her parents for Los Angeles, Jacob and Brian had to get on with their own lives. Then, 16 years later, Anna returns to New York on business and recaptures the hearts of her old friends, neither of whom are vocationally eligible to woo her... Somewhere in this somewhat laboured, self-indulgent movie is a lean, snappy comedy struggling to get out. This is a shame as Edward Norton's directorial debut (not counting his uncredited tinkering on *American History X*) is full of good things, some nice bits of comedy timing and a generous air of bonhomie that recalls a more innocent time.

● *Rabbi Jacob Schram* Ben Stiller, *Father Brian Kilkenny Finn* Edward Norton, *Anna Reilly* Jenna Elfman, *Rabbi Lewis* Eli Wallach, *Ruth Schram* Anne Bancroft, *Larry Friedman* Ron Rifkin, *Father Havel* Milos Forman, *Ali Decker* Lisa Edelstein, *Rachel Rose* Rena Sofa, *Don* Ken Leung, *Indian bartender* Brian George, *teenage Jacob* Sam Goldberg, *teenage Anna* Blythe Auffarth, *teenage Brian* Michael Roman, *T-Bone* Brian Anthony Wilson, *with* Holland Taylor, Catherine Lloyd Burns, Susie Essman, Stuart Blumberg, Jonathan Silver, Francine Beers.
● *Dir* Edward Norton, *Pro* Norton, Hawk Koch and Stuart Blumberg, *Ex Pro* Gary Barber, Roger Birnbaum and Jonathan Glickman, *Screenplay* Blumberg, *Ph* Anastas Michos, *Pro Des* Wynn P. Thomas, *Ed* Malcolm Campbell, *M* Elmer Bernstein; songs performed by Peter Salett, Ruben Gonzalez, Santana and Rob Thomas, Public Enemy, Jake Elwood Blues Band, Cheryl Lynn, Wild Cherry, Elliott Smith etc, *Costumes* Michael Kaplan.

Touchstone Pictures/Spyglass Entertainment/Koch Co./Norton-Blumberg-Buena Vista.
130 mins. USA. 2000. Rel: 15 September 2000. Cert 12.

## The King is Alive ★★★¹/₂

A bus breaks down in the African desert, leaving those aboard stranded and in conflict unless help arrives. What could be an adventure tale proves instead to be a well-acted, ambitious but sometimes obscure allegory which asks us to accept that the passengers might fill the time by staging *King Lear*. The improbability of this on a naturalistic level weakens the impact, as does a strong element of pretentiousness. All the same, we are left debating the film's meaning (possibly it shows the passing of a civilisation in which art and culture may pinpoint man's failings but cannot eradicate them) and, having been shot on digital video and blown up to 35mm, the film's beauty is remarkable. The open ending is appropriate and effective. For the record, this is the fourth feature made according to the Dogme rules of filming, formulated in Denmark in 1995. [*Mansel Stimpson*]

● *Jack* Miles Anderson, *Catherine* Romane Bohringer, *Henry* David Bradley, *Charles* David Calder, *Ray* Bruce Davison, *Ashley* Brion James, *Kanana* Peter Kubheka, *Moses* Vusi Kunene, *Gina* Jennifer Jason Leigh, *Liz* Janet McTeer, *Paul* Chris Walker, *Amanda* Lia Williams.
● *Dir* (uncredited) Kristian Levring, *Pro* Patricia Kruijer and Vibeke Windeløv, *Ex Pro* William A Tyer, Chris J Ball, David Linde and Peter Aalbæk Jensen, *Screenplay* Kristian Levring and Anders Thomas Jensen, inspired by William Shakespeare's *King Lear*, *Ph* Jens Schlosser, *Ed* Nicholas Wayman Harris.

New Market/Good Machine/Zentropa Ent./Danish Broadcasting Corp/Nordic Film and Television Fund, etc-Pathé.
109 mins. Denmark/USA/Sweden/Norway/Finland. 2000. Rel: 11 May 2001. Cert 15.

## Last Resort ★★★★

For Tanya, a Russian illustrator of children's books looking for love, Britain is a last resort. Arriving at Gatwick Airport with her ten-year-old son, Tanya finds herself branded an asylum seeker and is herded into a designated 'holding area' on the Kent coast. There she tries to contact her elusive fiancé, Mark, as 16 months' worth of bureaucratic paperwork stretches out in front of her. Suddenly, she finds herself a prisoner in a police state with only the kindly attentions of a local man to relieve the nightmare... Adopting a documentary realism, the Polish writer-director Pawel Pawlikowski has crafted a damning document of contemporary England. Painting Margate (doubling for the fictitious Stonehaven) as 'the armpit of the universe', the camera lingers on granite skies, driving rain and urban decay as Tanya struggles to make sense of this blighted isle. Introduced to the mysterious joys of bingo, greasy fish 'n' chips (without the fish) and a world of ritual vandalism, she becomes yet another victim of a moribund myth. Such a depressing reality is made all the stronger by Dina Korzun's remarkably naturalistic performance and by Pawlikowski's autobiographical take on the material. Quite unforgettable.

● *Tanya* Dina Korzun, *Alfie* Paddy Considine, *Artiom* Artiom Strelnikov, *Les* Lindsey Honey, *immigration officer* Perry Benson, *Katie* Katie Drinkwater, *Frank* Dave Bean, *with* Adrian Scarbrough, David Auker, Daniel Mobey.
● *Dir* Pawel Pawlikowski, *Pro* Ruth Caleb, *Ex Pro* David M Thompson and Alex Holmes, *Assoc Pro* Christopher Collins, *Screenplay* Pawlikowski and Rowan Joffe, *Ph* Ryszard Lenczewski, *Pro Des* Tom Bowyer, *Ed* David Charap, *M* Max De Wardener and Rowan Oliver; songs performed by Bromano Dives, Istanbul Oriental Ensemble, The Beach Boys, Petula Clark, Andy Williams, *Costumes* Julian Day.

BBC Films/BBC Documentaries-Artificial Eye.
77 mins. UK. 2000. Rel: 16 March 2001. Cert 15.

## Late Night Shopping ★★★¹/₂

Hospital porter Sean, shelf stacker Vincent, telephone operator Lenny and factory worker Jody chew the fat at an all-night café. They've been meeting up for months now and none of them are happy with their lives. And Sean has this little problem – he hasn't seen his girlfriend, who works a day shift, for three weeks... Inhabiting a nameless British city and proffering an unlikely quartet of stereotypes (the Lothario, the loser, the innocent, the female hanger-on), Saul Metzstein's debut feature starts out like a celluloid play suspended in a parallel universe. However, thanks to Jack Lothian's sharp writing and the spirited playing of an excellent cast, *Late Night*

*Above: Ire over England: Dina Korzun and Paddy Considine in Pawel Pawlikowski's immediate and haunting* Last Resort *(from Artificial Eye)*

***Right:***
*Beachspotting: James Lance, Enzo Cilenti, Kate Ashfield and Luke de Woolfson in Saul Metzstein's acrid, caffeine-enhancing* Late Night Shopping *(from FilmFour)*

*Shopping* evolves into something rather special. Boasting a visual freshness and a welcome freedom from drugs and alcohol (the characters are forever consuming cappuccinos and milkshakes), this is a quirky and charming diversion bursting with future talent. Filmed on location in Glasgow. Funniest scene: in which Lenny's car stereo gets stuck on an MOR radio station, doling out passé hits by Foreigner, T'Pau and Heart.

● *Sean* Luke de Woolfson, *Vincent* James Lance, *Jody* Kate Ashfield, *Lenny* Enzo Cilenti, *Madeline* Heike Makatsch, *Gail* Shauna MacDonald, *Susie* Sienna Guillory, *Joe* Laurie Ventry, *with* Bobby Finn, Claire Harman, Nigel Buckland.
● *Dir* Saul Metzstein, *Pro* Angus Lamont, *Ex Pro* Paul Webster and Lenny Crooks, *Co-Pro* Elinor Day, *Screenplay* Jack Lothian, *Ph* Brian Tufano, *Pro Des* Mike Gunn, *Ed* Justine Wright, *M* Alex Heffes; songs performed by Rush, Foreigner, Cutting Crew, The Ohio Players, Marillion, Heart, Finley Quaye etc, *Costumes* Eleanor Baker.

FilmFour/Glasgow Film Office/Scottish Screen/National Lottery/Senator Film/Ideal World-Film Four.
91 mins. UK/Germany. 2000. Rel: 22 June 2001. Cert 15.

## The Legend of Bagger Vance ★★★¹/₂

Savannah, Georgia; 1916-1931. Rannulph Junuh is Georgia's golden boy of the golf world and social set. However, following the Great War, he loses 'his authentic swing.' When his estranged girlfriend, Adele Invergordon, attempts to salvage her father's dream of mounting a historical golf tournament, she turns to Rannulph to represent Savannah against the two titans of the game: Bobby Jones and Walter Hagen. But Rannulph is not ready for public humiliation – until, that is, a black man called Bagger Vance offers to be his caddie... Much as fly-fishing in Redford's *A River Runs Through It* (1992) acted as a metaphor for life, so golf does the trick for the troubled Rannulph Junuh. And while the director's irritating penchant for filtered sunlight, piano chords and muted colour is much in evidence here, there is still a strong story and plenty of gentle humour. True, the narrative arc is predictable and much of the detail hokey (including the huffing Greek chorus of the town's dignitaries), but Bagger Vance is such an engaging character (and beautifully judged by Will Smith) that the end result is quite uplifting.

● *Bagger Vance* Will Smith, *Rannulph Junuh* Matt Damon, *Adele Invergordon* Charlize Theron, *Walter Hagen* Bruce McGill, *Hardy Greaves* J Michael Moncrief, *Bobby Jones* Joel Gretsch, *Grantland Rice* Lane Smith, *Neskaloosa* Peter Gerety, *with* Michael O'Neill, Thomas Jay Ryan, Dermot Crowley, Harve Presnell, Carrie Preston, Vijay Patel, and (*uncredited*) Jack Lemmon.
● *Dir* Robert Redford, *Pro* Michael Nozik and Jake Eberts, *Ex Pro* Karen Tenkhoff, *Co-Pro* Chris Brigham and Jospeh Reidy, *Screenplay* Jeremy Leven, *Ph* Michael Ballhaus, *Pro Des* Stuart Craig, *Ed* Hank Corwin, *M* Rachel Portman; songs performed by Arthur Fields, Josephine Baker, Duke Ellington, Fats Waller etc, *Costumes* Judianna Makovsky, *Sound* Gary Rydstrom, *Golf adviser* Tim Moss.

*Left:* Swing time: Will Smith and Matt Damon take to the fairway in Robert Redford's tasteful, gently humorous The Legend of Bagger Vance (from Twentieth Century Fox)

DreamWorks/Fox/Wildwood/Allied-Fox.
126 mins. USA. 2000. Rel: 23 February 2001. Cert PG.

## Liam ★★★¹/₂

Liam is seven years old and, in spite of a stutter and a partiality for the more risqué paintings of Ingres, he is a happy and normal enough lad. But this is Liverpool in the 1930s and when the Depression robs Liam's father of his job, poverty soon transforms the family's fortunes... If there's one thing worse than a miserable Irish Catholic childhood, it's a miserable Liverpudlian Catholic childhood. A sort of low-rent *Angela's Ashes*, Stephen Frears' celebration of childhood squalor is a little episodic but is redeemed by a wonderfully expressive performance from eight-year-old Anthony Borrows as the wide-eyed, stuttering Liam. *Liam*, the movie, is also mercifully succinct and has few pretensions to artistic integrity, even though, at times, it does feel a little too much like a TV drama. Nevertheless, the period detail and occasionally powerful vignettes, plus some savage satire of Catholicism, make this a memorable and affecting wallow in the impoverished childhood of a bygone era.

● *Dad, Tom Sullivan* Ian Hart, *Mam Sullivan* Claire Hackett, *Mrs Abernathy* Anne Reid, *Liam Sullivan* Anthony Borrows, *Teresa Sullivan* Megan Burns, *Con Sullivan* David Hart, *Father Ryan* Russell Dixon, *Auntie Aggie* Julia Deakin, *Uncle Tom* Andrew Schofield, *Mrs Samuels* Jane Gurnett, *Jane Samuels* Gema Loveday, *with* Bernadette Shortt, David Carey, David Knopov, Martin Hancock, Arnold Brown.
● *Dir* Stephen Frears, *Pro* Colin McKeown and Martin Tempia, *Ex Pro* David M Thompson, Tessa

Ross and Sally Hibbin, *Co-Pro* Ulrich Felsberg, *Screenplay* Jimmy McGovern, *Ph* Andrew Dunn, *Pro Des* Stephen Fineren, *Ed* Kristina Hetherington, *M* John Murphy, *Costumes* Alexandra Caulfield.

BBC Films/Liam Films/Road Movies/MIDA/ARTE/
Degeto Film, etc-Artificial Eye.
91 mins. UK/Germany/Italy. 2000. Rel: 23 February 2001. Cert 15.

## Le Libertin ★★★★

In the mid-18th century, knowledge remained the exclusive preserve of priests and academics and was not considered suitable material for the common man. However, resisting both the church and the state, the philosopher Denis Diderot sets about translating Ephraim Chambers' *Cyclopaedia* into French, dramatically altering the nature of the tome, introducing controversial revisions and filling it with revolutionary opinion. Hiding out at the country estate of the Baron d'Holbach, Diderot finds himself in a race against time as the Baron's censorious brother, a cardinal, attempts to discover the whereabouts of the printing press... What could have been an extremely dry piece of literary history is brought bounding to life in what is an outrageous French farce of the Feydeau school. Buoyed by spirited turns from Perez, Serrault, Balasko and Dombasle, the film makes the period seem incredibly modern, helped by the periodic introduction of such arcane delights as chocolate ('It looks like shit, but...'), magic mushrooms and 'popped corn.' There's also lashings of sex, opulent production values and insightful revelations on everything from Voltaire and Socrates to certain secrets concerning the hymen.

⬤ *Denis Diderot* Vincent Perez, *Madame Therbouche* Fanny Ardant, *The Cardinal* Michel Serrault, *Baroness d'Holbach* Josiane Balasko, *Madame de Jerfeuil* Arielle Dombasle, *Baron d'Holbach* François Lalande, *Julie d'Holbach* Audrey Tautou, *Madame Diderot* Françoise Lepine, *Angélique Diderot* Vahina Giocante, *Abraham* Yan Duffas, *with* Christian Charmetant, Véronique Vella.

⬤ *Dir* Gabriel Aghion, *Pro* Gaspard de Chavagnac, *Ex Pro* Raphaël Cohen, *Co-Pro* Pascal Houzelot, *Screenplay* Aghion and Eric-Emmanuel Schmitt, based on the play by Schmitt, *Ph* Jean-Marie Dreujou, *Pro Des* Dan Weil, *Ed* Luc Barnier, *M* Bruno Coulais, *Costumes* Olivier Beriot and Marie-Claude Brunet.

Bel Ombre Films/Mosca Films/TF1 Films/Josy Films/ Canal Plus-Gala.
102 mins. France. 2000. Rel: 25 May 2001. Cert 15.

## Liberty Heights ★★★¹/₂

Forest Park, the Jewish quarter of Baltimore, Maryland; 1954. For Ben Kurtzman, being Jewish was the only thing he knew until, at eight, he is invited over to a gentile's house and subjected to white bread, white mayonnaise and white milk. Then, in his teens, he is exposed to `coloured' students for the first time, while his father, who runs a songs racket from a burlesque hall, falls foul of a local black drug dealer... Strong on nuance and atmosphere, *Liberty Heights* marks Barry Levinson's fourth personal film set in his native Baltimore. At once intimate and far-reaching in its multi-tiered chronicle of the ethnic state of 1950s' America, this is a gentle, comic and poignant film, a work of observation and character that accumulates its power from a series of sharply detailed moments. Above all, it is a successful attempt to show the absurdity of cultural prejudice in a world in which we are all individuals, regardless of our creed, religion or colour.

⬤ *Van Kurtzman* Adrien Brody, *Ada Kurtzman* Bebe Neuwirth, *Nate Kurtzman* Joe Mantegna, *Ben Kurtzman* Ben Foster, *Little Melvin* Orlando Jones, *Sylvia* Rebekah Johnson, *Yussel* David Krumholtz, *Charlie* Richard Kline, *Pete* Vincent Guastaferro, *Trey* Justin Chambers, *Dubbie* Carolyn Murphy, *Sylvia's father* James Pickens Jr, *Scribbles* Anthony Anderson, *Sheldon* Evan Neuman, *Alan* Kevin Sussman, *Murray* Gerry Rosenthal, *James Brown* Carlton Smith, *with* Frania Rubinek, Kiersten Warren, Charley Scalies, Shane West, Cloie Wyatt Taylor, Susan Duvall, Elizabeth Ann Bennett, Ellyn O'Connell, Kenny Raskin, Brenda Russell, Stephen Williams, Ty Robbins, Emily Chamberlain, Paul Majors.

⬤ *Dir* and *Screenplay* Barry Levinson, *Pro* Levinson and Paula Weinstein, *Ex Pro* Patrick McCormick, *Ph* Chris Doyle, *Pro Des* Vincent Peranio, *Ed* Stu Linder, *M* Andrea Morricone; Elgar; songs performed by Patti Page, Barry Black, Crew-Cuts, Tom Waits, Tony Bennett, Bill Haley and His Comets, Jo Stafford, The Crows, Ray Charles, Big Joe Turner,

Frank Sinatra, Mandy Patinkin, Brenda Russell, Perry Como, James Brown, Elvis Presley, Orquesta Riverside, Louis Armstrong, Nat King Cole, Carl Perkins etc, *Costumes* Gloria Gresham.

Warner/Baltimore/Spring Creek-Warner.
127 mins. USA. 1999. Rel: 8 September 2000. Cert 15.

## Little Nicky ★★¹/₂

Harvey Keitel is awful as a Satan so unimpressed with his three boys that, rather than bequeath Hell to one of them, he decides to rule for another 10,000 years. While unobtrusive Nicky (Sandler) is thrilled that the father he obviously adores will be staying on, his two brutish brothers, Adrian (Ifans) and Cassius (Lister), opt to flee Hell and make their own domain out of the damned of an all-too-willing New York City. This upset in cosmic forces is terminal to their devilish dad, so Nicky heads to the Big Apple to restore order. Occasionally, one gets glimpses of how this could have been a good story. But, much like Adam Sandler himself, *Little Nicky* flip-flops between moments of genuine charm and being wholly offensive. Ultimately, it's a tedious duel that can't help but leave one unsatisfied. [*Scot Woodward Myers*]

● *Nicky* Adam Sandler, *Valerie* Patricia Arquette, *Dad* Harvey Keitel, *Adrian* Rhys Ifans, *Todd* Allen Covert, *Cassius* Tommy 'Tiny' Lister Jr., *gatekeeper* Kevin Nealon, *Peeper* Jon Lovitz, *Chief of Police* Michael McKean, *Deacon* Quentin Tarantino, *Peter* Peter Dante, *John* Jonathan Loughran, *Jimmy the Demon* Blake Clark, *street vendor* John Witherspoon, *Lucifer* Rodney Dangerfield, *Cardinal* Lewis Arquette, *referee* Dana Carvey, *with* Ellen Cleghorne, John Farley, Clint Howard, Leah Lail, Dan Marino, Ozzy Osbourne, Regis Philbin, Rob Schneider, Frank Sivero, Jackie Titone, George Wallace, Bill Walton, Carl Weathers, Henry Winkler, *Holly* Reese Witherspoon, Sylvia Lopez, Todd Holland, Mary Brill, Jana Sandler, Tom Winkler, *the voice of Beefy* Robert Smigel.
● *Dir* Steven Brill, *Pro* Robert Simonds and Jack Giarraputo, *Ex Pro* Robert Engelman, Adam Sandler, Michael De Luca and Brian Witten, *Screenplay* Sandler, Brill and Tim Herlihy, *Ph* Theo Van De Sande, *Pro Des* Perry Andelin Blake, *Ed* Jeff Gourson, *M* Teddy Castellucci; songs performed by POD, Kool & The Gang, Van Halen, Judy Garland, Dandy Warhols, Insolence, Zebrahead, Sinead O'Connor, Cypress Hill, Ozzy Osbourne, Chicago, Incubus, Lit, Filter, Scorpions, AC/DC, Disturbed, Deftones, Muse etc, *Costumes* Ellen Lutter, *Visual effects* John Sullivan.

New Line Cinema/Happy Madison/RSC Media-Entertainment.
90 mins. USA. 2000. Rel: 17 November 2000. Cert 12.

## The Little Vampire ★★★

Nine-year-old Tony Thompson from San Diego is not the most popular kid in his new school in rural Scotland. Not only does he have a funny accent but he can't stop talking about vampires. However, all that changes when he befriends Rudolph Sackville-Bagg, a local kid with bloodshot eyes and an ability to fly... As kids get increasingly sophisticated, so does the forum to entertain them. The German writer Angela Sommer-Bodenburg, being a fourth grade teacher at the time, knew what her students wanted: `something entertaining, funny, a little bit scary...' And so *The Little Vampire* was born, a 1976 novel that has grown into a multi-media phenomenon, spawning 16 books, two TV series, a musical and now the movie. Obviously, the subject, and the eccentric clan of the undead Sackville-Baggs in particular, has tapped into something that kids can't get enough of, although grown-ups, having been exposed to a huge backlog of vampiric culture, may find the antics here a little humdrum. Indeed, the icky imagination of Roald Dahl is sadly missed, the film often seeming little more than an extended TV drama. Nevertheless, there are a number of neat touches, not least a herd of flying cows.

● *Tony Thompson* Jonathan Lipnicki, *Frederick Sackville-Bagg* Richard E. Grant, *Rookery* Jim Carter, *Freda Sackville-Bagg* Alice Krige, *Dottie Thompson* Pamela Gidley, *Lord McAshton* John Wood, *Rudolph Sackville-Bagg* (aka *Rüdiger von Schlotterstein*) Rollo Weeks, *Anna Sackville-Bagg* Anna Popplewell, *Gregory Sackville-Bagg* Dean Cook, *Bob Thompson* Tommy Hinkley, *Lorna, the babysitter* Georgie Glen, *with* Jake D'Arcy, Iain De Caestecker, Scott Fletcher, Johnny Meres, Elizabeth Berrington.
● *Dir* Uli Edel, *Pro* Richard Claus, *Ex Pro* Alexander Buchman, Anthony Waller and Larry Wilson, *Screenplay* Wilson and Karey Kirkpatrick, *Ph* Bernd Heinl, *Pro Des* Joseph Nemec III, *Ed* Peter R Adam, *M* Nigel Clarke and Michael Csányi-Wills, *Costumes* James Acheson, *Visual effects* John Grower.

Comestone Pictures/Comet Film/Avrora Media/Stonewood Communications/Propaganda Films-Icon.
95 mins. Germany/Netherlands/UK/USA. 2000.
Rel: 20 October 2000. Cert U.

## The Lost Lover ★★

Following the death of their son in London, a Jewish couple, Adam and Asya, move to Tel Aviv where Adam starts up a garage and Asya pursues her historical research. It is there that their teenage daughter Dafi falls for an Arab mechanic and Asya herself takes a lover with a mysterious agenda... A rather plodding contemplation of loss, love and politics, Roberto Faenza's film takes itself far too seriously. Also, it's a little naïve in its optimism and yet still too sombre. Notwithstanding, the performances are creditable, not least Ciaran Hinds' turn as a man utterly devoted to and dependent upon his errant wife. [*Charles Bacon*]

● *Adam* Ciaran Hinds, *Asya* Juliet Aubrey, *Gabriel* Stuart Bunce, *the grandmother* Phyllida Law, *Herlich* Cyrus Elias, *Naim* Erick Vazquez, *Dafi* Clara Bryant, *Yigal* Edoardo Moscone.
● *Dir* Roberto Faenza, *Pro* Elda Ferri, *Co-Pro* Charles Steel, *Screenplay* Faenza and Sandro Petraglia, based on the novel by Abraham B Yehoshua, *Ph* José Luis Alcaine, *Pro Des* Giovanni Natalucci, *Ed* Massimo Fiocchi, *M* Paolo Buonvino, *Costumes* Alessandra Torella.

Jean Vigo Italia/Mikado Film/Steel Pictures/Rai Radio Televsione Italiana/Canal Plus/British Screen/British Sky Broadcasting/Tele +-Metrodome.
97 mins. Italy/UK. 1999. Rel: 19 January 2001. Cert PG.

## Lost Souls ★★¹/₂

New York City; today. Following the failed exorcism of a violent sociopath, seminary teacher Maya Larkin finds clues to the identity of the new Anti-Christ. Seeking the help of Peter Kelson, a charismatic authority on serial killers, Maya resolves to convince him that evil really does exist beyond the 'pathological narcissism' of mortal men... Recalling the stylistic texture of the similarly themed *Stigmata* (1999), *Lost Souls* is a handsome and serious contemplation of the nature of demonic possession. Drawn from extensive interviews with real exorcists, the film displays a considerable note of authenticity. It also has the courage to boycott the cheap thrills of gaudy effects, relying instead on visual deception and unnerving camera moves, engineered with considerable skill by first-time director Janusz Kaminski, the Oscar-winning cinematographer of *Schindler's List* and *Saving Private Ryan*. Yet, largely because of its stylisation, the film fails to bring the characters of Maya and Peter to flesh and blood dimensions, and thus falls down on creating real unease. It's a shame, too, that such demonic thrillers so often have to lead to the banality of a countdown to Armageddon. Co-produced by Meg Ryan.

● *Maya Larkin* Winona Ryder, *Peter Kelson* Ben Chaplin, *Father James* Philip Baker Hall, *John Townsend* Elias Koteas, *Claire Van Owen* Sarah Wynter, *Father Lareaux* John Hurt, *Mike Smythe* John Beasley, *Henry Birdson* John Diehl, *George Viznik* Brad Greenquist, *William Kelson* W Earl Brown, *Father Frank* Brian Reddy, *with* Victor Slezak, Paul Kleiman, Michael Mantell, Ming Lo, Anna Gunn, Cyd Strittmatter, James Lancaster, Robert Castle, Anna Berger, Kai Ephron, Jan Triska, *herself* Kaity Tong, and (*uncredited*) Alfre Woodard.
● *Dir* Janusz Kaminski, *Pro* Nina R Sadowsky and Meg Ryan, *Ex Pro* Donna Langley and Michael De Luca, and Betsy Stahl and Pierce Gardner, *Co-Pro*

Christopher Cronyn, *Screenplay* Pierce Gardner, from a story by Gardner and Stahl, *Ph* Mauro Fiore, *Pro Des* Garreth Stover, *Ed* Anne Goursaud and Andrew Mondshein, *M* Jan A P Kaczmarek; `Tijuana Lady' performed by Gomez, *Costumes* Jill Ohanneson.

New Line Cinema/Prufrock Pictures-Entertainment.
98 mins. USA. 2000. Rel: 12 January 2001. Cert 15.

## Love & Basketball ★★★

At first glance, this is yet another film expatiating on basketball being the only hope for Afro-Americans to achieve decent lives for themselves. The film itself is set up to run like a basketball game (divided into four quarters), starting in 1981. It follows the on-again/off-again coming together of Quincy and Monica, whose two passions are basketball and, of course, each other. Juxtaposing the inequities between male and female sports, it's clear from the word go that both Q and Monica got game. But, while Q easily follows the dream route of most urban young men (in cinema anyway), Monica challenges the expectations of a society that has already established what a woman's place is. Omar Epps and Sanaa Lathan are superb but it's Alfre Woodard's subtle and poignant depiction of Monica's mother which gives the film its extra pathos. Kudos to writer/director Gina Prince-Bythewood for creating a cast of rich and genuinely affecting characters undoubtedly drawn from her own experiences. [*Scot Woodward Myers*]

● *Quincy McCall* Omar Epps, *Monica Wright* Sanaa Lathan, *Camille Wright* Alfre Woodard, *Zeke McCall* Dennis Haysbert, *Nona McCall* Debbi Morgan, *Nathan Wright* Harry J Lennix, *with* Kyla Pratt, Glenndon Chatman, Christine Dunford, Erika Ringor, Regina Hall, Jess Willard, Tyra Banks, Gabrielle Union, Stu Lantz, Robin Roberts, Dick Vitale, Trevor Wilson, Gina Prince-Bythewood.
● *Dir* and *Screenplay* Gina Prince-Bythewood, *Pro* Sam Kitt and Spike Lee, *Ex Pro* Andrew Z Davis, Cynthia Guidry and Jay Stern, *Ph* Reynaldo Villalobos, *Pro Des* Jeffrey Howard, *Ed* Terilyn A Shropshire, *M* Terence Blanchard; songs performed by Al Green, New Edition, Marvin Gaye, Rufus and Chaka Khan, MC Lyte, Kool Moe Dee, Freddie Jackson, Herb Alpert, Bobby Brown, Roger, Maxwell, Guy, Hinda Hicks, Digital Underground, Melky Sedeck, Lucy Pearl etc, *Costumes* Ruth E Carter.

New Line Cinema/40 Acres and a Mule Filmworks-Entertainment.
124 mins. USA. 2000. Rel: 7 July 2000. Cert 12.

## Love & Sex ★★★¹/₂

Los Angeles; the present. With an intellect above her station (as a tabloid journalist) and the looks of a model, Kate Welles should have her pick of men. But she suffers the same dating problems as the next woman, in spite of her range of partners. Then she falls in with Adam, a sweet and funny, if disturbing, painter (think Lucien Freud on acid), whose inexperience with women is rather endearing. But then even their live-in friendship turns stale... Exhibiting a relaxed and confident directorial style, first-time filmmaker Valerie Breiman serves her material well, a compassionate and funny tale of love, tenderness and muddling through (and one obviously honed from experience). A wonderful showcase for the undervalued talents of Famke Janssen and Jon Favreau, the film displays a maturity that is surprising in a first-time director. Label this a *Love Story* for grown-ups or, better still, call it *Affection Story*. PS. Coincidentally, this serves as a neat counterpart to the Australian *Me Myself I*.

● *Kate Welles* Famke Janssen, *Adam Levy* Jon Favreau, *Eric* Noah Emmerich, *Ms Steinbacher* Ann Magnuson, *Mary* Cheri Oteri, *Joey Santino* Josh Hopkins, *Gerard* Robert Knepper, *Richard* Vincent Ventresca, *Savannah* Kristen Zang, *Peaches* Angela Marsden, *with* David Steinberg, Elimu Nelson, Yvonne Zima, Will Rothaar, Rance Howard and (*uncredited*) *the door-to-door religious guy* David Schwimmer.
● *Dir* and *Screenplay* Valerie Breiman, *Pro* Timothy Scott Bogart, Martin J Barab and Brad Wyman, *Ex Pro* Mark Damon, *Line Pro* Michelle Ledoux, *Ph* Adam Kane, *Pro Des* Sara Sprawls, *Ed* Martin Apelbaum, *M* Various; songs performed by Eddi Reader, Phil Roy, Marc Ford, Convoy, Dig, Todd Thibaud, Chucklehead, Steve Jeffries, The Merrymakers, Eric Caspar, Over the Rhine, Tim Easton, weaklazyliar, *Costumes* Sara Jane Slotnick.

Behaviour Worldwide/Bogart/Barab/Wyman-Inkpen Film Distribution.
82 mins. USA. 2000. Rel: 29 September 2000. Cert 15.

## The Low Down ★★

Frank makes props for a TV game show but would rather be doing something more creative. So, with his new girlfriend in tow, he and his twenty-something friends talk about art and stuff and drink too much and eat takeaway curries... A slice of contemporary London life, *The Low Down* might well look interesting in some future retrospective (at least for the first half hour). With characters united by a common inability to communicate, the film wears its naturalism on its sleeve, utilising probing close-ups, conversational pauses and banal small talk. But Gillen's character is an unsympathetic plonker and the lack of any story to speak of is irritatingly perverse. It's enough to put you off being 20.

● *Frank* Aidan Gillen, *Ruby* Kate Ashfield, *Mike* Dean Lennox Kelly, *John* Tobias Menzies, *Terry* Rupert Proctor, *with* Samantha Power, Dena Smiles, Maggie Lloyd Williams, Agnieszka Liggett, Adam Buxton, Joe Cornish, Paula Hamilton, Michael Hodgson, Vass Anderson.
● *Dir* and *Screenplay* Jamie Thraves, *Pro* John Stewart and Sally Llewellyn, *Ph* Igor Jadue-Lillo, *Pro Des* Lucy Reeves, *Ed* Lucia Zucchetti, *M* Nick Currie and Fred Thomas; songs performed by Human League, P J Harvey, Vuja-De, Groove Armada etc, *Costumes* Julie Jones.

FilmFour/British Screen/Bozie/Oil Factory/Sleeper Films-FilmFour.
96 mins. UK. 2000. Rel: 26 January 2001. Cert 18.

## The Luzhin Defence ★★★¹/₂

Northern Italy; 1929. At an exclusive Italian resort, the beautiful and independent Russian aristocrat Natalia is happy taking strolls alongside the lake or dipping into a book or two. Her domineering mother, however, feels that Natalia should be taking advantage of the eligible bachelors swanning around. Just then, a decidedly odd character in a rumpled, badly stained suit proposes to Natalia during a game of tennis. He is Alexander Luzhin, Russia's greatest living chess player... Following her eloquent adaptation of Virginia Woolf's *Mrs Dalloway*, the Dutch director Marleen Gorris returns to a literary source with this bewitching and elegant impression of Vladimir Nabokov's 1930 novella. Exquisitely crafted and photographed, the film is a treat to the eye, but it is the unique character of Luzhin that makes it so compelling. With his distracted air and dishevelled appearance, he is a most unconventional suitor for the beautiful Natalia, and is brought vividly to life by John Turturro in a performance that artfully circumvents caricature.

● *Alexander Luzhin* John Turturro, *Natalia* Emily Watson, *Vera* Geraldine James, *Valentinov* Stuart Wilson, *Stassard* Christopher Thompson, *Turati* Fabio Sartor, *Ilya* Peter Blythe, *Anna* Orla Brady, *Luzhin's father* Mark Tandy, *Luzhin's mother* Kelly Hunter, *young Luzhin* Alexander Hunting, *with* Luigi Petrucci, Carlo Greco.
● *Dir* Marleen Gorris, *Pro* Caroline Wood, Stephen Evans, Louis Becker and Philippe Guez, *Ex Pro* Jody Patton, *Co-Pro* Leo Pescarolo and Eric Robison, *Screenplay* Peter Berry, *Ph* Bernard Lutic, *Pro Des* Tony Burrough, *Ed* Michaël Reichwein, *M* Alexandre Desplat; Shostakovich, *Costumes* Jany Temime.

Renaissance Films/CBS/ICE3 Prods/Lantia Cinam/Magic Media-Entertainment.
109 mins. UK/France/Italy/Hungary/USA. 2000. Rel: 8 September 2000. Cert 12.

## Malèna ★¹/₂

Castelcuto, Sicily; 1940-1944. On the day that Mussolini declares war on Britain and France, 13-year-old Renato Amoroso has other things on his mind. He has just been given his first bicycle and has become transfixed by the vision of Malèna Scordía, `the most beautiful arse in Sicily.' But whereas the womenfolk pour scorn on this haughty stranger and the men stare with undisguised lechery, Renato falls deeply in love... Having lovingly chronicled the early days of cinema in *Cinema Paradiso* and the power of music in *Legend of 1900*, Giuseppo Tornatore now celebrates the crassness and cruelty of humanity. Painfully over-acted and visually sentimental, *Malèna* paints itself as an elegiac fable of war-time nostalgia and sexual awakening, but is in fact a crude and self-indulgent wallow in corporeal and social humiliation. To be fair, there is a poignant theme here (adapted from the short story by Luciano Vincenzoni), but Tornatore has over-baked the soufflé. FYI: The English subtitles were translated by director Anthony Minghella and scenarist Joseph Tropiano (*Big Night*).

● *Malèna Scordía* Monica Bellucci, *Renato Amoroso* Giuseppe Sulfaro, *Renato's father* Luciano Federico, *Renato's mother* Matilde Piana, *Professor Bonsignore* Pietro Notarianni, *Nino Scordía* Gaetano Aronica, *the lawyer Centorbi* Gilberto Idone, *political secretary* Angelo Pellegrino, *Lieutenant Cadei* Marcello Catalono, *with* Gabriella Di Luzio, Pippo Provvidenti, Maria Terranova, Elisa Morucci, Daniele Arena, Giovanni Litrico.
● *Dir* and *Screenplay* Giuseppe Tornatore, *Pro* Harvey Weinstein and Carlo Bernasconi, *Ex Pro* Bob Weinstein, Teresa Moneo, Fabrizio Lombardo and Mario Spedaletti, *Line Pro* Mario Cotone, *Ph* Lajos Koltai, *Pro Des* Francesco Frigeri, *Ed* Massimo Quaglia, *M* Ennio Morricone, *Costumes* Maurizio Millenotti.

Miramax International/Medusa Film/Pacific Pictures-Buena Vista.
92 mins. Italy/USA. 2000. Rel: 16 March 2001. Cert 15.

## The Man Who Cried ★★

At just six years of age, Fegele, a poor Jewish girl, is wrenched from the arms of her family and sent to England to escape the pogroms of 1920s' Russia. Moving to Paris as a teenager, Fegele, now called Suzie, is befriended by a Russian chorus girl, who instructs her in the ways of the world. While saving up enough money to sail to America to find her father, Suzie falls in with an enigmatic gypsy and a temperamental Italian singer... A chronicle of loss (the loss of family, culture and identity), *The Man Who Cried* was inspired by the director's love of opera, gypsy music and klezmer. Opening with a scene in which Fegele's father regales a crowd with a haunting folk ballad, the film certainly casts a lyrical spell. But murkier waters await our six-year-old heroine as she grows into Christina Ricci, a 20-year-old American actress who really isn't up to the demands of the part. It is also disconcerting to see such well-known stars as Cate Blanchett, John Turturro and Johnny Depp competing for the Meryl Streep foreign accent award, good as they all are. And with the narrative unfolded in erratic spits and bursts, the film seems at constant odds with the mood it is setting.

● *Fegele/Suzie* Christina Ricci, *Lola* Cate Blanchett, *Dante Dominio* John Turturro, *César* Johnny Depp, *Felix Perlman* Harry Dean Stanton, *Fegele's father* Oleg Yankovskiy, *young Fegele* Claudia Lander-Duke, *Madame Goldstein* Miriam Karlin, *with* Hana Maria Pravda, Diana Hoddinott, Alan David, Imogen Claire, Don Fellows, Cyril Shaps, David Baxt.
● *Dir* and *Screenplay* Sally Potter, *Pro* Christopher Sheppard, *Ex Pro* Tim Bevan and Eric Fellner, *Co-Pro* Simona Benzakein, *Ph* Sacha Vierny, *Pro Des* Carlos Conti, *Ed* Herve Schneid, *M* Osvaldo Golijov; Bizet, Verdi, Puccini, Purcell, Sapo Perapaskero etc, *Costumes* Lindy Hemming.

Canal Plus/Universal/Working Title/British Screen Finance-UIP.
100 mins. UK/France/USA. 2000. Rel: 8 December 2000. Cert 12.

## Meet the Parents ★★★★¹/₂

Chicago/New York; the present. Greg Focker is a caring and conscientious male nurse who is plucking up the courage to propose to his girlfriend, the lovely Pam Byrnes. However, before he pops the question, he is determined to make a good impression on Pam's parents, with whom he is to stay over the weekend. Unfortunately for Greg, though, good intentions really do pave the way to hell and the more he tries to impress, the more events conspire against him... The art of this sublimely funny film is that, while it teeters precariously between farce and tragedy, it seldom slips into either camp. Fuelled by a marvellous concept and story, the film's more farcical flights are stabilised by Ben Stiller's generally restrained central performance as the hapless Greg. At times, his plight is almost too painful to bear, all the more so as he is such an ordinary, credible and well-meaning guy. And while there are plenty of big laughs – Stiller inadvertently destroying the vase in which De Niro keeps his mother's ashes, Stiller giving Teri Polo's sister a black eye – there are priceless minor touches to, such as the rule-abiding flight attendant played by Kali Rocha (watch that name!).

● *Jack Byrnes* Robert De Niro, *Greg Focker* Ben Stiller, *Dina Byrnes* Blythe Danner, *Pam Byrnes* Teri Polo, *Larry Banks* James Rebhorn, *Denny Byrnes* Jon Abrahams, *Kevin Rawley* Owen Wilson, *Debbie Byrnes* Nicole Dehuff, *Bob Banks* Tom McCarthy,

**Left:** *There's something about Daddy... Robert De Niro and Blythe Danner entertain their prospective son-in-law Ben Stiller in* Meet the Parents, *one of the year's funniest movies (from UIP)*

*Linda Banks* Phyllis George, *flight attendant* Kali Rocha, *with* Bernie Sheredy, Judah Friedlander, Peter Bartlett, Mark Hammer.

● *Dir* Jay Roach, *Pro* Roach, Nancy Tenenbaum and Jane Rosenthal, *Co-Pro* Amy Sayres and Shauna Weinberg, *Screenplay* Jim Herzfeld and John Hamburg, from a story by Greg Glienna and Mary Ruth Clarke, *Ph* Peter James, *Pro Des* Rusty James, *Ed* Jon Poll, *M* Randy Newman; songs performed by The Beach Boys, Randy Newman, Lee Dorsey, Peter Paul and Mary, Pete Stringfellow and Jason Beltz, Dr John, Bobby Womack, Wayne Newton etc, *Costumes* Daniel Orlandi.

DreamWorks/Universal/ Nancy Tenenbaum Films/ Tribeca-UIP.
108 mins. USA. 2000. Rel: 15 December 2000. Cert 12.

## Memento ★★¹/₂

Los Angeles; the present. Since the rape and murder of his wife, Leonard Shelby has been struck down with a rare short-term memory disorder. He can still recall most things that happened before his wife's death, but he can't remember what happened two minutes ago. And so in the pursuit of revenge he props his life up with notes, charts, Polaroid snapshots and even tattooed instructions on his body. And now he's just killed a man whose name may be Teddy or perhaps John... Doesn't this sound like a fantastic premise for a thriller? The problem is that writer-director Christopher Nolan (*Following*) is so eager to superimpose the unhinged state of his protagonist on his audience, that he has decided to unfold the story *backwards*, much like Harold Pinter did with his play *Betrayal*. This unusual device does offer some rewards, such as shedding a fresh perspective on the trajectory of mundane events and changing the agenda of many of the protagonists (how often does an enemy turn out to be a former lover? – or perhaps vice versa). There's even some humour (at one point Leonard is not sure if he's running after somebody or whether he's being chased), but the gimmickry soon becomes tedious.

● *Leonard Shelby* Guy Pearce, *Natalie* Carrie-Anne Moss, *Teddy* Joe Pantoliano, *Burt* Mark Boone Junior, *Leonard's wife* Jorja Fox, *Sammy Jankis* Stephen Tobolowsky, *Mrs Jankis* Harriet Sansom Harris, *with* Russ Fega, Thomas Lennon, Callum Keith Rennie, Kimberly Campbell, Marianne Muellerleile, Larry Holden.

● *Dir* and *Screenplay* Christopher Nolan, *Pro* Suzanne Todd and Jennifer Todd, *Ex Pro* Aaron Ryder, *Co-Ex Pro* Will Tyrer and Chris Ball, *Co-Pro* Elaine Dysinger, *Assoc Pro* Emma Thomas, *Ph* Wally Pfister, *Pro Des* Patti Podesta, *Ed* Dody Dorn, *M* David Julyan; songs performed by David Bowie, Monc, Daniel May, *Costumes* Cindy Evans.

Newmarket/Team Todd/Summit Entertainment-Pathé.
113 mins. USA. 2000. Rel: 20 October 2000. Cert 15.

*Above: Dunkin'*
*Donuts! Jim Carrey*
*as the entirely*
*corruptible Hank*
*Baileygates in the*
*Farrelly brothers'*
*offensive, absurd and*
*gut-busting* Me,
Myself & Irene
*(from Twentieth*
*Century Fox)*

## Me, Myself & Irene ★★ ★¹/₂

Charlie Baileygates is an upstanding, public-serving officer of the Rhode Island State Police. However, when his wife leaves him for a black dwarf he is never the same again. Even so, while suspecting that people are laughing at him behind his back, Charlie struggles to put a brave face on things. Then, one day, following a queue-barging incident at the supermarket, a demon called Hank emerges from Charlie's inner soul... After two attempts at more serious comedy (with *The Truman Show* and *Man On the Moon*), Jim Carrey returns to his old form with a vengeance in this frequently hilarious farce from the sibling directors of *Dumb and Dumber* and *There's Something About Mary*. With two Carreys for the price of one, fans should be in seventh heaven as the elastic star is on suitably manic form, even if the demonic Hank is sometimes hard to decipher. Meanwhile, the Farrellys continue to push through the barriers of bad taste, making fun of blacks, dwarfs, cripples, albinos, dead animals and anal penetration with unabashed glee. Above all, though, the film works because of its comic invention, held together by characters that one can actually root for (not least Charlie's black, outsize and foul-mouthed sons).

● *Charlie Baileygates/Hank Baileygates* Jim Carrey, *Irene Waters* Renée Zellweger, *Lieutenant Gerke* Chris Cooper, *Colonel Partington* Robert Forster, *Agent Boshane* Richard Jenkins, *Jamaal Baileygates* Anthony Anderson, *Lee Harvey Baileygates* Mongo Brownlee, *Shonté Jr Baileygates* Jerod Mixon, *Whitey/Caspar* Michael Bowman, *Officer Stubie* Mike Cerrone, *Trooper Finneran* Rob Moran, *limo driver* Tony Cox, *with* Zen Gesner, Steve Sweeney, Traylor Howard, Googy Gress, Richard Tyson, *motel manager* Anna Kournikova, *narrator* Rex Allen Jr.
● *Dir* Bobby Farrelly and Peter Farrelly, *Pro* Bobby Farrelly, Peter Farrelly and Bradley Thomas, *Ex Pro* Charles B Wessler and Tom Schulman, *Co-Pro* Marc S Fischer, James B Rogers and Mark Charpentier, *Assoc Pro* Linda Fields-Hill and Kristofer W Meyer, *Screenplay* Bobby Farrelly, Peter Farrelly and Mike Cerrone, *Ph* Mark Irwin, *Pro Des* Sidney J. Bartholomew, *Ed* Christopher Greenbury, *M* Peter Yorn and Lee Scott; songs performed by Junior Brown, Wilco, Tom Wolfe, XTC, Cake, Ellis Paul, The Push Stars, Jimmy Luxury, Pete Yorn, The Dwarves, Foo Fighters, Hootie and the Blowfish, Ivy, Third Eye Blind, Smash Mouth, The Offspring etc, *Costumes* Pamela Withers.

Fox/Conundrum Entertainment-Fox.
116 mins. USA. 2000. Rel: 22 September 2000. Cert 15.

## Me Myself I ★★★¹/₂

Sydney, Australia; the present. Pamela Drury is a multi-award-winning journalist who is beginning to think that a top-flight career isn't necessarily every-

**Left:** *Cuba Gooding Jr (far right) prepares to meet his nemesis (centre, played by Robert De Niro) in George Tillman, Jr's cumbersome and overworked* **Men of Honor** *(from Twentieth Century Fox)*

thing. Unable to find a suitable mate, she dreams of the man she ditched 13 years ago and resolves to kill herself. Then, after being knocked down by a car, she is faced by her spitting image, a housewife and mother of three who happened to have married the man Pamela rejected. When the woman disappears, Pamela not only finds herself in the stranger's shoes but that her past has been completely erased... Once one accepts the total contrivance of the plot (think *Sliding Doors* Australian-style), the device of dropping a character slap-bang into an alternative reality is an effective one. Thankfully, writer-director Pip Karmel doesn't labour the gimmick, concentrating instead on the ramifications of tasting how the other half lives. Rachel Griffiths is terrific as the thirty-something human time bomb wanting the best of both worlds, parrying the horrors of domestic drudgery with a need for emotional fulfilment. A lively soundtrack and vivid camerawork adds to the enjoyment. FYI: The title is inspired by the 1980 Joan Armatrading song of the same name.

● *Pamela Drury/Pamela Dickson* Rachel Griffiths, *Robert Dickson* David Roberts, *Ben* Sandy Winton, *Stacey* Yael Stone, *Douglas* Shaun Loseby, *Rupert* Trent Sullivan, *Terri* Rebecca Frith, *Geoff* Felix Williamson, *Janine* Ann Burbrook, Maeliosa Stafford, Terence Crawford, Christine Stephen-Daly, *Brandy the Dog* Spud.
● *Dir* and *Screenplay* Pip Karmel, *Pro* Fabien Liron, *Co-Pro* Andrena Finlay, *Line Pro* Vicki Popplewell, *Ph* Graham Lind, *Pro Des* Murray Picknett, *Ed* Denise Haratzis, *M* Charlie Chan; Mozart; songs performed by Joan Armatrading, Peggy Lee, The Superjesus, T-Shirt, Regurgitator, Marie Wilson, The

Wiggles, Skyhooks, Charlie Chan, Simply Red, etc, *Costumes* Paul Warren and Ariane Weiss.

Gaumont/New South Wales Film and Television Office/ Australian Film Commission/Les Films du Loup-Buena Vista. 104 mins. Australia/France. 1999. Rel: 18 August 2000. Cert 15.

## Men of Honor ★★

The trouble with inspirational true-life stories is that there's often too much back story to fit into one film. Norman Jewison came undone with his over-reaching *The Hurricane*, and director Tillman has manoeuvred himself into a corner with this story of the first black diver in the US Navy. Opening with a shot of crashing waves and a setting sun, the film starts unpromisingly. We then segue into a 1966 news report, before cutting back to 1943 and the childhood of Carl Brashear on the Kentucky farm of his embittered, sharecropper father. This sets up Brashear's beginnings nicely, but it could have been done in a much more succinct way. We then have Brashear as a young man joining the Navy, establishing his chutzpah as he defies the segregation rules, getting promoted to seaman and then on to the long drawn-out struggle in Navy diving school. As much of Brashear's life is played out in broad strokes, we are allowed precious little insight into the man's character, as sympathetic as Gooding Jr is. As Brashear's demonised, racist trainer, Robert De Niro is given free rein to devour the scenery, while the action sequences are poorly executed and over-scored, depriving them of any suspense. Yet Brashear's agonising climb to the top of his profession is such a great story. Previously known as *Navy Diver*.

● *Billy Sunday* Robert De Niro, *Carl Brashear* Cuba Gooding Jr, *Gwen* Charlize Theron, *Mr Pappy* Hal Holbrook, *Snowhill* Michael Rapaport, *Jo* Aunjanue Ellis, *Captain Pullman* Powers Boothe, *Captain Hartigan* David Keith, *Ella Brashear* Lonette McKee, *Rourke* Holt McCallany, *Isert* Joshua Leonard, *Lt Hanks* David Conrad, *young Carl Brashear* Chris Warren Jr, *Mac Brashear, Carl's father* Carl Lumbly, *with* Dennis Troutman, Joshua Feinman, Theo Pagones, Ryan Honey, Lester B Hanson, Jack Frazier, Glynn Turman, Leon Russom.
● *Dir* George Tillman Jr, *Pro* Robert Teitel and Bill Badalato, *Ex Pro* Bill Cosby and Stanley Robertson, *Screenplay* Scott Marshall Smith, *Ph* Anthony B Richmond, *Pro Des* Leslie Dilley, *Ed* John Carter, *M* Mark Isham; Johann Strauss; songs performed by Will Schaefer, Frantic Faye Thomas, Bill Monroe, The Count, Sue Raney, Brenton Wood, The Temptations, Brian McKnight etc, *Costumes* Salvador Perez

Fox 2000/State Street Pictures-Fox.
129 mins. USA. 2000. Rel: 30 March 2001. Cert 15.

## Merci pour le chocolat ★★

Lausanne, Switzerland; today. Discovering that she may have been accidentally swapped as a baby, budding pianist Jeanne Pollet seeks out her alternative father, André Polonski, who happens to be a leading tickler of the ivories. Although snubbed by his son Guillaume, the cuckoo in the nest is welcomed with open arms by Polonski's wife, Marie-Claire. But what lies behind her obsessive desire to make hot chocolate for everyone she knows? … Although ostensibly a thriller, this has a wildly uneven pace which, at its slowest, makes one long for the excitement of staring at a goldfish bowl. Surprisingly uninvolving for a film from Claude Chabrol, this thriller is about as enticing as a long-lost bar of chocolate rediscovered under a sofa cushion. Chocolat? Non, merci. [*Simon Rose*]

● *Marie-Claire 'Mika' Muller-Polonski* Isabelle Huppert, *André Polonski* Jacques Dutronc, *Jeanne Pollet* Anna Mouglalis, *Guillaume Polonski* Rodolphe Pauly, *Louise Pollet* Brigitte Catillon, *Dufreigne* Michel Robin, *Axel* Mathieu Simonet, *man at gallery party* Hervé Dumont.
● *Dir* Claude Chabrol, *Pro* Marin Karmitz, *Ex Pro* Yvon Crenn, *Assoc Pro* Jean-Louis Porchet, *Screenplay* Chabrol and Caroline Eliacheff, based on the novel *The Chocolate Cobweb* by Charlotte Armstrong, *Ph* Renato Berta, *Pro Des* Yvan Niclass, *Ed* Monique Fardoulis, *M* Matthieu Chabrol; Liszt, Chopin, Schubert, Mahler, Debussy, Scriabin, *Costumes* Elisabeth Tavernier.

MK2 Prods/CAB Prods/France 2 Cinéma/Canal Plus, etc-Artificial Eye.
101 mins. France/Switzerland. 2000. Rel: 8 June 2001. Cert PG.

## Merlin the Return ★½

Having put King Arthur and his knights into a deep sleep and banished the evil Mordred to the Netherworld, the wizard Merlin has retired to a quiet life in an English village. But when an unscrupulous scientist communicates with Mordred through a medium and plots his escape from eternity, Merlin must once again enlist the help of Arthur and his men… Attempting to be all things to all schoolboys, this rip-roaring, time-travelling medieval romp throws too many possibilities into its convoluted stew. The bizarre casting (Rik Mayall as *Merlin*?) and some misconceived slapstick doesn't exactly help. [*Ewen Brownrigg*]

● *Merlin* Rik Mayall, *Joan Maxwell* Tia Carrere, *King Arthur* Patrick Bergin, *Lancelot* Adrian Paul, *Mordred* Craig Sheffer, *Guinevere* Julie Hartley, *Kate* Leigh Greyvenstein, *Ritchie* Byron Taylor, *Morgana* Grethe Fox, *Ritchie's mum* Jennifer Steyn, *Gawain* Anthony Bishop, *Aunt Evelyn* Lynne White, *Megan* Jocelyn Broderick, *with* Lee-Anne Liebenberg, Connie Giles, Elmi de Beer, Lizette van Heerden, Joanne Odendaal, Doriana Mastrogiuseppe.
● *Dir* and *Screenplay* Paul Matthews, *Pro* Matthews and Elizabeth Matthews, *Ph* Vincent G Cox, *Pro Des* Edward Thomas, *Ed* Peter Davies, *M* Mark Thomas, *Costumes* Pierre Vienings.

Peakviewing Transatlantic-Peakviewing Transatlantic.
91 mins. UK. 2000. Rel: 22 December 2000. Cert PG.

## The Mexican ★★★½

'The Mexican' is a hand-crafted pistol of legendary origin supposedly in the grip of a curse. When reluctant bagman Jerry Welbach is forced to retrieve it for his nefarious boss, he comes under the full scourge of the weapon's power. Meanwhile, his erstwhile bride-to-be is held captive by a notorious hitman with an ambiguous agenda should Jerry fail to deliver… Described as a romantic comedy with a Sam Peckinpah edge, *The Mexican* is an agreeably goofy road movie seasoned with some unexpected plot twists, plenty of colourful characters and a disarming visual style. Brad Pitt, in guileless, puppy dog mode, has seldom been more endearing, while Julia Roberts (as ever) gives her part more spark than it deserves. However, there is something mechanical about the film that, in spite of the odd glimpse of edge, prevents us from ever really fearing for the fate of these characters – and it does go on a bit. Still, director Verbinski (*Mouse Hunt*) provides the proceedings with an agreeable idiosyncrasy and there are some wonderful supporting performances, notably from James Gandolfini as a sexually ambiguous hitman and Bob Balaban as an icily detached racketeer.

● *Jerry Welbach* Brad Pitt, *Samantha Barzel* Julia Roberts, *Leroy* James Gandolfini, *Ted* J K Simmons, *Bernie Nayman* Bob Balaban, *Beck* David Krumholtz,

*well-dressed black man* Sherman Augustus, *Frank* Michael Cerveris, *car thief* Richard Coca, *Arnold Margulies* Gene Hackman, *gunsmith* Salvador Sanchez, *gunsmith's daughter* Melisa Romero, *Vegas onlooker* Lawrence Bender, *with* Castulo Guerro, Maira Serbulo, Ernesto Gomez Cruz, Daniel Escobar, Jeremy Roberts, Pedro Armendariz, Carlos LaCamara.
● *Dir* Gore Verbinski, *Pro* Lawrence Bender and John Baldecchi, *Ex Pro* William Tyrer, Chris J Ball, Aaron Ryder and J H Wyman, *Screenplay* Wyman, *Ph* Dariusz Wolski, *Pro Des* Cecilia Montiel, *Ed* Craig Wood, *M* Alan Silvestri and Abraham Laboriel; songs performed by Nancy Sinatra, WAR, Dean Martin, Men Without Hats, Esquivel, The Whitefield Brothers, *Costumes* Colleen Atwood, *Sound* Tom Myers.

DreamWorks/Newmarket-UIP.
123 mins. USA. 2001. Rel: 27 April 2001. Cert 15.

## Miss Congeniality ★★

When the FBI uncovers a plot to blow up the Miss United States Pageant, they must search for a suitable undercover agent to police the event. Their best bet is to find a female operative who can pass herself off as a contestant in the actual contest. But with the best-looking cop on maternity leave, they have no choice but to enlist Gracie Hart. Now, Gracie may look OK in a bathing suit, but her vocabulary, table manners and physical carriage call for the immediate attention of pageant consultant Victor Melling... Producer and star Sandra Bullock argued that the reason she took on the role of the slobbish, accident-prone Gracie Hart was to emulate Lucille Ball. And, fair enough, this proves to be a suitably energetic showcase for the screwball charms of the actress. Michael Caine is also on good form as a camp Professor Higgins to Bullock's Eliza Dolittle, but few others escape with their dignity intact. Drably photographed and tritely scored, *Miss Congeniality* is the worst kind of high concept Hollywood farce. Mechanical, predictable and hampered by weak dialogue, it barely generates a single belly laugh.

● *Gracie Hart* Sandra Bullock, *Victor Melling* Michael Caine, *Eric Matthews* Benjamin Bratt, *Kathy Morningside* Candice Bergen, *Stan Fields* William Shatner, *McDonald* Ernie Hudson, *Agent Clonsky* John DiResta, *Cheryl from Rhode Island* Heather Burns, *Karen from New York* Melissa De Sousa, *Frank Tobin* Steve Monroe, *Mary Jo from Texas* Deirdre Quinn, *Leslie from California* Wendy Raquel Robinson, *Alana from Hawaii* Asia DeMarcos, *with* Ken Thomas, Gabriel Folse, Christopher Shea, Ellen Schwartz.
● *Dir* Donald Petrie, *Pro* Sandra Bullock, *Ex Pro* Marc Lawrence, Ginger Sledge and Bruce Berman, *Screenplay* Lawrence, Katie Ford and Caryn Lucas, *Ph* Laszlo Kovacs, *Pro Des* Peter Larkin, *Ed* Billy Weber, *M* Edward Shearmur, *Costumes* Susie De Santo, *Choreography* Scott Grossman.

*Above:* Mexican stand-off: Brad Pitt and Julia Roberts fail to see eye-to-eye in Gore Verbinski's colourful, delightfully goofy The Mexican (from UIP)

Castle Rock-Warner.
111 mins. USA. 2000. Rel: 23 March 2001. Cert 12.

## Miss Julie ★★★

Over the course of a sultry midsummer night in the north of Sweden, the lady of a noble household takes advantage of her footman. However, the latter is more than she bargained for...

While adhering to the mechanics of Strindberg's original, Helen Cooper's screen adaptation certainly gives the 1888 play a fresh kick (for starters, Cooper has jettisoned many of the period's euphemisms). As the original was banned from the author's native Sweden for 16 years, Strindberg would surely have approved. And, while obviously remaining very much a filmed play, the piece is provided with a cinematic energy by director Figgis (utilising two handheld cameras) that serves it well. Figgis has also cranked up the subtext – and, indeed, the text – to a shocking degree of intensity, aided by a biting performance from Peter Mullan. And although both Mullan and Saffron Burrows seem wildly miscast, they certainly provide the dramatic fireworks. FYI: *Miss Julie* was previously filmed in 1912 (in Sweden), in 1922 (in Germany), in 1947 (in Argentina) and in 1950 (in Sweden).

● *Miss Julie* Saffron Burrows, *Jean* Peter Mullan, *Christine* Maria Doyle Kennedy, *with* Tam Dean Burn, Heathcote Williams, Eileen Walsh, Bill Ellis, Helen Cooper, Charlotte Mcleod.
● *Dir* and *M* Mike Figgis, *Pro* Figgis and Harriet Cruickshank, *Ex Pro* Annie Stewart, Willi Baer and Etchie Stroh, *Co-Pro* Jacquie Glanville, *Assoc Pro* Barney Reisz, *Screenplay* Helen Cooper, *Ph* Benoît Delhomme, *Pro Des* Michael Howells, *Ed* Matthew Hood, *Costumes* Sandy Powell, *Choreography* Scarlett Mackmin, *Food* Anna Bogue.

*Right: Tom Cruise in John Woo's grandiose, stylised and thoroughly entertaining Mission: Impossible 2 (from UIP)*

Daza Prods/Gallery Motion Pictures/Moonstone Entertainment/Red Mullet/European Script Fund/Left Handed Pictures-Optimum Releasing.
101 mins. UK/USA. 1999. Rel: 1 September 2000. Cert 15.

## Mission: Impossible 2 ★★★¹/₂

Sydney, Australia/The Rockies/Utah/Seville, Spain; today. When an eminent molecular biologist is killed in a plane crash, a terrible secret goes with him. It transpires that he was carrying a deadly virus in his system, the antidote to which has been abducted by terrorists. So it's up to special agent Ethan Hunt to

locate the mastermind behind the heist – with a little help from the terrorist's ex-girlfriend, a beautiful English thief... Considering the weaknesses of the first film, this $150 million sequel rises out of the ashes like a flaming phoenix. Provided with a complete face-lift by Hong Kong maestro John Woo, *M:I-2* is a grandiose, stylised and glorious piece of good fun. Making more entrances than a tube train in the rush hour, Tom Cruise is to the manner born, whether gliding into a Spanish casino in a suit or blasting his way into a subterranean hideout. At times the film does over-reach itself (as with the recurring trick of characters prosthetically disguised as each other), but it is directed with such an operatic sweep by Woo that we know exactly what to expect. And, with a major star like Cruise romancing an Anglo-Zimbabwean, the film is to be commended for its cultural daring (there is also the multi-national presence of American, Afro-American, English, Welsh, Scottish, Irish and Australian actors –and even a South African villain). PS. According to Woo, Tom Cruise performed 95 per cent of his own stunts.

● *Ethan Hunt* Tom Cruise, *Sean Ambrose* Dougray Scott, *Nyah Hall* Thandie Newton, *Hugh Stamp* Richard Roxburgh, *Billy Baird* John Polson, *McCloy* Brendan Gleeson, *Dr Nekhorvich* Radé Sherbedgia, *Luther Stickell* Ving Rhames, *Wallis* William Mapother, *Ulrich* Dominic Purcell, *Michael* Matthew Wilkinson, *with* Nicholas Bell, Kee Chan, Kim Fleming, Christian Manon, Antonio Vargas and (*uncredited*) Anthony Hopkins.
● *Dir* John Woo, *Pro* Tom Cruise and Paula Wagner, *Ex Pro* Terence Chang and Paul Hitchcock, *Assoc Pro* Michael Doven, *Screenplay* Robert Towne and (*uncredited*) Wesley Strick, William Goldman and Michael Tolkin, from a story by Ronald D Moore and Brannon Braga, *Ph* Jeffrey L Kimball, *Pro Des* Tom Sanders, *Ed* Christian Wagner and Steven Kemper, and (*uncredited*) Stuart Baird, *M* Hans Zimmer; Lalo Schifrin; songs performed by Limp Bizkit, Metallica, Zap Mama, Peret, Jose Manuel Lopez, Joaquina Lagar; *Costumes* Lizzy Gardiner, *Visual effects* Richard Yuricich.

Paramount/Cruise/Wagner/MFP Munich Film Partners-UIP. 124 mins. USA/Germany. 2000. Rel: 7 July 2000. Cert 15.

## The Monkey's Mask ★★

Broke, unhappily celibate and living in the Blue Mountains outside Sydney, Jill Fitzpatrick is a lesbian detective looking for work and love. She's then hired to find a poetry student, Mickey Norris, who has been missing for two weeks. Unfamiliar with Sydney's poetry scene, Jill approaches Mickey's tutor, Diana, and finds herself falling for the older woman... Here's a new one: an Australian thriller based on a novel written in verse featuring a lesbian PI. If that sounds like it has all the makings of a pretentious potboiler, then you'd be right. Vertically challenged, liberally freckled and with her hair cropped tight, Susie Porter is a refreshing cinematic presence, but can do little to salvage the film's clunky dialogue and pedestrian plot. And what sort of detective is Jill if, after several dates with Diana, she doesn't even notice her wedding ring?

● *Jill Fitzpatrick* Susie Porter, *Diana* Kelly McGillis, *Nick* Marton Csokas, *Lou* Deborah Mailman, *Mickey Norris* Abbie Cornish, *Tony Brach* Jean-Pierre Mignon, *Mr Norris* John Noble, *Mrs Norris* Linden Wilkinson, *Bill McDonald* Jim Holt,

*Det Sgt Wesley* William Zappa, *with* Caroline Gillmer, Brendan Cowell, Chris Haywood, Brian Wood, Billy Mitchell.
● *Dir* Samantha Lang, *Pro* Robert Connolly and John Maynard, *Co-Pro* Domenico Procacci, *Screenplay* Anne Kennedy, *Ph* Garry Philips, *Pro Des* Michael Philips, *Ed* Dany Cooper, *M* Andrew Kotatko; Schubert, Handel; songs performed by Single Gun Theory, Groove Armada, Deborah Conway and Neil Finn, Smoke City, Charlie Chan, Alan Wilder, Laila Engle and Roger Lock, *Costumes* Emily Seresin, *Sound* Annie Breslin, *Rock climbing supervisor* Andrew Penney, *Puppy wrangler* Dimity Bjork.

Arenafilm Prods/TVA International/New South Wales Film & Television Office/Canal Plus/Asmik Ace/Fandango/ Australian Film Commission-Momentum Pictures. 93 mins. Australia/France. 1999. Rel: 30 March 2001. Cert 18.

## The Mummy Returns ★★

Thebes, 3067 BC; London/Egypt; 1933. Eight years after legionnaire Rick O'Connell and Egyptologist Evelyn saw off the reincarnation of the vengeful high priest Imhotep, they have married, had a son and settled down in a nice English mansion. Then, on another recce to Egypt, they inadvertently unleash the almighty power of the Scorpion King and his invincible army of the undead... So, how do you follow an infantile, sub-Indiana Jones romp that grossed $413 million at the global box-office? Well, you throw in more money, add more computer-generated imagery, increase the number of sound effects, up the music and introduce a photogenic eight-year-old kid. There is obviously a market for this sort of thing (think *King Solomon's Mines* meets The Three Stooges), but that doesn't mean it has to be so lame. Spielberg introduced us all to the possibilities of the high-octane adventure ride, but *The Mummy Returns* mistakes bombast for panache and dulls the imagination with an overkill of screaming mummies and swirling skies. By the final credits we still haven't been treated to one decent line of dialogue or one defining, imaginative moment. Great battle scenes, though.

● *Rick O'Connell* Brendan Fraser, *Evelyn O'Connell* Rachel Weisz, *Jonathan* John Hannah, *Imhotep* Arnold Vosloo, *Ardeth Bay* Oded Fehr, *Anck-Su-Namun* Patricia Velasquez, *The Scorpion King* The Rock, *Alex O'Connell* Freddie Boath, *curator* Alun Armstrong, *Lock-Nah* Adewale Akinnuoye-Agbaje, *Izzy* Shaun Parkes, *Red* Bruce Byron, *The Pharaoh* Aharon Ipalé, *with* Joe Dixon, Tom Fisher, Quill Roberts, Donna Air.
● *Dir* and *Screenplay* Stephen Sommers, *Pro* James Jacks and Sean Daniel, *Ex Pro* Bob Ducsay and Don Zepfel, *Ph* Adrian Biddle, *Pro Des* Allan Cameron, *Ed* Bob Ducsay and Kelly Matsumoto, *M* Alan

**Right:** *Prince (and princess) of Egypt: Rachel Weisz and Brendan Fraser in Stephen Sommers' daft, overwrought and extremely successful* The Mummy Returns *(from UIP)*

Silvestri, *Costumes* John Bloomfield, *Visual effects* John Berton, *Sound* Leslie Shatz, *Creature/makeup effects* Nick Dudman.

Universal/Alphaville-UIP.
129 mins. USA. 2001. Rel: 18 May 2001. Cert 12.

## My Dog Skip ★★

Yazoo, Mississippi; 1942. An only child, eight-year-old Willie Morris craves companionship, a benefit denied him at school and even at home (his father is way out of touch with his inner child). Then his mother gives him a Jack Russell puppy, a gift that transforms Willie's life in the community... An adaptation of the late Willie Morris' 'heartfelt' memoir of his childhood, *My Dog Skip* is a casualty of shrewd marketing. With a poster of a Jack Russell terrier waiting patiently in front of a lavatory bowl, one expects something quirky and unusual. As it is, the film is a mawkish and awkwardly conceived tale of a boy, his dog, his stubborn father, the school bullies and the girl. And besides the glutinous overkill of William Ross' suffocating music (cry along the dotted line...), matters are further marred by the sort of acting in which someone claps a hand to their head to express disbelief or tiptoes emphatically to convey a sense of being quiet. Relish, then, the rich hues of James L Carter's lighting (obviously in deference to Norman Rockwell) and an uncanny performance from Enzo as Skip (Enzo being the son of Eddie, the terrier in TV's *Frasier*).

● *Willie Morris* Frankie Muniz, *Ellen Morris* Diane Lane, *Dink Jenkins* Luke Wilson, *Jack Morris* Kevin Bacon, *Big Boy Wilkinson* Bradley Coryell, *Rivers Applewhite* Caitlin Wachs, *with* Daylan Honeycutt, Cody Linley, Lucile Doan Ewing, Polly Craig, Elizabeth Rice, *Skip* Enzo (and Moose).
● *Dir* Jay Russell, *Pro* Broderick Johnson, Mark Johnson, John Lee Hancock and Andrew A. Kosove, *Ex Pro* Russell and Marty Ewing, *Screenplay* Gail Gilchriest, *Ph* James L Carter, *Pro Des* David J Bomba, *Ed* Harvey Rosenstock and Gary Winter, *M* William Ross; songs performed by Gene Krupa & His Orchestra, The Andrews Sisters, Harry James, Louis Jordan, Louis Prima, The Boswell Sisters, *Costumes* Edi Giguere, *Sound* Stephen Hunter Flick.

Alcon Entertainment-Warner.
95 mins. USA. 1999. Rel: 11 August 2000. Cert U.

## Nasty Neighbours ★★

West Midlands, England; today. When the Peaches' beloved next-door neighbours move to Australia, they dream of joining them. However, Harold Peach is behind with his mortgage payments (and just about everything else) and is on the downward path to financial ruin. Then the Chapmans move in next door...

Presumably *Nasty Neighbours* was intended to be a black comedy and/or a scathing social commentary on contemporary Britain. Unfortunately, it succeeds as neither. While periodically amusing in an uncomfortable way, it never attains the belly laughs of a Mike Leigh or Alan Ayckbourn farce, nor is it credible enough to fully draw us into the dysfunctional lives of these terrible people. Furthermore, it's a shame that its central character, Harold, is such a loathsome grotesque, thus dispelling any hope of empathy. While exhibiting a certain zesty style, first-time director Debbie Isitt would do well to check out Gary Oldman's *Nil By Mouth* (for a taste of realism) or Mike Leigh's *Secrets and Lies* (for sustained satire). Incidentally, Isitt not only wrote and directed, but plays the Peaches' forthright daughter – and was eight months pregnant at the time. PS. The subject of impossible neighbours was previously explored in the equally inept *Neighbors* (1981), John Belushi's last film.

● *Harold Peach* Ricky Tomlinson, *Jean Peach* Marion Bailey, *Robert Chapman* Phil Daniels, *Ellen Chapman* Rachel Fielding, *the boss* Hywel Bennett, *the estate agent* Nick Whitfield, *Pauline Peach* Debbie Isitt, *with* Gordon Coulson, Freda Barratt, Kenneth Hadley, Peter Isitt, Trevor Byfield.
● *Dir* and *Screenplay* Debbie Isitt, *Pro* Christine Alderson, *Ex Pro* Adam Page, Nadine Marsh Edwards, Terje Gaustad and Lukas Erni, *Ass Pro* Gary Tanner and Tim Webb, *Ph* Simon Reeves and Sam McCurdy, *Pro Des* Tim Streater, *Ed* Nicky Ager, *M* Jocelyn Pook, *Costumes* Sally Plum.

Ipso Facto Films/Glenrinnes Film Partnership/MPCE/Birmingham City Council-Redbus.
88 mins. UK. 2000. Rel: 13 October 2000. Cert 15.

## Nightfall
*See Abendland*

## Nowhere to Hide – Injeongsajeong bol geos eobsda ★★¹/₂

Inchon, the Republic of Korea; today. A drug dealer is stabbed to death by an unseen assailant and an attaché case is stolen. Woo, an unconventional and hot-headed detective with the Western Precinct, is called in to head the investigation. Woo will stop at nothing, but then his adversary is a very slippery fellow... Exuding the self-confident poise of Chow Yun-Fat and exhibiting a playfulness that recalls Jackie Chan, Park Joong-Hoon is an extremely watchable presence. There are also plenty of inventive set pieces courtesy of writer-director Lee Myung-Se, who films his action scenes in all weathers (but mainly in the rain and mainly at night) and is not afraid to use slow motion, stop motion and freeze framing in a welter of cartoon extravagance. However, the plotting is minimal (albeit convoluted), the villain a one-dimensional shadow and the credibility sorely lacking. Lee Myung-Se never lets us forget that we are watching a movie – and, after a while, the cumulative effect is about as invigorating as succumbing to two hours of commercials after the watershed.

● *Detective Woo* Park Joong-Hoon, *Chang Sungmin*

**Above:** A Reason to Leave: Renée Zellweger in her Golden Globe-winning performance as Nurse Betty (from Pathé)

Ahn Sung-Ki, *Detective Kim* Jang Dong-Kun, *Juyon* Choi Ji-Woo, *Fishhead* Kwon Yong-Wun, *Meathead* Park Sang-Myeon, *Woo's sister* Lee Hye-Eun, *with* Do Yong-Koo, Shim Cheol-Jong, Lee Wong-Jong.
● *Dir, Screenplay* and *Pro Des* Lee Myung-Se, *Pro* Chung Tae-Won, *Ex Pro* Kang Woo-Suk, *Ph* Jeong Kwang-Seok and Song Haeng-Ki, *Ed* Go Im Pyo, *M* Cho Sung-Woo, Kim Dae-Hong and Choi Young-Hoon, *Martial arts* Lee Koon-Ho.

Won Entertainment/Kook Min Tech Finance/Sam Soo Finance/Cinema Service/Fox Video Korea-Metro Tartan. 101 mins. The Republic of Korea. 1999. Rel: 29 June 2001. Cert 15.

## Nurse Betty ★★★★

Fair Oaks, Kansas/Arizona/Los Angeles; today. Blessed with a good heart and cursed with a bad marriage, Betty Sizemore escapes the drudgery of her life by immersing herself in the daytime soap opera *A Reason To Love*. Then, after witnessing a horrific crime, she packs up her bags and heads for California to woo the dashing, fictitious doctor of the series... It's a simple enough premise: take a Doris Day-like heroine, place her in a romantic fantasy of her own making and then introduce a jarring note of contemporary realism. But what is really disturbing about this sugar-coated *Pulp Fiction* is that it's meant to be a comedy – and it's hilarious. Thanks to casting-against-type (the noble Morgan Freeman as a hitman) and a general restraint in the acting (even Chris Rock plays down his lines), *Nurse Betty* constantly defies expectation. Playwright Neil LaBute, who directed the misanthropic, emotionally excoriating *In the Company of Men* and *Your Friends & Neighbors*, works from someone else's script for the first time and brings his own accomplished eye to the proceedings. And, in a performance of committed delusion, Renée Zellweger chills the marrow – even as we guiltily laugh at her.
● *Charlie* Morgan Freeman, *Betty Sizemore* Renée Zellweger, *Wesley* Chris Rock, *George McCord/Dr David Ravell* Greg Kinnear, *Del Sizemore* Aaron Eckhart, *Roy Ostrey* Crispin Glover, *Sheriff Eldon Ballard* Pruitt Taylor Vince, *Rosa Herrera* Tia Texada, *Lyla* Allison Janney, *Sue Ann Rogers* Kathleen Wilhoite, *Chloe* Elizabeth Mitchell, *Ellen* Harriet Sansom Harris, *Blake* Steven Gilborn, *Joyce* Sheila Kelley, *with* Susan Barnes, Sung Hi Lee, Laird Macintosh, Jenny Gago, Matthew Cowles, Alfonso Freeman, Steven Culp, Irene Olga Lopez, Steve Franken.
● *Dir* Neil LaBute, *Pro* Gail Mutrux and Steve Golin, *Ex Pro* Philip Steuer, Stephen Pevner, Moritz Borman and Chris Sievernich, *Screenplay* John C. Richards and James Flamberg, *Ph* Jean Yves Escoffier, *Pro Des* Charles Breen, *Ed* Joel Plotch and Steven Weisberg, *M* Rolfe Kent, songs performed by

Pink Martini, Della Reese, Ann-Margret, Hank Williams, Ricky Nelson, Eddy Arnold, Gus Gus, Slave, Texas Joe, Sugarman 3, Jula De Palma, Suga T, Willow Creek, Frankie, *Costumes* Lynette Meyer.

Gramercy Pictures/Pacifica Film Distrib./Propaganda Films/abstrakt pictures/IMF-Pathé. 110 mins. USA. 1999. Rel: 1 September 2000. Cert 18.

## Nutty Professor II: The Klumps ★½

Having ditched the lovely Carla Purty from the first film, the humble and overweight Professor Sherman Klump has made a hit with his scientific colleague Denise Gaines. But Sherman's brash and avaricious alter ego Buddy Love – an unsavoury side effect of the professor's experiment with a fat gene formula – is taking on a life of his own. So, with the help of Denise's DNA research, Sherman attempts to rid himself of Buddy for ever – with disastrous results... The real star of this redundant sequel is not Eddie Murphy (in spite of his eight roles), but make-up maestro Rick Baker, who has physically transformed Murphy into a variety of overweight Klumps of both genders. Murphy himself sacrifices intelligibility for overacting, thus destroying any humour the dialogue might have accommodated. So, deprived of verbal wit, one has the gross-out factor to revel in – if, that is, the sight of flying faeces, anal rape and involuntary boners is your cue for a hoot. But the main trouble is that the film's infantile mentality is wasted by its obsession with all things sexual, scatological and, well, nauseous, thus denying it its core audience.

● *Sherman Klump/Buddy Love/Granny Klump/Mama Klump/Papa Klump/young Papa Klump/Ernie Klump/Lance Perkins* Eddie Murphy, *Denise Gaines* Janet Jackson, *Dean Richmond* Larry Miller, *Jason* John Ales, *Leanne Guilford* Melinda McGraw, *Ernie Klump Jr* Jamal Mixon, *Old Willie* Sylvester Jenkins, *with* Richard Gant, Anna Maria Horsford, Gabriel Williams, Chris Elliott, Earl Boen, Freda Payne, George King, Naomi Kale, Charles Napier, Peter Segal, Nicole Segal.
● *Dir* Peter Segal, *Pro* Brian Grazer, *Ex Pro* Jerry Lewis, Eddie Murphy, Tom Shadyac, Karen Kehela and James D Brubaker, *Co-Pro* James Whitaker and Michael Ewing, *Screenplay* Barry W Blaustein, David Sheffield, Paul Weitz and Chris Weitz, from a story by Blaustein, Sheffield and Steve Oedekerk, *Ph* Dean Semler, *Pro Des* William Elliott, *Ed* William Kerr, *M* David Newman; songs performed by The Platters, Rufus, James Brown, Village People, Jerry Vale, *Costumes* Sharen Davis, *Visual effects* Jon Farhat, *Make-up effects* Rick Baker.

Universal/Imagine Entertainment-UIP. 106 mins. USA. 2000. Rel: 6 October 2000. Cert 12.

## O Brother, Where Art Thou? ★★★¹⁄₂

Mississippi; the 1930s. Breaking free from a chain gang, three unlikely convicts set off to find a stash of buried treasure worth $1.2 million. Along the way they encounter a variety of aberrant characters, not least the notorious gangster Baby Face Nelson... Only the Coen brothers could dream up a gospel crime musical based on Homer's *The Odyssey*. And only the Coen brothers could pull off such an audacious conceit with such aplomb, juggling stock elements of the Deep South – banjo-strumming minstrels, prison chain gangs and the Ku Klux Klan – with Cyclops, the Sirens and a blind prophet. As to be expected, the film is a visual feast, the dialogue consistently colourful and the *dramatis personae* a species unto themselves. And while the film lacks the comic momentum of *Raising Arizona* (which it most resembles in the Coens' canon), the eccentric detail is a constant pleasure. And, rest assured, all scenes involving cows were monitored by the American Humane Association. FYI: The title is actually the name of the 'meaningful' movie Joel McCrea set out to make in Preston Sturges' 1941 *Sullivan's Travels*.

● *Everett Ulysses McGill* George Clooney, *Pete* John Turturro, *Delmar* Tim Blake Nelson, *Pappy O'Daniel* Charles Durning, *George 'Baby Face' Nelson* Michael Badalucco, *Big Dan Teague* John Goodman, *Penny* Holly Hunter, *Tommy Johnson* Chris Thomas King, *Junior O'Daniel* Del Pentecost, *Homer Stokes* Wayne Duvall, *Vernon T Waldrip* Ray McKinnon, *Sheriff Cooley* Daniel Von Bargen, *Wash Hogwallop* Frank Collison, *Radio Station man* Stephen Root, *with* J R Horne, Brian Reddy, Ed Gale, Royce D Applegate, Quinn Gasaway, Lee Weaver, Milford Fortenberry, Gillian Welch, Mia Tate, Musetta Vander, Christy Taylor.

● *Dir* Joel Coen, *Pro* Ethan Coen, *Ex Pro* Tim Bevan and Eric Fellner, *Co-Pro* John Cameron, *Screenplay* Ethan Coen and Joel Coen, *Ph* Roger Deakins, *Pro Des* Dennis Gassner, *Ed* Roderick Jaynes and Tricia Cooke, *M* T Bone Burnett; Carter Burwell; songs performed by James Carter & The Prisoners, Alison Krauss, Emmylou Harris, Gillian Welch, The Whites, Tim Blake Nelson & Pat Enright, The Stanley Brothers, George Clooney, John Turturro etc, *Costumes* Mary Zophres, *Sound* Eugene Gearty.

Touchstone Pictures/Universal/Canal Plus/Working Title-Momentum Pictures.
107 mins. USA/France/UK. 2000. Rel: 15 September 2000. Cert 12.

## A One and a Two – Yi Yi ★★★★

Taipei; today. Starting with a wedding, this film looks at the lives of various individuals present as relatives or friends and also takes in the experiences of others known to them. Past emotions resurface and we observe relationships change as various interrelated

**Above:** *Chain of Fools: John Turturro, Tim Blake Nelson and George Clooney in the Coen brothers' gospel crime musical* O Brother, Where Art Thou? *(from Momentum)*

story threads are pursued. Less familiar in eastern cinema, this panoramic format is best known from many Robert Altman movies. It works here since, despite being almost three hours in length, Edward Yang's assured direction and his able cast hold your attention throughout. But, lacking the deep reality of Ozu's films, what it amounts to is soap opera of the very highest order. If you accept my view that the genre cannot yield a masterpiece, you will understand why, unlike many colleagues, I do not regard this as the best film of the year despite its many qualities. [*Mansel Stimpson*]

● *NJ Jian* Wu Nianzhen, *Mr Ota* Issey Ogata, *Min Min* Elaine Jin, *Ting Ting* Kelly Lee, *Yang Yang* Jonathan Chang, *A-Di* Chen Xisheng, *Sherry Chang-Breitner* Ke Suyun, *Da-Da* Michael Tao, *Xiao Yan* Xiao Shushen, *Lili* Adrian Lin, *Fatty* Chang Yu-Pang.
● *Dir* and *Screenplay* Edward Yang, *Pro* Shinya Kawai and Naoko Tsukeda, *Assoc Pro* Yu Weiyen and Kubota Osamu, *Ph* Yang Weihan, *Pro Des* Peng Kaili, *Ed* Chen Bowen, *M* Peng Kaili; Beethoven, J S Bach, *Sound* Du Duzhi

**Atom Films/Pony Canyon Prods-ICA Projects.**
173 mins. Taiwan/Japan. 1999. Rel: 6 April 2001. Cert 15.

## 101 Reykjavik ★★¹/₂

Concluding that life is nothing more than 'a break from death,' 28-year-old Hylnur still lives with his mother, collects social security and spends most of his time in the pub or surfing the Net for porn. Then his mother invites a friend from Spain for Christmas, a fun-loving lesbian who is not impressed by Hylnur's apathetic ways... Demonstrating a morose wit and painting his debut film in drab, washed-out colours, Iceland's Baltasar Kormakur can definitely count himself a student of the bleak comedy school of Northern Hemisphere filmmaking (whose most notable proponents include Aki Kaurismaki and fellow Iceman Fridrik Thor Fridriksson). However, besides some audacious thematic conceits and the occasional eccentric shot (Hylnur lying buried in snow limply clutching a packet of cigarettes), this lacks the bizarre beauty and humanity that makes the sub-genre so arresting. Besides, Hylnur is such a thoroughly unsympathetic dolt and the film so unremittingly ugly that things quickly become wearisome. There are some wonderful comic flourishes (Hylnur feeding parking metres in order to annoy a traffic warden) but they are not enough to make this anything more than a passing curiosity.

● *Lola Milagros* Victoria Abril, *Hylnur* Hilmir Snaer, *Berglind* Hanna Maria Karlsdottir, *Thröstur* Baltasar Kormakur, *Marri* Ólafur Darri Ólafsson, *Hofi* Thrúdur Vilhjalmdottir, *Brusi* Thröstur Leó Gunnarsson.

● *Dir* and *Screenplay* Baltasar Kormakur, from the novel by Hallgrímur Helgason, *Pro* Kormakur and Ingvar H. Thórdarson, *Ph* Peter Steuger, *Pro Des* Árni Páll Jóhannsson, *Ed* Stule Eriksen and Sigvaldi Karason, *M* Damon Albarn and Einar Örn Benediktsson.

**Filmhuset/Liberator/Zentropa/Troika Entertainment/ Icelandic Film Fund/Eurimages-Metrodome.**
88 mins. Iceland/Denmark/Norway/France/Germany. 2000. Rel: 1 June 2001. Cert 15.

## 102 Dalmatians ★★

Westminster, London; the present. It has been three years since Cruella De Vil was imprisoned for her canine cruelty, and now she is a changed woman. Thanks to the rehabilitation experiments of one Dr Pavlov (as in Ivan Pavlov's dogs – geddit?), Cruella (call me 'Ella') is now an ardent animal rights activist, with her own inimitable spin on the marketing of compassion. However, her probation officer, Chloe Simon, is not so easily convinced, although Kevin, the trusting proprietor of the dog's home 2nd Chance, is in thrall. Besides, should `Ella' stray from her new-found path of philanthropy, her entire fortune (£8 million) will go to Kevin's concern... The original live-action *101 Dalmatians* – based on the beloved children's novel by Dodie Smith – had a lot of slapstick, but it also boasted visual ingenuity, sharp dialogue ('You may have won the battle, but I'm about to win the wardrobe') and a high cute factor. This one seems content to have Cruella's hapless aide (McInnerny) repeatedly brutalised, although anybody who slams a door on his own hand gets what he deserves. The young human leads, Gruffudd and Evans, are sweet enough, but it's the literally spotless puppy Oddball that steals the show (even if his facial expressions are digitally enhanced).

● *Cruella De Vil* Glenn Close, *Kevin Shepherd* Ioan Gruffud, *Chloe Simon* Alice Evans, *Alonso* Tim McInnerny, *Jean-Pierre Le Pelt* Gérard Depardieu, *Ewan* Ben Crompton, *Detective Armstrong* Jim Carter, *Dr Pavlov* David Horovitch, *with* Carol MacReady, Ian Richardson, Ron Cook, Timothy West, Dick Brannick, June Watson, Kerry Shale, Thierry Lawson, Charles Simon, *voice of Waddlesworth* Eric Idle.
● *Dir* Kevin Lima, *Pro* Edward S Feldman, *Co-Pro* Paul Tucker and Patricia Carr, *Assoc Pro* Michelle Fox, *Screenplay* Kristen Buckley, Brian Regan, Bob Tzudiker and Noni White, *Ph* Adrian Biddle, *Pro Des* Assheton Gorton, *Ed* Gregory Perler, *M* David Newman, *Costumes* Anthony Powell, *Sound* Shannon Mills, *Visual effects* Jim Rygiel and Dan Deleeuw.

**Walt Disney Pictures-Buena Vista.**
100 mins. USA. 2000. Rel: 8 December 2000. Cert U.

## One Night at McCool's ★¹/₂

What a great cast. What a wonderful premise. A beautiful girl with a gun and an eye for interior decoration enters the lives of three men and changes them for ever. Unfortunately, Harald Zwart directs with the subtlety of a scout master and Liv Tyler isn't up to the task of playing this siren, providing little edge, credibility or even any real sex appeal. Instead, she delivers a watered-down impersonation of Marilyn Monroe which no amount of soft focus can bring to life. Interestingly, the only actor who doesn't behave as if he's in a burlesque is Matt Dillon, who last showed a talent for farce in the hilarious *There's Something About Mary*. It's a shame, then, that he's no more sympathetic than the rest of this tiresome bunch. Oh, and by the way, jokes about men caught in bondage apparel are past their laugh-by date. And so are jokes about Village People. The song 'YMCA' has already been used as a gag in *As Good As it Gets*, *At First Sight*, *Blast From the Past*, *In & Out*, *very Annie-Mary* and *Wayne's World 2*.

● *Jewel Valentine* Liv Tyler, *Randy* Matt Dillon, *Det Dehling* John Goodman, *Carl Lumpke* Paul Reiser, *Mr Burmeister* Michael Douglas, *Dr Green* Reba McEntire, *Utah/Elmo* Andrew Silverstein, *Father Jimmy* Richard Jenkins, *Karen Lumpke* Andrea Bendewald, *with* Mary Jo Smith, Tim deZarn, Leo Rossi, Eric Schaeffer, Vesleymoe Ruud Zwart.
● *Dir* Harald Zwart, *Pro* Michael Douglas and Allison Lyon Segan, *Ex Pro* Whitney Green, *Assoc Pro* Veslemoey Ruud Zwart, *Screenplay* Stan Seidel, *Ph* Karl Walter Lindenlaub, *Pro Des* Jon Gary Steele, *Ed* Bruce Cannon, *M* Marc Shaiman; songs performed by Johnny Cash, Jungle Brothers, Morcheeba, Ween, Touch and Go, Lisa Ekdahl, Joan Osborne, Bottlefly, Caleb, Village People, *Costumes* Ellen Mirojnick.

October Films/Furthur Films-Entertainment.
92 mins. USA. 2000. Rel: 20 April 2001. Cert 15.

## The Original Kings of Comedy ★★¹/₂

Humour is a very personal thing and this has seldom seemed more apparent than in this document of four black comics calling themselves the Kings of Comedy. Filmed live on stage during two concerts held at the Charlotte Coliseum in North Carolina, the movie is extraordinary in that the more incomprehensible the routine, the more the audience collapses into paroxysms of mirth. 'I try to make people laugh so hard so many times in a row,' admits D L Hughley, 'that they crack a rib.' What's also interesting is that in spite of the jokes about sex and bottom-wiping, the spectre of race is never far away. Each comic, addressing a predominantly black audience, talks about being black as if within a white context. Yet the performers insist that their act transcends race, class, gender and age,

Hughley noting that 'You don't have to be black to laugh – funny is funny is funny.' Be that as it may, much of the humour will be lost on audiences outside the US. As such, then, this is more successful as a social treatise than as a barrel of laughs. FYI: The tour, which grossed a staggering $37 million in ticket sales, is the most successful in the history of comedy.

● With Steve Harvey, D L Hughley, Cedric The Entertainer and Bernie Mac.
● *Dir* Spike Lee, *Pro* Lee, Walter Latham and David Gale, *Ex Pro* Van Toffler, *Co-Pro* Butch Robinson, *Ph* Malik Sayeed, *Pro Des* Wynn P Thomas, *Ed* Barry Alexander Brown, *M* Alex Steyermark; songs performed by Monifah and Chico Debarge, The O'Jays, Sticky Fingaz, King Floyd, Ohio Players, Earth Wind & Fire, Mystikal, Cedric The Entertainer and Chris Flores, One Way, Afrika Bambaataa and Soul Sonic Forces, Steve Harvey etc.

MTV Films/Latham Entertainment/40 Acres and a Mule Filmworks/A Spike Lee Joint/Paramount-UIP.
116 mins. USA. 2000. Rel: 24 November 2000. Cert 15.

## Out of Depth ★

When his mother is beaten and humiliated at the South London pub where she works, her son Paul decides to exact revenge. However, by hiring a professional gangster to do his dirty work, Paul finds himself trapped in a world where there are no painless resolutions… With its release delayed by three years, *Out of Depth* may actually have been ahead of its time – it was made concurrently with *Lock, Stock and Two Smoking Barrels*. As it is, it now looks terribly hackneyed, a situation that its risible dialogue really doesn't help. Strutting unconvincingly into a world of gangster stereotypes, the film just belittles the tragic true story on which it is based. FYI: As Sean Maguire was a character played by Robin Williams in *Good Will Hunting*, is it a coincidence that the actor's co-star Phil Cornwell now plays a character called Ed Harris? [*Ewen Brownrigg*]

● *Paul Nixon* Sean Maguire, *Steve Wilshin* Danny Midwinter, *Lenny Walker* Nicholas Ball, *Ed Harris* Phil Cornwell, *Sarah Callum* Josephine Butler, *Maggie Nixon* Rita Tushingham, *Andy O'Sullivan* Peter de Jersey, *Richard Tate* Leigh Lawson, *with* Gregor Trutor, David Battley, Karen Seacombe, Clive Russell, Paul Corrigan, Ian Brimble, Petra Markham, Rosemarie Dunham.
● *Dir* and *Screenplay* Simon Marshall, *Pro* Stephen Cranny, *Ex Pro* Paul Woolf, *Assoc Pro* Michael Riley, *Ph* Adam Suschitzky, *Pro Des* Philip Robinson, *Ed* St John O'Rorke, *M* Barry Adamson, *Costumes* Saffron Webb.

Redbus Films-Steon Films.
99 mins. UK. 1998. Rel: 29 June 2001. Cert 18.

And don't mistake this for history: even in war villains don't behave (or glower) like villains (and Jason Isaacs really does overdo the 'blank stare' school of villainy). FYI: For his part, Mel Gibson received an all-time record $25 million.

● *Benjamin Martin* Mel Gibson, *Gabriel Martin* Heath Ledger, *Charlotte Selton* Joely Richardson, *Col William Tavington* Jason Isaacs, *Col Harry Burwell* Chris Cooper, *Jean Villeneuve* Tcheky Karyo, *Rev Oliver* Rene Auberjonois, *General Charles Cornwallis* Tom Wilkinson, *Anne Howard* Lisa Brenner, *Dan Scott* Donal Logue, *John Billings* Leon Rippy, *Captain Wilkins* Adam Baldwin, *Occam* Jay Arlen Jones, *Peter Howard* Joey D Vieira, *Thomas Martin* Gregory Smith, *Margaret Martin* Mika Boorem, *Susan Martin* Skye McCole Bartusiak, *Nathan Martin* Trevor Morgan, *Samuel Martin* Bryan Chafin, *Brig General O'Hara* Peter Woodward, *General George Washington* Terry Layman, *with* Logan Lerman, Mary Jo Deschanel, Jamieson K Price, Grahame Wood, Beatrice Bush, Shan Omar Huey, Kirk Fox, Jack Moore, Mark Twogood, Colt Romberger, Shannon Eubanks, Bill Roberson, Charles Black, Andy Stahl, Kyle Richard Engels.
● *Dir* Roland Emmerich, *Pro* Mark Gordon and Gary Levinsohn, and Dean Devlin, *Ex Pro* William Fay, Ute Emmerich and Roland Emmerich, *Co-Pro* Peter Winther, *Screenplay* Robert Rodat, *Ph* Caleb Deschanel, *Pro Des* Kirk M Petruccelli, *Ed* David Brenner, *M* John Williams, *Costumes* Deborah L Scott.

Columbia Pictures/Mutual Film Company/Centropolis Entertainment-Columbia TriStar.
167 mins. USA. 2000. Rel: 14 July 2000. Cert 15.

*Above: Patriot games: Mel Gibson remakes* Braveheart *(without the skirt) in Roland Emmerich's sweeping, gripping and blood-broiling* The Patriot *(from Columbia TriStar)*

### The Patriot ★★★¹/₂

South Carolina; 1776. A hero of the French and Indian War, Benjamin Martin has settled down to tend his plantation and raise his seven children. Called upon to join the rebellion against the British, Martin resolutely refuses, knowing the terrible cost of battle. But when the leader of the Green Dragoons burns down Martin's home for nursing American wounded, he swears revenge... As a piece of sweeping, gripping and blood-broiling entertainment, *The Patriot* is extremely efficient, as one would expect from the director of *Independence Day*. However, if one is expecting anything remotely subtle, credible or non-manipulative, one should look elsewhere. Harrison Ford turned this down because of its violence (there is some serious cannon damage) but, in the tradition of *Braveheart*, this is pure Mel Gibson material: long, jingoistic and where every detail is planted for a dramatic payoff and where every emotional moment is underlined by an orchestral surge.

### Pay it Forward ★★★¹/₂

Eugene Simonet is a facially disfigured teacher starting work at a new school in Washington State. Shielded from the real world by a courteous reserve and a commanding vocabulary, Simonet sets his seventh grade students a challenge for the new year: to 'think of an idea to change our world – and then put it into action.' Troubled pupil Trevor McKinney takes Simonet's assignment literally and decides to kick-start a chain reaction of good deeds. The idea is that he helps three people and in return each of them helps three others – by 'paying it forward.' Four months later a cynical journalist, Chris Chandler, is given a brand-new Jaguar by a complete stranger and attempts to get to the bottom of this irrational act of altruism... Sometimes a film's concept and message are so original and courageous that any flaws in its execution cannot blunt its thrust. OK, so the characters here don't entirely ring true, and there's a whiff of

manipulation in the plotting, but films this inspirational are too few and far between for *Pay it Forward* to be ignored. Besides, Kevin Spacey and Haley Joel Osment are both terrific and there are enough moments of blistering truth to keep the mind churning for weeks afterwards. One quibble, though: how come Helen Hunt knew how to spell euphemism?

● *Eugene Simonet* Kevin Spacey, *Arlene McKinney* Helen Hunt, *Trevor McKinney* Haley Joel Osment, *Chris Chandler* Jay Mohr, *Jerry* James Caviezel, *Ricky* Jon Bon Jovi, *Grace* Angie Dickinson, *Sidney* David Ramsey, *Thorsen* Gary Werntz, *Adam* Marc Donato, *Bonnie* Kathleen Wilhoite, *with* Colleen Flynn, Liza Snyder, Jeannetta Arnette, Tina Lifford, Shawn Pyfrom, Alexandra Kotcheff, Bradley White, Bob McCracken, Eugene Osment.
● *Dir* Mimi Leder, *Pro* Peter Abrams, Robert Levy and Steven Reuther, *Ex Pro* Mary McLaglen and Jonathan Treisman, *Screenplay* Leslie Dixon, based on the novel by Catherine Ryan Hyde, *Ph* Oliver Stapleton, *Pro Des* Leslie Dilley, *Ed* David Rosenbloom, *M* Thomas Newman; songs performed by Sam Cooke, No Doubt, Los Hermanos Martinez Gil, POD, Jungle Brothers, Tracy Bonham, Papa Roach, Steve Earle etc, *Costumes* Renee Ehrlich Kalfus.

Warner/Bel-Air Entertainment/Tapestry Films-Warner. 123 mins. USA. 2000. Rel: 26 January 2001. Cert 12.

## Pearl Harbor ★★

Oahu Island, Hawaii; 1941-42. One woman. Two men. 423 Japanese aircraft. Rafe and Danny have been friends since childhood and have always dreamed of becoming fighter pilots. Now they're in the US Army Air Corps and, as the war rages in Europe, they find their hearts distracted by something a little more down-to-earth: the love of a beautiful nurse. Still, their romantic differences are nothing that a full-scale bombardment of America's prized Pacific Fleet can't sort out... The most expensive movie ever financed by a single studio (at a cost of $135,210,000), *Pearl Harbor* is not as historically inaccurate as the early word would have had us believe. Nevertheless, its credibility does leave a lot to be desired. Featuring characters with the complexity of a Levi's ad, the film cannot hope to sustain its elephantine running time, let alone place America's darkest hour of the 20th century into a tenable context. With nostril-nudging close-ups, duff dialogue, gushing orchestral riffs and endless sunsets, the corn not only prompts much unintentional laughter, but a bum-shifting impatience for the real action to start. However, with so much attention lavished on Japan's preparation for attack, the actual onslaught is completely deprived of surprise. When it does, eventually, come (90 minutes into the film), the blitz is so artlessly contrived that the sheer horror of it is completely lost. War, as Steven Spielberg showed us so brilliantly in *Saving Private Ryan*, is hell. Here, it is

*Above: Action men: Ben Affleck and Josh Hartnett in* Pearl Harbor *(from Buena Vista)*

*Right: Pushing the boat out: Mark Wahlberg and George Clooney battle the elements in Wolfgang Petersen's $140 million, jaw-dropping, stomach-knotting, true-life epic, The Perfect Storm (from Warner)*

nothing more than an MTV photo opportunity with big guns blowing the crap out of a Mills & Boon romance. FYI: To appease local environmental groups, divers combed the harbour for whales and turtles hours before each explosion.

● *Rafe McCawley* Ben Affleck, *Danny Walker* Josh Hartnett, *Evelyn Johnson* Kate Beckinsale, *Doris 'Dorie' Miller* Cuba Gooding Jr, *Earl* Tom Sizemore, *Franklin D Roosevelt* Jon Voight, *Admiral Kimmel* Colm Feore, *Colonel James H Doolittle* Alec Baldwin, *Billy* William Lee Scott, *Anthony R Fusco* Greg Zola, *Red* Ewen Bremner, *Betty* James King, *Barbara* Catherine Kellner, *Sandra* Jennifer Garner, *Gooz* Michael Shannon, *Admiral Isoroku Yamamoto* Mako, *Nishikura* John Fujioka, *Commander Minoru Genda* Cary-Hiroyuki Tagawa, *Captain Thurman* Dan Aykroyd, *young Danny* Reiley McClendon, *young Rafe* Jesse James, *General Marshall* Scott Wilson, *Jack Richards* Kim Coates, *Major Jackson* Leland Orser, *with* Matt Davis, William Fichtner, Graham Beckel, Howard Mungo, Tom Everett, Tomas Arana, Beth Grant, Peter Firth, Andrew Bryniarski, Tim Choate, John Diehl, Ted McGinley, Glenn Morshower, Guy Torry, and (*uncredited*) Nicholas Farrell.
● *Dir* Michael Bay, *Pro* Bay and Jerry Bruckheimer, *Ex Pro* Mike Stenson, Barry Waldman, Randall Wallace, Chad Oman and Bruce Hendricks, *Screenplay* Wallace, *Ph* John Schwartzman, *Pro Des* Nigel Phelps, *Ed* Chris Lebenzon, Steven Rosenblum and Mark Goldblatt, *M* Hans Zimmer; 'There You'll Be' sung by Faith Hill, *Costumes* Michael Kaplan, *Visual effects* Eric Brevig.

Touchstone Pictures/Jerry Bruckheimer Films-Buena Vista. 182 mins. USA. 2001. Rel: 1 June 2001. Cert 12.

## The Perfect Storm ★★★★

Gloucester, Massachusetts/The North Atlantic; October, 1991. When their last haul fails to bring the financial rewards that they had hoped for, the six fishermen of the *Andrea Gail* head out for a last-minute, late-season run. Just then Hurricane Grace, heading up the Atlantic from Bermuda, collides with two other weather fronts, creating, in meteorological terms, 'the perfect storm'… Like all good disaster movies, this $140 million adaptation of Sebastian Junger's best-selling account of 'the Storm of the Century' takes its time in setting up its *mise en scène* and characters. So, by the time George Clooney and his crew set off for the Grand Banks one can almost taste the salt, ice and fish guts in one's popcorn. And then the storm unleashes its ferocious power: with the help of cutting-edge computer-generated effects and a whole lot of authentic H20. At times it's almost *too* much of a good thing, *too* intense a ride for comfort. Full marks then to the muscular direction of Wolfgang Petersen, the highly efficient editing of Richard Francis-Bruce and some truly stomach-knotting photography. But let us not forget the emotional sustenance that makes the fate of the fisherman so unbearable, little moments of humour and some exceptional performances from a fine female cast: Diane Lane, Mary Elizabeth Mastrantonio, Rusty Schwimmer and Janet Wright. FYI: Amazingly, no live fish were used in the making of the film.

● *Billy Tyne* George Clooney, *Bobby Shatford* Mark

Wahlberg, *Dale 'Murph' Murphy* John C Reilly, *Christina Cotter* Diane Lane, *David 'Sully' Sullivan* William Fichtner, *Melissa Brown* Karen Allen, *Alfred Pierre* Allen Payne, *Alexander McAnally III* Bob Gunton, *Linda Greenlaw* Mary Elizabeth Mastrantonio, *Bob Brown* Michael Ironside, *Michael 'Bugsy' Moran* John Hawkes, *Irene 'Big Red' Johnson* Rusty Schwimmer, *Ethel Shatford* Janet Wright, *Dale Murphy Jr* Hayden Tank, *Debra Murphy* Merle Kennedy, *Quentin, the old timer* Sandy Ward, *with* Cherry Jones, ChristopherMcDonald, Dash Mihok, Josh Hopkins, Todd Kimsey, Chris Palermo, Jennifer Sommerfield.
● *Dir* Wolfgang Petersen, *Pro* Petersen, Paula Weinstein and Gail Katz, *Ex Pro* Barry Levinson and Duncan Henderson, *Screenplay* Bill Wittliff, *Ph* John Seale, *Pro Des* William Sandell, *Ed* Richard Francis-Bruce, *M* James Horner, *Costumes* Erica Edell Phillips, *Visual effects* Stefen Fangmeier.

Warner/Baltimore Spring Creek Pictures/Radiant Prods-Warner.
129 mins. USA. 2000. Rel: 28 July 2000. Cert 12.

## Pitch Black ★★★¹/₂

An interstellar passenger vessel crash-lands on a desert planet illuminated by three suns. Among those on board are a morphine-addicted lawman, a psycho-killer prisoner (now loose), a dead captain, a devout Muslim and an effete and ineffectual English antiques dealer. A rookie female docking pilot has to assume command. And that's just for starters. The bad news is that an eclipse is imminent that will plunge the planet into total darkness and release thousands of blind, flying predatory creatures which track and devour their prey by sensing movement... Although basically another version of the *Ten Little Aliens* theme, *Pitch Black* delivers on several levels and is stylishly shot in an inventive MTV way (taut editing, percussive sound, edgy camerawork, desaturated colour). Furthermore, by virtue of having a non A-list cast, the film attains a greater credibility, realism and power. Much of the latter comes courtesy of the aptly named Vin Diesel who, as the optically altered killer, delivers a magnificently brutal performance. [*Tim Dry*]

● *Riddick* Vin Diesel, *Fry* Radha Mitchell, *Johns* Cole Hauser, *Imam* Keith David, *Paris* Lewis FitzGerald, *Shazza* Claudia Black, *Jack* Rhiana Griffith, *Zeke* John Moore, *with* Simon Burke, Les Chantery, Sam Sari.
● *Dir* David Twohy, *Pro* Tom Engelman, *Ex Pro* Ted Field, Scott Kroopf and Anthony Winley, *Screenplay* Twohy, Jim Wheat and Ken Wheat, *Ph* David Eggby, *Pro Des* Graham 'Grace' Walker, *Ed* Rick Shaine, *M* Graeme Revell, *Costumes* Anna Borghesi, *Sound* Tom Myers, *Visual effects* Peter Chiang, *Creature design* Patrick Tatopoulos.

*Above: After dark: Vin Diesel gets tough in David Twohy's stylish, inventive and edgy* Pitch Black *(from UIP)*

Gramercy Pictures/Interscope Communications/Pacific Film and Television Commission-UIP.
110 mins. USA/Australia. 2000. Rel: 10 November 2000. Cert 15.

## Play It to the Bone ★★

When the supporting contestants in a Mike Tyson championship both become indisposed, the fight promoters call on Cesar Dominguez and Vince Boudreau as a last-minute replacement. Sparring partners and best friends, Cesar and Vince have been waiting for such an opportunity all their professional lives. But first they must get from Los Angeles to Las Vegas, a journey by car that fuels a sudden competitive spirit. If only they can save their mounting hatred for each other for the fight they're being paid for... Considering that writer-director Ron Shelton has cornered the market in smart and funny sports comedies (*Bull Durham, White Men Can't Jump, Tin Cup*), *Play It to the Bone* is a disappointment. Much of the earlier banter between Banderas and Harrelson doesn't ring true

*Above:* *With friends*
*like these…: Antonio*
*Banderas takes it*
*on the chin from*
*Woody Harrelson*
*in Ron Shelton's*
*disappointing* Play
It to the Bone
*(from Redbus)*

(and falls flat) and the film's first half drags considerably. Only with the introduction of fresh characters (Lucy Liu is a stand-out as a hedonistic hitchhiker) and the pivotal setting of Vegas does the film swing into its stride, before flopping into anticlimax. Very minor Shelton.

● *Cesar Dominguez* Antonio Banderas, *Vince Boudreau* Woody Harrelson, *Grace Pasic* Lolita Davidovich, *Joe Domino* Tom Sizemore, *Lia* Lucy Liu, *Hank Goody* Robert Wagner, *Artie* Richard Masur, *Cappie Caplan* Willie Garson, *Rudy* Cylk Cozart, *with* Aida Turturro, Louie Leonardo, Jim Lampley, Steve Lawrence, George Foreman, Larry Merchant, Mike Tyson, Michael Buffer, Rod Stewart, Marc Ratner, Bob and Lovey Arum, Kevin Costner, Drew Carey, Tony Curtis, Natasha Gregson Wagner, Angel and Yvette Manfredy, Wesley Snipes, Jennifer Tilly, James Woods, Buddy Greco, Dick Williams, Gennifer Flowers.
● *Dir* and *Screenplay* Ron Shelton, *Pro* Stephen Chin, *Ex Pro* David Lester, *Assoc Pro* Kellie Davis, *Ph* Mark Vargo, *Pro Des* Claire Jenora Bowin, *Ed* Paul

Seydor, *M* Alex Wurman; songs performed by Jacintha, Fishbone, John Lee Hooker, Jimmy Rogers, Los Lobos, Martin Blasick, Linda Jackson, BB King and Joe Cocker, Ann Farnsworth, Moby, Kirk Franklin's Nu Nation Project etc, *Costumes* Kathryn Morrison, *Sound* Stephen Hunter Flick.

Touchstone Pictures/Shanghai'd Films-Redbus.
124 mins. USA. 1999. Rel: 22 September 2000. Cert 18.

## Pokémon The Movie 2000 ★¹/₂

Lawrence III, a square-jawed megalomaniac, attempts to take control of the world's weather system by capturing three seminal Pokémon creatures: the fire-bird Moltres, the lightning-bird Zapdos and the ice-bird Articuno. However, Larry hadn't reckoned on the intervention of Pokémon trainer Ash Ketchum, who turns out to be the 'Chosen One'... While the animation is possibly superior to the first film (*Pokémon – The First Movie*), the excitement and charm factor is still woefully absent. Still, Lawrence III makes an articulate if unthreatening villain (with the mandatory English accent) and there's a built-in caution about Pokémon collecting.

Accompanied by the risible 22-minute short *Pikachu's Rescue Adventure*.

● *Voices*: *Ash Ketchum/Satoshi's mother* Veronica Taylor, *Misty Williams/Jessie Morgan/* Rachael Lillis, *Tracey Sketcher* Addie Blaustein, *James Morgan* Eric Stuart, *with* Ed Paul, Michelle Goguen, Eric Rath, Neil Stewart, Stan Hart, Kayzie Rogers.
● *Dir* Kunihiko Yuyama, *Dir of English adaptation* Michael Haigney, *Pro* Norman J Grossfeld, Choji Yoshikawa, Yukako Matsusako and Takemoto Mori, *Screenplay* Takeshi Shudo, *Screenplay of English adaptation* Grossfeld and Haigney, *Art Dir* Katsuyoshi Kanemura, *Ed* Jay Film, *M* Ralph Schuckett and John Loeffler; songs performed by Donna Summer, Youngstown and Nobody's Angel, Weird Al Yankovic, Westlife.

4 Kids Entertainment/TV Tokyo/Creatures Inc./Game Freak Inc./Wizards of the Coast/Media Factory/Nintendo, etc-Warner.
80 mins. Japan/USA. 1999/2000. Rel: 22 December 2000. Cert PG.

## Pourquoi pas moi? – Why Not Me?
★★★¹/₂

This pleasingly unpretentious French comedy incorporating enjoyable musical interludes takes a while to hit its stride because writer-director Stéphane Giusti rushes in with a large cast of characters who need to be more clearly introduced. But it soon settles down with its story of a collective 'coming out', as a gay man and a group of lesbians working in a small publishing house in Barcelona break the news to their parents. The weekend chosen for this revelation produces surprises for the younger generation as well as for the parents, and the piece is entertaining and well played. Modest but engaging, the only people likely to be seriously displeased by it are homophobes. A Patsy Cline song provides the musical finale, but it's a 1948 rarity from Betty Hutton which is heard over the end credits. [*Mansel Stimpson*]

● *Camille* Amira Casar, *Eve* Julie Gayet, *Nick* Bruno Putzulu, *Ariane* Alexandra London, *Lili* Carmen Chaplin, *José, Eve's father* Johnny Hallyday, *Irène, Ariane's mother* Marie-France Pisier, *Josepha, Camille's mother* Brigitte Roüan, *Diane, Lili's mother* Assumpta Serna, *with* Elli Medeiros, Vittoria Scognamiglio, Jean-Claude Dauphin.
● *Dir* and *Screenplay* Stéphane Giusti, *Pro* Caroloine Adrian and Marie Masmonteil, *Assoc Pro* Denis Carot, *Ph* Antoine Roch, *Pro Des* Rosa Ros, *Ed* Catherine Schwartz, *M* various; songs performed by Vittoria Scognamiglio, The Isley Brothers, Alexi Brothers, Patsy Cline, Musique, Eddy & Dan, Lisa Stansfield, Betty Haman etc, *Costumes* Catherine Rigault.

Elzevir Films/M6 Films/Glozel/Maestranza Films/ Sogedasa/Athena Films/Sofinergie 4/ Sofinergie 5/Canal Plus/Eurimages-millivres multimedia.
94 mins. France/Spain/Switzerland. 1998. Rel: 24 November 2000. Cert 15.

## The Princess and the Warrior – Der Krieger und die Kaiserin ★★★★¹/₂

Wuppertal, Germany; today. In a nondescript area of western Germany, Sissi works as a live-in nurse at the Birkenhof psychiatric clinic. Then, in a freak road accident, she is knocked down by an oil tanker and is rescued by a stranger who sheds tears as he enables her to breathe. On release from hospital, Sissi resolves to find out the identity of her saviour and to see if he is the man for her... A marked change in direction from the frenetic MTV-style of his runaway hit *Run Lola Run*, Tom Tykwer has, with his fourth film, fashioned a leisurely paced but densely plotted fable that owes as much to Antonioni as it does to Wenders and Herzog. At once extremely stylish yet profoundly surreal, the film casts a hypnotic spell even as it introduces some unexpected moments of humour and several scenes of wonderfully sustained suspense. Tykwer is also to be commended for creating a totally original story in which anything might, and frequently does, happen. The piano-driven score is another major plus, as is the final, superbly extended shot.

● *Simone 'Sissi'* Franka Potente, *Bodo Riehmer* Benno Fürmann, *Walter* Joachim Kròl, *Sissi's mother* Marita Breuer, *Schmatt* Jürgen Tarrach, *Steini* Lars

Rudolph, *Otto* Melchior Beslon, *Maria* Sybille Jacqueline Schedwill, *with* Ludger Pistor, Steffen Schult, Rolf Dennemann, Gottfried Breitfuss, Natja Brunckhorst.
● *Dir* and *Screenplay* Tom Tykwer, *Pro* Stefan Arndt and Maria Köpf, *Ph* Frank Griebe, *Pro Des* Uli Hanisch, *Ed* Mathilde Bonnefoy, *M* Tykwer, Johnny Kilmek and Reinhold Heil; songs performed by Brenda Lee, Arab Strap and Cora Bissett, Urmas Sisask etc, *Costumes* Monika Jacobs, *Sound* Dirk Jacobs.

X Filme creative Pool, etc-Pathé.
135 mins. Germany. 2000. Rel: 29 June 2001. Cert 15.

## Proof of Life ★★★★

In South America to construct a dam to ease local flooding, engineer Peter Bowman is consumed by his mission. It's causing a strain on his marriage and one morning he leaves for work without saying goodbye to his wife, Alice. Shortly afterwards, he is abducted by guerrillas and held to ransom for $3 million. With her husband cold-shouldered by his own company, Alice can only invest her trust in a stranger from London, a professional kidnapping negotiator... Strangely ridiculed by the press on its release, perhaps because of the romantic baggage brought with it by the Meg Ryan-Russell Crowe interface, *Proof of Life* is actually an extremely well-crafted, pertinent and heart-thumping drama. Inspired by real events and an article published in *Vanity Fair*, the film lifts the lid on the covert world of professional kidnapping and the secret organisations primed to combat it. With sterling performances from Ryan and Crowe, some deft storytelling and spectacular photography of Ecuador's rainforest, this is what film drama is all about. And with the added *frisson* of the ambiguous relationship between Alice and her husband's hunky rescuer, the film adds yet another string to its emotional bow.

● *Alice Bowman* Meg Ryan, *Terry Thorne* Russell Crowe, *Peter Louis Bowman* David Morse, *Janis Goodman* Pamela Reed, *Dino* David Caruso, *Ted Fellner* Anthony Heald, *Jerry* Stanley Anderson, *Eric Kessler* Gottfried John, *Wyatt* Alun Armstrong, *Ivy* Margo Martindale, *Fernandez* Mario Ernesto Sanchez, *with* Michael Kitchen, Pietro Sibille, Vicky Hernandez, Norma Martinez, Diego Trujillo, Aristoteles Picho, Sarahi Echeverria, Rowena King, Michael Byrne, Merlin Hanbury-Tenison, Stefan Gryff.
● *Dir* Taylor Hackford, *Pro* Hackford and Charles Mulvehill, *Ex Pro* Steven Reuther and Tony Gilroy, *Screenplay* Gilroy, inspired by William Prochnau's article `Adventures In the Ransom Trade' published in *Vanity Fair*, and by the book *Long March to Freedom* by Thomas Hargrove, *Ph* Slawomir Idziak,

Above: A dog's life: Greg McLane and Chris Beattie in Mark Herman's funny and touching Purely Belter (from FilmFour)

*Pro Des* Bruno Rubeo, *Ed* John Smith and Sheldon Kahn, *M* Danny Elfman; 'I'll Be Your Lover, Too' sung by Van Morrison, *Costumes* Ruth Myers, *weight loss advisor* Dr Paul McAuley.

Castle Rock/Bel-Air Entertainment/Anvil Films-Warner. 135 mins. USA/UK. 2000. Rel: 2 March 2001. Cert 15.

## Purely Belter ★★★★

Newcastle; today. In the lexicon of Northern English, 'purely belter' means 'so dead good' that there isn't a word to describe it. Best friends Gerry, 15, and Sewell, 17, don't ask for much, but they would give everything just to see their football team, Newcastle United, play. So, sacrificing such daily niceties as booze, cigarettes and glue, they start saving up enough money to buy themselves a season ticket. But they need £500 *each*, so their ploys to raise money quickly transgress the law... Yet another portrait of the oppressed underclass of contemporary Britain (afflicted by crime, unemployment and parental abuse), *Purely Belter* manages to be funny and touching without resorting to mawkishness. Armed with two extraordinary performances from his young leads, writer-director Herman (*Brassed Off, Little Voice*) has fashioned an engaging odyssey that is authentic and heart-breaking but never down-

beat. With an enormous compassion and a wilful resolve not to cop out ('Life is shite but it could be worse'), *Purely Belter* reinstates one's faith in the British cinema.

● *Mrs McCarten* Charlie Hardwick, *Mr McCarten* Tim Healy, *Mr Sewell* Roy Hudd, *Mr Caird* Kevin Whately, *Gerry McCarten* Chris Beattie, *Sewell* Greg McLane, *Clare* Tracy Whitwell, *Gemma* Jody Baldwin, *Bridget* Kerry Ann Christiansen, *Mrs Brabin* Sue Elliott, *Maureen* Val McLane, *Ginga* Willie Ross, *himself* Alan Shearer, *with* Daniel James Lake, Tracey Wilkinson, Libby Davison, Adam Fogerty, Charlie Richmond, Chris Wiper, Adam Moran, Brendan Healy, *Rusty the dog* Ben.
● *Dir* and *Screenplay* Mark Herman, from the novel *The Season Ticket* by Jonathan Tulloch, *Pro* Elizabeth Karlsen, *Ex Pro* Stephen Woolley, *Line Pro* Kathy Lord, *Ph* Andy Collins, *Pro Des* Don Taylor, *Ed* Michael Ellis, *M* Ian Broudie and Michael Gibbs; songs performed by Tim Healy, Gabrielle, John Lennon and Yoko Ono, Wizzard, Shed Seven, The Animalhouse, Bleachin', The Prodigy, Charlie Hardwick, Ian Broudie and Terry Hall, *Costumes* Jill Taylor.

FilmFour/Mumbo Jumbo-Film Four.
99 mins. UK. 2000. Rel: 3 November 2000. Cert 15.

## Quills ★★★¹⁄₂

Paris/Charenton; 1794-1814. Adapted by Doug Wright from his own play, *Quills* is an articulate and full-blooded account of what might have occurred within the walls of the Charenton lunatic asylum (in western France) where the Marquis de Sade was held captive. Supplied with all the luxuries that a man of his aristocratic station was heir to, the novelist and playwright was permitted to continue his depraved writing in order to cleanse 'the toxins of his soul.' However, due to the enormous public demand for his degenerate literature, Sade was able to smuggle out his work courtesy of a star-struck chambermaid. Following the publication of the scandalous *Justine*, Napoleon himself ordered the ruthless physician Dr Royer-Collard to purge the Marquis of his madness... Besides being a fascinating look at an extraordinary man (played by Geoffrey Rush with his customary dementia), *Quills* offers plenty of food for thought regarding artistic freedom and oppression mirrored in the continuing debate over censorship today. In the end, it is the madmen themselves who are roused to violence by the Marquis' words, a fact that holds enormous contemporary resonance. FYI: Sade was previously played by Patrick Magee, Klaus Kinski, Michel Piccoli and Keir Dullea in four films between the years 1967 and 1969, and then again by Daniel Auteuil in last year's *Sade*.

● *Donatien Alphonse François, Comte de Sade* Geoffrey Rush, *Madeleine* Kate Winslet, *Abbé Coulmier* Joaquin Phoenix, *Dr Royer-Collard* Michael Caine, *Madame LeClerc* Billie Whitelaw, *Delbené* Patrick Malahide, *Simone Royer-Collard* Amelia Warner, *Renée Pelagie* Jane Menelaus, *Prouix* Stephen Moyer, *Valcour* Tony Pritchard, *Cleante* Michael Jenn, *Bouchon* Stephen Marcus, *Charlotte* Elizabeth Berrington, *Napoleon Bonaparte* Ron Cook, *with* Danny Babington, George Yiasoumi, Edward Tudor-Pole, Harry Jones, Bridget McConnel, Pauline McLynn, Rebecca Palmer, Daniel Ainsleigh, Terry O'Neill, Carol MacReady, *girl on guillotine* Diana Morrison.
● *Dir* Philip Kaufman, *Pro* Julia Chasman, Nick Wechsler and Peter Kaufman, *Ex Pro* Des McAnuff, Sandra Schulberg and Rudolf Wiesmeier, *Co-Pro* Mark Huffam, *Screenplay* Doug Wright, *Ph* Rogier Stoffers, *Pro Des* Martin Childs, *Ed* Peter Boyle, *M* Stephen Warbeck, *Costumes* Jacqueline West.

Fox Searchlight Pictures/Industry Entertainment/Walrus & Associates/Hollywood Partners-Fox.
124 mins. USA. 2000. Rel: 19 January 2001. Cert 18.

*Above: By the book: Joaquin Phoenix and Kate Winslet in Philip Kaufman's articulate and provocative Quills (from Twentieth Century Fox)*

## Rage ★★¹/₂

Peckham, South London; today. 'Rage' is the moniker Jamie adopts for his rap persona and 'rage' is what he feels about his hopeless life stacking shelves and living in a run-down estate. But he is determined to find the £4000 he needs to cut his first record with his friends Thomas, a white DJ, and Godwin, a talented black pianist. Of course, crime offers the quickest solution... Marking the feature-length directorial debut of the Nigerian-born Newton I Aduaka, *Rage* trawls through familiar waters and wears its non-existent budget on its sleeve. Having said that, Aduaka has coaxed some very fine performances from his largely unknown cast (OK, so Shaun Parkes did make a vivid impression in *Human Traffic*) and knows how to move his camera for dramatic effect. But there is a naïveté and confusion of intent that sits uncomfortably with too many clichés about what it means to be black, underprivileged and angry in contemporary Britain. [*Ewen Brownrigg*]

● *Jamie* (aka 'Rage') Fraser Ayres, *Godwin* (aka 'G') Shaun Parkes, *Thomas* (aka 'T') John Pickard, *Marcus* Shango Baku, *Pin* Wale Ojo, *Ellen, Godwin's mother* Alison Rose, *Lola* Rebecca Ella, *Cindy* Sian Adams, *Shona* Landy Oshinowa, *Razor* Cornell John, *Razz* Norman Roberts, *Thomas' mother* Sheridan MacDonald, *Godwin's father* Ewart James Walters.
● *Dir* and *Screenplay* Newton I Aduaka, *Pro* Aduaka and Maria-Elena L'Abbate, *Ph* Carlos Arango, *Pro Des* Kathryn Bates, *Tone* Emblemsvaag and Charlotte Hanson, *Ed* Marcela Cuneo, *M* various; songs performed by Andre Gurov, Styly Cee, Mao, Mark B, Ming, Swollen Members, Redhed, Def Tex, Third Order, DJ Vadim, Son, The Isolationists, DJ Food, Fraser Ayres, UK Kartel etc, *Costumes* Julian Day, *Sound* Tim Parker.

Granite FilmWorks-Metrodome.
96 mins. UK. 2000. Rel: 12 January 2001. Cert 15.

## Ready to Rumble ★

Continuing the Hollywood trend for milking comedy out of mentally arrested losers, *Ready to Rumble* wrestles to reach a new low. Here, David Arquette (brother of Patricia and Rosanna) and Scott Caan (son of James) play a pair of dumb and dumbers who empty Porta-Potties for a living. Deprived of any romantic distraction, they focus their energy on the stars of World Championship Wrestling, whom Caan likens to 'heroes of history.' When their favourite bone-breaker is thrashed in a local contest, they resolve to restore the latter's self-esteem and get him in shape in time for a Vegas rematch. Sloppily written and poorly performed, this is not only unfunny but inflicts more pain than any WCW 'fighter' could hope to mete out in the ring. [*Ewen Brownrigg*]

● *Gordie Boggs* David Arquette, *Jimmy King* Oliver Platt, *Sean Dawkins* Scott Caan, *himself* Bill Goldberg, *Sasha* Rose McGowan, *himself* Diamond Dallas Page, *Titus Sinclair* Joe Pantoliano, *Sal Bandini* Martin Landau, *Mr Boggs* Richard Lineback, *with* Chris Owen, Steve `Sting' Borden, Caroline Rhea, Tait Smith, Ellen Albertini Dow, Kathleen Freeman, Lewis Arquette, Ahmet Zappa, Bam Bam Bigelow, Gorgeous George, Juventud Guerrero, Van Hammer, Booker T, Sid Vicious.
● *Dir* Brian Robbins, *Pro* Bobby Newmyer and Jeffrey Silver, *Ex Pro* Steven Reuther and Mike Tollin, *Co-Pro* Herb Gains and Scott Strauss, *Assoc Pro* Susan E Novick, *Screenplay* Steven Brill, *Ph* Clark Mathis, *Pro Des* Jaymes Hinkle, *Ed* Ned Bastille, *M* George S Clinton; Wagner, Aaron Copland; songs performed by Starling, Lit, Mötley Crüe, Dweezil Zappa, Run-DMC, Van Halen, Ahmet Zappa, The Commodores, FAT, POD, House of Pain, Kool & The Gang, Bee Gees, Martin Denny, Tex Ritter, Kid Rock, Inner Circle, Bif Naked, Ol' Dirty Bastard, DJ Hurricane and Scott Weiland etc, *Costumes* Carol Ramsey.

Warner/Bel-Air Entertainment/Outlaw/Tollin/Robbins Prods-Warner.
106 mins. USA. 2000. Rel: 24 November 2000. Cert 15.

## Red Planet ★★★

Outer space/Mars; 2050. With the Earth virtually depleted of its natural resources, a plan to oxygenate its nearest neighbour has been put into action. However, when the Mars Terraforming Project fails, a group of elite astronauts are dispatched to investigate the problem in the first manned expedition to Mars. And, as the mission's chief science officer predicts, 'the universe is full of surprises'... Arriving half a year after *Mission to Mars*, *Red Planet* was due for a bumpy ride. With less fleshed-out characters than the former (Val Kilmer is in particularly uncharismatic mode) and a general lack of humour, the film is a largely anodyne trip. However, there are some intriguing concepts at work (colonisation through the seeding of oxygen-producing algae), plenty of nifty gimmicks (such as a flexy navigational map) and a spectacular depiction of the planet itself (recreated in the deserts of Jordan and Australia). Good, too, is Carrie-Anne Moss in the Sigourney Weaver school of ballsy, creditable heroines. When the latter says, 'I don't mind dying, I just hate being alone,' she makes it a plausible sentiment.

● *Mechanical Systems Engineer Robby Gallagher* Val Kilmer, *Dr Quinn Burchenal* Tom Sizemore, *Lt Commander Kate Bowman* Carrie-Anne Moss, *Air Force Captain Ted Santen* Benjamin Bratt, *Dr Chip Pettengil* Simon Baker, *Chief Science Officer Bud Chantilas* Terence Stamp, *voice of Houston* Bob Neill.
● *Dir* Antony Hoffman, *Pro* Mark Canton, Bruce

Berman and Jorge Saralegui, *Ex Pro* Charles J D Schlissel and Andrew Mason, *Screenplay* Jonathan Lemkin and Channing Gibson, from a story by Chuck Pfarrer, *Ph* Peter Suschitzky, *Pro Des* Owen Paterson, *Ed* Robert K Lambert and Dallas S Puett, *M* Graeme Revell, *Costumes* Kym Barrett, *Sound* Dane A Davis.

Warner/Village Roadshow/NPV Entertainment-Warner. 106 mins. USA/Australia. 2000. Rel: 1 December 2000. Cert 12.

## Remember the Titans ★★★¹/₂

TC Williams High School, Alexandria, Virginia; 1971. When a white and black school are integrated, Herman Boone, a black coach from North Carolina, is brought in to groom the prized football team, the TC Williams High Titans. While the move is nothing but a gesture, Boone takes his appointment extremely seriously, although ingrained prejudice and bureaucratic red tape conspire to make his job almost impossible... As an ethnic citizen of the US, it stands to reason that director Boaz Yakin would have a passion for the subjects of race and American football. Here, he takes a formulaic story – albeit based on fact – and with the failsafe ingredients of morale-boosting speeches, male bonding, soaring music, lashings of testosterone and classic songs, has fashioned an extremely watchable movie. But it's the quality of the performances that separates this from the run-of-the-mill sports programmer, from Denzel Washington's uncompromising coach and Will Patton's man of principle to an extraordinary turn from the young Hayden Panettiere as Patton's football-centric, tough-as-boots nine-year-old daughter. In the end, even those unfamiliar with the rules of American football will find it hard not to get caught up in the excitement of it all.

● *Coach Herman Boone* Denzel Washington, *Coach Bill Yoast* Will Patton, *Julius Campbell* aka 'Big Ju' Wood Harris, *Gerry Bertier* Ryan Hurst, *Petey Jones* Donald Faison, *Jerry Harris* aka 'The Rev' Craig Kirkwood, *Lewis Lastik* Ethan Suplee, *Ronnie Bass* aka 'Sunshine' Kip Pardue, *Sheryl Yoast* Hayden Panettiere, *Carol Boone* Nicole Ari Parker, *Emma Hoyt* Kate Bosworth, *Blue Stanton* Earl C Poitier, with Ryan Gosling, Burgess Jenkins, Neal Ghant, David Jefferson Jr, Gregalan Williams, Brett Rice.
● *Dir* Boaz Yakin, *Pro* Jerry Bruckheimer and Chad Oman, *Ex Pro* Mike Stenson and Michael Flynn, *Screenplay* Gregory Allen Howard, *Ph* Philippe Rousselot, *Pro Des* Deborah Evans, *Ed* Michael Tronick, *M* Trevor Rabin; songs performed by Buddy Miles, Marvin Gaye and Tammi Terrell, Buck Owens, Norman Greenbaum, The Sea Shells, Leon Russell, The Temptations, Cat Stevens, Ike & Tina Turner, Creedence Clearwater Revival, Eric Burdon and WAR, Steam, Shocking Blue, The Hollies, James Taylor etc, *Costumes* Judy Ruskin Howell.

Walt Disney Pictures/Jerry Bruckheimer Films-Buena Vista. 113 mins. USA. 2000. Rel: 9 February 2001. Cert PG.

## Requiem For a Dream ★★★★

Brighton Beach, Brooklyn, New York; the present. Since her beloved son Harry left home, Sara Goldfarb lives on her own in a small apartment eating chocolates and watching TV. Periodically, Harry turns up to take the TV in order to pay for his heroin habit, a dependence he shares with his beautiful girlfriend, Marion, and his best friend, Tyrone. Sara then buys the TV back. Then, out of the blue, Sara receives a telephone call to say that she is to appear on a national TV show. Determined to fit into her favourite red dress, the widow embarks on a ruthless, pill-popping diet regimen... Having demonstrated his stark originality with the $60,000 mathematical mind-trip *Pi*, writer-director Darren Aronofsky takes on the more familiar subject of drug addiction with this, his second movie. Collaborating with Hubert Selby Jr on the adaptation of the latter's novel, Aronofsky reaffirms his status as one of America's most distinctive filmmakers, creating a chamber piece that artfully penetrates the psyche of its four characters. Utilising the process of split-screen, speeded-up film, hallucinogenic effects and a score that recalls the electronic seduction of Michael Nyman, Aronofsky has fashioned a stylish, dream-like fable that escalates into nightmare. He has also secured an emotionally numbing performance from Ellen Burstyn and good ones from Connelly, Wayans and Leto, tipping the drama off the edge into madness. A film that has the courage of its own convictions, *Requiem For a Dream* is one of the most potent and disturbing indictments of drug abuse ever committed to celluloid.

● *Sara Goldfarb* Ellen Burstyn, *Harry Goldfarb* Jared Leto, *Marion Silver* Jennifer Connelly, *Tyrone C Love* Marlon Wayans, *Tappy Tibbons* Christopher McDonald, *Ada* Louise Lasser, *Arnold, the shrink* Sean Gullette, *Rae* Marcia Jean Kurtz, *Mrs Pearlman* Janet Sarno, *Mr Rabinowitz* Mark Margolis, *Dr Pill* Peter Maloney, *Alice* Aliya Campbell, *Big Tim* Keith David, *Southern doctor* Dylan Baker, with Suzanne Shepherd, Joanne Gordon, Charlotte Aronofsky, Abraham Aronofsky, Jimmie Ray Weeks, *laughing guard* Hubert Selby Jr.
● *Dir* Darren Aronofsky, *Pro* Eric Watson and Palmer West, *Ex Pro* Nick Wechsler, Beau Flynn and Stefan Simchowitz, *Screenplay* Aronofsky and Hubert Selby Jr, *Ph* Matthew Libatique, *Pro Des* James Chinlund, *Ed* Jay Rabinowitz, *M* Clint Mansell; string quartets performed by Kronos Quartet, *Costumes* Laura Jean Shannon, *Sound* Brian Emrich.

Artisan Entertainment/Thousand Words/Sibling/ Protozoa/Industry and Bandeira Entertainment/ Sundance-Momentum Pictures. 101 mins. USA. 2000. Rel: 19 January 2001. Cert 18.

## Ring – Ringu ★★★¹/₂

Japan; the present. Two teenage schoolgirls discuss the urban legend about a certain video that, once watched, is followed up by a mysterious phone call announcing that you have one week left to live. Investigating the inexplicable death of one of the girls, TV reporter Reiko Asakawa hears of the myth and decides to watch the video herself. She then receives an unexpected telephone call... Where the American horror film tends to play with the viewer's gut, its Japanese equivalent messes with the mind. This ingenious, unsettling and commendably original psychological thriller delves into territory previously explored by *Videodrome* and *Candyman*, but replaces the gore with a chilling placidity and naturalism. Like Cronenberg reinvented by Ozu, it transmutes its warning of the ills of violent videos into a riveting take on the 'sins of the fathers.'

● *Reiko Asakawa* Matsushima Nanako, *Ryuji Takayama* Sanada Hiroyuki, *Mai Takano* Nakatani Miki, *Masami Kurahashi* Sato Hitomi, *Tomoko Oishi* Yûko Takeuchi, *Masami Kurahashi* Hitomi Sato.
● *Dir* Nakata Hideo, *Pro* Shinya Kawai, Takashige Ichise and Takenori Sentô, *Ex Pro* Masato Hara, *Screenplay* Takahashi Hiroshi, from the novel by Suzuki Koji, *Ph* Hayashi Junichiro, *Pro Des* Iwao Saitô, *Ed* Takahashi Nobuyuki, *M* Kawai Kenji.

Omega Project Inc./Kadokawa/Pony Canyon/Toho/
Imagica/Ace Pictures, etc-ICA.
95 mins. Japan. 1997. Rel: 18 August 2000. No Cert.

## The Road Home ★★★

Sanhetun, north China. Returning to the village of his youth for the funeral of his father, Luo Yusheng discovers that his mother wants an old-fashioned ceremony. However, with most of the young men now living in the city, such a convention – in which the coffin is carried rather than driven from the hospital – proves untenable. But then Luo recalls his parents' ineffably romantic courtship, played out at a time when such attention to detail had a significant resonance... A little more Hollywood-friendly than most Chinese films that reach these shores, *The Road Home* is pretty and poignant if not exactly profound. Indeed, with its gushing music and flashbacks bathed in resplendent colour, this is a surprisingly sentimental work from the director of *Not One Less* and *Raise the Red Lantern*. Be that as it may, Zhang's attention to the little things is most rewarding while Zhang ZiYi – who plays Jen in *Crouching, Tiger, Hidden Dragon* – substantiates her position as a major rising star. [*Ewen Brownrigg*]

● *the young Zhao Di* Zhang ZiYi, *Luo Yusheng* Sun Honglei, *Luo Changyu* Zheng Hao, *the elderly Zhao Di* Zhao Yuelin, *grandmother* Li Bin, *elderly mayor* Chang Guifa, *young mayor* Sung Wencheng, *with* Liu Qi, Ji Bo, Zhang Zhongxi.

● *Dir* Zhang Yimou, *Pro* Zhao Yu, *Ex Pro* Zhang Weiping, *Screenplay* Bao Shi, *Ph* Hou Yong, *Pro Des* Cao Jiuping, *Ed* Zhai Ru, *M* San Bao, *Costumes* Dong Huamiao.

Columbia Pictures/Guangxi Film Studios/Beijing New Picture Distribution-Columbia TriStar.
89 mins. China. 1999. Rel: 13 October 2000. Cert U.

## The Road to El Dorado ★★★★

After winning a map to El Dorado in a crap shoot, the endearing rapscallions Tulio and Miguel end up as prisoners of the Spanish conqueror Hernando Cortes. However, with the help of a spirited horse, they escape Cortes' ship and find their way to the mythical city of gold... Proving yet again that DreamWorks is Disney's equal in the animation department, this hugely enjoyable romp succeeds on every level – and then some. Kevin Kline and Kenneth Branagh make a wonderful partnership as the mischievous Tulio and Miguel (erasing any unsavoury memories of their collaboration on *Wild Wild West*), while Rosie Perez's sultry, streetwise 'Chel' is not the sort of heroine you come across often in family cartoons (even though her thighs scream out for liposuction). Add the rousing songs of Elton John and Tim Rice, some breathtaking vistas of South American jungle and a genuinely witty script, and you have a slice of entertainment that really does capture that elusive element of 'adventure'. PS. There are some delicious jabs at the twee heritage of Disney, not least the unexpected appearance of a seagull (surely modelled on Scuttle from *The Little Mermaid*), who instantly ends up as shark lunch.

● Voices: *Tulio* Kevin Kline, *Miguel* Kenneth Branagh, *Chel* Rosie Perez, *Tzekel-Kan* Armand Assante, *The Chief* Edward James Olmos, *Hernando Cortes* Jim Cummings, *Altivo* Frank Welker, *Zaragosa* Tobin Bell, *with* Duncan Marjoribanks, Elijah Chiang, Cyrus Shaki-Khan; *narrator* Elton John.
● *Dirs* Don Paul and Éric 'Bibo' Bergeron, *Pro* Bonne Radford and Brooke Breton, *Ex Pro* Jeffrey Katzenberg, *Co-Ex Pro* Bill Damaschke, *Screenplay* Ted Elliott and Terry Rossio, *Pro Des* Christian Schellewald, *Art* Raymond Zibach, Paul Lasaine and Wendell Luebbe, *Ed* John Carnochan and Dan Molina, *M* Hans Zimmer and John Powell; *songs*: Elton John (*music*), Tim Rice (*lyrics*), *Digital supervisor* Dan Philips.

DreamWorks-UIP.
90 mins. USA. 2000. Rel: 4 August 2000. Cert U.

## Road Trip ★★★

Josh and Tiffany have been dating forever, so when they go their separate ways to college – she to Texas, he to New York – they keep in constant touch by phone. Then, when Tiffany stops returning Josh's calls, he succumbs to a night of glorious seduction with Beth. But Beth videoed their nookie and Josh's roommate has popped the wrong cassette into Tiffany's jiffy bag. So can Josh get to Texas in time to intercept the incriminating package? … The latest in a string of gross-out comedies, *Road Trip* achieves a few firsts of its own (the prostate-stimulated orgasm springs to mind), but manages a little bit more. For the most part avoiding the humiliation of its characters, the comedy presents a cross-section of likeable and credible college types, while even the bit-part actors get their turn in the spotlight (such as Andy Dick's sarcastically disinterested hotel manager, Mary Lynn Rajskub's no-nonsense blind girl, Edmund Lyndeck's Viagra-empowered geriatric). There's also a splendid turn from MTV's Tom Green as the dryly manic tour guide of Ithaca University and a storyline that's strong enough to keep the interest when the gags aren't making you gag (such as Green popping a live mouse into his mouth). Pure summer madness.

● *Josh* Breckin Meyer, *E L* Seann William Scott, *Beth* Amy Smart, *Rubin* Paulo Costanzo, *Kyle Edwards* D J Qualls, *Tiffany* Rachel Blanchard, *Jacob* Anthony Rapp, *Earl Edwards* Fred Ward, *Barry Manilow* Tom Green, *sperm bank nurse* Marla Sucharetza, *with* Andy Dick, Ethan Suplee, Horatio Sanz, Rhoda Griffis, Ellen Albertini Dow, Edmund Lyndeck, Jessica Cauffiel, Kohl Sudduth, Wendell B Harris Jr, Rini Bell, Jaclyn DeSantis, Mary Lynn Rajskub, Cleo King, *foot lover* Todd Phillips.
● *Dir* Todd Phillips, *Pro* Daniel Goldberg and Joe Medjuck, *Ex Pro* Ivan Reitman and Tom Pollock, *Screenplay* Phillips and Scot Armstrong, *Ph* Mark Irwin, *Pro Des* Clark Hunter, *Ed* Sheldon Kahn, *M* Mike Simpson; songs performed by Gordon Henderson & His Midnight Music Makers, Breckin Meyer, Tom Green, The KGB, Black Eyed Peas, Jungle Brothers, Ash, eels, Jessica Andrews, Randy Travis, Ween, Bloodstone, E40, Run-DMC, Minnie Riperton, Kid Rock, Twisted Sister, Groove Armada, The Jon Spencer Blues Explosion, Supergrass, Buckcherry, *Costumes* Peggy Stamper.

DreamWorks/Montecito Picture Company-UIP.
94 mins. USA. 2000. Rel: 13 October 2000. Cert 15.

## Romeo Must Die ★¹/₂

Oakland, San Francisco Bay; the present. In cahoots with a white businessman to secure a major waterfront property, the heads of rival black and Chinese gangs are eager to get along. However, when the son of Chinese crime lord Ch'u Sing is found strung up by his neck, dissent starts brewing. Further complications ensue when the victim's brother, Han Sing, and the daughter of the black crime lord, Trish, strike up a friendship... Relocating *Romeo and Juliet* to contemporary San Francisco (courtesy of Vancouver), *Romeo Must Die* is a routine martial arts endeavour replete with squandered

opportunities. While the 'blacks' and Chinese stand in for the Capulets and Montagues, little is developed from this unusual cultural friction, whereas the fights themselves are stylised beyond any hope of excitement. Jet Li himself is an engaging presence but is given little to do, while his scenes with Aaliyah are sadly lacking in pheromonal activity. Laughably, both leads are credited with an acting coach, although neither gleaned much from their tutelage.

● *Han Sing* Jet Li, *Trish O'Day* Aaliyah, *Mac* Isaiah Washington, *Kai Sing* Russell Wong, *Silk* DMX, *Isaak O'Day* Delroy Lindo, *Ch'u Sing* Henry O, *Colin O'Day* D.B. Woodside, *Vincent Roth* Edoardo Ballerini, *Maurice* Anthony Anderson, *with* Matthew Harrison, Terry Chen, Fatima Robinson.
● *Dir* Andrzej Bartkowiak, *Pro* Joel Silver and Jim Van Wyck, *Ex Pro* Dan Cracchiolo, *Co-Pro* Warren Carr, *Screenplay* Eric Bernt and John Farrell, from a story by Mitchell Kapner and William Shakespeare, *Ph* Glen MacPherson, *Pro Des* Michael Bolton, *Ed* Derek G Brechin, *M* Stanley Clarke and Timbaland; songs performed by DMX, Chanté Moore, Confidential, Fatboy Slim, Groove Armada and Gram'ma Funk, Aaliyah, Destiny's Child, The Crystal Method, Joe, Timbaland and Magoo, Ohio Players, Dave Bing and Lil' Mo etc, *Costumes* Sandra J Blackie, *Sound* Dane A Davis.

Warner/Silver Pictures-Warner.
114 mins. USA. 2000. Rel: 13 October 2000. Cert 15.

## Room to Rent ★¹/₂

For some reason, Ali Radwan, an Egyptian immigrant and aspiring screenwriter, wants to stay in London in spite of the rain and poor job prospects. Given 12 weeks to leave the country, he struggles to find a wife, but cannot come up with the money to pay for a bride of convenience... It's not often that Egyptian directors make films set in Britain and Khaled El Hagar has blown a wonderful opportunity to lift the lid on the North African community in London. Instead, he has created a banal and charmless comedy that sits uncomfortably in the company of such efforts as *Foreign Body* and *Guru in 7* detailing the 'Adventures of an Immigrant in England'. Rich with stereotypes, hackneyed situations and terrible performances (Juliette Lewis as a Marilyn Monroe wannabe), the film might have ended on a promising note had it not flown in the face of implausibility.

● *Ali Radwan* Saïd Taghmaoui, *Linda* Juliette Lewis, *Mark* Rupert Graves, *Sarah Stevenson* Anna Massey, *Ahmed aka Farouk* Karim Belkhadra, *Vivienne* Clémentine Cèlariè, *Pedro* Louis Hammond, *Mr Paul* Chris Langham, *Mark's father* Robert Lang, *Sam* Richard Lumsden, *Martin* Roger Frost, *young Sarah* Lisa Kay, *with* Flaminia Cinque, Shobu Kapur, Badia Obaid, Christopher Simon,

Kevin Wainwright, Ian Puleston Davies.
● *Dir* Khaled El Hagar, *Pro* Ildiko Kemeny, *Ex Pro* Robert Buckler and George Benayoun, *Co-Pro* Marina Gefter and Amanda Mackenzie Stuart, *Screenplay* El Hagar and Mackenzie Stuart, *Ph* Romain Winding, *Pro Des* Eli Bø, *Ed* John Richards, *M* Safy Boutella; songs performed by Malika Abbes, Safy Boutella, Mehdi Askeur, Juliette Lewis, Oum Kalsoum, Lisa Kay etc, *Costumes* Janice Rider, *Choreography* Juliette Lewis.

Film Consortium/Canal Plus/Renegade Films/Ima Films/FilmFour/Arts Council of England-Pathé.
95 mins. UK/France. 2000. Rel: 22 June 2001. Cert 15.

## Rugrats in Paris: The Movie ★★¹/₂

When Stu Pickles is summoned to Paris to help fix a design fault on his giant Reptar appearing at a theme park, he takes along his wife, the kids and his buddy Charles and the latter's toddler, Chuckie. Recently widowed, Charles falls for the romantic overtures of the conniving Coco La Bouche, who needs an instant kid to ensnare her promotion as overseer of EuroReptarland. And she finds a wily ally in Angelica, Stu's self-seeking eldest daughter... With the first film grossing over $100 million in the US alone, it was inevitable that a follow-up would not be long in coming. But, like the *Pokémon* sequel, this is actually better than the original, with a stronger storyline, more vivid characters and some choice film references (Spike, emulating Disney's Tramp, ends up being stuck to a French poodle with Mozzarella cheese). However, the crude animation, some unintelligible dialogue and a preoccupation with bodily functions will hardly endear this to those not already entranced by the TV series.

● Voices: *Coco La Bouche* Susan Sarandon, *Jean-Claude* John Lithgow, *Lulu Pickles* Debbie Reynolds, *Tommy Pickles* E G Daily, *Chuckie Finster* Christine Cavanaugh, *Phil, Betty* and *Lil Deville* Kath Soucie, *Angelica Pickles* Cheryl Chase, *Dil Pickles* Tara Charendoff, *Didi Pickles* Melanie Chartoff, *Stu Pickles* Jack Riley, *Chas Finster* and *Drew Pickles* Michael Bell, *Charlotte Pickles* Tress MacNeille, *Kira Watanabe* Julia Kato, *Kimi Watanabe* Dionne Quan, *Princess* Lisa McClowry, with Tim Curry, Casey Kasem, Cree Summer Franck, Joe Alasky, Phil Proctor, Mako.
● *Dir* Stig Bergqvist and Paul Demeyer, *Pro* Arlene Klasky and Gabor Csupo, *Ex Pro* Albie Hecht, Julia Pistor, Eryk Casemiro and Hal Waite, *Co-Pro* Tracy Kramer, Terry Thoren and Norton Virgien, *Screenplay* J David Stem and David N Weiss and Jill Gorey & Barbara Herndon and Kate Boutilier, *Pro Des* Dima Malanitchev, *Ed* John Bryant, *M* Mark Mothersbaugh; songs performed by Tracey Amos, Big Bad Voodoo Daddy, Geri Halliwell, Sinéad O'Connor, T-Boz, Cyndi Lauper, Mylène Farmer, Baha Men, Jessica Simpson, Cheryl Chjase and Tim Curry, No Authority, Amanda, Aaron Carter, Isaac

Hayes and Robert Casale etc, *Ms Sarandon's language advisers* Timothy Monich and Mariko Kitamura Bird.

Paramount/Nickleodeon Movies/MFP Munich Film Partners-UIP.
78 mins. USA/Germany. 2000. Rel: 6 April 2001. Cert U.

## Rules of Engagement ★★★★

Vietnam/Yemen/Camp Lejeune, North Carolina; 1968-2000. A recipient of the Navy Cross and two silver stars, Colonel Terry Childers is a 30-year veteran of the Marines who has served his country in Vietnam, Beirut and the Gulf. But, following his direct involvement in the massacre of 83 men, women and children in Yemen, he is hauled up in front of a court martial. With his sole three witnesses shot dead by Arab snipers, Childers has only his lifelong friend, fellow veteran and retired lawyer Colonel Hays Hodges, to help clear his name. But with Hodges' dodgy legal record and the National Security Agency's resolve to sacrifice Childers as a scapegoat, the prognosis does not look good... With its noble ideals and inflexible codes of honour, the US army is always good for a rousing counter-attack from Hollywood (cf *A Few Good Men, Courage Under Fire, The General's Daughter*). Boasting an articulate screenplay and well-researched story (the latter concocted by former Secretary of the Navy James Webb), this slick, gung-ho courtroom thriller punches its emotional buttons with military precision. A terrific return to form for director Friedkin (whose last outing was the lamentable *Jade*), the film also spotlights charismatic turns from Messrs Jones and Jackson and extra-strong support from Guy Pearce as Childers' wily prosecutor.

● *Colonel Hays Hodges* Tommy Lee Jones, *Colonel Terry Childers* Samuel L Jackson, *Major Mark Biggs* Guy Pearce, *National Security Advisor William Sokal* Bruce Greenwood, *Captain Lee* Blair Underwood, *General H Lawrence Hodges* Philip Baker Hall, *Mrs Mourain* Anne Archer, *Ambassador Mourain* Ben Kingsley, *General Perry* Dale Dye, *Doctor Ahmar* Amidou, *Captain Tom Chandler* Mark Feuerstein, *with* Richard McGonagle, Baoan Coleman, Nicky Katt, Ryan Hurst, Gordon Clapp, Hayden Tank, Ahmed Abounouom, William Gibson, Bonnie Johnson, David Graf, G Gordon Liddy.
● *Dir* William Friedkin, *Pro* Richard D Zanuck and Scott Rudin, *Ex Pro* Adam Schroeder and James Webb, *Co-Pro* Arne L Schmidt, *Screenplay* Stephen Gaghan, from a story by James Webb, *Ph* William Fraker and Nicola Pecorini, *Pro Des* Robert Lang, *Ed* Augie Hess, *M* Mark Isham, *Costumes* Gloria Gresham, *Sound* Steve Boeddeker, *Military adviser* Dale Dye.

Paramount/Seven Arts Pictures/MFP Munich Film Partners GmbH & Co ROE Prods-UIP.
127 mins. USA/Germany. 2000. Rel: 11 August 2000. Cert 15.

Robert Walpole, *Ex Pro* David M Thompson, Rod Stoneman and Clare Duigan, *Ph* Oliver Curtis, *Pro Des* Luana Hanson, *Ed* Emer Reynolds, *M* The Plague Monkeys, *Costumes* Kathy Strachan, *Second unit dir* Paddy Breathnach.

BBC Films/ Bord Scannán na hÉireann/Irish Film Board/Alta Films/Treasure Films-Artificial Eye. 95 mins. Ireland/UK. 1999. Rel: 5 January 2001. Cert 15.

**Left:** *A cut above the rest: Heather Graham plays the world's worst hairdresser in J.B. Rogers' sweet and outrageous Say It Isn't So (from Twentieth Century Fox)*

## Save the Last Dance ★★★¹/₂

When her mother is killed in a car crash on the way to her ballet audition, Sara finds that her life is stopped in its tracks. Abandoning her aspirations for dance, she moves to Chicago to stay with her estranged father and is enrolled in a predominantly African-American high school. There she meets the cocky, self-assured Derek Reynolds, a black student who is the local prince of hip-hop dance... While essentially a formulaic dance romance in the tradition of, oh, *Saturday Night Fever*, *Dirty Dancing*, *Flashdance*, *Strictly Ballroom* and everything else inbetween, *Save the Last Dance* manages to rise above the nuts and bolts of its mechanics. This is due in part to the striking cinematography of former stills cameraman Robbie Greenberg who, in spite of having worked with Robert Redford, refrains from too much filtered sunlight. There is also some wonderfully colourful dialogue which makes the most of the cultural clash between hip-hop and rural, middle class America. Above all, though, director Thomas Carter has managed to coax some beautifully nuanced performances from his young cast, creating credible, flesh-and-blood characters from stock stereotypes. Julia Stiles and Sean Patrick Thomas are particularly impressive in the leads.

● *Sara* Julia Stiles, *Derek Reynolds* Sean Patrick Thomas, *Chenille* Kerry Washington, *Malakai* Fredro Starr, *Roy* Terry Kinney, *Nikki* Bianca Lawson, *Snookie* Vince Green, *Kenny* Garland Whitt, *Mr Campbell* Tab Baker, *with* Elisabeth Oas, Artel Jarod Walker, Cory Stewart, Jennifer Anglin, Dorothy Martin, Kim Tlusty, Felicia Fields, Andrew Rothenberg.
● *Dir* Thomas Carter, *Pro* Robert W Cort and David Madden, *Co-Pro* Marie Cantin, *Screenplay* Duane Adler and Cheryl Edwards, *Ph* Robbie Greenberg, *Pro Des* Paul Eads, *Ed* Peter E Berger, *M* Mark Isham; Tchaikovsky, Ravell; songs performed by Blackout, Kevon Edmonds, Shawty Redd, Shyne, Grace Jones, Chaka Demus and Pliers, Methodman/Redman, Faith Evans, Chic, Donell Jones, Lucy Pearl with Snoop Dogg & Q-Tip, Pink, The Lovin' Spoonful, 112 and The Notorious BIG, KC & The Sunshine Band, Ice Cube, Mase, Curtis Mayfield, Jill Scott and Fredro Starr, Soulbone, Montell Jordan, Claudja Barry etc, *Costumes* Sandra Hernandez, *Choreography* Fatima.

Paramount/MTV Films-UIP.
113 mins. USA. 2000. Rel: 30 March 2001. Cert 12.

## Saltwater ★★★¹/₂

At an off-season coastal resort in Ireland, the Beneventi family is having a rough week. George Beneventi is finding it increasingly hard to pay off his debt to a loan shark. His eldest son, Frank, who runs the family café, decides to take the law into his own hands by robbing the local bookie. Joe, the youngest Beneventi, falls in with a trouble-maker at school. And Ray, the teacher boyfriend of Frank and Joe's sister Carmel, is caught having an affair with a student... Utilising an economic narrative style and a humour so dry it's almost imperceptible, playwright Conor McPherson (*The Weir*, *Port Authority*) has pulled off an accomplished directorial debut. His strength is his juxtaposition of surreal black comedy with naturalistic drama and he juggles the two styles extremely efficiently. And thanks to plausible performances from an excellent cast, the hiccoughs thrown up by an increasingly tightening plot always take one by surprise. Interestingly, the film was developed from a set of stage monologues (*This Lime Tree Bower*) by the author.

● *Frank Beneventi* Peter McDonald, *George Beneventi* Brian Cox, *Dr Ray Sullivan* Conor Mullen, *Joe Beneventi* Laurence Kinlan, *'Simple' Simon McCurdie* Brendan Gleeson, *Deborah* Eva Birthistle, *Carmel Beneventi* Valerie Spelman, *Damien Fitzgibbon* David O'Rourke, *Tara* Caroline O'Boyle, *Sgt Duggan* Gina Moxley, *Professor Tony Regan* Garrett Keogh, *John Traynor* Michael McElhatton, *Mr Fanning* Pat Shortt, *Professor Konisberg* Carl Duering, *Dr Trish Meehan* Olwen Fouere, *Michelle* Nuala O'Neill, *with* Maria McDermottroe, Alan King, Mark Dunne, Billy Roche.
● *Dir* and *Screenplay* Conor McPherson, *Pro*

*Above: Scream, groan and groan again: the spoof reaches new depths in Keenen Ivory Wayans' redundant Scary Movie (from Buena Vista)*

### Say It Isn't So ★★★

Shelby, Indiana/Beaver, Colorado; today. 'Gilly' Noble is a sweet, upstanding employee of an animal shelter who is looking for the right woman with whom to share the rest of his life. When klutzy but amazingly beautiful hairdresser Jo Wingfield cuts off his right ear, it's love at first blood. After a whirlwind romance and lots of humping, Gilly proposes marriage – and then discovers that Jo is his sister... A typically outrageous farce from the brothers Farrelly (*Dumb and Dumber/There's Something About Mary/Me, Myself & Irene*), *Say It Isn't So* makes fun of incest, strokes, amputees and any number of other sacred cows (in one case, literally). And like previous Farrelly hits, the film spins its gags off a strong storyline and vivid characters, elevating this free-for-all burlesque above the likes of more aimless, scattershot fare (qv *Scary Movie*). Young lovers Chris Klein and Heather Graham are to be commended for playing their roles absolutely straight (well, almost), while Sally Field, erstwhile *Flying Nun*, may shock her fans as Jo's foul-mouthed, abusive mother-from-hell. FYI: First-time helmer J B Rogers previously worked as assistant director on all of the Farrellys' films.

● *Josephine Wingfield* Heather Graham, *Gilbert 'Gilly' Noble* Chris Klein, *Dig McCaffey* Orlando Jones, *Valdine Wingfield* Sally Field, *Walter Wingfield* Richard Jenkins, *Larry Falwell* John Rothman, *Leon Pitofsky* Jack Plotnick, *Jack Mitchelson* Eddie Cibrian, *Jimmy Mitchelson* Mark Pellegrino, *Streak* Brent Hinkley, *Ruthie Falwell* Julie White, *Cher Falwell* Courtney Peldon, *Gina* Sarah Silverman, *with* Henry Cho, Richard Riehle, Brent Briscoe, Ezra Buzzington, David L Lander, Lin Shaye, C Ernst Harth, Matthew Peters, Jackie Flynn, Suzanne Somers.

● *Dir* J B Rogers, *Pro* Bobby Farrelly, Bradley Thomas and Peter Farrelly, *Screenplay* Peter Gaulke and Gerry Swallow, *Ph* Mark Irwin, *Pro Des* Sidney J Bartholomew Jr, *Ed* Larry Madaras, *M* Mason Daring, *Costumes* Lisa Jensen, *Make-up effects* Tony Gardner.

Twentieth Century-Fox/Conundrum Entertainment-Fox. 96 mins. USA. 2001. Rel: 15 June 2001. Cert 15.

### Scary Movie ★¹/₂

Last Halloween six classmates accidentally knocked down a man in the road and disposed of his body in the sea, swearing never to speak of the incident again. Then, a year later, a hooded figure in a white mask turns up wielding a large hunting knife, a hook and a mobile phone... Intriguingly, *Scary Movie* was the original title of *Scream*, of which this is a parody. But *Scream* itself is a parody of the slash-er pic, which makes this over-the-top spoof redundant to say the least. But then everything from *The Matrix* to *The Usual Suspects* gets the ridicule treatment, which is fine if you've seen the film in question. But citing other movies is not in itself a show of wit, so *Scary Movie* reaches into its bag of tricks to try and out-do the extremes of *American Pie* and its ribald rip-offs. So, while it may delight this year's devotees of the tasteless limit, next year jokes about explosive orgasms and mutilated foreskins may seem old hat. Scary, indeed.

● *Bobby* Jon Abrahams, *Drew Decker* Carmen Electra, *Buffy* Shannon Elizabeth, *Cindy Campbell* Anna Faris, *Sheriff* Kurt Fuller, *Brenda* Regina Hall, *Greg* Lochlyn Munro, *Gail Hailstrom* Cheri Oteri, *Officer Doofy* Dave Sheridan, *Shorty* Marlon Wayans, *Ray* Shawn Wayans, *Miss Thing* Kendall Saunders, *Miss Mann* Jayne Trcka, Rick Ducommun, David L Lander, Keenen Ivory Wayans, and (uncredited) *Dawson Leery* James Van Der Beek.
● *Dir* Keenen Ivory Wayans, *Pro* Eric L Gold and Lee R Mayes, *Ex Pro* Bob Weinstein, Harvey Weinstein, Cary Granat, Peter Schwerin, Brad Grey, Peter Safran and Bo Zenga, *Co-Pro* Lisa Suzanne Blum, *Assoc Pro* and *Pro Des* Robb Wilson King, *Screenplay* Shawn Wayans, Marlon Wayans, Buddy Johnson, Phil Beauman, Jason Friedberg and Aaron Seltzer, *Ph* Francis Kenny, *Ed* Mark Helfrich, *M* David Kitay; songs performed by Paula Cole, Public Enemy, Save Ferris, Silverchair, Robert Barry and Monet, The Unband, Bender, Black Eyed Peas, Tupac Shakur & Nate Dogg, Da Beat Bros, Radford etc, *Costumes* Darryle Johnson, *Visual effects* Brian Jennings.

Miramax/Dimension Films/Wayan Bros. Entertainment/ Gold-Miller/Brad Grey Pictures-Buena Vista. 88 mins. USA. 2000. Rel: 8 September 2000. Cert 18.

## Second Skin – Segunda piel ★★

Although Elena loves her husband to distraction, she is concerned that she and Alberto have so little sex these days. Then she discovers a hotel receipt in Alberto's jacket and suspects the worst. But Alberto is not seeing another woman, he is seeing another man... Former costume designer Gerardo Vera has cooked up an intriguing premise for his third film as director (adapted by Angeles Gonzáles-Sinde from Vera's idea). However, in spite of the painstaking detail lavished on its characters (we know what they eat, what music they listen to, how they walk down a corridor), the film fails to make them either plausible or interesting. It's also unfortunate that Jordi Mollá, as the bisexual Alberto, is so unremittingly unsympathetic and uncharismatic. He's a self-pitying bore and he brings the film down with him.

**Above:** A man and a woman and a man: Javier Bardem and Cecilia Roth in Gerardo Vera's intriguing but implausible Second Skin (from Gala)

● *Diego* Javier Bardem, *Alberto* Jordi Mollá, *Elena* Ariadna Gil, *Eva* Cecilia Roth, *Rafael* Javier Albalá, *Manuel* Adrian Sac, *with* Mercedes Sampietro, Cristina Espinosa, Pilar Castro.
● *Dir* Gerardo Vera, *Pro* Andres Vicente Gomez, *Screenplay* Angeles Gonzáles-Sinde, from an idea by Vera, *Ph* Julio Madurga, *Pro Des* Ana Alvargonzález, *Ed* José Antonio Bermudez, *M* Roque Baños, *Costumes* Macarena Soto.

Lolafilms/Via Digital/Antena 3 de Televisión-Gala. 104 mins. Spain. 1999. Rel: 2 February 2001. Cert 18.

## Secrets of the Heart – Los secretos del corazón ★★★★

Oddly akin to those London buses which eventually arrive together, this 1997 production from Spain's Montxo Armendáriz shares much in common with José Luis Cuerda's *Butterfly's Tongue* (1998), which reached us a few months earlier. Cuerda's film, by being set just before the Spanish Civil War, had greater ambitions and wider horizons, but both works (this one set in and around Pamplona in the 1960s) are centred on a schoolboy's rites of passage as he becomes aware of sex and of the complexities of the adult world. This film may be more modest, but it's equally well played and endearing, and it eschews sentimentality. Indeed, it reveals enough pain to make the ending ambiguous: it smiles on the boy by allowing him a dance with his first girlfriend, while the music heard is a tune associated with a brutish husband anguished by having driven his wife to suicide. [*Mansel Stimpson*]

● *Uncle Ignacio* Carmelo Gómez, *Aunt María* Charo López, *Teresa, the mother* Silvia Munt, *Aunt Rosa* Vicky Peña, *Javi* Andoni Erburu, *with* Alvaro Nagore, Iñigo Garcés.
● *Dir* and *Screenplay* Montxo Armendáriz, *Pro* Imanol Uribe and Andres Santana, *Ph* Javier Aguirresarobe, *Pro Des* Félix Murcia, *Ed* Rori Sáinz de Rozas, *M* Bingen Mendizábal, *Costumes* Josune Lasa.

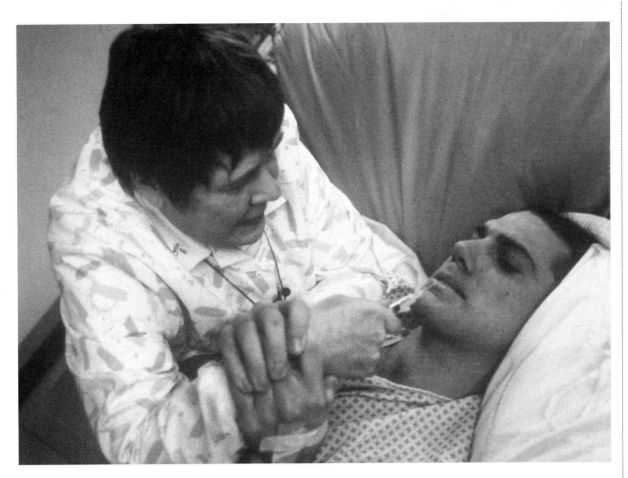

**Above:** *Needling the competition: Marylouise Burke and Glenn Fitzgerald in Daniel Minahan's camp, compelling and macabre 'Series 7':The Contenders (from FilmFour)*

Aiete Films/Ariane Films/Sogepaq/Canal Plus/Eurimages, etc-Metrodome.
105 mins. Spain/France/Portugal. Rel: 22 September 2000. Cert 12.

## See Spot Run ★

Seattle; today. The story of a canine FBI agent on the run from the Mafia, *See Spot Run* throws together those ingredients designed to appeal to nose-picking, poo-obsessed youngsters who live for the day that *The Rugrats in Ibiza* turns up at their local. However, this film's over-complicated plot and sluggish pace may leave even them disappointed. David Arquette, a poor man's Jim Carrey, tries hard, but he is outclassed both by co-star Anthony Anderson and the bull mastiff. [*Ewen Brownrigg*]

● *Gordon Smith* David Arquette, *Agent Murdoch* Michael Clarke Duncan, *Stephanie* Leslie Bibb, *Gino Valente* Joe Viterelli, *James* Angus T Jones, *Benny* Anthony Anderson, *Sonny Talia* Paul Sorvino, *Arliss Santino* Steven R. Schirripa, *with* Kim Hawthorne, Kavan Smith, Roger Haskett, *voice of Spot* Dan O'Connell.
● *Dir* John Whitesell, *Pro* Robert Simonds, Tracey Trench and Andrew Deane, *Ex Pro* Michael Alexander Miller and Bruce Berman, *Screenplay*

George Gallo, Gregory Poirier, Danny Baron and Chris Faber, *Ph* John Bartley, *Pro Des* Mark Freeborn, *Ed* Cara Silverman, *M* John Debney; songs performed by George Clinton, Barry Manilow, Young MC, Etta James, The Chordettes, Milo Z, Hampton the Hamster, Stevie Wonder, Vitamin C, *Costumes* Diane M. Widas.

Warner/Village Roadshow/NVP Entertainment-Warner.
97 mins. USA/Australia. 2001. Rel: 25 May 2001. Cert PG.

## 'Series 7':The Contenders ★★★¹/₂

Newbury, Connecticut; the very near future. The highest-rated reality programme on US television, *The Contenders* pits six random citizens against each other in a fight to the death. After six extremely successful series, the show has made a star of Dawn, now eight months pregnant. But, in *'Series 7'*, can she stay alive long enough to have her baby? And will she really terminate childhood sweetheart Jeff Norman to do so? … Taking reality TV to a new level, 'Series 7' is real enough in itself that, with naturalistic performances and a hand-held DV camera, it exudes a documentary immediacy. However, it has just enough humour to tip the wink to the viewer, thus transcending the pretentious silliness of similar fare (notably the futuristic Schwarzenegger vehicle *The*

**Above:** Black as blue: Samuel L. Jackson as John Singleton's cool, stylish and damn baaaad Shaft (from UIP)

*Running Man*, in which TV contestants also fight for their lives). Above all, the film is extremely compelling viewing and succeeds so beautifully because it manages to run along the thin edge between high camp and genuine unease. By making voyeurs of us all, *'Series 7'* rams its message home with the efficiency of a hypodermic needle.

● *Dawn* Brooke Smith, *Jeffrey Norman* Glenn Fitzgerald, *Connie* Marylouise Burke, *Franklin* Richard Venture, *Tony* Michael Kaycheck, *Lindsay* Merritt Wever, *Doria* Angelina Phillips, *Laura* Jennifer Van Dyck, *with* Donna Hanover, Tom Gilroy, Nada Despotovich, Alex Yershov, Tanny McDonald, *narrator* Will Arnett.
● *Dir* and *Screenplay* Daniel Minahan, *Pro* Jason Kliot, Joana Vicente, Christine Vachon and Katie Roumel, *Ex Pro* Charles J Rusbasan, *Co-Ex Pro* Judith Zarin and Michael Escott, *Co-Pro* Evan T. Cohen and Gretchen McGowan, *Assoc Pro* Pamela Koffler, *Line Pro* Libby Richman, *Ph* Randy Drummond, *Pro Des* Gideopn Ponte, *Ed* Malcolm Jamieson, *M* Girls Against Boys; songs performed by Joy Division, MenKing, Girls Against Boys, Eli Janney and Julie Stapanek, *Costumes* Christine Beiselin.

USA Films/Blow Up Pictures/Killer Films/Open City Films/Sundance Institute-Film Four.
87 mins. USA. 2000. Rel: 1 June 2001. Cert 18.

## Sexy Beast ★★★

Gary Dove has never been happier. After a life of crime, he's retired to the Costa del Sol with his beautiful wife and enough money never to have to work again. Then he gets word that a certain London gangster, Don Logan, wants him for another job. And the trouble with Don Logan is that he can never take `no' for an answer – and he's on his way to Spain... Cockney gangsters, a bank heist, Ray Winstone... If all that sounds too familiar to be true, this debut feature from pop promo maker Jonathan Glazer does make up for its *déjà vu* with a commanding visual style and a potent visceral kick. Constructed like a three-act play, the film gains the lion's share of its power from an extraordinarily pungent performance from Ben Kingsley, who manages to be simultaneously comic and terrifying. And while the plot is a tad undernourished and the pacing far too deliberate, the overall effect is quite unnerving.

● *Gary 'Gal' Dove* Ray Winstone, *Don Logan* Ben Kingsley, *Teddy Bass* Ian McShane, *DeeDee Dove* Amanda Redman, *Harry* James Fox, *Aitch* Cavan Kendall, *Jackie* Julianne White, *Enrique* Alvaro Monje, *with* Robert Atiko, Nieves del Amo Oruet, Gerard Barray, Andy Lucas, Eddie O'Connell, Terry Plummer.
● *Dir* Jonathan Glazer, *Pro* Jeremy Thomas, *Co-Pro* Denise O'Dell, *Screenplay* Louis Mellis and David Scinto, *Ph* Ivan Bird, *Pro Des* Jan Houllevigue, *Ed* John Scott and Sam Sneade, *M* Roque Baños and UNKLE with South; songs performed by The Stranglers, The

Gibson Brothers, Wayne Marshall, Dean Martin, Derek Martin, *Costumes* Louise Stjernsward.

Recorded Picture Company/FilmFour/Fox Searchlight/Zanzaman S.A.-FilmFour.
88 mins. UK/Spain/USA. 2000. Rel: 12 January 2000. Cert 18.

### Shadow of the Vampire ★★★

Eastern Europe; 1921. The great German director F W Murnau is determined to make the most authentic film yet. Denied the rights to Bram Stoker's *Dracula*, he names his vampire picture *Nosferatu* and hires an unknown performer called Max Schreck to play Count Orlok. But Schreck is no ordinary actor and commands a terrible price for Murnau's realism... A sly supposition of what could have been during the making of *Nosferatu*, Merhige's fiction is fun while it lasts but is also rather unfulfilling. John Malkovich is an excellent choice as Murnau but turns in one of his least mysterious performances, leaving Willem Dafoe to guzzle the scenery and steal the acting honours. In a perfect world, Werner Herzog would've made a perfect Murnau, particularly as he directed the remake himself (in 1979). Filmed in Luxembourg.

● *F W Murnau* John Malkovich, *Max Schreck* Willem Dafoe, *Fritz Wagner, the second cameraman* Cary Elwes, *Henrik Galeen, the screenwriter* John Aden Gillet, *Gustav Von Wangenheim, the leading man* Eddie Izzard, *Albin Grau, the producer* Udo Kier, *Greta Schroeder, the leading lady* Catherine McCormack, *Wolfgang Muller, the first cameraman* Ronan Vibert, *with* Marja-Leena Junker, Sacha Ley, Nicholas Elliot.
● *Dir* E Elias Merhige, *Pro* Nicolas Cage and Jeff Levine, *Ex Pro* Paul Brooks, *Co-Pro* Richard Johns and Jimmy de Brabant, *Screenplay* Steven Katz, *Ph* Lou Bogue, *Pro Des* Assheton Gorton, *Ed* Chris Wyatt, *M* Dan Jones, *Costumes* Caroline de Vivaise.

Saturn Films/Long Shot Films/BBC Films/DeLux Prods/Pilgrim Films-Metrodome.
92 mins. UK/USA/Luxembourg. 2000. Rel: 2 February 2001. Cert 15.

### Shaft ★★★¹/₂

New York City; today. He's the baddest mother on the NYPD and he engenders respect, fear and frustration in equal measure. Then, when John Shaft encounters what looks like an open-and-shut case of racial murder, he vows to see the Yuppie killer put away when the latter is released on $200,000 bail. Shaft knows there was a witness to the crime, but she has disappeared into thin air. Why is she so frightened and who will get to her first? ... From the stylish opening credit sequence to the appearance of Samuel L Jackson sporting a shaved head, pencil-thin beard and leather Armani overcoat, this rein-vention of the 1970s' phenomenon is an exercise in sheer cool. Thanks to a muscular story and some vivid underworld characters, it's also an extremely gripping ride. In fact, the original *Shaft*, which was so explosive in its day, pales in comparison to this slick update featuring the nephew of the original private eye. But then Mr Jackson is given full rein to flaunt his considerable presence and Sam is indisputably *the* man now.

● *John Shaft* Samuel L Jackson, *Carmen Vasquez* Vanessa Williams, *Peoples Hernandez* Jeffrey Wright, *Walter Wade Jr* Christian Bale, *Rasaan* Busta Rhymes, *Jack Roselli* Dan Hedaya, *Diane Palmieri* Toni Collette, *Uncle John Shaft* Richard Roundtree, *Jimmy Grovitch* Ruben Santiago-Hudson, *Curt Fleming* Josef Sommer, *Carla Howard* Lynne Thigpen, *Walter Wade Snr* Philip Bosco, *Hon Dennis Bradford* Pat Hingle, *Trey Howard* Mekhi Phifer, *with* Leet Ergesen, Daniel Von Bargen, Francisco 'Cogui' Taveras, Sonja Sohn, Peter McRobbie, Zach Grenier, Ron Castellano, Catherine Kellner, John Cunningham, Gordon Parks, and (*uncredited*) Gloria Reuben.
● *Dir* John Singleton, *Pro* Singleton and Scott Rudin, *Ex Pro* Adam Schroeder, Paul Hall and Steve Nicolaides, *Screenplay* Singleton, Richard Price and Shane Salerno, based on the novel *Shaft* by Ernest Tidyman, *Ph* Donald E Thorin, *Pro Des* Patrizia Von Brandenstein, *Ed* John Bloom, *M* David Arnold and Isaac Hayes; songs performed by Isaac Hayes, Fulanito, Sleepy Brown, R. Kelly, Oro Solido, OutKast etc, *Costumes* Ruth Carter and Giorgio Armani, *Samuel L Jackson's hair* [!] Robert Stevenson.

Paramount/Scott Rudin/New Deal/MFP Munich Film Partners-UIP.
99 mins. USA/Germany. 2000. Rel: 15 September 2000. Cert 18.

### Shanghai Noon ★★★

The Forbidden City, Peking, China/Nevada; 1881. When the beautiful Princess Pei Pei is spirited beyond the walls of the Imperial Palace, three of the Emperor's finest guards are appointed to track her all the way to Nevada. Her humble servant, Chon Wang (sort of pronounced 'John Wayne'), tags along for the ride, meeting up with affable train robber Roy O'Bannon (real name Wyatt Earp) en route... Having rumbled the Bronx and chopped up half of LA, Asia's biggest superstar, Jackie Chan (5'6"), turns his attention to the Wild West. Again, Chan's self-deprecatory humour and acrobatic fighting skills defuse the stock clichés of a familiar genre (the barroom brawl, the posse, the bordello, the Indians, the peace pipe...), this time with some glorious cinematography of Alberta doubling for Nevada. However, as Chan's stunts are inevitably less energetic this time round (the guy *is* 46 now, after all), it is Owen Wilson who takes up the slack, being an amiable presence not unlike the Sundance Kid with verbal diarrhoea.

● *Chon Wang* Jackie Chan, *Roy O'Bannon* Owen Wilson, *Princess Pei Pei* Lucy Liu, *Falling Leaves* Brandon Merrill, *Lo Fong* Roger Yuan, *Van Cleef* Xander Berkeley, *with* Rong Guang Yu, Cui Ya Hi, Eric Chi Cheng Chen, Walton Goggins, P. Adrien Dorval, Rafael Baez, *Andrews* Jason Connery, Henry O, Simon Baker, Rick Ash, James Baker, Christy Greene, Lisa Stafford.

● *Dir* Tom Dey, *Pro* Roger Birnbaum, Gary Barber and Jonathan Glickman, *Ex Pro* Jackie Chan, Willie Chan and Solon So, *Co-Pro* Ned Dowd and Jules Daly, *Screenplay* Alfred Gough and Miles Millar, *Ph* Dan Mindel, *Pro Des* Peter J Hampton, *Ed* Richard Chew, *M* Randy Edelman; songs performed by ZZ Top, Kid Rock, Aerosmith, Uncle Kracker, *Costumes* Joseph Porro, *Sound* Tim Chau.

Touchstone Pictures/Spyglass Entertainment-Buena Vista. 110 mins. USA. 2000. Rel: 25 August 2000. Cert 12.

## Shower – Xizao ★★★★½

Beijing; today. Like Joseph Losey's 1985 film *Steaming*, which was based on Nell Dunn's stage play, *Shower* is set almost entirely within the confines of a steam bath facility. Here, however, it is a disparate group of men, not women, who share their innermost demons as they unwind from the pressures of the outside world. Cunningly set up with a scene in a fully automated sidewalk shower cubicle (the ablutionary equivalent of a Portaloo), the film goes on to observe the ritualistic detail of pedicures, back scrubs, suction cupping and wet shaves in an old bath house, neatly highlighting the contrast between the time-saving, impersonal efficiency of the new world with the reassuring, leisurely values of the old. By turns fascinating, touching, funny, poignant and charming, *Shower* is a film of enormous heart that leaves one with a bittersweet glow, the spiritual complement to a full body massage.

● *Master Liu* Zhu Xu, *Da Ming* Pu Cun Xin, *Er Ming* Jiang Wu, *He Bing* He Zheng, *Hu Bei Bei* Zhnag Jim Hao, *Li Ding* Lao Lin, *Feng Shun* Lao Wu.

● *Dir* Zhnag Yang, *Pro* Peter Loher, *Ex Pro* Sam Duann, *Screenplay* Liu Fen Dou, Zhang Yang, Huo Xin, Diao Yi Nan and Cai Xiang Jun, *Ph* Zhang Jian, *Pro Des* Tian Meng, *Ed* Yang Hong Yu, *M* Ye Xiao Gang, *Costumes* Hao Ge.

Imar Film Co/The Xi'an Film Studio-Momentum Pictures. 94 mins. China. 1999. Rel: 30 March 2001. Cert 12.

## Shrek ★★★★★

In a land far, far away, an ugly green ogre called Shrek defends his right to be on his own. Feared by the local populace for his unconventional appearance and flatulence, the ogre suddenly finds his swamp overrun by fairy tale characters. In order to return his home to its former solitude, Shrek is compelled to rescue the Princess

**Above:** How the West Was Wang: Jackie Chan horses around in Tom Dey's silly and completely engaging Shanghai Noon (from Buena Vista)

Fiona from the clutches of a fire-breathing dragon... A hideously entertaining cartoon which, as it reaches new heights in what is possible in computer animation, breaks the narrative and thematic rules of what is permissible in family entertainment. Borrowing more than a nod from Raymond Briggs' *Fungus the Bogeyman* (in which subterranean beings reverse the social order of hygiene and cleanliness) and using contemporary songs on the soundtrack (see music credits), *Shrek* tweaks the tradition of fairy tale cinema as it repeatedly thumbs its nose at the conventional cosiness of Disney. Thus, Geppetto sells off Pinocchio, the Seven Dwarfs are pressed into a chain gang and the Gingerbread Man chides an aggressor with a curt 'Eat me!' Yet *Shrek* never rests on its irreverent laurels for a second: it is as visually inventive as the best Disney 'toons and a whole lot funnier. A real tonic for the whole family of which Roald Dahl would most wholeheartedly have approved (while Walt Disney will be spinning in his cryogenic chamber).

● Voices: *Shrek/blind mouse* Mike Myers, *Donkey* Eddie Murphy, *Princess Fiona* Cameron Diaz, *Lord*

*Farquaad* John Lithgow, *Monsieur Hood* Vincent Cassel, *Captain of the Guards* Jim Cummings, *Geppetto/Magic Mirror* Chris Miller, *Pinocchio/Three Pigs* Cody Cameron, *old woman* Kathleen Freeman, *Peter Pan* Michael Galasso, *Gingerbread Man* Conrad Vernon, *Bishop* Val Bettin.

● *Dir* Andrew Adamson and Vicky Jenson, *Pro* Aron Warner, John H Williams and Jeffrey Katzenberg, *Ex Pro* Penney Finkelman Cox and Sandra Rabins, *Co-Pro* Ted Elliott and Terry Rossio, *Co-Ex Pro* David Lipman, *Assoc Pro* Jane Hartwell, *Screenplay* Elliott, Rossio, Joe Stillman and Roger S H Schulman, based upon the book by William Steig, *Pro Des* James Hegedus, *Ed* Sim Evan-Jones, *M* Harry Gregson-Williams and John Powell; songs performed by Smash Mouth, Eddie Murphy, Joan Jett, The Proclaimers, Vincent Cassel, eels, Jason Wade, John Cale, Self, Baha Men, Leslie Carter, Dana Glover etc, *Visual effects* Ken Bielenberg, *Animation* Raman Hui.

DreamWorks/PDI-UIP.
90 mins. USA. 2001. Rel: 29 June 2001. Cert U.

## Siam Sunset ★★¹/₂

Some men have all the luck but Perry isn't one of them. After his wife is killed by a fridge that has fallen off a plane, Perry, who creates colours for a paint company, decides to find a hue that will prove to be his salvation: siam sunset. Before then, however, he wins a tour of the Australian outback, only to find himself stuck on a run-down bus with a surly driver and his Anglophobic passengers. And then things take a turn for the worse… A crazy mix of affectionate observation, black humour, sudden violence and the unpredictable, *Siam Sunset* is another startling original from Al Clark, producer of *The Adventures of Priscilla, Queen of the Desert*. With Linus Roache providing a sympathetic and gently charismatic performance and with the writers' canny observation of human character, *Siam Sunset* is enjoyable and quirky even when it's at its most uneven and contrived. FYI: After this, director John Polson went on to star opposite Tom Cruise in *Mission: Impossible 2*. [*Charles Bacon*]

● *Perry* Linus Roache, *Grace* Danielle Cormack, *Martin* Ian Bliss, *Bill* Roy Billing, *Stuart* Alan Brough, *with* Rebecca Hobbs, Terry Kenwrick, Deidre Rubenstein.
● *Dir* John Polson, *Pro* Al Clark, *Ex Pro* Andrew Knight and Peter Beilby, *Screenplay* Max Dann and Andrew Knight, *Ph* Brian Breheny, *Pro Des* Steven Jones-Evans, *Ed* Nicholas Beauman, *M* Paul Grabowsky, *Costumes* Louise Wakefield.
Australian Film Finance Corporation/Showtime Australia/Artists Services/Channel 4 UK, etc-Blue Dolphin.
92 mins. Australia/UK. 1999. Rel: 10 November 2000. Cert 15.

## Siberia ★¹/₂

Hanging out in the city centre of Amsterdam, Hugo and Goof are two young bucks who prey on young female tourists. Promising the girls a good time, they bed them, steal their money and camera and, for a memento, rip out the essential page of their passport. Then, on a whim, they make a bet that the first to collect 15 passport pages from girls of different nationalities gets to keep all the money… A couple of decades ago one knew more or less what to expect from a foreign-language film. Nowadays too many resemble pale imitations of American independents, complete with the grainy, in-yer-face, hand-held camerawork that has become *de rigueur*. Even the leading actor in *Siberia* looks like an American star – Matthew McConaughey in *EDtv* mode – while half the dialogue is in English (the international tongue of Amsterdam). Furthermore, films about miscreants present a major drawback for, unless the protagonists are wildly charismatic, they are hard to spend time with. Here, the abhorrent Hugo and Goof commit despicable crimes against a range of helpless and lovely girls and show no remorse. So what's the point?

● *Hugo* Hugo Metsers, *Goof* Roeland Fernhout, *Lara* Vlatka Simac, *Kristy* Nicole Eggert, *Freddy* Johnny Lion, *Marina* Nefeli Anthopoulou, *with* Alessia Sorvillo, Francesca Rizzo, Syan Blake, Katja Dreyer, Jessica Stockmann, Bente Jonker.
● *Dir* Robert Jan Westdijk, *Pro* Clea De Koning, *Screenplay* Westdijk and Jos Driessen, *Ph* Bert Pot, *Pro Des* Anouk Damoiseaux, *Ed* Herman P Koerts and Peter Alderliesten, *M* Junkie XL and Fons Merkies, *Costumes* Ciska Nagel, *Hair adviser* Wouter Segers.

Partners of the Siberia Experience/Stichting Nederlands Fonds voor de Film, etc-Metro Tartan.
87 mins. The Netherlands/France. 1998. Rel: 18 August 2000. Cert 18.

## The 6th Day ★★★¹/₂

In the not too distant future, smoking will be illegal, 'virtual' girlfriends will be commonplace and you'll be able to tune into the news headlines on your bathroom mirror. In addition, the science of genetics will have become so sophisticated that you'll be able to replace your dead pet with an exact replica in an afternoon. Human cloning, though, will of course be strictly illegal. Crack pilot Adam Gibson prefers the old world, so he's more than a little unnerved when he arrives home one day to find a replica of himself blowing out the candles on his birthday cake… Juggling action, humour and a handful of intriguing moral issues, *The 6th Day* is a welcome return to form for Arnold Schwarzenegger. A sly cocktail of *Total Recall*, *Gattaca* and *Multiplicity*, it moves fast enough to cover any lapses in logic while never failing to poke fun at Schwarzenegger's celebrity (Arnie even gets to say, 'Look, I might be back'). However, the best line comes when, following a discussion on whether or not a

clone has a soul, Arnie terminates the discourse with a succinct, 'Alright, enough philosophy.'

● *Adam Gibson* Arnold Schwarzenegger, *Hank Morgan* Michael Rapaport, *Michael Drucker* Tony Goldwyn, *Robert Marshall* Michael Rooker, *Talia Elsworth* Sarah Wynter, *Dr Griffin Weir* Robert Duvall, *Natalie Gibson* Wendy Crewson, *Wiley* Rod Rowland, *Vincent* Terry Crews, *Clara Gibson* Taylor-Anne Reid, *Tripp* Colin Cunningham, *Katharine Weir* Wanda Cannon, *with* Ken Pogue, Jennifer Gareis, Don McManus, Steve Bacic, Ellie Harvie, Don S Davis, Gillian Barber.
● *Dir* Roger Spottiswoode, *Pro* Jon Davison, Arnold Schwarzenegger and Mike Medavoy, *Ex Pro* David Coatsworth and Dan Petrie Jr, *Screenplay* Cormac Wibberley and Marianne Wibberley, *Ph* Pierre Mignot, *Pro Des* John Willett and Jim Bissell, *Ed* Mark Conte and Dominique Fortin, *M* Trevor Rabin, *Costumes* Trish Keating.

Columbia/Phoenix Pictures-Columbia TriStar. 123 mins. USA. 2000. Rel: 15 December 2000. Cert 15.

## The Skulls ★★★

For over 200 years secret societies have flourished in the upper echelons of American life, priming three presidents, various senators and assorted captains of industry. For Luke McNamara, a gifted but financially strapped law aspirant, acceptance into The Skulls – New Haven's

most elite secret society – would almost guarantee his passage into the legal profession. But the moral cost is higher than he had anticipated... A former member of a secret society himself, screenwriter and Yale alumni John Pogue knows a thing or two about the closed world of the privileged and the elite. And he has cooked up an entertaining little conspiracy thriller that has the decency to throw out some food for thought. Rob Cohen steers things along with the proficiency one would expect from the director of *Dragonheart* and *Daylight* and Joshua Jackson (reminiscent of a cross between a young Tom Hanks and Kiefer Sutherland) makes a watchable and unconventional leading man.

● *Luke McNamara* Joshua Jackson, *Caleb Mandrake* Paul Walker, *Will Beckford* Hill Harper, *Chloe* Leslie Bibb, *Martin Lombard* Christopher McDonald, *Det. Sparrow* Steve Harris, *Ames Levritt* William Petersen, *Litten Mandrake* Craig T Nelson, *Dr Rupert Whitney* Nigel Bennett, *with* David Asman, Scott Gibson, Andrew Aasland, Jennifer Melino, Ken Campbell, Paul Walker III.
● *Dir* Rob Cohen, *Pro* Neal H Moritz and John Pogue, *Ex Pro* William Tyrer, Chris J Ball and Bruce Mellon, *Co-Pro* Fred Caruso, *Screenplay* Pogue, *Ph* Shane Hurlbut, *Pro Des* Bob Ziembicki, *Ed* Peter Amundson, *M* Randy Edelman; songs performed by 3 Day Wheely, Papa Roach, Eman, BTK, Hednoize, Collective Soul, Lorna Vallings, Creed, Fatboy Slim, Sourcerer, *Costumes* Marie-Sylvie Deveau.

**Above:** *Send in the clones: Arnold Schwarzenegger and Sarah Wynter in Roger Spottiswoode's fast-moving, engrossing and surprisingly topical* The 6th Day *(from Columbia TriStar)*

Universal/Original Film/Newmarket Capital Group-UIP. 107 mins. USA. 2000. Rel: 24 November 2000. Cert 15.

## Small Time Crooks ★★★

New York (where else?); today. Ray Winkler is a dishwasher who dreams up an audacious plan to tunnel into a high street bank. Having persuaded his wife to set up a cookie shop as a front, Ray, along with three cronies, sets about executing what should be the perfect heist. But things are never as straightforward as they seem... Returning to the madcap comedy of his earlier career, Woody kicks off his 30th film as writer-director with enormous zest and comic invention, as if re-born. Then, halfway through, the momentum slows down to an amble and the filmmaker falls back on the kind of smug humour that draws laughs from the ridicule of those less culturally enlightened than himself. However, Woody does have some fun by casting himself against intellectual type, as a schlemiel who would rather slump in front of a TV with a 'Bud' than discuss the geographical import of Henry James ('Who cares where he lives? Where did he eat?'). He has also found a wonderful sparring partner in Tracey Ullman and has hung his miscellaneous dopey characters on a story that actually throws up some inspiring U-turns.

● *Ray Winkler* Woody Allen, *Tommy* Tony Darrow, *David* Hugh Grant, *George Blint* George Grizzard, *Benny* Jon Lovitz, *May Sloane* Elaine May, *Denny* Michael Rapaport, *Chi Chi Potter* Elaine Stritch, *Frances 'Frenchy' Winkler* Tracey Ullman, *cop* Brian Markinson, *Langston Potter* Howard Erskine, *with* Crystal Field, Steve Kroft, Brian McConnachie, Isaac Mizrahi, Kristine Nielsen, Larry Pine, John Doumanian, Maurice Sonnenberg, Richard Mawe, Ruth Laredo, Peter McRobbie, Douglas McGrath, Ira Wheeler, Marvin Chatinover.

● *Dir* and *Screenplay* Woody Allen, *Pro* Jean Doumanian, *Ex Pro* J E Beaucaire, *Co-Ex Pro* Jack Rollins, Charles H Joffe and Letty Aronson, *Co-Pro* Helen Robin, *Ph* Zhao Fei, *Pro Des* Santo Loquasto, *Ed* Alisa Lepselter, *M* Rachmaninoff, J S Bach; songs performed by Hal Kemp, Benny Goodman & His Orchestra, Stephen Lang, Harry James, The Champs, Carmen Cavallaro, Lester Lanin etc, *Costumes* Suzanne McCabe.

Sweetland Films-Film Four. 95 mins. USA. 2000. Rel: 1 December 2000. Cert PG.

## Snatch ★★★¹/₂

London; the present. When a notorious diamond thief arrives in London en route to New York to off-load some stolen gems, he is set up by a ruthless Russian mobster. However, the latter's cronies, a trio of cack-handed pawnbrokers, mess up the abduction and come into the line of fire of some brutal East End gangsters. Meanwhile, an illegal bare-knuckle boxing fight is thrown into disarray when a volatile Irish gypsy knocks out the star player, complicating events considerably... If you loved *Lock, Stock and Two Smoking Barrels*, then there's a fair chance that you'll get off on this gimmicky, violent carbon copy. Tough, funny and stylish to a fault, *Snatch* punches the visceral buttons of the *Loaded* brand of cinema with more vigour than wit, but delivers, in spades, pikes, kikes, cockneys, Russians and even a quartet of gun-wielding Hasidic Jews. Of course, the advantage of such a large ensemble cast is that you can gun down a large number of characters and still keep several plot twists flexing. There's a great soundtrack, too, albeit one using old songs as familiar as many of the movie's recycled gags (such as the dog swallowing the prize diamond).

● *Frankie Four Fingers* Benicio Del Toro, *Avi* Dennis Farina, *Darren* Jason Flemyng, *Bullet Tooth Tony* Vinnie Jones, *Mickey O'Neill* Brad Pitt, *Boris the Blade* Rade Sherbedgia, *Turkish* Jason Statham, *Brick Top* Alan Ford, *Doug the Head* Mike Reid, *Tyrone* Ade, *Errol* Andy Beckwith, *Mum O'Neill* Sorcha Cusack, *Vinny* Robbie Gee, *Tommy* Stephen Graham, *Sol* Lennie James, *with* Ewen Bremner, Jason Buckham, Nikki Collins, Teena Collins, Sam Douglas, Adam Fogerty, Goldie, Jason Ninh Cao, Trevor Steedman, Andy Till, Austin Drage, Tim Faraday.
● *Dir* and *Screenplay* Guy Ritchie, *Pro* Matthew Vaughn, *Co-Pro* Michael Dreyer, *Ph* Tim Maurice-Jones, *Pro Des* Hugo Luczyc-Wyhowski, *Ed* Jon Harris, *M* John Murphy; songs performed by Klint, Overseer, The Johnston Brothers, The Stranglers, 10CC, Maceo & The Macks, Mirwais, Bobby Byrd, Madonna, The Specials, The Herbaliser, Massive Attack, Oasis, Huey 'Piano' Smith & The Clowns, *Costumes* Verity Hawkes.

Columbia Pictures/SKA Films-Columbia TriStar. 102 mins. UK. 2000. Rel: 1 September 2000. Cert 18.

## Some Voices ★★¹/₂

West London; the present. Ray has a tendency to hear voices but is deemed well enough to leave the psychiatric hospital at which he has been staying for a number of years. Moving in with his brother, the owner of and cook for a small restaurant, Ray aimlessly strolls around the streets of Shepherd's Bush. There he intercepts a romantic squabble and ends up falling for the girl... A slice of London life, *Some Voices* wins points for authenticity (hand-held camera, natural lighting), but seems an odd choice for the big screen. Adapted by Joe Penhall from his award-winning play, the film displays some grit and energy but doesn't seem to know where it's going. And while Daniel Craig is a compulsive figure as Ray, he seems a little old for the part and slips into standard English once too often. Kelly Macdonald, David Morrissey and Julie Graham are all very good, though.

● *Ray* Daniel Craig, *Pete* David Morrissey, *Laura* Kelly Macdonald, *Mandy* Julie Graham, *Dave* Peter

**Above:** *Fight cub: Brad Pitt puts his best fist forward in* Snatch *(from Columbia TriStar)*

McDonald, *with* Nicholas Palliser, Edward Tudor Pole, Ashley Walters, Cate Fowler.
● *Dir* Simon Cellan Jones, *Pro* Damian Jones and Graham Broadbent, *Co-Pro* Fiona Morham, *Screenplay* Joe Penhall, *Ph* David Odd, *Pro Des* Zoe MacLeod, *Ed* Elen Pierce Lewis, *M* Adrian Johnston; songs performed by Alabama 3, Squeeze, Imogen Heap, Grand Theft Auto, Toots and the Maytals, Françoise Hardy, *Costumes* James Keast.

FilmFour/Dragon Pictures/British Screen-Film Four. 101 mins. UK. 2000. Rel: 25 August 2000. Cert 15.

## Songs From the Second Floor – Sånger Från Andra Våningen ★★★¹/₂

Summing up the tone of the film, Kalle, a furniture salesman, reveals, 'It's not easy being human.' It is close to the new Millennium and the city is gripped in an inexplicable traffic jam. An ageing magician accidentally saws a volunteer's stomach open. On the subway, Kalle tries to ignore a ghost speaking to him in Russian. Kalle's son, meanwhile, has become insane writing poetry... To fully appreciate Roy Andersson's extraordinarily dyspeptic, stylised comic Armageddon, one will need considerable patience and a profound appreciation of the unusual. A series of loosely connected skits in search of a punch line, the film took Andersson four years to complete as he scrambled to finance his unique vision. Visually sparse, the film makes every detail count, near-empty rooms arranged like surreal tableaux, his characters' ghostly pallor beaded with sweat, the noise of car horns constantly bleating in the background... In the end it all goes on too long, but its power – and unexpected flashes of humour – are undeniable. Like an unsettling dream that won't go away, it leaves a distinct taste in the mind. FYI: Roy Andersson made his last feature, *Giliap*, in 1975 and directed this without a script or storyboard.

● *Kalle* Lars Nordh, *Stefan, Kalle's son* Stefan Larsson, *Pelle Wigert* Torbjörn Fahlström, *Lasse* Sten Andersson, *magician* Lucio Vucino, *Sven* Sture Olsson, *with* Hanna Eriksson, Peter Roth, Tommy Johansson, Joran Mueller, Hasse Soderholm, Eva Stenfelt, Rolando Nunez, Klas Gosta Olsson, Helene Mathiasson, Fredrik Sjogren.
● *Dir* and *Screenplay*: Roy Andersson, *Pro* Lisa Alwert, *Ex Pro* Philippe Bober, *Ph* Istvan Borbás and Jesper Klevenas, *M* Benny Andersson, *Costumes* Leontine Arvidsson.

Roy Andersson Filmproducktion AB/Sveriges Television AB/Danmarks Radio/Arte France Cinema/Easy Film/ARTE/La Sept/Canal Plus, etc-ICA Projects.
98 mins. Sweden/France/Denmark/Norway/Germany. 2000. Rel: 16 February 2001. Cert 15.

## Sorted ★★

Carl leaves Scunthorpe for the glamour of London so as to unearth the facts surrounding his brother's apparently accidental death at a rave. With his brother's ex-girlfriend in tow, he ventures into the underbelly of the urban club scene, befriending various head-nodding, suppository-popping characters who know more about his brother than they are telling… Immaculately styled and fronted by an achingly attractive couple in Rhys and Guillory, *Sorted* nevertheless travels trite territory, parodying rather than exposing the alternative lifestyles of London's ravers. Rhys' crash course in the strobe-lit under-culture is a too-familiar essay in the dangers of freelance hedonism, while the villainous menace of a grotesquely caricatured Tim Curry is a pitiful foil which crumbles under the weight of DJ-turned-director Alex Jovy's admirably high ambitions. [*Adam Keen*]

● *Carl* Matthew Rhys, *Sunny* Sienna Guillory, *Damian Kemp* Tim Curry, *Tiffany* Fay Masterson, *Rob* Stephen Marcus, *Martin* Jason Donovan, *Jake* Sebastian Knapp, *Sarah* Kelly Brook, *with* Michael Price, Charlotte Bicknell, Idris Elba, Gina Murray, Martin Wimbush, Tim Vincent, Mary Tamm, Mark Crowdy.
● *Dir* Alexander Jovy, *Pro* Fabrizio Chiesa and Mark Crowdy, *Ex Pro* Jovy and Steve Clark-Hill, *Line Pro* Peter La Terriere, *Screenplay* Nick Villiers, from a story by Jovy, *Ph* Mike Southon, *Pro Des* Eve Stewart,

*Ed* Justin Krish, *M* Guy Farley; songs performed by Morcheeba, Leftfield, Elvis Presley, Public Enemy, Lost Tribe, Twisted Pair, The Turtles, Southsugar, Agnelli & Nelson, Aphrodite, St Etienne, Funky G with the Gibson Bros, Disposable Disco Clubs, Hi Gate, Scott 4, Depeche Mode, CRW, Atlantis, Art of Trance etc, *Costumes* Ffion Elinor.

Jovy Junior-Metrodome.
102 mins. UK. 2000. Rel: 6 October 2000. Cert 18.

## Space Cowboys ★★★

Back in 1958 Frank Corvin, Hawk Hawkins, Jerry O'Neil and Tank Sullivan were the most promising test pilots America could call its own. But after crashing three planes in ten months, the flyboys were grounded forever, dashing their hopes of ever getting into space. Then, 40 years later, a crucial Soviet communications satellite is headed for self-destruction and only its original designer, Frank Corvin, can save it. But in order to do so, Frank insists that his original team head out for space to intercept it... One of the key elements in Clint Eastwood's lasting success is that he has never been afraid to play his own age. Here, he almost takes a masochistic delight in flexing his geriatric muscles, while there's the supplementary pleasure of watching three other old farts strutting their stuff. Although this grey-haired variation of *Armageddon* is a tad long in the tooth, as well as in the telling, it is consistently amiable with charm to spare. Only in the last half hour does a certain predictability creep in, as the old standbys of the space mission genre are played out to diminishing returns. FYI: *Space Cowboys* marks Clint's 22nd outing as director.

● *Frank D Corvin* Clint Eastwood, *Hawk Hawkins* Tommy Lee Jones, *Jerry O'Neil* Donald Sutherland, *Tank Sullivan* James Garner, *Sara Holland* Marcia Gay Harden, *Eugene Davis* William Devane, *Ethan Glance* Loren Dean, *Roger Hines* Courtney V Vance, *Bob Gerson* James Cromwell, *General Vostov* Rade Sherbedgia, *Barbara Corvin* Barbara Babcock, *Dr Anne Caruthers* Blair Brown, *himself* Jay Leno, *Tiny* Nils Allen Stewart, *young Frank D Corvin* Toby Stephens, *with* Kate McNeil, Karen Mistal, Cooper Huckabee.
● *Dir* Clint Eastwood, *Pro* Eastwood and Andrew Lazar, *Ex Pro* Tom Rooker, *Screenplay* Ken Kaufman and Howard Klausner, *Ph* Jack N Green, *Pro Des* Henry Bumstead, *Ed* Joel Cox, *M* Lennie Niehaus; songs performed by Mitch Holder, Joshua Redman, *NSYNC, Willie Nelson, Alison Eastwood, Frank Sinatra with Count Basie & His Orchestra etc, *Costumes* Deborah Hopper, *Sound* Christopher Boyes and David Farmer, *Visual effects* Michael Owens.

Warner/Village Roadshow/Clipsal Films/Malpaso/Mad Chance-Warner.
130 mins. USA/Australia. 2000. Rel: 22 September 2000. Cert PG.

**Left:** *Pet detectives: Alexa Vega and Daryl Sabara in Robert Rodriguez's cunning, fast-moving and totally entertaining* Spy Kids *(from Buena Vista)*

## Spy Kids ★★★¹/₂

Gregorio and Ingrid Cortez were the world's most valued spies until, ordered to knock each other off, they fell in love, married and had kids. Now they've been kidnapped by the dastardly Fegan Floop, an eccentric children's TV host and criminal mastermind. However, Floop hadn't reckoned on the wily intervention of Carmen and Juni Cortez – his captives' son and daughter! … Adopting a deliciously straight face, writer-director Robert Rodriguez gives the James Bond genre an irreverent face-lift with this slick, pacey adventure for all the family. Peppered with eye-popping gimmicks, genuinely amusing set-ups and some priceless throwaway gags, the film should appeal equally to children and their guardians – and without condescension. The young at heart are treated to some ingenious slapstick and inspired flights of espionage fancy, while grownups are provided with an adult morality tale that has as much to say about marriage and responsibility as it does about living up to one's potential. Some of the effects are a little 1980s, but then the action moves so fast that one shouldn't really care. Favourite innovation: Fegan Floop's robotic sidekicks which are, literally, 'all thumbs.' Filmed on location in Austin, Texas.

● *Gregorio Cortez* Antonio Banderas, *Ingrid Cortez* Carla Gugino, *Fegan Floop* Alan Cumming, *Ms Gradenko* Teri Hatcher, *Felix Gumm* Cheech Marin, *Machete* Danny Trejo, *Mr Lisp* Robert Patrick, *Alexander Minion* Tony Shalhoub, *Carmen Cortez* Alexa Vega, *Juni Cortez* Daryl Sabara, *Donnagon/Donnamight* Mike Judge, *cool spy* Richard Linklater, *Pastor* Guillermo Navarro, *Devlin* George Clooney, *with* Johnny Reno, Jeff Dashnaw, Rachel Duhame.
● *Dir, Screenplay* and *Ed* Robert Rodriguez, *Pro* Rodriguez and Elizabeth Avellán, *Ex Pro* Bob Weinstein, Harvey Weinstein and Cary Granat, *Line Pro* Bill Scott, *Ph* Guillermo Navarro, *Pro Des* Cary White, *M* Danny Elfman, Gavin Greenaway, Heitor Pereira, John Debney, Robert Rodriguez, Los Lobos and Harry Gregson-Williams, *Costumes* Deborah Everton, *Make-up* Robert Kurtzman, Gregory Nicotero and Howard Berger.

Miramax International/Dimension Films-Buena Vista. 90 mins. USA. 2001. Rel: 13 April 2001. Cert U.

## State and Main ★★★★★

In the gentle heart of Vermont, the denizens of Waterford are discussing the excitement of a new traffic light when a film crew arrives. Having blown his surplus budget on the construction of a water mill in New Hampshire (now held hostage by the locals), director Walt Price is determined to cut his losses. But his writer is refusing to change the script, his star is romancing an underaged girl and his leading lady has changed her mind about baring her breasts... Having got the plotless profanity of his early plays out of his system, and changed gear dramatically with his adaptation of *The Winslow Boy*, David Mamet continues to hone his creative genius. Here, the writer-director combines both a threadbare premise (the hardship of shooting a movie) with the trickiest of genres (farce) and comes up with a comic masterpiece. He gives us an array of juicy, unexpected characters (Paymer's ruthless producer, Hoffman's inarticulate writer, Macy's multi-faced director, Pidgeon's sanguine bookseller), a compendium of great lines ('I didn't say anything, I was just talking out loud'), a non-interfering score and a fat-free pace. The result: a canny, smart, devilishly funny (and affectionate) middle finger to the movie business. Even the final credit sequence is priceless ('Only two animals were harmed during the making of this film').

● *Bob Barrenger* Alec Baldwin, *Mayor George Bailey* Charles Durning, *Doug MacKenzie* Clark Gregg, *Joseph Turner White* Philip Seymour Hoffman, *Sherry Bailey* Patti LuPone, *Walt Price* William H Macy, *Claire Wellesley* Sarah Jessica Parker, *Marty Rossen* David Paymer, *Ann Black* Rebecca Pidgeon, *Carla Taylor* Julia Stiles, *Jack Taylor* Ricky Jay, *Tommy Max, first assistant director* Jim Frangione, *Doc Wilson* Michael Higgins, *Uberto Pazzi* Vinne Gustafero, *Bill Smith* Lonnie Smith, *with* Linda Kimbrough, Morris Lamore, Alan Soule, Chris Kaldor, Laura Silverman, J J Johnston, Matt Malloy, Tony Mamet, Charlotte Potok, Jordan Lage, Leo Burns, Matthew Pidgeon.
● *Dir* and *Screenplay* David Mamet, *Pro* Sarah Green, *Ex Pro* Alec Baldwin and Jon Cornick, *Line Pro* Dorothy Aufiero, *Ph* Oliver Stapleton, *Pro Des* Gemma Jackson, *Ed* Barbara Tulliver, *M* Theodore Shapiro, *Costumes* Susan Lyall.

Fine Line Features/Filmtown Entertainment/Green/Renzi/El Dorado Pictures-Redbus.
106 mins. USA. 2000. Rel: 16 February 2001. Cert 15.

## Stuart Little ★★★

New York City; the recent past. Desperate to adopt a second child, Mr and Mrs Little are won over by the character and charm of Stuart, a dapper little mouse holed up at the local orphanage. But the Little's nine-year-old son and Persian cat are not so enamoured of the new family member... If you can get over the idea of Hugh Laurie and Geena Davis adopting a talking mouse as *a son*, then you are halfway there. Thanks to some priceless dialogue and miraculous digital effects, this adaptation of the E B White classic is one of the better children's offerings of 1999. Still, one can't help wondering why Laurie and Davis played their thankless roles so straight and what happened to the original structure of the plot. No sooner has Stuart been accepted by his human brother (*Jerry Maguire*'s Jonathan Lipnicki) than he's whisked away by his rodent guardians. But then the

film really belongs to the Littles' cat Snowbell, superbly voiced by Nathan Lane (who previously vented his hatred of rodents in *Mouse Hunt*).

● *Mrs Little* Geena Davis, *Mr Little* Hugh Laurie, *George Little* Jonathan Lipnicki, *voice of Stuart Little* Michael J Fox, *voice of Snowbell* Nathan Lane, *voice of Smokey* Chazz Palminteri, *voice of Monty* Steve Zahn, *voice of Mr Stout* Bruno Kirby, *voice of Mrs Stout* Jennifer Tilly, *Uncle Crenshaw* Jeffrey Jones, *Grandma Estelle* Estelle Getty, *Mrs Keeper* Julia Sweeney, *voice of Lucky* Jim Doughan, *voice of Red* David Alan Grier, *with* Connie Ray, Allyce Beasley, Brian Doyle-Murray, Harold Gould, Patrick O'Brien, Dabney Coleman, Miles Marsico, Jon Polito, Jim Doughan, Taylor Negron.
● *Dir* Rob Minkoff, *Pro* Douglas Wick, *Ex Pro* Jason Clark, Jeff Franklin and Steve Waterman, *Screenplay* M. Night Shyamalan and Greg Brooker, *Ph* Guillermo Navarro, *Pro Des* Bill Brzeski, *Ed* Tom Finan, *M* Alan Silvestri; songs performed by Lyle Lovett, Dean Martin, Lou Bega, Trisha Yearwood, *Costumes* Joseph Porro, *Visual effects* John Dykstra.

Global Entertainment Prods/Columbia Pictures-Columbia TriStar.
84 mins. USA. 1999. Rel: 21 July 2000. Cert U.

## Suzhou River – Su Zhou He ★★★¹/₂

Shanghai; today. A tale is told concerning a courier's deep love for a girl who disappears and his subsequent pursuit of someone who claims not to be her despite their similar looks (the excellent Zhou Xun plays both roles)... This issue of uncertain identity has prompted comparisons with *Vertigo*, but this is more indebted to French arthouse cinema than to Hitchcock, since it plays with the issue of whether obsessional romantic love can only exist in fiction and encourages the audience to ask if the narrator is inventing what he tells us and what we see. Lou Ye's film has emotional force and may well please those who like movies which invite discussion afterwards, but the rough video style of shooting (supposedly that of the narrator, a videographer) soon becomes tiresome. [*Mansel Stimpson*]

● *Moudan/Meimei* Zhou Xun, *Mardar* Jia Hongsheng, *boss* Yao Anlian, *Mada* Nai An, *Lao B* Hua Zhongghkai.
● *Dir* and *Screenplay* Lou Ye, *Pro* Nai An and Philippe Bober, *Assoc Pro* Jian Wei Han, Asai Takashi, Brock Norman Brock and Susanne Marian, *Ph* Wang Yu, *Pro Des* Li Zhuoyi, *Ed* Karl Riedl, *M* Jörg Lemberg.

Essential Film (Berlin)/Dream Factory (Beijing)-Artificial Eye.
83 mins. China/Germany/Netherlands/Japan/France. 1999. Rel: 17 November 2000. Cert 12.

## The Tailor of Panama ★★

Berated for his gambling and womanising, unscrupulous M16 operative Andrew Osnard is dispatched to Panama. There, he quickly infiltrates the smart set, befriending a cockney tailor to the rich and powerful. Using the latter's inside knowledge, Osnard hatches a plan that could have far-reaching consequences... Adapted by John Le Carré from his 1996 novel (in collaboration with director Boorman and the award-winning scenarist Andrew Davies), *The Tailor of Panama* is a wannabe espionage thriller hammering its political point home with what is, presumably, meant to be black farce. Saddled with unwieldy dialogue and sabotaged by an extraordinary range of fluctuating accents, the film feels like a 1960s' programmer calling out for the additional services of Michael Caine and Leslie Phillips. As it is, Geoffrey Rush cuts an irritating figure as the tailor, scuttling about like a beetle and pulling off an odd vocal inflection that recalls Tommy Cooper. Indeed, had Tommy Cooper ever made a James Bond film, it could well have looked like this. Filmed in Panama.

● *Andrew Osnard* Pierce Brosnan, *Harry Pendel* Geoffrey Rush, *Louisa Pendel* Jamie Lee Curtis, *Mickie Abraxas* Brendan Gleeson, *Francesca* Catherine McCormack, *Marta* Leonor Varela, *Teddy* Martin Ferrero, *Uncle Benny* Harold Pinter, *Luxmore* David Hayman, *Ramon Rudd* Jon Polito, *Rafi Domingo*

Mark Margolis, *Dusenbaker* Dylan Baker, *Maltby* John Fortune, *Mark Pendel* Daniel Radcliffe, *Sara Pendel* Lola Boorman, *with* Ken Jenkins, Jonathan Hyde, Paul Birchand, Harry Ditson, Martin Savage. ● *Dir* and *Pro* John Boorman, *Ex Pro* John Le Carré, *Co-Pro* Kevan Barker, *Screenplay* Le Carré, Boorman and Andrew Davies, *Ph* Philippe Rousselot, *Pro Des* Derek Wallace, *Ed* Ron Davis, *M* Shaun Davey, *Costumes* Maeve Paterson.

Columbia Pictures/Merlin Films/Irish Film Industry-Columbia TriStar.
109 mins. USA/Ireland. 2001. Rel: 20 April 2001. Cert 15.

## The Tao of Steve ★★★★

Santa Fe, New Mexico; the present. Steve is not so much a name as a state of mind. Think Steve McGarrett, Steve Austin, Steve McQueen. Dex, a part-time kindergarten teacher, is pure Steve and attracts women like moths to a searchlight. His maxim is simple: be desireless, be excellent and be God. Dex is also a compulsive liar, an unrepentant under-achiever and about 200 pounds overweight. Then he breaks his first rule of seduction. He starts to fall in love... Originally conceived as a documentary, *The Tao of Steve* is based on the lifestyle and philosophy of one Duncan North, who has co-scripted this fresh, perceptive and hilarious film with his friend Jenniphr

*Above:* Sexism rules: Greer Goodman takes Donal Logue for a ride in Jenniphr Goodman's fresh, perceptive and hilarious **The Tao of Steve** (from Entertainment)

Goodman and her sister, Greer, a former lover. To add to the air of authenticity, Jenniphr directs, Greer plays Duncan's girlfriend and Donal Logue, as Duncan, wears his real-life character's wardrobe. Logue won the best actor award at Sundance and deservedly so: he manages to transform a manipulative, overweight slob into a loveable, charismatic charmer. Of course, he is aided by a terrific premise and a canny and witty screenplay (Syd: 'What do you look for in a woman?' Dex: 'Low expectations.').

● *Dex* Donal Logue, *Syd* Greer Goodman, *Dave* Kimo Wills, *Beth* Ayelet Kaznelson, *Rick* David Aaron Baker, *Maggie* Nina Jaroslaw, *Ed* John Hines, *Julie* Dana Goodman, *with* John Harrington Bland, Matt Hotsinpiller, Sue Cremin, *Duncan* Duncan North, *himself* Astro the Dog.
● *Dir* Jenniphr Goodman, *Pro* Anthony Bregman, *Ex Pro* Ted Hope, *Screenplay* Duncan North, Greer Goodman and Jenniphr Goodman, *Ph* Teodoro Maniaci, *Pro Des* Rosario Provenza, *Ed* Sarah Gartner, *M* Joe Delia; songs performed by Epperley, The Marathons, The Bugaloos, Eytan Mirsky, Stereo Total, Adventures in Stereo, Lemonheads, The Blue Hawaiians, *Costumes* Birgitta Bjerke, *Steve consultant* Bruce Robertson.

Good Machine/Thunderhead Prods-Entertainment. 87 mins. USA. 2000. Rel: 2 March 2001. Cert 15.

## Taxi 2 ★★★

Marseilles; today. When speedaholic taxi driver Daniel Morales is introduced to his girlfriend's father, the disciplinarian Général Bertineau, he is eager to make a good impression. Then the chauffeur of a visiting Japanese minister – in Marseilles to study the anti-terrorist techniques of the city's elite police force – is injured and the General suggests that Daniel take his place. But even with Daniel at the wheel, the minister is kidnapped by members of the Japanese Yakuza… Blending elements of *Meet the Parents* with the high-octane stunt work *of The Fast and the Furious*, this sequel to the 1998 Luc Besson-penned hit certainly delivers the goods. With a considerably bigger budget this time round, the film expands on the running gags of the original and delivers the same breathless action, charm and sexiness. Expect *Taxi 3* any time soon. FYI: During one particularly harrowing stunt, two stuntmen were seriously injured and a cameraman killed. [*Charles Bacon*]

● *Daniel Morales* Samy Naceri, *Émilien Coutan Kermadec* Frédéric Diefenthal, *Petra* Emma Sjöberg, *Chief Inspector Gibert* Bernard Farcy, *Lilly Bertineau* Marion Cotillard, *Général Bertineau* Jean-Christophe Bouvet, *Ministre français* Marc Faure, *Rachid* Malek Bechar, *with* Edouard Montoute, Sébastien Pons, Tsuyu Shimizu.
● *Dir* Gérard Krawczyk, *Pro* Luc Besson, Laurent

Pétin and Michèle Pétin, *Ex Pro* Bernard Grenet and Antoine Simkine, *Screenplay* Besson, *Ph* Gérard Sterin, *Pro Des* Jean-Jacques Gernolle, *Ed* Thierry Hoss, *M* Al Khemya, *Costumes* Martine Rapin.

Luc Besson/Leeloo Prods/ARP Prods/TF1 Films/Canal Plus-Metrodome.
82 mins. France. 2000. Rel: 29 June 2001. Cert 15.

## The Terrorist ★★★½

Sri Lanka/southern India; the present. Just a young girl when her brother sacrificed himself for the 'good of the cause,' Malli is proud to be chosen as the assassin of an Indian dignitary known only as the 'VIP'. And so she prepares herself for the ultimate act of martyrdom, in which, corseted in dynamite, she will honour the name of her brother and her people... Inspired by the assassination of the Indian prime minister Rajiv Gandhi in 1991, *The Terrorist* explores the psychology of the executioner, in this case a 19-year-old woman trained from an early age to kill without compunction. As embodied by the Anglo-Indian actress Ayesha Dharkar, Malli is a photographic presence whose looks are devoured by the camera in a series of pore-probing close-ups. With the few acts of violence committed off-screen, this is essentially a character piece, underscored by an overactive soundtrack of melodramatic music and, in its quieter moments, heavy breathing. Best known for his cine-

matography of large-scale musicals, director Satosh Sivan is hardly a subtle filmmaker, but he has a good eye, even though he lets us know it rather too often.

● *Malli* Ayesha Dharkar, *Thyagu* Vishnu Vardhan, *Perumal* Bhanu Prakash, *Vasu* Parmeshwaran, *with* Lotus Vishwas, K Krishna, Sonu Sisupal, Anuradha, Bhavani.
● *Dir* and *Ph* Satosh Sivan, *Pro* Shree Prasad and Jit Joshi, *Ex Pro* Ravi Sunil Doshi, Vikram Singh and Mark Burton, *Screenplay* Santosh Sivan, Ravi Deshpande and Vijay Deveshwar, *Pro Des* Shyam Sunder, *Ed* Sreekar Prasad, *M* Sonu Sisupal and Rajamani, *Costumes* Anu Radha.

Modern Gallerie/Motion Pictures New York/Indian Image Prods-Metro Tartan.
99 mins. India/USA. 1998. Rel: 11 May 2001. Cert 12.

## There's Only One Jimmy Grimble
★★★½

A fairy story in Manchester – how very modern. John Hay's charming feature debut stars Lewis McKenzie as a young lad who rises above the playground bullies when he's given a pair of ancient footie boots. Jimmy's belief that the boots are magic gives him unstoppable abilities both on and off the pitch, the moral being that we can achieve our dreams when we have faith (even if it comes via boots from a spooky old bag

*Above:* The kids are alright: A scene from John Hay's charming, involving There's Only One Jimmy Grimble (from Pathé)

lady). McKenzie carries the film impressively, especially when you note the big Brit line-up. Robert Carlyle provides bitter humour as Jimmy's dejected PE teacher, Gina McKee is quietly fraught as Jimmy's caring but ineffective mum, and Ray Winstone puts in a surprising turn as the nice bloke. The point of view scenes of Jimmy being taunted highlight our emotional connection with him. In fact, other than Billy Elliot, Jimmy becomes a far greater hero than any character I've met in a British movie recently. The film doesn't break new ground, nor justify big screen viewing, but it's not a bad benchmark for intimate storytelling. [*Wendy Lloyd*]

● *Eric Wirral* Robert Carlyle, *Harry* Ray Winstone, *Donna* Gina McKee, *Jimmy Grimble* Lewis McKenzie, *Two Dogs* Ben Miller, *with* Wayne Galtrey, John McArdle, Michael J Jackson, Andrew Schofield, Dave Hill, Julie Brown.
● *Dir* John Hay, *Pro* Sarah Radclyffe, Jeremy Bolt and Alison Jackson, *Screenplay* Simon Mayle, John Hay and Rik Carmichael, *Ph* John de Borman, *Pro Des* Michael Carlin, *Ed* Oral Norrie Ottey, *M* Simon Boswell and Alex James; songs performed by The Charlatans, Freestylers, Public Enemy, Orbital, Frankie Goes To Hollywood, Happy Mondays, Stone Roses, Bananarama, Echo and the Bunnymen, Fatboy Slim, The Chemical Brothers etc, *Costumes* Mary-Jane Reyner.

Pathé Pictures/Arts Council of England/Canal Plus/Impact Films/National Lottery- Pathé.
105 mins. UK/France. 2000. Rel: 25 August 2000. Cert 12.

## Thirteen Days ★★¹/₂

Washington DC; October 1962. When John F Kennedy discovers that Cuba is installing medium-range ballistic missiles, he knows that he must act immediately. But the last thing he wants is a nuclear showdown, or even a national panic. Knowing that if the missiles are armed Cuba could wipe out 80 million US citizens in five minutes, Kennedy calls on the expertise of all the advisers, diplomats and generals at his disposal... The problem with a thriller based on known facts is that, like *Titanic* and *Apollo 13*, the outcome is predetermined. Yet, as filtered through the corridors of the White House, David Self's intelligent script allows the viewer a fresh, fly-on-the-wall perspective, even though the human impact is merely touched on. And, at two-and-a-half hours, the film does get bogged down in a war of words uttered by countless suited dignitaries. Meanwhile, Kevin Costner, who also produced, sounds a discordant note (where *did* he get that accent from?), adding a slight imbalance to what is basically an ensemble drama peopled by little-known but creditable actors. Of the latter, Steven Culp is particularly impressive as Bobby Kennedy, while Trevor Jones' urgent score propels the action along nicely.

● *Kenneth O'Donnell* Kevin Costner, *John F Kennedy* Bruce Greenwood, *Robert F Kennedy* Steven Culp, *Robert McNamara* Dylan Baker, *Adlai Stevenson* Michael Fairman, *Dean Rusk* Henry Strozier, *National Security Adviser McGeorge Bundy* Frank Wood, *General Curtis LeMay* Kevin Conway, *Ted Sorensen* Tim Kelleher, *Dean Acheson* Len Cariou, *General Maxwell Taylor* Bill Smitrovich, *Arthur Lundahl* Dakin Matthews, *Commander William B Ecker* Christopher Lawford, *Andrei Gromyko* Olek Krupa, *Helen O'Donnell* Lucinda Jenney, *Jacqueline Kennedy* Stephanie Romanov, *with* Madison Mason, Ed Lauter, Elena Baskin, James Karen, Tim Jerome, Shawn Driscoll, Drake Cook, Caitlin Wachs, Jon Foster, *NPIC photo interpreter* Kevin O'Donnell, Jack McGee, John Aylward, David O'Donnell, Michael Gaston
● *Dir* Roger Donaldson, *Pro* Armyan Bernstein, Peter O Almond and Kevin Costner, *Ex Pro* Ilona Herzeberg, Michael De Luca, Thomas A. Bliss and Marc Abraham, *Co-Pro* Paul Deason and Mary Montiforte, *Screenplay* David Self, based on the book *The Kennedy Tapes – Inside the White House during the Cuban Missile Crisis*, *Ph* Andrzej Bartkowiak, *Pro Des* Dennis Washington, *Ed* Conrad Buff, *M* Trevor Jones, *Costumes* Isis Mussenden.

Beacon Pictures-Buena Vista.
145 mins. USA. 2000. Rel: 16 March 2001. Cert 12.

## Thomas and the Magic Railroad ★★

Thomas the Tank Engine steams up a siding in his journey from page to big screen when he interacts with human characters on the magical island of Sodor and battles the evil Diesel 10, a nasty new train with no rail manners. Mara Wilson stars as a young girl sent to spend time with her reclusive grandfather (Fonda) whose life has been blighted by his inability to mend a steam engine called Lady. Meanwhile, back at the station Mr Conductor has more problems than BR's proverbial leaves-on-the-track. An uneasy mix of models and animation. [*Marianne Gray*]

● *Grandpa Burnett Stone* Peter Fonda, *Lily* Mara Wilson, *Mr Conductor* Alec Baldwin, *Stacy* Didi Conn, *Billy Twofeathers* Russell Means, *Patch* Cody McMains, *Junior* Michael E Rodgers, *young Burnett Stone* Jared Wall; voices: *Thomas the Tank Engine* Edward Glen, *Diesel 10/Splatter/Gordon* Neil Crone, *Toby* Colm Feore, *Percy* Linda Ballantyne, *Lady* Britt Allcroft, etc.
● *Dir* and *Screenplay* Britt Allcroft, *Pro* Allcroft and Phil Fehrle, *Ex Pro* Charles Falzon, Nancy Chapelle, Barry London, Brent Baum and John Bertolli, *Co-Pro* Mark Jacobson, *Ph* Paul Ryan, *Pro Des* Oleg Savytski, *Ed* Ron Wisman, *M* Hummie Mann; 'Locomotion' performed by Atomic Kitten, *Costumes* Luis M. Sequeira, *Visual effects* Bill Neil.

Destination Films/Gullane Pictures/The Isle of Man Film Commission, etc-Icon.
85 mins. USA/UK. 2000. Rel: 14 July 2000. Cert U.

## Those Who Love Me Can Take the Train – Ceux qui m'aiment prendront le train ★★

The title of this contemporary French drama from Patrice Chéreau, best known here for *La Reine Margot*, refers to travellers leaving Paris to attend a funeral in Limoges. The deceased was a bisexual painter and the mourners include family, friends, ex-students and lovers. As a detailed study of relationships, many of them precarious, this is promising material, and it's aided by a strong cast (not least Jean-Louis Trintignant, seen briefly in flashback as the deceased and more fully as his twin brother). What infuriates is that the potential is lost through Chéreau's decision to have 15 leading characters and to tell their stories so confusingly that it's a full-time distraction just to work out who is who and what their relationships are. There's passing consolation in the Scope view of the cemetery in Limoges, a breathtaking moment and an unforgettable cinematic image. [*Mansel Stimpson*]

● *François* Pascal Greggory, *Claire* Valéria Bruni-Tedeschi, *Jean-Marie* Charles Berling, *Lucien/Jean-*

*Baptiste Emmerich* Jean-Louis Trintigant, *Viviane* Vincent Perez, *Louis* Bruno Todeschini, *Bruno* Sylvian Jacques, *Thierry* Roschdy Zem, *Catherine* Dominique Blanc, *Elodie* Delphine Schiltz, *with* Nathan Cogan, Marie Daems, Chantal Newirth, Thierry De Peretti, Olivier Gourmet, Geneviève Brunet, Didier Brice.
● *Dir* Patrice Chéreau, *Pro* Charles Gassot, *Ex Pro* Jacques Hinstin, *Screenplay* Chéreau, Danièle Thompson and Pierre Trividic, *Ph* Eric Gautier, *Pro Des* Richard Peduzzi and Sylvian Chauvelot, *Ed* François Gedigier, *M* various; songs performed by Massive Attack & Tracey Thorn, John Parish & P.J. Harvey, Jeff Buckley, The Divine Comedy, James Brown, Cake, Björk, The Doors, Nina Simone, Charles Aznavour, Portishead etc, *Costumes* Caroline De Vivaise.

Canal Plus/Téléma/France 2 Cinema/France 3 Cinema/Azor Films-Artificial Eye.
122 mins. France. 1998. Rel: 18 August 2000. Cert 15.

## Tigerland ★★

Fort Polk/Tigerland, Louisiana; 1971. If war is hell, then it's up to the army to prepare its men for the worst. Thus, the grunts of A-Company, Second Platoon, are given a taste of what is to come as they are verbally degraded by their superiors, physically

**Above:** *Fight club: Colin Farrell prepares for action in Joel Schumacher's dreary, superfluous and muddled* Tigerland *(from Twentieth Century Fox)*

abused by their peers and deprived of sleep. So, are they man enough to die for their country? ... Just what we need: another soul-destroying drama about men humiliating other men in boot camp. Yet, unlike such films as *An Officer and a Gentleman*, *Full Metal Jacket* and *Biloxi Blues*, this one underscores its integrity with queasy hand-held camerawork, murky photography and an unknown cast. Of course, the trouble with unknown casts is that when men are reduced to their bare essentials – shaved heads, mud-caked faces, surly stares – it's hard to tell them apart, particularly when the camera is zooming all over the place. Still, with his confident masculinity and innate charisma, the Irish-born Colin Farrell cuts an imposing figure as an embryonic George Clooney.

● *Roland Bozz* Colin Farrell, *Pvt Jim Paxton* Matthew Davis, *Miter* Clifton Collins Jr, *Cantwell* Thomas Guiry, *Wilson* Shea Whigham, *Johnson* Russell Richardson, *Captain Saunders* Nick Searcy, *Sergeant Landers* Afemo Omilami, *Sergeant Thomas* James McDonald, *Sergeant Cota* aka *NCO* Cole Hauser, *with* Keith Ewell, Matt Gerald, Stephen Fulton, Arian Ash, Haven Gaston, Michael Shannon, Marc MacCaulay, Chris Huvane.
● *Dir* Joel Schumacher, *Pro* Arnon Milchan, Steven Haft and Beau Flynn, *Ex Pro* Ted Kurdyla, *Screenplay* Ross Klavan and Michael McGruther, *Ph* Matthew Libatique, *Pro Des* Andrew Laws, *Ed* Mark Stevens, *M* Nathan Larsen; songs performed by Steppenwolf, Adam Kay, Tory Kittles and Rhynell Brumfield, *Costumes* Linda Gennerich, *Military adviser* Dale Dye.

Regency Enterprises/Haft Entertainment/New Regency/ Kirch Media-Fox.
101 mins. USA. 2000. Rel: 18 May 2001. Cert 18.

## Timecode ★★¹/₂

Contrary to the central conceit of the film, *Timecode* is not the future of cinema. Writer/director Mike Figgis challenges the traditional editing of modern movies by showing the product of four unedited, continuously running Sony DSR-1 digital cameras in a quartered screen for his film's entire running time. While admirable for its challenge to both the actors and the viewer, the interrelated, mostly improvised stories of an adulterous film producer, his suspicious wife, his bisexual mistress and her jealous lover are simply too flimsy to sustain the choppy narrative. If anything, *Timecode* merely demonstrates the cinema's need for good editors. Were it a film school project, it would have definite merit. As a video resumé for its participating actors, it should prove invaluable for far less tedious work. Xander Berkeley truly stands out as the producer on the verge of a nervous breakdown and Julian Sands alternately amuses and annoys as a wandering masseuse. [*Scot Woodward Myers*]

● *Evan Watz* Xander Berkeley, *Emma* Saffron Burrows, *Victoria Cohen* Viveka Davis, *Lester Moore* Richard Edson, *Sikh nurse* Aimee Graham, *Rose* Salma Hayek, *therapist* Glenne Headley, *executive* Holly Hunter, *Randy* Danny Huston, *Bunny Drysdale* Kyle MacLachlan, *Ana Pauls* Mia Maestro, *Cherine* Leslie Mann, *Dava Adair* Laurie Metcalf, *Joez Z* Alessandro Nivola, *Quentin* Julian Sands, *Alex Green* Stellan Skarsgård, *Lauren Hathaway* Jeanne Tripplehorn, *Darren Fetzer* Steven Weber, *Onyx Richardson* Golden Brooks, *with* Andrew Heckler, Patrick Kearney, Daphna Kastner, Elizabeth Low, Suzy Nakamura, Zuleikha Robinson, Holly Houston.
● *Dir* and *Screenplay* Mike Figgis, *Pro* Figgis and Annie Stewart, *Co-Pro* Dustin Bernard and Gary Scott Marcus, *Ph* Patrick Alexander Stewart, *Pro Des* Charlotte Malmlöf, *M* Figgis and Anthony Marinelli; Mahler; songs performed by Skin, Arlen Figgis, Everything But the Girl, *Costumes* Donna Casey.

Screen Gems/Red Mullet-Columbia TriStar.
93 mins. USA. 2000. Rel: 18 August 2000. Cert 15.

## Titan A.E. ★★★★

In mankind's evolutionary cycle, the great stepping stones have been the discovery of fire, the harnessing of electricity, the splitting of the atom and now, in the year 3028, the creation of the Titan project. With this last breakthrough, Earth suddenly becomes a threat to a previously tolerated enemy, the Drej, who immediately annihilate our planet. Only a few space-bound humans remain, one of whom, Cale, holds a map to the whereabouts of the missing Titan ship holographically encased in his signet ring... *Titan A.E.* is to be commended for taking animated science fiction into a new area, particularly where the computer-generated effects are concerned. Like a Yes album cover sprung to life, the film is a banquet to the eye. There is also a strong story, vivid characters and an off-hand sense of humour that constantly defuses any delusions of pomposity. While teenagers should get plenty of entertainment out of repeated viewings, their parents shouldn't be bored either. Without wishing to sound too grandiose about it, this is a real milestone in animation.

● Voices: *Cale* Matt Damon, *Korso* Bill Pullman, *Gune* John Leguizamo, *Preed* Nathan Lane, *Stith* Janeane Garofalo, *Akima* Drew Barrymore, *Professor Sam Tucker* Ron Perlman, *young Cale* Alex D Linz, *Tek* Tone-Loc, *with* Jim Breuer, Chris Scarabosio, Jim Cummings, Charles Rocket, Ken Campbell, Tsai Chin, Crystal Scales, David L Lander.
● *Dir* Don Bluth and Gary Goldman, *Pro* Bluth, Goldman and David Kirschner, *Ex Pro* Paul Gertz, *Screenplay* Ben Edlund, John August and Joss

Whedon, from a story by Hans Bauer and Randall McCormick, *Pro Des* Philip A. Cruden, *M* Graeme Revell, *Sound* Christopher Boyes, *Animation* Len Simon.

Twentieth Century Fox Animation-Fox. 97 mins. USA. 2000. Rel: 28 July 2000. Cert PG.

### Titus ★★★¹/₂

Playing at his kitchen table with a jumble of toys of destruction, young Lucius loses control and, following a sudden explosion, his Roman soldiers take on a life of their own. Transposed to the Coliseum in Rome, the boy becomes a spectator to a tale of unspeakable savagery and barbarism as a single act of ritual violence unleashes a vicious cycle of betrayal and revenge... Juggling the artefacts of war throughout the ages, theatre director Julie Taymor has brought what is arguably Shakespeare's bloodiest play resoundingly to life. Dominated by a magnificent turn from Anthony Hopkins as the manic Roman general, the film is a vivid interpretation of a work that has shocked society for centuries. Bringing out the black comedy that she insists Shakespeare intended, Taymor exhibits a ferocious cinematic talent linked with a deep understanding for the language. Pulling no punches in a frenzied collision of styles (utilising chariots, tanks, swords and guns), Taymor animates the repercussions of violence in a fresh and orgiastic way.

● *Titus* Anthony Hopkins, *Tamora* Jessica Lange, *Saturninus* Alan Cumming, *Marcus* Colm Feore, *Bassianus* James Frain, *Lavinia* Laura Fraser, *Aaron* Harry Lennix, *Lucius* Angus Macfadyen, *Demetrius* Matthew Rhys, *Chiron* Jonathan Rhys Meyers, *young Lucius* Osheen Jones, *Alarbus* Raz Degan, *Quintus* Kenny Doughty, *Mutius* Blake Ritson, *Martius* Colin Wells, *Aemelius* Constantine Gregory, *Nurse* Geraldine McEwan, *Caius* Leonardo Treviglio.
● *Dir* and *Screenplay* Julie Taymor, *Pro* Taymor, Jody Patton and Conchita Airoldi, *Ex Pro* Paul G Allen, *Co-Ex Pro* Ellen Little, Robbie Little and Stephen K Bannon, *Assoc Pro* Karen L Thorson, *Ph* Luciano Tovoli, *Pro Des* Dante Ferretti, *Ed* Francoise Bonnot, *M* Elliot Goldenthal, *Costumes* Milena Canonero, *Choreography* Giuseppe Pennese.

Clear Blue Sky Prods/Overseas Filmgroup/Urania Pictures/NDF International-Buena Vista. 162 mins. USA/UK. 1999. Rel: 1 September 2000. Cert 18.

### Tom's Midnight Garden ★¹/₂

When his younger brother contracts measles, Tom Long is packed off to stay with his boring aunt and

**Above:** 'Nobility's true badge': Anthony Hopkins takes on the title role of Shakespeare's tragically betrayed warrior Titus Andronicus (from Buena Vista)

uncle at a block of flats near Ely, Cambridgeshire. Then, when the grandfather clock on the ground floor strikes 13, Tom discovers a whole new world beyond the back door. Here there is a beautiful Victorian garden in which resides a lonely orphan girl called Hatty. While others in the garden fail to notice Tom, Hatty sees him and the children strike up a unique friendship... Writer-director Willard Carroll should have taken a long hard look at Agnieszka Holland's *The Secret Garden* to see how magical, and beautiful, a children's film can really be. As it is, Carroll has made a disastrous job of adapting Philippa Pearce's 1958 classic to the screen, depriving it of rhythm, structure, credibility and charm. And while Carroll coaxed fine performances out of Sean Connery and Angelina Jolie in his subsequent *Playing by Heart*, he's extracted nothing but a series of cheesy grins out of young Anthony Way. For God's sake read the book.

● *Gwen Kitson* Greta Scacchi, *Alan Kitson* James Wilby, *Mrs Bartholomew* Joan Plowright, *Tom Long* Anthony Way, *Abel* David Bradley, *Aunt Melbourne* Penelope Wilton, *adult Tom Long* Nigel Le Vaillant, *Mrs Willows* Liz Smith, *young Hatty* Florence Hoath, *Hatty* Caroline Carver, *Alice Long* Mel Martin, *Melody Long* Serena Gordon, *Peter Long* Nick Robinson, *youngest Hatty* Laurel Melsom, *with* Marlene Sidaway, Arlene Cockburn, Tom Bowles, Rory Jennings, Noah Huntley, Daniel Betts, Arthur Cox.
● *Dir* and *Screenplay* Willard Carroll, *Pro* Adam Shapiro, Charles Salmon and Tom Wilhite, *Ex Pro* Marie Vine and Yukio Sonoyama, *Ph* Gavin Finney, *Pro Des* James Merifield, *Ed* Les Healey, *M* Debbie Wiseman, *Costumes* Deirdre Clancy.

Hyperion/Isle of Man Film Commission/BS24 (Japan)/
Isis Prods-Downtown Pictures.
92 mins. USA/UK/Japan. 1998. Rel: 13 October 2000.
Cert U.

*Above:* Judge
dreading: Michael
Douglas finds himself
in a terrible dilemma
in Steven Soderbergh's
provocative and
disturbing Traffic
(from Entertainment)

## Town & Country ★¹/₂

Manhattan/Mississippi/Sun Valley; the present.
When renowned and extremely wealthy architect
Porter Stoddard discovers that his best friend's infidelity is costing him his marriage, he decides to put
his own (extramarital) affairs in order. However, the
more Stoddard attempts to mend the error of his
ways, the more he seems to court romantic disaster…
As the wit of its title would indicate, comic invention
is not exactly in ample supply in this tediously nepo-
tistic comedy. With Warren Beatty's imprint obvious
from the start, the film's bloated mediocrity (and
apparent budget of $100 million) is too much for
Blackpool-born director Chelsom to salvage. Sadly,
none of the inspired quirkiness of Chelsom's *Hear My
Song*, *Funny Bones* or *The Mighty* is evident here, as
the film plods from one inconsequential situation to
another. Desperately over-produced, re-shot and over-
written, the film's attempt at resurrecting the star-
laden screwball comedies of Capra and Sturges is truly

soul-destroying. FYI: Having grossed a mere $7m in
the US, *Town & Country* now rates as the biggest flop
in Hollywood history. [*Ewen Brownrigg*]

● *Porter Stoddard* Warren Beatty, *Ellie Stoddard*
Diane Keaton, *Eugenie Claybourne* Andie
MacDowell, *Griffin* Garry Shandling, *Auburn* Jenna
Elfman, *Alex* Nastassja Kinski, *Mona* Goldie Hawn,
*Mr Claybourne, Eugenie's father* Charlton Heston,
*Mrs Claybourne, Eugenie's mother* Marian Seldes, *Tom
Stoddard* Josh Hartnett, *Alice Stoddard* Tricia Vessey,
*Barney* William Hootkins, *Holly* Katherine Towne,
*Peter Principal* Ian McNeice, *Suttler* Buck Henry,
*with* Eve Crawford, Azura Skye, Chris Tuttle,
Holland Taylor.
● *Dir* Peter Chelsom, *Pro* Andrew Karsch, Fred
Roos and Simon Fields, *Ex Pro* Sidney Kimmel,
Michael De Luca and Lynn Harris, *Co-Pro* Cyrus
Yavneh, *Screenplay* Michael Laughlin and Buck
Henry, *Ph* William A. Fraker, *Pro Des* Caroline
Hanania, *Ed* David Moritz and Claiere Simpson,
*M* Rolfe Kent and John Altman; songs performed
by Djano Reinhardt, Marilyn Monroe, Pink
Martini, Patsy Cline, Louis Armstrong, etc,
*Costumes* Molly Maginnis.

New Line Cinema/Sidney Kimmel Entertainment/FR
Prods/ Longfellow Pictures/Simon Fields Prods-
Entertainment.
104 mins. USA. 2001. Rel: 29 June 2001. Cert 15.

## Traffic ★★★★★

Javier Rodriguez is a Mexican cop determined to resist
the corruption ingrained in the legal hierarchy. Ohio
State Supreme Court Justice Robert Wakefield is
appointed by the White House to head the American
war against drugs. San Diego housewife and expectant
mother Helena Ayala discovers that she is married to
a notorious drug baron. Wakefield's 16-year-old
daughter Caroline responds to her parents' antago-
nism by taking up freebasing… A sweeping, circling
mosaic that reaches into every pore of society conta-
minated by drugs, from the upper reaches of
Washington DC to the streets of the ghetto, *Traffic*
tackles perhaps the most damaging social plague of
our age with intelligence, eloquence, edge, excitement
and even humour. Superbly orchestrated by Steven
Soderbergh (now, surely, America's most accomplished filmmaker – see *sex, lies, and videotape*, *Erin
Brockovich* and everything in between), the film spills
into the consciousness as more and more characters –
some sympathetic, some despicable, others somewhere in between – are sucked into a maelstrom of
greed, deceit and despair. Exceptionally well-acted by
a genuinely outstanding cast (who to praise? Cheadle,
Del Toro, Guzman, Zeta-Jones, Irving, Milian, young
Erika Christensen as Wakefield's disillusioned daughter), edited and photographed (Mexico filmed in a

gritty orange as if occupying another world), *Traffic* is provocative, gripping, disturbing, disorientating and terrifying cinema.

● *Robert Wakefield* Michael Douglas, *Montel Gordon* Don Cheadle, *Javier Rodriguez Rodriguez* Benicio Del Toro, *Arnie Metzger* Dennis Quaid, *Helena Ayala* Catherine Zeta-Jones, *Ray Castro* Luis Guzman, *Manolo Sanchez* Jacob Vargas, *General Arturo Salazar* Tomas Milian, *Eduardo Ruiz* Miguel Ferrer, *Seth Abrahms* Topher Grace, *Caroline Wakefield* Erika Christensen, *Chief of Staff* Albert Finney, *Jeff Sheridan* D W Moffett, *General Ralph Landry* James Brolin, *Carlos Ayala* Steven Bauer, *Ana Sanchez* Marisol Padilla Sanchez, *Barbara Wakefield* Amy Irving, *Francisco Flores* Clifton Collins Jr., *Attorney Michael Adler* Peter Riegert, *Porfilio Madrigal* Joel Torres, *Juan Obregon* Benjamin Bratt, *with* Jose Yenque, Michael O'Neill, Rick Avery, Brian Avery, Corey Spears, Majandra Delfino, Alec Roberts, Stacey Travis, Governor Bill Weld, George Blumenthal, Senator Don Nickles, Margaret Travolta, Senator Harry Reed, Jeff Podolsky, Senator Barbara Boxer, Senator Charles Grassley, James Pickens Jr, Elaine Kagan, John Slattery, Yul Vazquez, Jack Conley, Eddie Velez, Steve Rose, Vincent Ward, and (*uncredited*) Salma Hayek.
● *Dir* Steven Soderbergh, *Pro* Edward Zwick, Marshall Herskovitz and Laura Bickford, *Ex Pro* Richard Solomon, Mike Newell, Cameron Jones, Graham King and Andreas Klein, *Screenplay* Stephen Gaghan, inspired by the Channel 4 TV series *Traffik*, created by Simon Moore, *Ph* Peter Andrews (aka Steven Soderbergh), *Pro Des* Philip Messina, *Ed* Stephen Mirrione, *M* Cliff Martinez, *Costumes* Louise Frogley, *Consultant* Tim Golden.

USA Films/Initial Entertainment/Bedford Falls-Entertainment.
147 mins. USA. 2000. Rel: 26 January 2001. Cert 18.

## 24 Hours in London ★★

London; 2009. When crime lord Christian decides to cut a deal with an American counterpart, he determines to tidy up a few loose ends in his administration. However, when Martha Bedford, an innocent bystander, witnesses one of Christian's 'hits', the police take her into custody. Be that as it may, the law has seldom been a deterrent to Christian's reign of terror... With his tight budget, first-time director Alexander Finbow makes the most of what he has, but he could have spent more time on his script. A mildly futuristic take on *The Long Good Friday*, the film stocks its succinct running time with saleable ingredients (sex, guns, blood), but doesn't have the flair to take them any further. Obviously a fan of John Woo and his successors, Finbow borrows generously from

other films without displaying his own stamp of distinction. [*Charles Bacon*]

● *Christian* Gary Olsen, *Martha Bedford* Anjela Lauren Smith, *Leon* Tony London, *Bubbles Healy* David Sonnenthal, *Simone* Sara Stockbridge, *Richard* Luke Garrett, *Antonia* Wendy Cooper, *Tony* John Sharian, *Miss Lloyd* Lorelei King, *with* Sean Francis, Katia Caballero, Richard Graham, John Benfield, James Olivier, Amita Dhiri.
● *Dir* and *Screenplay* Alexander Finbow, *Pro* Fergal McGrath, *Ex Pro* Peter Jaques, *Line Pro* Bob Portal, *Ph* Chris Plevin, *Pro Des* Matthew Davies, *Ed* Ian Farr, *M* Edmond Butt; Mozart; songs performed by Silver Sun, The Infidels, Faithless, Baby Fox, Headrillaz etc, *Costumes* Fiona Chilcott, *Special effects* Richard Reeve.

One World Films-Blue Dolphin.
92 mins. UK. 1999. Rel: July 2000. Cert 18.

## Twin Falls Idaho ★★★

Blake and Francis Falls have two heads, two arms and three legs between them. Conjoined from birth, they live a life of extraordinary intimacy, their reliance on one another augmented by their constant aversion to so-called 'normal' people. Then, one day, a young woman enters their lives and, hesitantly, falls for the right-hand brother... Drawing on their own closeness as identical twins, first-time filmmakers Mark and Michael Polish have fashioned a truly original film. Creating a surreal netherworld in contemporary New York through their attention to offbeat detail (a taxi driver with a mechanical claw, the elevator that sticks a foot beneath the seventh floor), the Polish brothers imbue the unconventional with a poetic sensibility. *Twin Falls Idaho* is perhaps a little slow and studied for its own good but eminently haunting nonetheless.

● *Blake Falls* Mark Polish, *Francis Falls* Michael Polish, *Penny* Michele Hicks, *Jay Harrison* Jon Gries, *Miles* Patrick Bauchau, *Jesus* Garrett Morris, *surgeon* William Katt, *Francine* Lesley Ann Warren, *Sissy* Teresa Hill, *D'Walt* Robert Beecher, *with* Jill Andre, Ant, Holly Woodlawn.
● *Dir* Michael Polish, *Pro* Marshall Persinger, Rena Ronson and Steven J Wolfe, *Ex Pro* Joyce Schweickert, *Co-Pro* Paul Torok, *Screenplay* Mark and Michael Polish, *Ph* M David Mullen, *Pro Des* Warren Alan Young, *Ed* Leo Trombetta, *M* Stuart Matthewman; songs performed by Fong Naam, Cottonbelly, Lisa Ekdahl, Mark and Michael Polish, Aubrey Ghent, Marc Anthony Thompson, *Costumes* Bic Owen, *Twin effects* Gary J Tunnicliffe.

Seattle Pacific Investments/Fresh Produce Co./Sneak Preview Entertainment-Downtown.
110 mins. USA. 1998. Rel: 1 September 2000. Cert 15.

## Unbreakable ★★★

Philadelphia; the present. David Dunn is the sole survivor of a train wreck that killed 125 people – yet he doesn't have so much as a scratch. Elijah Price suffers from osteogenesis imperfecta, a rare hereditary disease that has turned his bones into brittle sticks. Somehow, these two men could be connected, albeit at opposite ends of the same metaphysical spectrum... M Night Shyamalan, the writer-director of *The Sixth Sense*, certainly has some intriguing ideas up his sleeve, and that must count for something. Yet, like the former, *Unbreakable* is a hard film to describe without giving the game away. It also stars Bruce Willis in another somnambulant performance as a man trapped in a disintegrating marriage. And – this is hard to believe – his character has only just realised, in his mid-forties, that he's never been ill in his life. This being a hard premise to swallow, Shyamalan cloaks it with a plodding style that creaks with its own self-importance. Shooting several key sequences in long shot and at odd angles, Shyamalan seems to be saying *this is serious*, a technique that becomes tiresome soon enough. Still, *Unbreakable* does boast a great central idea and is beautifully shot.

● *David Dunn* Bruce Willis, *Elijah Price* Samuel L Jackson, *Audrey Dunn* Robin Wright Penn, *Joseph Dunn* Spencer Treat Clark, *Elijah's mother* Charlayne Woodard, *Dr Mathison* Eamon Walker, *Kelly* Leslie Stefanson, *priest* James Handy, *nurse* Elizabeth Lawrence, *with* Richard E Council, Marsha Dietlein, Whitney Sugarman, *stadium drug dealer* M Night Shyamalan.
● *Dir* and *Screenplay* M Night Shyamalan, *Pro* Shyamalan, Barry Mendel and Sam Mercer, *Ex Pro* Gary Barber and Roger Birnbaum, *Ph* Eduardo Serra, *Pro Des* Larry Fulton, *Ed* Dylan Tichenor, *M* James Newton Howard, *Costumes* Joanna Johnston, *Sound* Richard King.

Touchstone Pictures-Buena Vista.
118 mins. USA. 2000. Rel: 29 December 2000. Cert 12.

## Under Suspicion ★★

Port San Juan, Puerto Rico; the present. On his way to make a speech at a fund-raising gala, eminent tax attorney and local dignitary Henry Hearst is called in for questioning by the police. It transpires that two young girls have been found raped and murdered and Hearst's report on finding the second body just doesn't add up. Hearst obviously has much to hide, but what exactly? ... Considering the film's claustrophobic setting and relatively short time span, it's surprising to learn that *Under Suspicion* is actually a remake of a French film (Claude Miller's 1981 *Garde à vue*), itself adapted from an English novel by John Wainwright

(*Brainwash*). Yet the leaden proceedings here bear all the hallmarks of a stage play, except with the sort of clichéd dialogue you expect to find in a B-film ('I'm as well as can be expected under the circumstances,' 'the patter of tiny feet', etc). But the real trouble is that it's all so unbelievable, which arty flashbacks, slow motion and speeded-up shots of Puerto Rico just don't help. It goes without saying that Morgan Freeman and Gene Hackman are wonderful actors, but they can't bring this material alive. Formerly known as *Third Degree*.

● *Captain Victor Benezet* Morgan Freeman, *Henry Hearst* Gene Hackman, *Det Felix Owens* Thomas Jane, *Chantal Hearst* Monica Bellucci, *Isabella* Nydia Caro, *with* Miguel Angel Suárez, Pablo Cunqueiro, Isabel Algaze, Jackeline Duprey, Luis Caballero, Patricia Beato.
● *Dir* Stephen Hopkins, *Pro* Hopkins, Lori McCreary and Anne Marie Gillen, *Ex Pro* Morgan Freeman, Gene Hackman, Maurice Leblond and Ross Grayson Bell, *Line Pro* Llewellyn Wells, *Screenplay* Tom Provost and W Peter Iliff, *Ph* Peter Levy, *Pro Des* Cecilia Montiel, *Ed* John Smith, *M* BT; Mozart, *Costumes* Francine Jamison-Tanchuck.

Revelations Films/TF1 International-Redbus.
111 mins. USA/France. 1999. Rel: 12 January 2001. Cert 15.

## Under the Sand – Sous le sable ★★★★

Marie Drillon is an English college lecturer in her fifties living in Paris. Married to Jean for the past 25 years, she is happy with her life and content with her familiar routine. Then, during a holiday in Lit-et-Mixe, Les Landes, Jean vanishes on the beach... While pursuing the same thematic threads as Polanski's *Frantic* and the more recent *Deep End of the Ocean* with Michelle Pfeiffer, François Ozon's psychological drama takes a much more profound look at the process of denial in the person left behind. Dwelling on the minutiae of Marie's everyday life, Ozon manages to draw a very exact and intelligent portrait of the complex barriers we affect just to cope with the emotional exigencies of our daily routine. Giving arguably the best performance of her career, Charlotte Rampling adapts to Ozon's unblinking camera with a naked otherworldliness that is nothing short of mesmerising. And, at 55, she is as sexy as ever, whether romping naked in bed or just rustling up some spaghetti. FYI: Intriguingly, Ozon filmed the first part of his story before even knowing how the second half would turn out.

● *Marie Drillon* Charlotte Rampling, *Jean Drillon* Bruno Cremer, *Vincent* Jacques Nolot,

*Amanda* Alexandra Stewart, *Suzanne Drillon* Andrée Tainsy, *with* Maya Gaugler, David Portugais, Michel Cordes.
● *Dir* François Ozon, *Pro* Olivier Delbosc and Marc Missonnier, *Screenplay* Ozon, Emmanuèle Bernheim, Marina De Van and Marcia Romano, *Ph* Jeanne Lapoirie (winter) and Antoine Heberlé (summer), *Pro Des* Sandrine Canaux, *Ed* Laurence Bawedin, *M* Philippe Rombi; Dvořák, Mahler, Chopin; songs performed by Barbara, Portishead, *Costumes* Pascaline Chavanne.

Fidélité Prods/Euro Space Inc./Haut et Court/Arte France Cinéma/Canal Plus-Artificial Eye.
96 mins. France/Japan. 2000. Rel: 20 April 2001. Cert 15.

## Uneasy Riders – Nationale 7 ★★★¹/₂

Var, south-east France; the present. Intelligent, belligerent and horny as hell, René Amistadi is victim of a terminal wasting disease and is confined to a wheelchair at a home for the physically handicapped. As contemptuous of his carers as his fellow residents, René has become a major problem. Then he suggests a solution which, in its simplicity, threatens to engulf the home in bureaucratic red tape – he needs a prostitute to help relieve him of his pent-up sexual aggression... The message is clear: the physically handicapped are just as funny, unpleasant and sexually driven as the rest of us. Filmed in and around a real home for the handicapped and mixing professional actors with the residents, the film, based on a true story, has an almost documentary feel, aided by the use of hand-held DV cameras. It's certainly an eye-opener and is to be commended for presenting its rich tapestry of characters without a whiff of sentimentality. And, unlike most films about the handicapped, it invites us to laugh at the absurdity of the human condition, whether it be psychological or sexual.

● *Julie* Nadia Kaci, *René Amistadi* Olivier Gourmet, *Roland* Lionel Abelanski, *Sandrine* Chantal Neuwirth, *the psychiatrist* Julien Boisselier, *Florèle* Nadine Marcovici, *Father Gilbert* François Sinapi, *Solange* Isabelle Mazin, *director of the home* Jean-Claude Frissung, *Rabah* Saïd Taghmaoui, *with* Gérald Thomassin, Franck Desmaroux, Manuela Gourary, Nicolas Lecuyot.
● *Dir* Jean-Pierre Sinapi, *Pro* Jacques Fansten, *Screenplay* Jean-Pierre Sinapi and Anne-Marie Catois, *Ph* Jean-Paul Meurisse, *Pro Des* Erminia Sinapi and Jean-Noël Borecek, *Ed* Catherine Schwartz, *M* Jean Musy; Richard Cocciante; Vivaldi *Costumes* Valérie Denieul.

La Sept ARTE/Télécip/Gimages 3-Blue Light.
95 mins. France. 1999. Rel: 30 March 2001. Cert 15.

## Urban Legends: Final Cut ★¹/₂

Alpine University is, apparently, 'the greatest film school ever'. Here, the student whose thesis film wins the annual Hitchcock award is virtually guaranteed an entrée into Hollywood. In fact, it is such a coveted prize that maybe somebody would kill for it... While the inevitable sequel to the 1998 *Urban Legend* is to be applauded for taking a different tack to the original, it does, alas, adopt the same derivative format and false-alarm shock tactics. Thus, a variety of sudden noises interact with a few gruesome murders (a decapitation, electrocution, death by camera lens), although *still* the school's security guard isn't suspicious (where do they *get* these people?). Furthermore, the opening scene is a rip-off from *Passenger 57* and it doesn't get any better, although there is the occasional amusing line ('You stole my fucking genre!,' 'Digital sucks, latex rules!'). There are also some in-jokes, but they are so obscure as to be subliminal (the surname of Amy's character is taken from the director of the actress' first film). FYI: Director/composer John Ottman was composer and editor of *The Usual Suspects*.

● *Amy Mayfield* Jennifer Morrison, *Travis/Trevor* Matthew Davis, *Graham Manning* Joseph Lawrence, *Reese* Loretta Devine, *Professor Solomon* Hart Bochner, *Toby* Anson Mount, *Vanessa* Eva Mendes, *Sandra* Jessica Cauffiel, *Stan* Anthony Anderson, *Dirk* Michael Bacall, *Simon* Marco Hofschneider, *with* Derek Aasland, Jacinda Barrett, Peter Millard.
● *Dir* and *M* John Ottman, *Pro* Neal H Moritz, Gina Matthews and Richard Luke Rothschild, *Ex Pro* Brad Luff and Nicholas Osborne, *Co-Pro* Michael McDonnell, *Screenplay* Paul Harris Boardman and Scott Derrickson, *Ph* Brian Pearson, *Pro Des* Mark Zuelzke, *Ed* Rob Kobrin, *Costumes* Marie-Sylvie Deveau and Trysha Bakker.

Phoenix Pictures/Canal Plus-Columbia TriStar.
98 mins. USA. 2000. Rel: 1 December 2000. Cert 15.

## Valentine ★

This is what video bargain bins are for. Seldom do films this vapid and artless make it to a cinema screen these days, but then horror still sells at the megaplex. Anyway, for the record this is the tiresome story of a bevy of lovelies who meet a variety of ends at the hands (and big knife) of a 'mysterious' psycho. It transpires that, 13 years earlier, a sixth grade Valentine's Day dance went sour when the school geek was humiliated by his female classmates and then beaten by the boys. Now He's Back and there's no *Scream*-like parody to hide behind. The film features mainly TV graduates and is directed by none other than Jamie Blanks of *Urban Legend* fame, which should tell you something. [*Ewen Brownrigg*]

● *Paige* Denise Richards, *Adam* David Boreanaz, *Kate* Marley Shelton, *Dorothy* Jessica Capshaw, *Lily* Jessica Cauffield, *Shelley* Katherine Heigl, *Ruthie* Hedy Burress, *Det Vaughn* Fulvio Cecere, *with* Daniel Cosgrove, Johnny Whitworth, Woody Jeffreys, Adam Harrington.
● *Dir* Jamie Blanks, *Pro* Dylan Sellers, *Ex Pro* Grant Rosenberg and Bruce Berman, *Screenplay* Donna Powers, Wayne Powers, Gretchen J Berg and Aaron Harberts, based on the novel by Tom Savage, *Ph* Rick Bota, *Pro Des* Stephen Geaghan, *Ed* Steve Mirkovich, *M* Don Davis; songs performed by Star, Tipsy, Goldo, DJ Sonic, Rob Zombie, Marilyn Manson, Carter Armstrong, Deftones, Static-X, Linkin Park, Filter, Amanda Ghost, BT, Disturbed, Beautiful Creatures, Orgy, Snake River Conspiracy etc, *Costumes* Karin Nosella.

Warner/Village Roadshow/NPV Entertainment-Warner. 96 mins. USA/Australia. 2001. Rel: 13 April 2001. Cert 15.

## Vertical Limit ★★★¹/₂

The Karakorum Range of the western Himalayas, Pakistan; the present. It has been three years since National Geographic photographer Peter Garrett and his sister Annie, a world-class mountaineer, lost their father in a horrific climbing accident. Peter has given up climbing for good, but Annie is intent on fulfilling her father's dreams. Then she gets stranded 26,000 feet up the face of K2 and Peter is forced to enlist an eccentric gaggle of mountaineers to save her life... As formulaic movies go, *Vertical Limit* supplies some mighty knee-trembling thrills. Shot primarily in the Southern Alps of New Zealand (with Mount Cook doubling for K2), it not only boasts some heart-stopping scenery but many stunts performed by the actors themselves. There are also some nice touches of humour (the Pakistanis hanging on to their English heritage), some grisly sound effects and a few good lines (Le Marquand to O'Donnell: 'One hundred thousand sperm and you were the fastest?'). However, it's time for the helicopter-appearing-out-of-nowhere cliché to be put to bed – helicopters make a lot of noise and can be heard a mile off.

● *Peter Garrett* Chris O'Donnell, *Elliot Vaughn* Bill Paxton, *Annie Garrett* Robin Tunney, *Montgomery Wick* Scott Glenn, *Monique Aubertine* Izabella Scorupco, *Major Rasul* Temuera Morrison, *Royce Garrett* Stuart Wilson, *Colonel Amir Salim* Roshan Seth, *Tom McLaren* Nicholas Lea, *Malcolm Bench* Ben Mendelsohn, *Cyril Bench* Steve Le Marquand, *Skip Taylor* Robert Taylor, *with* Ed Viesturs, Augie Davis, Alejandro Valdes-Rochin, Rod Brown, Alexander Siddig, David Hayman, Robert Mammone, Leela Patel.

● *Dir* Martin Campbell, *Pro* Campbell, Lloyd Phillips and Robert King, *Ex Pro* Marcia Nasatir, *Screenplay* King and Terry Hayes, *Ph* David Tattersall, *Pro Des* Jon Bunker, *Ed* Thom Noble, *M* James Newton Howard; songs performed by Dean Martin, Bekka & Billy, *Costumes* Graciela Mazon, *Visual effects* Kent Houston, *Special effects* Neil Corbould.

Columbia Pictures-Columbia TriStar. 124 mins. USA. 2000. Rel: 19 January 2001. Cert 12.

## very Annie-Mary ★★★¹/₂

Ogw, Wales; today. Subjugated by her domineering father, an opera-singing baker in a small Welsh town, Annie-Mary Pugh has lost her own voice. Once a great singer herself – as a teenager she won the most prestigious singing competition in Wales – Annie-Mary has now become an insecure, accident-prone and rather timorous person. She dreams of moving out and buying her own house, but her father refuses to let her go... Rachel Griffiths is always a pleasure to watch, whether playing a giggly American bridesmaid in *My Best Friend's Wedding*, a Yorkshire prostitute in *My Son the Fanatic* or a suicidal Australian journalist in *Me Myself I*. Here she exhibits a self-effacing skill with slapstick and fits in seamlessly with a cast of genuine Welsh character actors. But Sara Sugarman's second film (following the critically mauled *Mad Cows*) is by no means a star vehicle, being a richly comic, endearing ensemble piece that recalls the eccentric whimsy of the Irish *Hear My Song* (acknowledged in the name of a horse which Annie-Mary backs in the Grand National). Previously known as *Pavarotti in Dad's Room*.

● *Annie-Mary Pugh* Rachel Griffiths, *Jack Pugh* Jonathan Pryce, *Hob* Ioan Gruffudd, *Nob* Matthew Rhys, *minister* Kenneth Griffith, *Mrs Ifans* Ruth Madoc, *Bethan Bevan* Joanna Page, *Colin Thomas* Rhys Miles Thomas, *ginger gravedigger* Llyr Evans, *Nerys* Cerys Matthews, *with* Grafton Radcliffe, Ray Gravell, Donna Edwards, Rhian Grundy, Wendy Phillips, Anna Mountford, Gwenllian Davies.
● *Dir* and *Screenplay* Sara Sugarman, *Pro* Graham Broadbent and Damian Jones, *Co-Pro* Lesley Stewart, *Ph* Barry Ackroyd, *Pro Des* Alice Normington, *Ed* Robin Sales, *M* Stephen Warbeck; songs performed by Jonathan Pryce, Ioan Gruffud and Matthew Rhys, Rednex, Cerys Matthews, The Village People, Fleetwood Mac etc, *Costumes* Caroline Harris.

Canal Plus/FilmFour/Arts Council of Wales/Arts Council of England/Dragon Pictures-Film Four. 104 mins. UK/France. 2000. Rel: 25 May 2001. Cert 15.

**Right:** *A kiss before crying: Rhys Miles Thomas turns down the advances of Rachel Griffiths in Sara Sugarman's richly comic and endearing very Annie-Mary (from FilmFour)*

## La Veuve de Saint-Pierre ★★★★

French Canada; 1849-50. On the island of Saint-Pierre, off Newfoundland, Neel Auguste is found guilty of a murder he cannot remember committing and is condemned to death. However, with no guillotine and no executioner on the island, the authorities are forced to petition Paris and to await their endorsement. As the weeks turn into months and the months into seasons, Neel is befriended by the wife of the Captain of the Guard and through her care and his good deeds he becomes something of a local hero... A fascinating chronicle adapted from court records, this is a beautifully realised tragedy that draws its power from the understatement of its protagonists and from a skilful economy in the telling. Indeed, the presentation is so stiff-upper-lip that were it not for the sweeping cadence of Pascale Estève's music, little emotion would be in evidence at all. Yet by investing so much trust in his story, director Leconte has created an enticing, accomplished and ultimately deeply moving testament to the healing power of pure forgiveness. FYI: The real-life tale actually took place in the 1920s, but was moved back to the mid-nineteenth century for dramatic effect (and to incorporate the powerful motif of the guillotine).

● *Pauline, 'Madame La'* Juliette Binoche, *Jean, the Captain* Daniel Auteuil, *Ariel Neel Auguste* Emir Kusturica, *Judge Venot* Philippe Magnan, *Governor* Michel Duchaussoy, *Widow Malvilain* Catherine Lascault, *with* Christian Charmetant, Philippe du Janerand, Marc Beland, Ghyslain Tremblay, Marianne Miron.
● *Dir* Patrice Leconte, *Pro* Gilles Legrand and Frédéric Brillion, *Assoc Pro* Denise Robert and Daniel Louis, *Screenplay* Leconte and Claude Faraldo, *Ph* Eduardo Serra, *Pro Des* Ivan Maussion, *Ed* Joëlle Hache, *M* Pascale Estève, *Costumes* Christian Gasc.

Epithète Films/Cinémaginaire/France 3 Cinéma/Universal Pictures (France)/Canal Plus/Téléfilm Canada/Radio Canada, etc-Film Four.
112 mins. France/Canada. 2000. Rel: 4 August 2000. Cert 15.

## The Watcher ★★

Stressed out by the sickening crime rate of Los Angeles, FBI agent Jack Campbell moves to the quieter streets of Chicago to rediscover himself. But when the distinctive murders of one David Allen Griffin start to happen all over again, Campbell realises that Griffin is actually committing his murders as a way of 'bonding' with him... Do FBI agents *ever* have wives (or, for that matter, hobbies?). Do serial killers *ever* kill spontaneously? These are serious questions one must ask before approaching this umpteenth thriller about the cop and the sociopath. Besides the novelty of having Keanu Reeves play the killer (he's one cool psycho), *The Watcher* is numbingly predictable and looks like it was directed by someone who has spent his whole career making music videos (it was).

● *Jack Campbell* James Spader, *Polly* Marisa Tomei, *David Allen Griffin* Keanu Reeves, *Ibby* Ernie Hudson, *Hollis* Chris Ellis, *Mitch* Robert Cicchini, *Lisa* Yvonne Niami, *Ellie Buckner* Rebakah *with* Louise Smith, Jennifer McShane, Gina Alexander, Joe Sikora.
● *Dir* Joe Charbanic, *Pro* Christopher Eberts, Elliot Lewitt, Jeff Rice and Nile Niami, *Ex Pro* Patrick Choi and Paul Pompian, *Screenplay* David Elliot and Clay Ayers, from a story by Elliot and Darcy Meyers, *Ph* Michael Chapman and Ric Waite, *Pro Des* Brian Eatwell and Maria Caso, *Ed* Richard Nord, *M* Marco Beltrami; songs performed by Portishead, Rob Zombie, Sneaker Pimps, Sharkfin, Jacqui Lynn, *Costumes* Jay Hurley.

Universal/Interlight-UIP.
97 mins. USA. 2000. Rel: 2 March 2001. Cert 15.

## Water Drops on Burning Rocks – Gouttes d'eau sur pierres brûlantes ★★★★

This fascinating hybrid finds the talented young French director François Ozon filming an early play by Rainer Werner Fassbinder. He applies camera movement as Fassbinder himself did with *The Bitter Tears of Petra von Kant* to render it essentially cinematic without hiding its stage origin. Relationships both gay and straight are here studied to illustrate the belief that intimacies are more likely to be built on power games than on true love. The outlook of the then 19-year-old Fassbinder, expressed through the intertwined relationships of four characters (all well played here), was sharp and cynical and wittily expressed. Ozon is faithful to this, but also increases the impact by incorporating issues touched on by Fassbinder much later in the movie *In the Year of 13 Moons*. That still doesn't quite make for a masterpiece, but on its own circumscribed terms this is admirably assured and true to both Ozon and Fassbinder. [*Mansel Stimpson*]

● *Léopold Blum* Bernard Giraudeau, *Franz Meister* Malik Zidi, *Anna* Ludivine Sagnier, *Véra* Anna Thomson.
● *Dir* and *Screenplay* François Ozon, from the play *Tropfen auf Heisse Steine* by Rainer Werner Fassbinder, *Pro* Olivier Delbosc and Marc Missonnier, *Ph* Jeanne Lapoirie, *Pro Des* Arnaud de Moléron, *Ed* Laurence Bawedin and Claudine Bouché, *M* various; including songs performed by Françoise Hardy, Tony Holiday etc, *Costumes* Pascaline Chavanne.

Fidélité Prods/Les Films Alain Sarde/Eurospace/Studio Images 6-Artificial Eye.
86 mins. France/Japan. 2000. Rel: 6 October 2000. Cert 18.

## The Way of the Gun ★★★★¹⁄₂

While waiting to be approved as donors at a sperm bank, Parker and Longbaugh overhear a conversation about a doctor, a surrogate mother and a millionaire. Sensing a quick buck, Parker and Longbaugh draw up a hurried plan of abduction and ransom before they head for the border. However, the kidnappers have failed to do their homework and find themselves up against a seriously powerful, merciless and pissed-off kingpin... With an opening scene that stops one in one's tracks, and which sets the tone for things to come, this stylish, excessively violent thriller from the Oscar-winning writer of *The Usual Suspects* is like a shot of caffeine after a season of tea dances. The enigmatically named Parker and Longbaugh are the sort of career criminals who don't care who gets killed – men, women, innocent passers-by – so long as they get what they want. But then, as the good guys don't come off smelling of roses either, one is faced with an intriguing moral dance and a scenario in which each narrative layer is ripped off like sticky plaster from hairy skin. Recalling the breathless, strutting tone of *Reservoir Dogs* – Sam Peckinpah with great dialogue – *The Way of the Gun* is actually a better film than *The Usual Suspects* in that McQuarrie manages to juggle the numerous balls of his complex story with greater clarity. Not for the weak of heart, though. Filmed in Salt Lake City, Utah.

● *'Parker'* Ryan Phillippe, *'Longbaugh'* Benicio Del Toro, *Robin* Juliette Lewis, *Mr Jeffers* Taye Diggs, *Mr Obecks* Nicky Katt, *Hale Chidduck* Scott Wilson, *Joe Sarno* James Caan, *Dr Allen Painter* Dylan Kussman, *Francesca Chidduck* Kristin Lehman, *Abner* Geoffrey Lewis, *P Whipped* Henry Griffin, *raving bitch* Sarah Silverman, *with* Neil Pollock, Irene Santiago, Jan Jensen.
● *Dir* and *Screenplay* Christopher McQuarrie, *Pro* Kenneth Kokin, *Ex Pro* Russ Markowitz, *Ph* Dick Pope, *Pro Des* Maia Javan, *Ed* Stephen Semel, *M*

Joe Kraemer; Mozart; songs performed by The Rolling Stones, Johnny Dilks, Casalando, Daniel Indart, *Costumes* Genevieve Tyrell and Heather Neely McQuarrie.

Artisan Entertainment/Aqaba-Momentum Pictures. 119 mins. USA. 2000. Rel: 17 November 2000. Cert 18.

## Weak at Denise ★★

Colin is in his mid-forties, lives with his mum and, for recreation, listens to recordings of aeroplane engines. He thinks love has passed him by until, one day, he meets Denise at the hospital. He used to steal her knickers at school, but he is a changed man now... After a promising start, this 'comic' take on Graham Williams' literary thriller deteriorates into over-plotted farce. Still, Bill Thomas retains an endearingly straight face throughout and there are a few choice moments and some amusing dialogue. But the triple-twist format has been done to death now and some incongruous moments of bad taste sit uneasily within the gentle flow of Colin's voice-over narrative. FYI: First-time director Julian Nott previously composed the music to Nick Park's Oscar-winning shorts *The Wrong Trousers* and *A Close Shave*.

● *Colin* Bill Thomas, *Denise* Chrissie Cotterill, *Roy* Craig Fairbrass, *Wendy* Tilly Blackwood, *Sharon* Claudine Spiteri, *Iris* Edna Doré, *Colin's mum* Jean Ainslie, *with* Indira Joshi, Vivien Douglas, Richard Dixon, Dawn Davis, Alexis Saunders, Margaret Holmes-Drewry.
● *Dir, Pro* and *M* Julian Nott, *Co-Pro* Clare Erasmus, *Screenplay* Nott and Graham Williams, *Ph* Marco Windham, *Pro Des* Kate Woodman, *Ed* Simon Beeley and Melanie Adams, *Costumes* Julie Nelson.

Peninsula Films-Guerilla Films. 87 mins. UK. 2000. Rel: 1 June 2001. Cert 18.

## The Wedding Planner ★★

San Francisco; the present. Mary Fiore is to weddings what MacArthur was to the 42nd US Division. Armed with bottles of sedatives, a hands-free headset and comforting patter, she has engineered Whitney Houston's nuptials and is now moving up in the world. She's just landed her biggest matrimonial account yet but then discovers that the groom happens to be the man she's just fallen in love with... While Jennifer Lopez and Matthew McConaughey have never been more appealing, they are given little to work with here other than glutinous close-ups. Unashamedly old-fashioned and impossibly romantic, the film might have pulled off such rarefied reality if it had had a stronger story tugging at the heartstrings.

**Above:** *Always a bridesmaid? Jennifer Lopez provides a pep talk for a client in Adam Shankman's old-fashioned and impossibly romantic* The Wedding Planner *(from Pathé)*

● *Mary Fiore* Jennifer Lopez, *Dr Steve James 'Eddy' Edison* Matthew McConaughey, *Fran Donolly* Bridget Wilson-Sampras, *Massimo* Justin Chambers, *Penny Nicholson* Judy Greer, *Salvatore* Alex Rocco, *Mrs Donolly* Joanna Gleason, *Mr Donolly* Charles Kimbrough, *Basil St Mosely* Fred Willard, *Burt Weinberg* Lou Myers, *Dottie* Frances Bay, *Dr John Dojny* Kevin Pollak, *Geri* Kathy Najimy, *Mary Fiore, aged 7* Cortney Shounia, *with* Philip Pavel, F William Parker, Caisha Williams, Fabiana Udenio, Bree Turner, Susan Mosher.
● *Dir* Adam Shankman, *Pro* Gigi Pritzker and Deborah Del Prete, Peter Abrams, Robert L Levy and Jennifer Gigbot, *Ex Pro* Moritz Borman, Guy East and Nigel Sinclair, Nina R Sadowsky and Chris Sievernich, *Co-Pro* Mary Gail Artz and Barbara Cohen, *Screenplay* Pamela Falk and Michael Ellis, *Ph* Julio Macat, *Pro Des* Bob Ziembicki, *Ed* Lisa Zeno Churgin, *M* Mervyn Warren; Pachelbel, Mendelssohn, Richard Wagner; songs performed by Lisa Stansfield, Sourcerer, Olivia Newton-John, John Denver, Nikki Hassman, Sister Hazel, Jennifer Lopez, Dick Powell and Ruby Keeler etc, *Costumes* Pamela Withers.

Columbia/Intermedia Films/Tapestry Films/Dee Gee Entertainment/IMF/Prufrock Pictures-Pathé. 110 mins. USA. 2001. Rel: 6 April 2001. Cert PG.

*Above: Running scared: Harrison Ford finds himself up against unseen forces in Robert Zemeckis's atmospheric if clichéd What Lies Beneath (from Twentieth Century Fox)*

## The Wedding Tackle ★★

London; today. Hal, an over-sexed photographer, has one week to go before his wedding day. But now he's got cold feet and so calls on his three best mates to help bail him out. And so, one fateful day, the four losers tie themselves into ever tighter knots as they struggle to find a solution to Hal's, and indeed their own, escalating problems... An old-fashioned comedy of almost Shakespearean design, *The Wedding Tackle* proffers a number of promising situations. Yet, in spite of a spirited cast, the film's conceit fails to gather momentum due to poor pacing and barely any comic timing. The fact that we can't believe these idiotic male caricatures is not the point; we shouldn't just be bored by them. Still, a lively soundtrack of 1960s songs and some isolated moments of high comedy – Tony Slattery poking in his contact lenses, Neil Stuke's ill-fated attempt to order a soft drink – take up some of the slack.

● *Mr Mac* Adrian Dunbar, *Hal* James Purefoy, *Petula* Amanda Redman, *George* Leslie Grantham, *Clodagh Donovan* Victoria Smurfit, *Vinni* Susan Vidler, *Little Ted* Tony Slattery, *Salty* Neil Stuke, *Felicity Adams* Sara Stockbridge, *Trev* Martin Armstrong, *with* Al Hunter Ashton, Roger Gartland, Diane Worswick.
● *Dir* Rami Dvir, *Pro* and *Screenplay* Nigel Horne, *Ex Pro* Donald Horne, *Line Pro* Anne Boyd, *Ph* Shelley Hirst, *Pro Des* Sarah Beaman, *Ed* Matthew Tabern, *M* Charles Hodgkinson and Kirk Zavich; songs performed by Dusty Springfield, Sandy Shaw, Cilla Black, Helen Shapiro, Peter Sarstedt, Freddie and The Dreamers, The Fortunes, Frank Ifield, Kathy Kirby, Lulu, Lou Christie, Susan Maughan, The Box Tops, *Costumes* Jane Spicer, *Cartoons* Jed Stone.

Viking Films-Ratpack Films.
93 mins. UK. 1999. Rel: 11 August 2000. Cert 15.

## What Lies Beneath ★★★

Vermont; the present. After their teenage daughter moves to college, Norman and Claire Spencer find themselves alone for the first time in years. But with Norman's demanding workload in genetic research, Claire is left to her own devices. And soon she is going out of her mind as the front door of their house takes on a life of its own and the bath repeatedly fills itself... Few big-budget films have ever got close to creating a tenable ghost story, but this has a darned good try. Thanks to a skillfully pitched performance from Michelle Pfeiffer – is she mad? is she seeing things? is she possessed? – and considerable restraint in the effects department, the film gains substantial atmospheric mileage. Equally, though, it fails to convince in human terms, leaving plot points dangling and back stories unresolved. What is the significance of Claire's first husband? Why was Mary Feur acting that way in the garden? And so on. Indeed, both the film's strengths and weaknesses are pinpointed in one scene, near the end: as Claire backs away from her tormentor, she does so in complete silence (and you can hear the audience hold its breath), but then she walks down the stairs *backwards*, perpetrating one of the cheapest (and dumbest) clichés in the horror movie lexicon.

● *Norman Spencer* Harrison Ford, *Claire Spencer* Michelle Pfeiffer, *Jody* Diana Scarwid, *Dr Drayton* Joe Morton, *Warren Feur* James Remar, *Mary Feur* Miranda Otto, *Madison Elizabeth Frank* Amber Valletta, *Caitlin Spencer* Katharine Towne, *Dr Stan Powell* Ray Baker, *Elena* Wendy Crewson, *with* Victoria Bidewell, Elliott Goretsky, Sloane Shelton, Tom Dahlgren, Micole Mercurio.

● *Dir* Robert Zemeckis, *Pro* Steve Starkey, Robert Zemeckis and Jack Rapke, *Ex Pro* Joan Bradshaw and Mark Johnson, *Screenplay* Clark Gregg, from a story by Gregg and Sarah Kernochan, *Ph* Don Burgess, *Pro Des* Rick Carter and Jim Teegarden, *Ed* Arthur Schmidt, *M* Alan Silvestri, *Costumes* Susie DeSanto, *Visual effects* Robert Legato.

Twentieth Century Fox/DreamWorks/Imagemovers-Fox. 130 mins. USA. 2000. Rel: 20 October 2000. Cert 15.

## What Women Want ★★★★

Chicago; the present. Having grown up surrounded by Vegas showgirls, advertising exec Nick Marshall has always found it a cinch to get into women's pants. But getting into their psyche has been another ball game (so to speak). So when an electric shock enables him to eavesdrop on women's innermost thoughts, the world would appear to be his... Of the recent crop of Hollywood confections about male workaholics transformed by supernatural intervention, *What Women Want* hits its marks with the greatest proficiency. Courting the *Sleepless in Seattle* crowd with its romantic inevitability and soundtrack of brassy classics, the film is broad, silly and calculating. It is also smart, very funny and full of those little moments that distinguish a really special entertainment from a merely adequate one. So, whether it's Mel Gibson giving a fruity impersonation of Sean Connery or doing a Fred Astaire dance routine, or the secretaries who don't think when they're not talking (as played by Delta Burke and Valerie Perrine), the film provides plenty of incidental meat. As for stereotyping women as oestrogen-powered, professionally and sexually insecure victims of fashion, it racks up some equally comic mileage at the expense of male arrogance, narcissism and insensitivity.

● *Nick Marshall* Mel Gibson, *Darcy Maguire* Helen Hunt, *Lola* Marisa Tomei, *Morgan Farwell* Mark Feuerstein, *Gigi* Lauren Holly, *Dan Wanamker* Alan Alda, *Alex Marshall* Ashley Johnson, *Eve* Delta Burke, *Margo* Valerie Perrine, *Erin* Judy Greer, *Annie* Sarah Paulson, *Sue Cranston* Ana Gasteyer, *Dina* Lisa Edelstein, *Flo* Loretta Devine, *with* Diana-Maria Riva, Eric Balfour, Andrea Taylor, Robert Briscoe Evans, Hallie Meyers Shyer, Laura Quicksilver, and (*uncredited*) Bette Midler.

● *Dir* Nancy Meyers, *Pro* Meyers and Bruce Davey, Matt Williams, Susan Cartsonis and Gina Matthews, *Ex Pro* Stephen McEveety, David McFadzean and Carmen Finestra, *Co-Pro* Bruce A Block, *Screenplay* Josh Goldsmith and Cathy Yuspa, from a story by Goldsmith, Yuspa and Diane Drake, *Ph* Dean Cundey, *Pro Des* Jon Hutman, *Ed* Stephen A Rotter and Thomas J Nordberg, *M* Alan Silvestri; songs performed by Sammy Davis Jr, Nancy Wilson, Bobby Darin, Meredith Brooks, Groove Armada, Lou Rawls, Joel Evans and Patrick Maier, Frank Sinatra, B*witched, Christine Aguilera, The Temptations, Raining Stones, Wild Orchid, Peggy Lee, Nnenna Freelon, *Costumes* Ellen Mirojnick, *Choreography* Keith Young.

Icon Prods/Paramount/Winddancer-Icon. 126 mins. USA. 2000. Rel: 2 February 2001. Cert 12.

## Whatever – Extension du Domaine de la Lutte ★★★¹/₂

Amusing, provocative and disturbing by turn, this is a challenging dissection of contemporary society by a French filmmaker, Philippe Harel, who himself plays the lead role in his adaptation with the author of Michel Houellebecq's novel *Extension du Domaine de la Lutte*. Its bracing intelligence and literacy recall sixties cinema as, illustrated by the experiences of two travelling computer programmers, it exposes the lack of meaning in life today. On occasion it confronts us with explicit sexual imagery, but, in a world short on ideals and beliefs, it also suggests that sex, desperately pursued as a panacea, fails to supply the satisfaction missing elsewhere. The acting is excellent (José Garcia plays Harel's partner brilliantly), and the film would warrant a higher rating but for a seriously misjudged conclusion which ineptly challenges the convincingly pessimistic viewpoint of all that precedes it. [*Mansel Stimpson*]

● *Our Hero* Philippe Harel, *Tisserand* José Garcia, *the psychologist* Catherine Mouchet, *Catherine Lechardoy* Cécile Reigher, *Henri La Brette* Philippe Agael, *with* Marie Charlotte Leclaire, Alain Guillo, Christophe Rossignon, *voice of the narrator* Philippe Bianco.

● *Dir* Philippe Harel, *Ex Pro* Adeline Lécallier, *Screenplay* Philippe Harel and Michel Houellebecq, *Ph* Gilles Henry, *Pro Des* Louise Marzaroli, *Ed*

Bénédicte Teiger, *M* Novo Navis, *Costumes* Anne Schotte, *Sound* Joël Flesher.

Lazennec/Canal Plus-Artificial Eye.
121 mins. France. 1999. Rel: 1 September 2000. Cert 18.

## When Brendan Met Trudy ★★¹/₂

Dublin; the present. Brendan, schoolteacher, amateur chorister and one-track-minded film buff, is possibly the world's most boring and anally retentive human being. He is the sort of sad sack who, to virtual strangers, expounds on the 'courageous editing' of Sergio Leone and gives a biography of Martin Scorsese to his pre-adolescent nephew. Then, one night in the pub, he meets the dynamic, down-to-earth Trudy, who shows him that life can even be more thrilling without subtitles... When the two funniest moments in a film are a clip from an old movie (Gene Wilder in *The Producers*) and the closing credits, you know something is wrong. A jumble of purloined ideas peppered with moments of inspired comedy (such as a scene re-enacted straight from *A Bout de Soufle*, complete with subtitles), *When Brendan Met Trudy* ultimately falls down due to the flawed credibility of the central relationship. And, in spite of his final redemption through crime, Brendan remains an insufferable cipher. Still, first-time director Kieron J Walsh glosses over the gaps with some gusto, a buoyant soundtrack and a string of choice clips from both the large and small screen.

● *Brendan* Peter McDonald, *Trudy* Flora Montgomery, *Mother* Marie Mullen, *Nuala* Pauline McLynn, *Niall* Don Wycherley, *Edgar* Maynard Eziashi, *Siobhan* Eileen Walsh, *headmaster* Barry Cassin, *with* Niall O'Brien, Rynagh O'Grady, Ali White, Jack Lynch, Robert O'Neill, Eoin Manley, Gabriel Byrne, *young man at Filmhaus* Kieron J Walsh.
● *Dir* Kieron J Walsh, *Pro* Lynda Myles, *Ex Pro* David M Thompson, Mike Phillips, Rod Stoneman and Clare Duignan, *Line Pro* Mary Alleguen, *Screenplay* and *Co-Pro* Roddy Doyle, *Ph* Ashley Rowe, *Pro Des* Fiona Daly, *Ed* Scott Thomas, *M* Richard Hartley; Bizet; songs performed by John McCormack, Elvis Costello and the Attractions, Folk Implosion, Iggy Pop, The Divine Comedy, Arnold etc, *Costumes* Consolata Boyle.

BBC Films/Bord Scannán na hÉireann/Irish Film Board/
Deadly Films 2/Collins Avenue-Momentum.
95 mins. Ireland/UK. 2000. Rel: 25 May 2001. Cert 15.

## Where the Heart Is ★★★¹/₂

Accompanying her boyfriend on a trip to Vegas, Novalee Nation, 17 years old and seven months pregnant, is left abandoned at an Oklahoma Wal-Mart.

Using the supermarket as a makeshift hotel, Novalee ends up giving birth in the kitchen utensils aisle and becomes a local celebrity (`the Wal-Mart Mom'). She is then adopted by the locals and gradually finds her feet as a single parent in a community where tragedy is never far away... Bearing in mind that this is an adaptation of a title selected by the Oprah Book Club, the heartstrings are plucked with some dexterity. Aside from the misfortune of adding a song to a key love scene, first-time director (and TV executive) Matt Williams shows considerable restraint in unfolding the events of this big, sprawling tale. He has also secured some exemplary performances, particularly from his female stars, while Natalie Portman is a revelation as the innocent savant who ages from 17 to her mid-twenties. In addition, Mason Daring's score for the most part lets the performers do their own acting.

● *Novalee Nation* Natalie Portman, *Lexie Coop* Ashley Judd, *Sister Husband* Stockard Channing, *Ruth Meyers* Joan Cusack, *Willy Jack Pickens* Dylan Bruno, *Moses Whitecotton* Keith David, *Forney Hull* James Frain, *Mr Sprock* Richard Jones, *Mama Lil* Sally Field, *Ray* T J McFarland, *with* Alicia Godwin, Kathryn Esquivel, John Daniel Evermore, David Alvarado, Margaret Ann Hoard, Rodger Boyce, Richard Nance, Cheyenne Rushing.
● *Dir* Matt Williams, *Pro* Williams, Susan Cartsonis, David McFadzean and Patricia Whitcher, *Ex Pro* Carmen Finestra and Rick Leed, *Co-Pro* Gerrit Folsom and Dianne Minter Lewis, *Screenplay* Lowell Ganz and Babaloo Mandel, *Ph* Richard Greatrex, *Pro Des* Paul Peters, *Ed* Ian Crafford, *M* Mason Daring; songs performed by Big Sugar, Shannon Curfman, Joan Osborne and Tommy Sims, John Hiatt, Girlfriendz, Michael McCarthy, The Corrs, Lonestar, NRBQ, The Warren Brothers, Beth Nielsen Chapman, Lyle Lovett, Jennifer Day, Emmylou Harris and Patty Griffin, Martina McBride, Coley McCabe etc, *Costumes* Melinda Eshelman.

Fox/Wind Dancer-Fox.
120 mins. USA. 2000. Rel: 17 November 2000. Cert 12.

## Where the Money Is ★★★

Henry Manning is a master thief who only got caught when a power cut stranded him in a Denver bank vault. Carol is a nurse at an old people's home who is becoming disillusioned with her small-town life. Then Henry is, literally, wheeled into her life, into her care, following a stroke. But Carol is nobody's fool and suspects that there's more to this handsome old vegetable than meets the eye. But Henry is cleverer than Carol thinks. They could make a perfect team for the perfect crime... *Where the Money Is* is not a particularly ingenious or stylish crime caper. However, thanks to engaging terms from Paul Newman and

Linda Fiorentino, a welcome lightness of touch and a succinct running time, it is a highly enjoyable trifle. And there are a number of scenes to relish, all of them with Newman playing down his legendary sex appeal, either as a wily stroke victim or as a doddery security guard. Once again, the actor gives eternal hope to everyone over 70.

● *Henry Manning* Paul Newman, *Carol Ann McKay* Linda Fiorentino, *Wayne McKay* Dermot Mulroney, *Karl* Bruce MacVittie, *with* Susan Barnes, Anne Pitoniak, Irma St Paul, Michel Perron, Dorothy Gordon, Rita Tucket, T J Kenneally, Charles Doucet, Arthur Holden, Frankie Faison, Vlasta Vrana, Jayne Eastwood.
● *Dir* Marek Kanievska, *Pro* Ridley Scott, Charles Weinstock, Chris Zarpas and Christopher Dorr, *Ex Pro* Tony Scott, Guy East, Nigel Sinclair, Chris Sievernich and Moritz Borman, *Co-Pro* Beau E L Marks, *Screenplay* E Max Frye, Topper Lilien & Carroll Cartwright, *Ph* Thomas Burstyn, *Pro Des* Andre Chamberland, *Ed* Garth Craven, Samuel Craven and Dan Lebental, *M* Mark Isham; songs performed by The Cars, Ron Keel, Scott Eversoll, William Joseph Martin, Mersh Bros Band, Johnny Lang, Barry Omarr & Stephen Lang, *Costumes* Francesca Chamberland.

Intermedia Films/Pacifica Film Dist/Scott Free/IMF-Warner. 88 mins. USA/UK/Germany. 1999. Rel: 6 October 2000. Cert 15.

## Woman on Top ★½
Bahia, north eastern Brazil/San Francisco; the present. While blessed with extraordinary beauty and culinary expertise, Isabella Oliveira suffers dramatically from motion sickness. This means that wherever movement is concerned she has to be in the driver's seat, whether commandeering a taxi, taking the stairs or just adopting the dominant position in sex. Then, one night, her husband Toninho takes to another's bed and Isabella flees to San Francisco to stay with her transvestite friend, Monica. There, her cooking skills quickly replace the void in her heart... The word 'dopey' springs to mind, as does 'twee' and 'silliest movie of the year.' Even romantic fantasies need some rooting in reality, but this tepid fable makes a mockery of anything approaching real life. As if conceived in a vacuum of the writer's imagination, the film is narratively deficient, chemically barren and saddled with a leading man (Murilo Benício) who inspires nothing but contempt for his ineptitude and dilettante ways.

● *Isabella Oliveira* Penélope Cruz, *Toninho Oliveira* Murilo Benício, *Monica Jones* Harold Perrineau Jr, *Cliff Lloyd* Mark Feuerstein, *Alex Reeves* John De Lancie, *TV director* Anne Ramsay, *Rafi* Wagner Moura, *with* Ana Gasteyer, June A Lomena, Bob Greene.

● *Dir* Fina Torres, *Pro* Alan Poul, *Ex Pro* Torres and Bronwen Hughes, *Co-Pro* Nancy Paloian-Breznikar, *Screenplay* Vera Blasi, *Ph* Thierry Arbogast, *Pro Des* Philippe Chiffre, *Ed* Leslie Jones, *M* Luis Bacalov, *Costumes* Elisabeth Tavernier.

Fox Searchlight/Alan Poul-Fox. 91 mins. USA. 2000. Rel: 22 January 2001. Cert 15.

## Wonder Boys ★★★★
Pittsburgh; the present. In his own words, English professor Grady Tripp is having 'one fucked-up day.' His wife has just left him, the wife of his head has discovered that she is pregnant with his baby and his most gifted student has just shot his lover's dog. And with his gay editor in town baying to look at his stubbornly unfinished novel and his car about to be repossessed, Tripp is having a problem juggling his priorities... *Wonder Boys* is a rare animal in that it is a beautifully crafted black comedy that draws its humour from painfully recognisable situations. And while replete with eccentric characters and unexpected plot twists, the film manages to retain a sense of credibility, thanks largely to excellent playing from the ensemble cast and the director's good sense never to push a scene too far. Michael Douglas reveals an unexpected talent for sardonic humour as Grady, a drowning man who offers a scabrous commentary on those around him even as his own life self-destructs. The film is further to be commended for refusing to succumb to the standard campus clichés.

● *Grady Tripp* Michael Douglas, *James Leer* Tobey Maguire, *Sara Gaskell* Frances McDormand, *Terry Crabtree* Robert Downey Jr, *Hannah Green* Katie Holmes, *Quentin Moorehead* aka 'Q' Rip Torn, *Walter Gaskell* Richard Thomas, *Hank Winters* Philip Bosco, *Oola* Jane Adams, *Vernon Hardapple* Richard Knox, *Miss Sloviak/Tony* Michael Cavadias, *Sam Traxler* Alan Tudyk, *Fred Leer* George Grizzard, *Amanda Leer* Kelly Bishop, *with* Bill Velin, Charis Michelsen, James Ellroy.
● *Dir* Curtis Hanson, *Pro* Hanson and Scott Rudin, *Ex Pro* Adam Schroeder and Ned Dowd, *Screenplay* Steve Kloves, based on the novel by Michael Chabon, *Ph* Dante Spinotti, *Pro Des* Jeannine Oppewall, *Ed* Dede Allen, *M* Christopher Young; songs performed by Tom Rush, Johnny Hodges, Jr Walker & the All Stars, Little Willie John, Clarence Carter, Buffalo Springfield, Bob Dylan, John Lennon, Judy Garland and Mickey Rooney, Neil Young, Leonard Cohen, Van Morrison, Lee Wiley, *Costumes* Beatrix Aruna Pasztor, *Snow effects* Snow Business.

Mutual Film Co/Paramount/BBC/Marubeni, etc-UIP. 111 mins. USA/Germany/Japan/UK. 2000. Rel: 3 November 2000. Cert 15.

Above: Patrick
Stewart realises that
his comb-over just
doesn't look like the
real thing – in Bryan
Singer's lean and
entertaining X-Men
(from Twentieth
Century Fox)

### X-Men ★★★¹/₂

Every few thousand millennia or so evolution takes a giant leap forward. Thus, in the not too distant future, a race of *homo sapiens* develops genetic anomalies, bestowing on them superhuman powers such as telepathy, telekinesis, metamorphosis and unnatural strength. Feared and shunned by society, this breed of *homo superior* pool their resources at Xavier's School for Gifted Youngsters (aka `Mutant High'), to perfect and control their potential so as to safeguard the future of mankind. However, not every mutant has such a benevolent objective... While the countless loyal fans of this enormously popular comic-book series may have one opinion, general cinemagoers should glean enormous enjoyment from this amalgam of high concepts, vivid characters and special effects. Packed into a lean 104 minutes and regulated by lashings of humour, *X-Men* displays none of the self-reverence and indigestibility of the *Batman* movies and is fun from the word go. FYI: Hugh Jackman snared the role of the metallically enhanced Wolverine when Dougray Scott was forced to bow out after *Mission: Impossible 2* ran over schedule.

● *Professor Charles Francis Xavier* Patrick Stewart, *Wolverine* aka *Logan* Hugh Jackman, *Magneto* aka *Erik Lehnsherr* Ian McKellen, *Storm* aka *Ororo Munroe* Halle Berry, *Jean Grey* aka *Phoenix* aka *Marvel Girl* Famke Janssen, *Cyclops* aka *Scott Summers* James Marsden, *Mystique* aka *Raven Darkholme* Rebecca Romijn-Stamos, *Senator Robert Kelly* Bruce Davison, *Toad* aka *Mortimer Toynbee* Ray Park, *Rogue* Anna Paquin, *Sabretooth* aka *Victor Creed* Tyler Mane, *Henry Guyrich* Matthew Sharp, *Bobby* Shawn Ashmore, *Toad cop* Tom DeSanto, *President* David Black, *museum cop* David Hayter, with Brett Morris, Kevin Rushton, Sumela Kay, *hot dog vendor* Stan Lee.

● *Dir* Bryan Singer, *Pro* Lauren Shuler Donner and

Ralph Winter, *Ex Pro* Avi Arad, Stan Lee, Richard Donner and Tom DeSanto, *Co-Pro* Joel Simon and William S Todman, *Screenplay* David Hayter, from a story by DeSanto and Singer, *Ph* Newton Thomas Sigel, *Pro Des* John Myhre, *Ed* Steven Rosenblum, Kevin Stitt and John Wright, *M* Michael Kamen, *Costumes* Louise Mingenbach, *Sound* Steve Boeddeker and Craig Berkey, *Visual effects* Michael Fink, *Make-up* Gordon Smith.

Fox/Marvel Entertainment Group/Bad Hat Harry-Fox. 104 mins. USA. 2000. Rel: 18 August 2000. Cert 12.

## The Yards ★★★¹/₂

Queens, New York; today. In the railway yards and industrial repair plants of New York, big business flourishes under the counter as contracts are bought and sold. Into this netherworld comes young Leo Handler, fresh out of prison, who wants to make amends for his wrongs. Taken under the wing of Willie Gutierrez, a flash social climber in the employ of Leo's uncle, the ex-con is plunged into a 'situation' for which he takes the rap... Imbuing his crime drama with an understated power that recalls the tone of *The Godfather*, director/co-writer James Gray (*Little Odessa*) has created an intelligent and atmospheric saga strong on character and suspense. Leisurely paced and underlit, it displays a confidence in its material so often lacking in the hyperventilating thrillers of today. And there are convincing performances from all concerned (and anybody who can persuade Faye Dunaway to underplay her lines deserves some kind of accolade). FYI: To create the pictorial palette for his film, James Gray painted over 40 watercolours depicting scenes from the script.

● *Leo Handler* Mark Wahlberg, *Willie Gutierrez* Joaquin Phoenix, *Erica Stoltz* Charlize Theron, *Kitty Olchin* Faye Dunaway, *Val Handler* Ellen Burstyn, *Frank Olchin* James Caan, *Raymond Price* Andrew Davoli, *Arthur Mydanick* Steve Lawrence, *Paul Lazarides* Victor Argo, *Hector Gallardo* Robert Montano, *with* Chad Aaron, Tony Musante, Victor Arnold, Louis Guss, Domenick Lombardozzi, Joe Lisi, David Zayas, Jack O'Connell, Andi Shrem.
● *Dir* James Gray, *Pro* Nick Wechsler, Paul Webster and Kerry Orent, *Ex Pro* Bob Weinstein, Harvey Weinstein and Jonathan Gordon, *Co-Pro* Matt Reeves and Christopher Goode, *Screenplay* Gray and Reeves, *Ph* Harris Savides, *Pro Des* Kevin Thompson, *Ed* Jeffrey Ford, *M* Edward Shearmur and Howard Shore; Holst; songs performed by Les McCann, Macy Gray, Peggy Lee, KRS-One, Howard Jones, Clinton, George Benson, D Walter, P-18, *Costumes* Michael Clancy.

Miramax/Paul Webster/Industry Entertainment-Film Four. 116 mins. USA. 2000. Rel: 10 November 2000. Cert 15.

## You Can Count On Me ★★★★★

Scottsville; upstate New York; the present. A cheerful, hard-working, church-going single mother, Samantha Prescott has pretty much got her life in order. Then she gets a letter from her brother Terry, who's coming to visit. Thrilled with the prospect of getting to know her younger sibling again, Samantha is unprepared for the changes in Terry's outlook on life... Marking the directorial debut of playwright-scenarist Kenneth Lonergan, *You Can Count On Me* is a funny, poignant and perceptive look at the clash of American extremes as embodied in a sister and brother who, growing up in the same rural New York community, used to be so close. Beautifully written and observed, the film furnishes Laura Linney with the performance of her career, an accomplishment perfected in its unscripted moments, like when she's driving in her car after an unexpected step off the moral path (neatly mirroring Julia Roberts' brilliant scene in *Erin Brockovich* where, driving through the night, she lets a myriad of emotions wash over her face). But then, under Lonergan's subtly invisible direction, everybody excels, from Matthew Broderick's hilariously anal bank manager to Jon Tenney's awkward, perpetually embarrassed suitor, not to mention an astonishingly naturalistic reading from Rory Culkin, the youngest of the Culkin clan. Displaying the courage of its silences, *You Can Count On Me* reminds one of how good American cinema can be.

● *Samantha 'Sammy' Prescott* Laura Linney, *Terry Prescott* Mark Ruffalo, *Brian Everett* Matthew Broderick, *Bob* Jon Tenney, *Rudy Prescott* Rory Culkin, *Sheriff Darryl* Adam LeFevre, *Mabel* J Smith-Cameron, *Sheila* Gaby Hoffman, *Ron* Kenneth Lonergan, *Rudy Sr* Josh Lucas, *with* Halley Feiffer, Betsy Aiden, Nina Garbiras, Kim Parker.
● *Dir* and *Screenplay* Kenneth Lonergan, *Pro* Barbara De Fina, John N Hart, Larry Meistrich and Jeff Sharp, *Ex Pro* Martin Scorsese, Steve Carlis, Donald C Carter and Morton Swinsky, *Line Pro* Jill Footlick, *Ph* Stephen Kazmierski, *Pro Des* Michael Shaw, *Ed* Anne McCabe, *M* Lesley Barber; J S Bach; songs performed by Loretta Lynn, 6 String Drag, Steve Earle and the Del McCoury Band, Marah, Sue Foley, The V-roys, Cheri Knight etc, *Costumes* Melissa Toth.

Paramount Classics/Hart Sharp Entertainment/Shooting Gallery/Cappa Prods-Momentum Pictures. 111 mins. USA. 2000. Rel: 23 March 2001. Cert 15.

# Video Releases

## from July 2000 through to June 2001

### Compiled by Daniel O'Brien

## The Adventures of Sebastian Cole

An evocative teenage rites-of-passage tale, set during the early 1980s, which covers the well-worn territory with unexpected wit and subtlety. In Duchess County, New York, young Sebastian Cole (Adrian Grenier) contends with the usual high school angst and the unexpected news that his stepfather is to undergo a sex change. Clark Gregg gives a commendably restrained performance as the transgender Hank/Henrietta, who proves to be Sebastian's strongest ally in a hostile world. Written and directed by Tod Williams, this original, well-handled film incurred the wrath of the BBFC, losing footage of 'instructional' drug use.
● Also starring Aleksa Palladino, Margaret Colin, John Shea.
Paramount. July 2000. Cert 15.

## Airtight

Oddly titled Australian-made action movie, with little to distinguish it from several billion others of the same ilk. The unlikely Grayson McCouch stars as one Rat Lucci, equipped with the standard heavy-duty firepower and a severe haircut. As the 12 certificate suggests, the violence/gore quotient is on the low side. The supporting cast includes former Hammer contract artist Shane Briant.
● Also starring Andrew McFarlane, John Noble. *Dir* Ian Barry.
Paramount. September 2000. Cert 12.

## Annie

Made-for-television version of the hit Broadway musical, with Victor Garber as Daddy Warbucks and Alicia Morton as everybody's favourite singing orphan. Kathy Bates and Alan Cumming provide some high-class villainy and the end result is markedly superior to the lumpen 1982 film, directed by John Huston, which discarded some of the best songs. Spirited newcomer Morton steers clear of nauseating cuteness, while Andrea McArdle, the original Broadway Annie, makes a cameo appearance as 'Star to Be'.

● *Dir* Rob Marshall.
Buena Vista. November 2000. Cert U.

## Beethoven's 3rd

The less than pedigree canine franchise develops a severe case of mange with this belated third instalment, which features none of the original cast. Judge Reinhold takes over from Charles Grodin as the bemused family patriarch, and his game performance is the only bright spot in a sea of doggy dross. Co-star Frank Gorshin, a memorable Riddler to Adam West's 1960s tv Batman, must have wished he was back in the tight green leotard. On this evidence, the prospects for a *Beethoven's 5th* look mercifully remote.
● Also starring Julia Sweeney. *Dir* David M Evans.
Universal. December 2000. Cert U.

## The Bogus Witch Project

This shockingly awful *Blair Witch* spoof is actually a series of short films, all of which ineptly parody the same bits of the original movie. Top-billed performer Pauly Shore features for a mere ten minutes. Co-directors Steve Agee and Kelly Anne Conroy, who also appear in their respective segments, should be dumped in a remote and spooky wood and left there for good.
● Also starring Bino Bates.
High Fliers. November 2000. Cert 15.

## The Brutal Truth

A young woman named Emily (Christina Applegate) invites nine close friends to her remote mountain cabin for the weekend. Upon their arrival, she hangs herself. Trapped in the cabin by a sudden earthquake, the understandably shaken friends attempt to work out what caused Emily to take her own life. While the premise suggests a *Ten Little Indians*-style thriller, the film unreels as a flashback-laden exploration of tangled relationships, past misdeeds and collective guilt. Most viewers will find it difficult to care. Originally released in the United States as *The Giving Tree*.

● Also starring Molly Ringwald, Moon Unit Zappa.*Dir* Cameron Thor.
High Fliers. December 2000. Cert 18.

## Chain of Command

During a sensitive diplomatic visit to China, US President Roy Scheider is kidnapped, along with a briefcase containing the controls to America's entire nuclear arsenal. Special agent Patrick Muldoon goes off in hot pursuit, despite his personal antipathy towards Scheider. A decent thriller with enough sustained tension to offset the more contrived plot twists. Maria Conchita Alonzo turns up as Scheider's Vice President, a piece of casting that can be seen as either commendably progressive or a token sop to political correctness.
● Also starring Michael Biehn.
*Dir* John Terlesky.
Paramount. September 2000. Cert 15.

## Children of the Corn V – Fields of Terror

*Children of the Corn* (1984) diluted its Stephen King source material into a standard shocker, lent some flavour by the scythe-wielding Bible Belt teen psychopaths. Nearly a decade later, the title and concept were revived for a series of straight-to-video 'sequels', of which this may well be the worst. Writer-director Ethan Wiley does nothing remotely interesting with the material, and star Alexis Arquette demonstrates why he's yet to match the screen success of siblings Rosanna, Patricia and David. Season Hubley, the gutsy prostitute in Paul Schrader's *Hardcore*, makes a brief appearance. The film's only novelty value is its casting of exploitation regulars David Carradine and Fred Williamson.
● Also starring Diva Zappa, Ahmet Zappa.
Buena Vista. January 2001. Cert 18.

## Children of the Corn 666 – Isaac's Return

Searching for her natural mother, Hannah Martin (Natalie Ramsay) travels to the rural ghost town of Gatlin, scene of the original Bible-inspired corn carnage. The surviving cult children are now adults, some with children of their own, and Hannah discovers a little too late that she has been chosen to bear the cult's new leader… Some rate this as the best of the *Corn* sequels, which isn't saying a great deal. Well-enough made, the film suffers from a trite script and an unappealing heroine. Original cast member John Franklin reprises his 1984 role as creepy, diminutive cult leader Isaac, who has spent the last 19 years in a coma; sadly, he's a lot less spooky as an adult. Best line: 'How dare you castrate my words, you fuck?'

● Also starring Nancy Allen, Stacy Keach, Paul Popowich. *Dir* Kari Skogland.
**Buena Vista. April 2001. Cert 18.**

## The Convent

A group of college students – don't these people ever go to lectures? – decide to check out the local abandoned convent and soon discover why the nuns left, experiencing a bad case of demonic possession. A bog-standard horror premise is harnessed to duff dialogue and some less than cutting-edge special effects. That said, the movie is reasonable fun for genre fans in indulgent mood. Adrienne Barbeau appears in a typically tough, ass-kicking role. Badass rap star Coolio and Bill Moseley (who played the monstrous Chop-Top in *Texas Chainsaw Massacre 2*) co-star as a couple of cops.

● *Dir* Mike Mendez.
**Metrodome. July 2000. Cert 18.**

## The Defender

Also known as *Bodyguard from Beijing*, this solid Jet Li vehicle delivers the action goods, though the expected martial arts take a back seat to more conventional gunplay. A blatant, if superior, rip-off of the Kevin Costner-Whitney Houston hit *The Bodyguard*, the film was one of the first to locate Li in a contemporary setting, rather than the mythologised historical past of *Once Upon A Time in China* and *Fong Sai Yuk*. When a corrupt Hong Kong businessman orders the murder of a rival, the only witness is a young woman (Christy Chung), whose executive boyfriend has strong ties with the Chinese government. The latter assign their top police bodyguard (Li) to protect her. Struggling to adapt to Hong Kong culture, Li's strait-laced character also finds himself falling for his spoiled charge. The climactic fight scene, staged in a room steadily filling with natural gas, is riddled with continuity errors, not that Li fans will be bothered.

● Also starring Ngai Sing. *Dir* Cory Yuen.
**Buena Vista. March 2001. Cert 18.**

## Desert Blue

Morgan J Freeman's second film as a writer-director, following *Hurricane Streets*, is a quirky comedy set in the small town of Baxter, California, home of the world's largest ice cream cone. After an Empire Cola truck crashes in Baxter, spilling the company's secret, and possibly toxic, main ingredient all over the place, the entire town is put under quarantine. The bored and disaffected local teenagers, previously trapped by their own apathy, finally begin to think about the possibilities of a life beyond Baxter. Despite a strong cast and some nice observation, Freeman doesn't handle the material with much assurance, and the film is often as static and dull as the lives it depicts.

● Starring Kate Hudson, John Heard, Sara Gilbert, Brendan Sexton, Ethan Suplee, Christina Ricci.
**Columbia Tristar. October 2000. Cert 15.**

## Dirty Pictures

In 1990, a Cincinnati museum director is prosecuted for displaying sexually explicit photographs by Robert Mapplethorpe. Made for television, this powerful drama is based on the true story of Dennis Barrie, played by James Woods, effectively cast against type as a decent family man who will not compromise his principles. Craig T Nelson, the sympathetic father in the first two *Poltergeist* films, plays the vindictive local sheriff who wants Barrie jailed on obscenity charges. Giving a fair hearing to both sides of the argument, scriptwriter Ilene Chaiken handles the issues of censorship and freedom of expression with some assurance. The personal cost to Barrie is not downplayed, his high-profile court case leading to the breakdown of his marriage, while his kids are taunted by their classmates.

● Also starring Diana Scarwid, Ann Marin, Leon Pownall. *Dir* Frank Pierson.
**Fox Pathe. March 2001. Cert 18.**

## Dragonheart: A New Beginning

Made-for-video sequel to the 1996 hit, starring Christopher Masterson as an orphaned stable boy whose dreams of becoming a knight are realised when he discovers the last living dragon. Robby Benson provides the voice of Drake, son of the original film's Draco. Despite the film's unmistakably 'B'-grade feel, the special effects-driven plot provides reasonable entertainment, though former teen star Benson makes an inadequate vocal substitute for Sean Connery.

● Also starring Harry Van Gorkum, Rona Figueroa. *Dir* Doug Lefler.
**Universal. July 2000. Cert PG.**

## Dudley Do Right

Made before star Brendan Fraser hit the big time with *The Mummy*, this live action version of the 1960s cartoon tv show is marginally better than it sounds. Fraser plays the heroic, though utterly incompetent, Canadian Mountie Dudley Do Right, who must thwart the evil schemes of old adversary Snidely Whiplash (Alfred Molina). The plot, involving a fake gold rush and a property conspiracy, is negligible and the pacy action scenes seem a little intense for the intended juvenile audience. Writer-director Hugh Wilson got his big break with the first *Police Academy*, and his comedic style has remained reassuringly constant.

● Also starring Sarah Jessica Parker, Eric Idle, Robert Prosky, Alex Rocco.
**Universal. March 2001. Cert PG.**

## The End of Innocence

In the town of Jefferson Creek, North Carolina, a retarded teenager shoots dead his violent, abusive redneck father while the latter is beating the boy's mother. Showing an unusual sense of team spirit, his high school football buddies decide to shield him from the law. Needless to say, the attempted cover-up goes horribly wrong, leading to the accidental killing of a witness. Writer-director James Rowe supplements the grim main storyline with subplots involving impending graduation, football scholarships and strained relationships. Rodney Eastman gives a forceful performance as the abused boy, and singer Chris Isaak makes an appearance as the town's increasingly suspicious sheriff. Released in the United States as *Blue Ridge Fall*.

● Also starring Tom Arnold, Amy Irving, Garvin Funches, Peter Facinelli.
**High Fliers. March 2001. Cert 18.**

## For Love or Country

A made-for-television biopic of world-class Cuban trumpet player Arturo Sandoval, who defected to the United States with his family. Produced by Home Box Office, the film features strong performances from Andy Garcia as Sandoval and Charles S Dutton as American jazz legend Dizzy Gillespie. Timothy J Sexton's script perhaps overplays the predictable anti-Castro angle; if nothing else, Cuba's Communist regime gave Sandoval a career break impossible under the Batista dictatorship. Also known as *For Love or Country: The Arturo Sandoval Story*.

● Also starring Mia Maestro, Gloria Estefan, David Paymer, Tomas Milian. *Dir* Joseph Sargent.
**High Fliers. June 2001. Cert 12.**

## The 4th Floor

New York interior designer Juliette Lewis inherits her grandmother's rent-controlled apartment after the latter is killed in a strange accident. Her fellow residents, at first merely eccentric, become increasingly weird and menacing. Writer-director Josh Klausner borrows heavily from Roman Polanski, lifting ideas and images from *Repulsion*, *Rosemary's Baby* and *The Tenant*. Is Lewis really being threatened by a mysterious neighbour or is it all in her increasingly disturbed mind? Unfortunately, Klausner seems unable to fashion a satisfactory or even coherent narrative, throwing in swarms of rats and flies to distract the viewer from the gaping holes in his story. Furthermore, Lewis' character is just too dumb to stir up the necessary audience identification.
● Also starring William Hurt, Austin Pendleton, Shelley Duvall.
**Paramount. May 2001. Cert 15.**

## Freedom Song

Writer-director Phil Alden Robinson, whose career has been a little quiet since *Field of Dreams*, delivers an effectively understated account of the 1960s Civil Rights movement, seen through the eyes of teenager Vicellous Reon Shannon. Danny Glover co-stars as the boy's father, ever more aware of the increasing generation gap in their relationship. Miles away from the crudely emotive approach of *Mississippi Burning*, this modest tv movie makes the point that the movement's non-violent tactics did work, in time.
● Also starring Vondie Curtis Hall.
**Warner Home Video. July 2000. Cert 12.**

## From Dusk Till Dawn 3 – The Hangman's Daughter

This second straight-to-video sequel to Robert Rodriguez's blood-spattered 1995 original is a distinct improvement on the tiresomely camp *FDTD2: Texas Blood Money*. Rodriguez had a hand in the storyline, which might explain its structural similarity to the first *Dusk*, starting off as an ersatz spaghetti western before plunging into full-blown horror. Set in 1914 Mexico, the film explains the origins of vampire queen Santanico Pandemonium (Ara Celi), later top dancer at the Titty Twister. (Presumably Salma Hayek wasn't available to reprise her role.). Real-life American journalist Ambrose Bierce, author of *The Devil's Dictionary*, appears as a main character, well played by Michael Parks (Adam in John Huston's 1966 epic *The Bible*). A veteran of the American Civil War, Bierce is looking for revolutionary leader Pancho Villa when the film begins, a trip which cost the real Bierce his life. Brazilian actress Sonia Braga plays the bordello's vampire madam and Maori actor Temuera Morrison, star of *Once Were Warriors*, gives a forceful performance as the doomed hangman.
● Also starring Marco Leonardi.
*Dir* P J Pesce.
**Buena Vista. August 2000. Cert 18.**

## God's Favourite

A made-for-television biopic of tinpot Panamanian dictator, CIA operative and drug dealer Manuel Noriega (Bob Hoskins), who was first backed, then squashed, by the United States. Hoskins, who previously played Italian despot Benito Mussolini, manages to suggest the warped humanity behind the public 'monster'. Also known as *Noriega: God's Favourite*.
● Also starring Rosa Blasi, Jeffrey De Munn, Richard Masur. *Dir* Roger Spottiswoode.
**Fox Pathe. September 2000. Cert 15.**

## Gorgeous

While *Rush Hour* gave Jackie Chan his long-awaited break into Hollywood, the Hong Kong megastar has not abandoned his home turf by any means. This gentle romantic comedy, co-written by Chan, is a real change of pace from his usual action fare, with only a few token fights to placate the fans. A Taiwanese girl (Shu Qi) from a small fishing village travels to Hong Kong in search of love and adventure, after finding a romantic message in a bottle. Discovering that the message's author is the charming but gay Tony Leung, Qi switches her attentions to the macho yet sensitive Jackie. Meanwhile, her boyfriend from the fishing village arrives in search of her. *Note*: The dubbing for the English-language print is unusually poor.
● *Dir/co-sc* Vincent Kok.
**Columbia Tristar. September 2000. Cert PG.**

## Gun Shy

A veteran agent of the Drug Enforcement Agency, Charlie (Liam Neeson) is facing an emotional meltdown. At the centre of an elaborate sting operation set up to nail a local mobster, a corrupt Wall Street broker and a Colombian drug cartel, he has lost control of both his cool and his bowels. Meanwhile, psychotic Mafia bone-breaker Fulvio Nesstra (Oliver Platt) is having trouble with his wife and his tomatoes... While first-time director Eric Blakeney is to be commended for turning the clichés of the crime thriller on their collective head, he is a little late in the day. Trailing in the wake of *Jane Austen's Mafia!*, *Analyze This* and *Mickey Blue Eyes*, Blakeney's black comedy has a few nice moments (mainly supplied by Oliver Platt's shifty-eyed, hen-pecked mobster) but is too uncertain in tone to get a comic grip. Also, to cast a non-genre actor as the jittery hero seems something of a wasted opportunity (imagine Steven Seagal in the same role!). [JC-W]
● Also with Sandra Bullock, José Zuniga, Richard Schiff, Mary McCormack, Frank Vincent. *Pro* Sandra Bullock.
**Warner Home Video. May 2001. Cert 15.**

## Here on Earth

A spoiled rich kid by the name of Kelvin Morse trashes a small-town restaurant while out racing his new Mercedes. Taken to court, his sentence is to spend the summer vacation rebuilding the diner, during which time he learns some valuable lessons in life. Throwing in class rivalry and a wrong-side-of-the-tracks romance, this inconsequential film seems to be arguing that an expensive private education is no substitute for a taste of the real world. Fair enough. The romantic resolution is likely to cause serious viewer irritation.
● With Chris Klein, Leelee Sobieski, Josh Hartnett, Michael Rooker, Annette O'Toole. *Dir* Mark Piznarski.
**Fox Pathe. October 2000. Cert 15.**

## Highlander: Endgame

Long-lived brothers Connor and Duncan Macleod team up to defeat evil Immortal Kell (Bruce Payne), who threatens to give the entire human race a really bad time. Uniting Christopher Lambert and Adrian Paul, respective stars of the movie and TV *Highlanders*, doesn't add much to a series that ran out of surprises, and entertainment, with part one. Original cast members Beatie Edney and Sheila Gish make brief appearances, presumably to add some sense of continuity. The action scenes are staged with some flair but Hong Kong martial arts star Donnie Yen is sadly wasted. *Note*: Like its predecessors, this film exists in a number of different versions; serious fans should seek out the DVD release, which includes the longer director's cut and a number of deleted scenes.
● *Dir* Douglas Aarniokoski.
**Buena Vista. May 2001. Cert 18.**

## I Dreamed of Africa

Based on the autobiographical novel by Kuki Gallmann, this *Out of Africa* wannabe performed a spectacular belly flop at the US box-office, and it's not difficult to see why. Kim Basinger stars as a forceful Italian divorcee who

decides to turn her life around after a serious car accident. She relocates her family to a cattle ranch in rural Kenya, where their hopes of a peaceful existence undergo a predictable series of setbacks, including storms, lions, snakes and poachers. On top of all this, Basinger has serious problems with new husband Vincent Perez, a dangerously reckless man she barely knows. Director Hugh Hudson, whose career never recovered from the *Revolution* fiasco, concentrates on picturesque travelogue, and the native Kenyans are depicted in a very superficial way.
● With Eva Marie Saint, Daniel Craig. **Columbia TriStar. February 2001. Cert 12.**

## If These Walls Could Talk 2

Three stories of lesbian relationships, set in the same house over different decades:

*1961.* When a woman loses her female partner of 50 years to a fatal stroke, she finds herself shunned by the dead lover's family, who exclude her from the funeral, unwilling to acknowledge her existence. *1972.* A militant college student is ostracised by other feminists over her sexuality. *2000.* A well-heeled lesbian couple wants to have a baby via anonymous sperm donation. This HBO TV movie handles its potentially tricky subject matter with some assurance, though the short story format doesn't allow for a great deal of character development. For all its merits, the film is likely to be remembered for the third episode, a collaboration between writer-director Anne Heche and executive producer-star Ellen DeGeneres. At the time, Heche and DeGeneres were Hollywood's only celebrity lesbian couple; they later cited relentless media exposure as one reason for their break-up.
● Also with Vanessa Redgrave, Elizabeth Perkins, Chloe Sevigny. *Co-dir* Jane Anderson, Martha Coolidge. **Mosaic. November 2000. Cert 15.**

## In the Company of Spies

On assignment in North Korea, CIA operative Clancy Brown is arrested before he can transmit his intelligence report. Veteran agent Tom Berenger is brought out of retirement to lead the rescue mission. Favouring suspense over action, this above-average TV movie features vivid location work and some ingenious gadgetry. The characters tend towards stereotypes, however, and while the unconditionally pro-American stance makes a change from the usual CIA dirty tricks scenario, it doesn't ring true. Also known as *The Agency*.
● With Alice Krige, Arye Gross, Ron Silver, Al Waxman. *Dir* Tim Matheson. **Paramount. July 2000. Cert 15.**

## Intern

Viewers curious about the post-*Lolita* career of Dominique Swain can check out this middling comedy. Swain plays a young intern at the hip New York fashion magazine 'Skirt', dealing with models' tantrums and her editor's bulimia. She also vies with a top supermodel for the affections of a dashing British art director. Throwing in elements of romance, satire and even a little whodunit, the script badly lacks focus. That said, it's a lot shorter than *Prêt à Porter*. Gwyneth Paltrow makes a cameo appearance as herself, for what it's worth.
● With Joan Rivers, Ben Pullen, Kathy Griffin, Peggy Lipton. *Dir* Michael Lange. **High Fliers. April 2001. Cert 15.**

## The Intruder

Top 1960s fashion photographer David Bailey directed this dreary psychological thriller, with Charlotte Gainsbourg as a woman who suspects her husband is up to no good. The extremely weak script is a blend of ghost story, paranoia movie and science fiction, harnessed to a clumsy flashback structure, none of which can disguise the poor characterisation or central miscasting. Bailey's own still photographs hang on the walls of Gainsbourg's apartment, the film's main location, a shameless piece of self-promotion. Nastassja Kinski makes a brief appearance as a friend who may or may not have sexual designs on Gainsbourg.
● With John Hannah. **High Fliers. May 2001. Cert 15.**

## Island of Fire

This tense, if scrappily written, 1990 prison drama offers an impressive line-up of Hong Kong stars: Jackie Chan, Sammo Hung, Andy Lau and Tony Leung. An undercover cop infiltrates a prison run by a corrupt warden, discovering that supposedly executed prisoners are being used as covert assassins, their deaths faked. Chan fans may be disappointed, as the top-billed star is confined to a supporting role, disappearing for large chunks of the film (he seems to have participated as a favour). Sammo Hung gives a touching performance as an inmate who regularly escapes to visit his beloved son. The disparate plot strands are resolved with a big shootout. *Note*: The UK DVD edition of the film features a number of deleted scenes, which flesh out the supporting characters.
● *Dir* Chu Yin Ping. **Hong Kong Legends. September 2000. Cert 18.**

## It's the Rage

An extraordinary cast is utterly wasted in this made-for-TV satire on America's out-of-control gun culture. Depicting all gun owners as foaming lunatics itching to pull the trigger is not going to win many converts for the anti-firearm cause. For all its laudable intentions, the film works neither as black comedy nor social commentary. A misfire on every level. Original US title: *All the Rage*.
● With Joan Allen, Jeff Daniels, Robert Forster, Andre Braugher, Anna Paquin, David Schwimmer, Gary Sinise, Josh Brolin. *Dir* James D Stern. **Columbia TriStar. January 2001. Cert 15.**

## Just a Little Harmless Sex

An alleged romantic comedy notably lacking in either ingredient. A happily married, strictly monogamous man finds that a spur-of-the-moment roadside sexual encounter leads to arrest, eviction and social ridicule. What did he expect? Laden with stupid, unpleasant characters, this laboured farce has nothing to say about relationships or sexual behaviour. On this evidence, co-star Alison Eastwood needs a little career advice from her dad.
● With Rachel Hunter, Lauren Hutton, Tito Larriva, Michael Ontkean, Jonathan Silverman. *Dir* Rick Rosenthal. **Fox Pathe. September 2000. Cert 15.**

## Kiss the Sky

Bored with their dull, unfulfilled lives back in the US, two middle-aged men, an architect and a lawyer, head for the Philippines to recapture their youth through a haze of booze and drugs. Currently riding high in the hit TV show *CSI: Crime Scene Investigation*, William Petersen is still best known for his starring role in *Manhunter*. Here, he gives a believable performance in an effective tale of mid-life crisis. Terence Stamp makes a cameo appearance as a Zen Buddhist monk with a line in pithy epigrams. The title refers to the Jimi Hendrix song 'Purple Haze', one of the top 1960s drug anthems.
● With Gary Cole, Sheryl Lee, Patricia Charbonneau, Season Hubley. *Dir* Roger Young. **Fox Pathe. October 2000. Cert 18.**

## K-9 II

James Belushi returns as the canine-friendly cop, now widowed and stalked by a lunatic who blames him for his wife's death. Anyone who thought the original *K-9* was a howling dog of a comedy would be pretty close to the mark. This made-for-video

sequel manages to be even worse, which is some kind of achievement.
● With Christine Tucci, Wade Williams. *Dir* Charles T Kanganis.
Universal. August 2000. Cert 12.

## The Legend aka Fong Sai-Yuk

Having achieved Asian superstardom in *Once Upon a Time in China* (1991), martial arts virtuoso Jet Li consolidated his new status with this 1993 period action comedy, which he also executive-produced. The plot involves a former bandit turned 'legitimate' businessman who organises a kung fu tournament, with his daughter the prize. Meanwhile, agents of the Manchurian emperor attempt to track down members of the dissident Red Flower Society. *The Legend*'s sudden switches from broad, almost slapstick comedy to dead serious violence may prove disconcerting for Western viewers, with some bone-shattering, face-ripping kung fu near the beginning of the film. *Note*: The BBFC cut one second from this video release, involving a horse being trip-wired, on the grounds of animal cruelty.
● With Michelle Reis Lee Kar-yan, Sibelle Hu Hui-ching, Paul Chu Kong, Zhao Wen Zhou, Chen Sung Yung. *Dir* Cory Yuen Kwai.
Buena Vista. June 2001. Cert 15.

## Let the Devil Wear Black

A Los Angeles college student suspects his mother and uncle of murdering his wealthy father, especially after they announce their forthcoming marriage. This risible updating of *Hamlet* retains the basic story elements – treachery, greed, infidelity, revenge – yet somehow lacks the Shakespearean touch. Director-writer Stacy Title's most memorable innovation is to have the Ophelia character eat dog food.
● With Jonathan Penner, Jacqueline Bisset, Mary Louise Parker, Philip Baker Hall, Chris Sarandon.
High Fliers. July 2000. Cert 18.

## Live Virgin

An unscrupulous porn video director – is there any other kind? – plots to have his arch-rival's alienated teenage daughter lose her virginity live on cable television, the media event of the year. Don't be fooled by the presence of Bob Hoskins and Mena Suvari: this tasteless comedy is as bad as it sounds. If the makers intended to satirise the public's insatiable appetite for voyeuristic 'reality' television, something went badly wrong. Hoskins' worst film since *Super Mario Bros.* While *American*

*Beauty* put Suvari on the Hollywood map, she won't stay there long if she carries on making movies like this one. Original US title: *American Virgin*.
● With Robert Loggia, Sally Kellerman. *Dir/co-sc* Jean Pierre Marois.
Metrodome. February 2001. Cert 18.

## A Man Called Hero

A Chinese martial arts master flees to the US after the murder of his family. He helps fellow immigrants establish their own community in New York, all the time awaiting his chance for vengeance. Based on a phenomenally popular Hong Kong comic strip, this relentlessly action-packed film attempts to find an equivalent visual style, employing extensive digital effects. A fight on top of the Statue of Liberty makes for an interesting comparison with *X-Men*'s climactic punch-up, though many will prefer the more conventional martial arts sequences.
● With Ekin Cheng, Kristy Yang, Yuen Biao, Anthony Wong, Shu Qi. *Dir* & *ph* Andrew Lau.
Hong Kong Legends. May 2001. Cert 15.

## The Mating Habits of the Earthbound Human

An alien anthropologist studies human behaviour, delivering a *National Geographic*-style commentary on the more bizarre aspects of mating rituals. David Hyde Pierce does an amusing turn as the unseen narrator, not a million miles removed from Niles in *Frasier*, as he follows The Male (Mackenzie Astin) and The Female (Carmen Electra) from their first meeting, through regular dating, to long-term commitment. Writer-director Jeff Abugov sustains the laughs for most of the running time, though the material is better suited to a television sitcom episode than a feature-length movie. Carmen Electra certainly wasn't cast for her acting ability.
● With Lucy Liu, Markus Redmond, Marc Blucas.
Columbia TriStar. January 2001. Cert 15.

## Molly

Molly, a 28-year-old autistic woman, is released from an institution into the care of her brother, who allows her to undergo experimental medical treatment. Loosely based on a true story, this disappointing romantic comedy is effectively a gender-reversal remake of *Charly* (1968). Elisabeth Shue gives an engaging performance in the title role, but the script and supporting cast leave a lot to be desired. *Note*: The North American theatrical

release date for *Molly* was pushed back by several months and the film had its premiere on a US airline, in a version running 20 minutes longer than the cinema print. The shorter version is noticeably disjointed in places, with sudden narrative jumps.
● With Aaron Eckhart, Jill Hennessy, Lucy Liu. *Dir* John Duigan
Warner Home Video. September 2000. Cert 15.

## Mystery, Alaska

The anonymous small town of Mystery, Alaska becomes the focus of media attention when its amateur ice hockey team is chosen to play the major league New York Rangers in a televised game. Directed by Jay Roach, Mike Myers' collaborator on the *Austin Powers* films, and co-written by *Ally McBeal* creator David E Kelley, this alleged comedy is a tedious misfire. The level of wit rarely gets above having old people and young children mouth obscenities, and the theme of the townspeople pulling together for the big win is lame. The presence of Russell Crowe is the main attraction for prospective viewers, most of who will be crying for blood by the end.
● With Hank Azaria, Mary McCormack, Burt Reynolds, Colm Meaney, Lolita Davidovich
Buena Vista. August 2000. Cert 15.

## Passion of Mind

Marie (Demi Moore), a single mother in Provence, dreams of Marty (Moore again), a New York literary agent who resembles her. Or is it the other way round? Demi Moore's career freefall continues unabated with this misbegotten, poorly scripted psycho-drama. Playing with themes of identity and fantasy versus reality has defeated better talents than the ones at work here. Co-star Joss Ackland, cast as Marty's psychiatrist, described the film as 'terrible' and few are likely to disagree. Chilean writer-director Raul Ruiz handled a similar idea with much greater assurance in *Shattered Image* (1998).
● With Eloise Eonnet, Sinead Cusack, Peter Riegert, Stellan Skarsgaard. *Dir* Alain Berliner.
Buena Vista. May 2001. Cert 15.

## Permanent Midnight

Yet another cautionary tale of substance abuse, with high-flying television writer Ben Stiller brought violently down to earth by his heroin addiction. Working from Jerry Stahl's much sharper autobiography, writer-director David Veloz delivers the expected scenes of personal and professional trauma, without adding anything fresh. Producers

Jane Hamsher and Don Murphy worked on Oliver Stone's speed-freak, psycho-nutter satire *Natural Born Killers* (1994), which at least kept moving. By contrast, *Permanent Midnight* feels like a real downer.

● With Elizabeth Hurley, Owen Wilson, Cheryl Ladd, Janeane Garofalo and Jerry Stahl.

**Columbia TriStar. October 2000. Cert 18.**

## Prophets Game

In not-so-sunny Los Angeles, a game of wits is being played to lethal extremes by the Prophet, a serial killer with a liking for riddles and detached body parts. Retired police detective Vincent Swann (Dennis Hopper) begins to suspect that his murdered daughter was an earlier victim of the Prophet, rather than of the man convicted of the crime. Aside from Hopper, effectively cast against type as a good (ish) guy, this thriller is a wasted opportunity, undermining its premise with tired clichés, absurd plot turns and a largely lacklustre supporting cast. *Spoiler*: If the producers wanted to maintain the element of suspense – such as it is – they should have introduced Sondra Locke's character a bit sooner.

● With Stephanie Zimbalist, Robert Yocum, Don Swayze, Joe Penny, Robert Ginty, Michael Dorn. *Dir* David Worth.

**High Fliers. April 2001. Cert 18.**

## The Proposal

Undercover cop Nick Moran gets too involved in his latest assignment, no longer certain who he can trust. Teamed with supposedly inexperienced colleague Jennifer Esposito, Moran starts to feel she knows a lot more about lead villain Stephen Lang than she's telling. Scripted by Maurice Hurley, a veteran of *Star Trek: The Next Generation*, this is an effective tale of mounting paranoia and suspected double-cross.

● *Dir* Richard Gale.

**Mosaic. October 2000. Cert 18.**

## Rat

An unassuming bread delivery man (Pete Postlethwaite) wakes up as a rat after a hard night's drinking, much to the irritation of his wife (Imelda Staunton). As his family attempt to adjust to his new rodent state, an unscrupulous journalist tries to exploit the bizarre situation for personal gain. This Irish-set comic fantasy has a pleasantly surreal premise, which is developed along enjoyable if predictable lines. While the script makes occasional nods to Franz Kafka's much darker *Metamorphosis*, the debates about identity, loyalty and preju-

dice are kept on a safely superficial level.

● With Frank Kelly, Ed Byrne, Niall Tobin, Geoffrey Palmer. *Dir* Steve Barron.

**Universal. April 2001. Cert PG.**

## The Replacements

Faced with a professional footballers' strike, team manager Gene Hackman brings in amateur 'scab' players, including washed-up ex-pro Keanu Reeves, substance-abusing Welshman Rhys Ifans and a Sumo wrestler. Reeves' success with *The Matrix* hasn't sharpened his instinct for good film roles and this dreary comedy never scores a decent touchdown. Hackman, a vastly superior actor with an equally dubious collection of career choices, does his best with the feeble script. In fairness to director Howard Deutch, *The Replacements* was heavily re-edited by the studio without his input or consent. Inspired by a real American football players' strike in 1987.

● With Brooke Langton, Orlando Jones.

**Warner Home Video. June 2001. Cert 12.**

## The St Francisville Experiment

Yet another *Blair Witch Project*-derived spookumentary, featuring a supposedly haunted house being investigated by a talent-lite documentary team badly in need of a decent camera tripod. Shaky in more ways than one.

● With Tim Baldini, Madison Charap, Paul James, Ryan Larson.

**High Fliers. March 2001. Cert 15.**

## Screw Loose

After suffering a serious heart attack, a Milan 'natural food' magnate wants to be reunited with the American GI who saved his life during World War II. Sent to the United States, the magnate's idiot son (Enzo Greggio) discovers that the former GI (Mel Brooks) is now incarcerated in an insane asylum. Director-star Greggio, a popular comic on Italian TV, previously gave the world *The Silence of the Hams*, one of the worst film parodies of all time. This isn't much of an improvement, the mix of juvenile humour and softcore titillation suggesting extreme creative desperation. Original title: *Svitati*.

● With Julie Condra.

**Columbia. March 2001. Cert 12.**

## The Serpent's Kiss

In spite of a starry British cast, this flawed but intriguing companion piece to Peter Greenaway's *The Draughtsman's Contract* failed to secure a theatrical release in the UK. Set in 1699, it centres on the short-lived fashion for Dutch parterre gardens and

man's arrogant belief that he could control nature. The acting and fabulous garden sets stand out, although the direction by the Oscar-winning cinematographer Philippe Rousselot is rather flabby. Nonetheless, this is a compelling curiosity item worth renting on a cold winter's night [JCW].

● With Ewan McGregor, Greta Scacchi, Pete Postlethwaite, Richard E. Grant, Donal McCann, Gerard McSorley.
*Screenplay* Tim Rose Price.

**Guerilla Films. November 2000. Cert 15.**

## Seven Days to Live

Plodding Euro shocker set in a supposedly haunted house, where Amanda Plummer has troubling visions of her own impending death. Borrowing a little too freely from *The Shining*, this German-produced, English-language horror movie has a confused, unresolved storyline. There is very little sense of time or place, which could be a deliberate touch to disorientate the viewer, but is probably just the result of co-production compromise and plain carelessness (the cars have British number plates, yet are all left-hand drive).

● With Sean Pertwee, Nick Brimble, Gina Bellman. *Dir* Sebastian Niemann.

**Mosaic. March 2001. Cert 18.**

## The Sex Monster

Bored with his sex life, a Los Angeles interior designer persuades his reluctant wife to participate in a threesome. While he is only moderately turned on, she discovers an insatiable appetite for lesbian sex. Writer-director-star Mike Binder attempts a humorous dissection of modern relationships, where one man's casual voyeurism threatens to unleash uncontrollable sapphic forces. The film might have worked better with a more expressive co-star than Mariel Hemingway, whose performance as the suddenly liberated wife is curiously inert. Viewers hoping for some hot all-girl action will be disappointed to learn that the sex takes place offscreen, with just a few suggestive noises on the soundtrack.

● With Missy Crider, Stephen Baldwin, Robin Curtis.

**High Fliers. September 2000. Cert 15.**

## Shriek If You Know What I Did Last Friday the 13th

This dismal straight-to-video horror spoof deserved to go straight-to-hell. Throwing in the usual masked serial killer, assorted high school kids and nosy reporter, the script bears little sign that the makers ever saw the films being parodied. Coolio turns up as the school

principal, probably the movie's highpoint, while co-star Kim Greist looks like she'd rather be elsewhere. Some people rate this higher than *Scary Movie*, for what that's worth.
● With Julie Benz, Harley Cross, Majandra Delfino, Tom Arnold. *Dir* John Blanchard. **High Fliers. May 2001. Cert 15.**

## Soft Fruit

Written and directed by Christina Andreef, this Australian comedy-drama is light years away from the standard Hollywood soap opera. Three sisters and their criminal brother return home for the first time in 15 years to nurse their terminally ill mother. As the ill-matched siblings attempt to honour her last wishes, they have to deal with their suppressed emotions and troubled relationships, both with their parents and each other. Avoiding cliché and sentimentality, Andreef makes her flawed, unglamorous characters both plausible and sympathetic. Linal Haft (Maureen Lipman's son in the 'Beatie' British Telecom adverts) gives a fine performance as the distant, repressed father, who seems unable to cope with either his dying wife or dysfunctional children.
● With Jeanie Drynan, Russell Dykstra, Genevieve Lemon, Sacha Horler, Dion Bilios. **Fox Pathe. April 2001. Cert 18.**

## Sugar Town

Would-be rock stars hustle their way through the Los Angeles music scene, searching for the elusive big break. Gwen (Jade Gordon) is determined to reach the top by any means necessary. Writer-directors Alison Anders and Kurt Voss don't have anything particularly new or profound to say in this heavily improvised comedy, yet the end result is reasonably effective. Stronger on atmosphere and character observation than plot, the tone is both unsentimental and non-judgmental. British pop stars John Taylor (Duran Duran) and Martin Kemp (Spandau Ballet) give creditable performances as members of a defunct glam-rock group, offered the chance of a comeback.
● With Rosanna Arquette, Beverly D'Angelo, Ally Sheedy, Michael Des Barres. **FilmFour/VCI. May 2001. Cert 18.**

## Teaching Mrs Tingle

Grandsboro High, California; the present. Leigh Ann Watson (Katie Holmes) has worked her butt off to get top marks in her history exam. But her teacher, Mrs Tingle, gets a perverse satisfaction in humiliating and flunking her students. Facing expulsion

for nothing more than a misunderstanding, Leigh Ann – with the aid of two fellow students – takes Mrs Tingle hostage... The directorial debut of horror scenarist Kevin Williamson (*Scream*s 1-2, *I Know What You Did Last Summer*), *Teaching Mrs Tingle* is a so-so black comedy enlivened by a great part. At first glance a one-dimensional gorgon, Mrs Tingle – played with appropriate irony by Helen Mirren in her trashiest role for aeons – reveals greater and greater depths of cunning and even humanity. There's also a priceless turn from Marisa Coughlan, whose skit from *The Exorcist* belongs in a much better movie. Original title: *Killing Mrs Tingle* (which was changed in the aftermath of the Columbine massacre). [JC-W]
● Also with Jeffrey Tambor, Barry Watson, Liz Stauber, Molly Ringwald, Vivica A. Fox, Michael McKean, the dog Jill and (uncredited) Lesley Ann Warren (as Faye Watson). **Buena Vista. January 2001. Cert 15.**

## Texas Chainsaw Massacre: The Next Generation aka The Return of the Texas Chainsaw Massacre

Writer-director Kim Henkel co-scripted the original *Texas Chain Saw Massacre* (1974), but had no real involvement with the first two sequels, Tobe Hooper's *The Texas Chainsaw Massacre 2* (1986) and Jeff Burr's *Leatherface: The Texas Chainsaw Massacre III* (1990), both of which flopped in the US and received a big thumbs-down from the British censor. Henkel claimed he wanted a return to cannibal basics for the fourth instalment, recruiting original cast members Marilyn Burns and Paul A Partain plus then-unknowns Matthew McConaughey and Renée Zellweger. Released in the US as *The Return of the Texas Chainsaw Massacre* in October 1994, the disappointingly inept end result received only limited distribution and was picked up in 1997 by Columbia TriStar, who, after some strategic re-editing, gave it a small-scale re-release as *Texas Chainsaw Massacre: The Next Generation*. This new version ran ten minutes shorter than the original print, dropping a scene where Zellweger's character is violently abused by her stepfather (which probably wouldn't have gone down well with her post-*Jerry Maguire* fans). In the event, nobody really cared. It says something about the film's fundamental timidity that Leatherface (played this time by Robert Jacks) doesn't even get to slay anyone with his trademark weapon. The buzz is off. *Note*:

UK pre-release publicity confused the film with Hooper's vastly superior *Texas Chainsaw Massacre 2*, starring Dennis Hopper, which was finally offered a BBFC 18 certificate for cinema release, dependent on nearly *25 minutes* of cuts.
**Columbia TriStar. October 2000. Cert 18.**

## The Thirteenth Floor

Following the mysterious death of his employer, a computer programmer becomes involved in time travel and virtual reality. A solid enough science fiction premise leads to nowhere in particular here. The intricate storyline is confusing rather than labyrinthine, and the cast seems adrift in a sea of indifference. Co-producer Roland Emmerich knows a thing or two about s-f blockbusters but doesn't appear to have communicated his wisdom to director Josef Rusnak, who also co-wrote the script.
● With Craig Bierko, Armin Mueller-Stahl, Gretchen Mol, Vincent D'Onofrio, Dennis Haysbert.
**Columbia TriStar. July 2000. Cert 15.**

## Tokyo Raiders

Hectic comedy thriller which travels from Las Vegas to Hong Kong to Tokyo, with a plot involving an absent groom, a bad cheque and the Japanese criminal underworld. Despite the presence of Asian star Tony Leung, die-hard Hong Kong action fans tend to find the movie disappointing, while newcomers will probably be a little bewildered. Worth a look for those in an open frame of mind.
● With Ekin Chen, Kelly Chen. *Dir* Jingle Ma.
**Columbia TriStar. May 2001. Cert 12.**

## The Virginian

Owen Wister's Western novel about a ranch foreman who tangles with the local villain was first filmed in 1929 with Gary Cooper and remade in 1946 with Joel McCrea. Despite the famous line 'Smile when you say that,' neither version achieved classic status and the book is probably best known as the inspiration for the hit 1960s television series. Director-star Bill Pullman has come up with a decent made-for-TV remake, though some feel that the budget-friendly Canadian locations lack authenticity. Former TV *Virginian* James Drury makes a cameo appearance, alongside long-serving *Gunsmoke* co-star Dennis Weaver.
● With Diane Lane, John Savage, Harris Yulin, Colm Feore.
**Warner Home Video. August 2000. Cert PG.**

# Faces of the Year

## Javier Bardem

**Born:** 1 March 1969 in Las Palmas de Gran Canaria, Gran Canaria, Spain
**Full name:** Javier Encinas Bardem
**Education:** studied painting at the Escuela de Artes y Officios in Madrid
**Previous occupation:** rugby player (for the Spanish National Team), bouncer, construction worker, waiter, security guard, cartoonist, exotic dancer (male stripper)
**Film debut:** aged six, in *El Pícaro* (*The Scoundrel*)
**The other films:** *The Ages of Lulu* (1990), Pedro Almodóvar's *High Heels*, Bigas Luna's *Jamon Jamon*, *The Bilingual Lover*, Luna's *Golden Balls*, Luna's *The Tit and the Moon*, *Dias contados*, *The Detective and Death*, *Mouth to Mouth*, *La Madre*, *Ecstasy*, *Not Love Just Frenzy*, *El Amor perjudica seriamente la salud*, *Airbag*, Almodóvar's *Live Flesh*, *Perdita Durango*, *Torrente, el brazo tonto de la ley*, *Between Your Legs*, *Los Lobos de Washington*, *Second Skin*, *Before Night Falls*
**Next up:** the lead in *The Dancer Upstairs*, the film version of Nicholas Shakespeare's novel, marking the directorial debut of John Malkovich
**Strengths:** willingness to try anything, rough-hewn good looks, does nude scenes
**Weakness:** incomprehensible English accent
**Famous relative:** his uncle, the celebrated writer-director Juan Antonio Bardem
**Infamy:** he got his broken nose in a childhood brawl
**Awards:** voted best actor of 2000 for his role as the Cuban writer Reinaldo Arenas in *Before Night Falls* by the National Board of Review, the National Society of Film Critics and the Venice Film Festival. He also snagged an Oscar nomination
**Also:** he turned down the role of the villain played by Robert Carlyle in *The World is Not Enough*
**Idol:** Ken Loach
**He said it:** 'To be compared to [Antonio] Banderas is an honour, because he's done a lot for Spanish movies. But his career and what I want from my work are not the same. He's a star, a celebrity. I'd hate all that.'
**They said it:** 'Bardem [is] … an outmoded sexual stereotype … a male Jane Russell.' Liese Spencer in the *Independent*

## Jack Black

**Born:** 7 April 1969 in Edmonton, Alberta, Canada
**Real name:** Jack Black
**Education:** University of California, Los Angeles
**Film debut:** Roger in Tim Robbins' *Bob Roberts* (1992)
**The other films:** *Demolition Man*, *Airborne*, *The NeverEnding Story III*, *Blind Justice*, *Bye Bye Love*, *Waterworld*, *Dead Man Walking*, *Bio-Dome*, *The Cable Guy*, *The Fan*, *Mars Attacks!*, *Crossworlds*, *The Jackal*, *Johnny Skidmarks*, *Bongwater*, *I Still Know What You Did Last Summer* (uncredited), *Enemy of the State*, *Cradle Will Rock*, *Jesus' Son*, *High Fidelity*, *Saving Silverman*, *Run Ronnie Run*, *Orange County*
**Next up:** the starring role of Hal in the Farrelly brothers' *Shallow Hal*, co-starring Gwyneth Paltrow and Jason Alexander
**Strengths:** high energy level, deadpan comic delivery
**Significant other:** Laura Kightlinger
**Claim to fame:** scene-stealing turns in *Jesus' Son* and *High Fidelity*, in the latter playing John Cusack's manic vinyl-selling colleague who says things like, 'We're no longer called Sonic Death Monkey. We're on the verge of becoming Kathleen Turner Overdrive, but just for tonight, we are Barry Jive and his Uptown Five!'
**Also:** lead singer of the cult group Tenacious D and guest star in the Foo Fighters' 'Learn to Fly' video and Beck's 'SexxLaws'
**He said it:** 'Once you have a career, it's like a tangible thing. You don't want to lose it. And you become protective, like, "What do I do to keep it?" And that's kind of a bummer.'
**A bit like:** Chris Farley disguised as a disgruntled badger

## Alice Evans

**Born:** 2 August 1974 in New Jersey, USA
**Full name:** Alice Jane Evans
**Education:** London University (graduating in languages), Cour Florent drama school, Paris
**Previous occupation:** Model, TV presenter
**Film debut:** the Franco-Italian thriller *Rewind* (1988)
**The other films:** *Monsieur Naphtali* (1999), *10 Things I Hate About You* (billed as 'perky girl'), *The Escort*, *Une pour toutes* (aka *One 4 All*), *102 Dalmatians*
**TV:** *Highlander*, *Elisa top modèle*, *Le ragazze di Piazza di Spagna*, *Best of Both Worlds* (BBC)
**Next up:** *The Abduction Club*, with Liam Cunningham and Matthew Rhys
**Strengths:** ability to speak fluent French and Italian, stunning beauty, great figure, coquettish innocence, slow-burn sexuality
**Significant other:** the entrepreneur Olivier Picasso, grandson of the artist, who now acts as her manager
**Claim to fame:** the ingenue role in *102 Dalmatians* and the starring role in the BBC's *Best of Both Worlds*, in which she played a bigamist. Also extremely famous in France as the glamorous girlfriend of Olivier Picasso
**Good friends:** Matthew Rhys, Ioan Gruffudd, supermodel Karen Mulder,

TV presenter Tania Bryer

**She said it:** 'When you go out in Paris it always has to be some bloody dinner. Why can't they just go out and get drunk like we do in London?'

**They said it:** 'She is very famous in France. One year I went to the Cannes Film Festival with her. People would go crazy every time we stepped out of the hotel, shouting "Aleece! Aleece!"' TV presenter Tania Bryer

## Colin Farrell

**Born:** 31 March 1976 in Castleknock, Dublin

**Education:** the Gaiety School of Drama, Dublin

**Previous occupations:** aspiring footballer, waiter

**Film debut:** *Drinking Crude* (1997)

**The other films:** *The War Zone*, *Ordinary Decent Criminal* (cast after the film's star, Kevin Spacey, saw Farrell in the Donmar Warehouse production of *A Little World of Their Own*), Joel Schumacher's *Tigerland*, *American Outlaws* (as Jesse James), Schumacher's *Phone Booth*, the Second World War epic *Hart's War*, with Bruce Willis

**TV:** *Ballykissangel* (as Danny Byrne), *Falling for a Dancer*, *David Copperfield*, *Love in the 21st Century*

**Next up:** Steven Spielberg's sci-fi thriller *Minority Report*, based on the short story by Philip K Dick, and *The Farm* with Al Pacino

**Strengths:** slow-burning presence, soulful eyes, great American accent

**Famous relative:** his father Eammon Farrell, who played pro' football for Shamrock Rovers

**Wife:** Actress Amelia Warner (*Quills*), married 17 July 2001 on a beach in Tahiti

**Awards:** voted best actor by the Boston Society of Film Critics for his part in *Tigerland*

**He said it:** 'Who wants to be a movie star? Oh, well I do. Well, do I? Do I? I dunno.'

**They said it:** 'He's got that thing with the camera that I'll never understand. Some people have it. Others don't. It's like a magic potion.' Joel Schumacher, director of *Tigerland* and *Phone Booth*

## Kate Hudson

**Born:** 19 April 1979 in Los Angeles

**Full name:** Kate Garry Hudson

**Film debut:** *Desert Blue* (1998), in which she played an egotistical TV starlet

**The other films:** *Ricochet River*, *200 Cigarettes*, *About Adam*, *Gossip*, *Almost Famous*, *Dr T & the Women*

**Next up:** Shekhar Kapur's *The Four Feathers*, in which she plays Ethne Eustace opposite Heath Ledger and Wes Bentley

**Strengths:** sunny personality, strong work ethic, good singing voice

**Famous relative:** mother Goldie Hawn, stepfather Kurt Russell

**Husband:** Chris Robinson, lead singer of the Black Crowes, whom she wed on 31 December 2000

**Awards:** Golden Globe and Oscar nomination for Best Supporting Actress in *Almost Famous*

**Also:** the career-making role of Penny Lane in *Almost Famous* was originally intended for Sarah Polley, who turned it down to pursue another project

**Idol:** Bette Davis

**She said it:** 'I accepted who I was and what pod I came from. I didn't fall too far from the tree, and I'm OK with that. I'm never going to try to be anything I'm not – and if I do, I'm going to ask one of my brothers to shoot me.'

**They said it:** 'Kate had this terrible Irish accent when she first auditioned for the role, really appalling. She had to work very hard on that accent.' Then, afterwards: 'She's so convincing that any Irish person who has seen it [the film] thinks she's Irish.' Gerard Stembridge, director of the Irish comedy *About Adam*

'There's something that makes movie stars, and I think Kate Hudson has got

that magic. She just lights up the scene, and the screen.' Robert Altman, director of *Dr T & the Women*

## Hugh Jackman

**Born:** 12 October 1968 in Sydney, Australia

**Education:** Knox Grammar, Sydney; University of Technology, Sydney; Actors Centre, Sydney; Academy of Performing Arts, Melbourne

**Previous occupation:** TV presenter

**Film debut:** *Paperback Hero* (1998)

**The other films:** *Erskineville Kings*, *X-Men* (as Wolverine), *Someone Like You* (aka *Animal Attraction*), *Swordfish*

**Next up:** James Mangold's *Kate & Leopold*, in which he plays a 19th century English duke transported into the present. Meg Ryan co-stars

**Strengths:** impeccable American accent, rugged handsomeness, rock-solid philosophical outlook

**Wife:** Australian actress Deborra-Lee Furness (*Angel Baby*)

**Son:** Oscar, adopted

**Good friend:** Russell Crowe

**Also:** he is an excellent singer and dancer, plays the piano, practises Transcendental Meditation and is even a bit of a juggler

**He said it:** 'I didn't want to be an actor for all these things that have happened to me – making more money than I ever thought I'd earn, the places I've travelled, the people I've met ... It's been wild. But I never did it for that, and I'd be just as happy being on stage back in my hometown.'

## Lucy Liu

**Born:** 2 December 1967 in Queens, New York City (to Chinese immigrants)

**Nickname:** Curious George

**Education:** Stuyvesant High School, University of Michigan (where she studied Asian languages and cultures), Beijing University (where she studied Chinese art, philosophy and religion)

**Previous occupation:** ice cream scooper, clothes clerk, restaurant hostess, aerobics instructor, caterer. Once upon a time she wanted to be a cop

**Film debut:** *Bang* (1995), a low-budget comedy-drama written and directed by Ash [sic]. Lucy played a prostitute

**The other films:** *Jerry Maguire*, *Guy*, *Gridlock'd*, *City of Industry*, *Flypaper*, *Payback*, *True Crime*, *The Mating Habits of*

the Earthbound Human, Play It to the Bone, Molly, Shanghai Noon, Charlie's Angels (as Alex) and Mike Figgis' Hotel, with Lysette Anthony, Salma Hayek and Burt Reynolds
**TV:** L.A. Law, Coach, Beverly Hills 90201, Home Improvement, NYPD Blue, The X-Files, ER, Nash Bridges, Michael Hayes and, of course, Ally McBeal
**Next up:** Vincenzo Natali's Company Man with Jeremy Northam
**Strengths:** extraordinary beauty, fantastic cheekbones, cut-glass delivery
**Significant other:** in the summer of 2000 she was romantically linked with George Clooney
**Claim to fame:** her scene-stealing turn as the outspoken, venomous lawyer Ling Woo in TV's Ally McBeal. She originally read for the role of Nelle Porter, but was considered too cold for the part. So the show's creator, David E Kelly, wrote Ling Woo especially for her
**Also:** Lucy is an accomplished 'mixed media' avant-garde photographer, a talented accordion player and an avid rock climber, skier and rider. She has also trained in the martial arts
**She said it:** 'I do not think men like spanking as much as women like spanking. I myself like a good spanking on occasion – if it's done right.'
**They said it:** 'Lucy is an incredibly gentle person. She's a deep river.' Greg Germann, who plays Lucy's boss and lover, Richard Fish, in Ally McBeal, and, like his co-star, is a keen accordion player

## Franka Potente

**Born:** 22 July 1974 in Dülmen, Germany
**Education:** Otto Falckenberg School,

Munich; Lee Strasberg Theatre Institute, New York
**Previous occupation:** schoolgirl
**Film debut:** Nach fünf im Urwald (aka After Five in the Forest Primevall/It's a Jungle Out There) (1996)
**The other films:** Babe's Petrol, Run Lola Run, Am I Beautiful?, Downhill City, Our Island in the South Pacific, Schlaraffenland, Anatomy, The Princess and the Warrior, Blow
**Next up:** The Bourne Identity, a Euro-thriller with Matt Damon and Clive Owen
**Strengths:** beauty, a solid understanding of the English language and a chameleon-like ability to change her appearance from film to film
**Significant other:** writer-director Tom Tykwer, who has directed her in Run Lola

Run and The Princess and the Warrior
**Claim to fame:** the bright red-haired look she adopted for Run Lola Run started a cult in Germany, where dyed red hair became de rigueur for teenagers and TV models
**Idol:** Danish filmmaker Lars von Trier
**She said it:** 'I'm childish, down-to-earth and punctual – but, of course, I am German.'
**A bit like:** Swiss star Marthe Keller

## Michelle Rodriguez

**Born:** 12 July 1978 in Bexar County, Texas
**Previous occupation:** clerk at Toys 'R' Us
**Film debut:** Girlfight (2000)
**The other films:** 3 a.m., The Fast and the Furious
**Next up:** Paul Anderson's action thriller Resident Evil (based on the video game), in which she plays a 'zombie fighter' opposite Milla Jovovich and James Purefoy
**Strengths:** no-nonsense attitude to

Hollywood, physical strength, presence
**Awards:** named Best Newcomer by the National Board of Review and in the Independent Spirit Awards
**Significant other:** actor Vin Diesel, who, she told Howard Stern in a radio interview, 'will be a part of my life for a very long time'
**Claim to fame:** her astonishing, brutally honest performance in Girlfight; her turn as a fist-loose racer in the $140-million-grossing The Fast and the Furious didn't do her any harm, either
**Infamy:** demanded to have her skirt hems lowered and her tops loosened for the role of Letty in The Fast and the Furious
**She said it:** 'I like to explore my dementia' and 'I've never really fallen in love. I just love the sex, that's all – I'm just being honest.'
**A bit like:** a young female Marlon Brando mixed with Ice Cube

## Mark Ruffalo

**Born:** 1968 in Kenosha, Wisconsin
**Alternative occupation:** stage director
**Film debut:** There Goes My Baby (aka The Last Days of Paradise) (1993)
**The other films:** Mirror Mirror 2: Raven Dance, Mirror Mirror 3: The Voyeur, The Dentist, The Last Big Thing, The Destiny of Marty Fine, Blood Money, On the 2nd Day of Christmas (TV), Safe Men, 54, Ride With the Devil, Life/Drawing (aka Low Rent), Houdini (TV), A Fish in the Bathtub, You Can Count On Me, Committed, XX/XY, John Woo's Windtalkers, Bruno Barreto's A View from the Top
**Next up:** Rod Lurie's The Last Castle, with Robert Redford
**Wife:** Sunrise Coigney
**Strengths:** a theatre-honed talent, a healthy connection to his dark side, malleable appearance
**Awards:** presented with the New Generation Award by the Los Angeles Film Critics' Association for his performance in You Can Count On Me
**Also:** voted 'Most Fun to Be Around' at school ('but it was tears of a clown – I was always really miserable inside, but no one would've ever known that')
**He said it:** 'I had a questionable self-image coming into the game. I wasn't like the best candidate to become an actor. I was really insecure and I didn't particularly like myself very much.'
**A bit like:** A good-looking Vincent D'Onofrio

# Film World Diary
## July 2000 – June 2001

## JULY 2000

*The Perfect Storm* grosses $100 million in the US ● **Mike Myers** is sued by Imagine Entertainment for backing out of their production of *Sprockets*, following their failure to meet his unexpected demand for a bigger wage packet ● **Gerard Depardieu** is secretly admitted to hospital outside Paris for a quintuple heart bypass operation. Apparently, the actor and wine entrepreneur had been consuming up to three packets of Gitanes and five bottles of wine a day ● **Liam Neeson**'s pelvis is shattered when his motorcycle collides with a deer on a country road near his home in Connecticut. The deer doesn't make it ● **Jean-Claude Van Damme** is fined $1200 and placed on three years' probation after pleading guilty to drink-driving and driving without a licence ● **Patsy Kensit** and her rock star husband **Liam Gallagher** decide to split ● *Big Momma's House* grosses $100 million in the US ● *Mission: Impossible 2* grosses $200 million in the US ● It's official: **Drew Barrymore**, 25, is to marry her boyfriend, MTV comedian **Tom Green**, who is recovering from treatment for testicular cancer ● *Scary Movie* grosses $100 million in the US ● After 27 years of retirement, **Brigitte Bardot**, 69, agrees to appear in a low-budget film about the Nazis ● *X-Men* grosses $100 million in the US ● **Brad Pitt** and **Jennifer Aniston** tie the knot at a security-conscious ceremony in Malibu that costs the couple $1 million. Celebrity guests include **David Arquette**, **Courteney Cox Arquette**, **Cameron Diaz**, **Morgan Freeman**, Anthony Hopkins, Lisa Kudrow, Edward Norton, Matthew Perry and **David Schwimmer** ● Three years after tabloid speculation that **Keanu Reeves** was engaged to **Amanda De Cadenet**, fresh rumour has it that the couple really *are* engaged now. Yet only last year Keanu and his girlfriend Jennifer Syme were expecting a baby (which was stillborn on Christmas Eve) ● *The Patriot* grosses $100 million in the US ● **Richard Attenborough**, **Judi Dench**, **Jeremy Irons**, **Kevin Spacey** and **David Suchet** announce plans to restore London's Old Vic Theatre to its former glory ● *The Mirror* newspaper reveals that **Steve Martin** and **Helena Bonham Carter** are now a couple. The actor and actress met while filming the comedy *Novocaine* in Chicago.

**Right:** *Catherine Zeta-Jones: The mother of all Hollywood wives*

## AUGUST 2000

**Macaulay Culkin**, 19, and his wife of two years, Rachel Miner, 20, are calling it quits ● *What Lies Beneath* grosses $100 million in the US ● **Michael Douglas** and **Catherine Zeta-Jones** are the proud parents of a 7lb 7oz baby boy, Dylan Michael ● *Chicken Run* grosses $100 million in the US ● On the day that her relationship with fellow actress **Ellen DeGeneres** is confirmed to be over, **Anne Heche** is found 'dazed and confused' on the side of the road in Fresno, near Los Angeles. The star is later hospitalised ● *Nutty Professor II: The Klumps* grosses $100 million in the US.

## SEPTEMBER 2000

*Mission: Impossible 2* grosses $500 million worldwide ● More than 5000 actors and their champions turn out on the streets of Los Angeles to protest against the unfair structure of residual payments. The grievance began when advertising agencies decided to dismantle the pay-per-play policy, thus negating repeat fees for performers. **Kevin Spacey**, who has donated over $100,000 to the cause, argued that

'80 per cent of Screen Guild members earn less than $5000 per year.' Other supporters of an imminent strike include **Ben Affleck, Kevin Bacon, Marlon Brando, Richard Dreyfuss, Tim Robbins, Susan Sarandon** and **Tom Selleck ● Al Gore**, in a TV interview with **Oprah Winfrey**, warns that if the film industry doesn't tone down its violence he will impose legislation if he makes it to the White House (he doesn't) ● **Al Pacino**, 60, and his girlfriend, actress **Beverly D'Angelo**, 46, discover that they are to become parents of twins ● **Brad Renfro**, 18, star of *Apt Pupil* and *Ghost World*, is charged with grand theft following his attempt to steal a 45-foot yacht in Fort Lauderdale ● According to the *New York Post*, **Lara Flynn Boyle** has left **Jack Nicholson** for **Bruce Willis** ● The British Board of Film Classification unveils plans to relax laws governing sex and violence in adult films and videos. However, the censor intends to toughen up on sexual violence and scenes depicting drug-taking, particularly those that seem to 'instruct' ● Having broken up with actor **Hank Azaria**, her husband of 12 months, **Helen Hunt** falls for the charms of **Kevin Spacey** (according to the *National Enquirer*) ● **Justin Pierce**, the star of Larry Clark's controversial *Kids* (1995), is found hanged in his hotel room in Las Vegas. He leaves behind a wife, new baby and two suicide notes ● **Jamie Lee Curtis** reveals that she has been fighting a battle against alcoholism, ten years after overcoming her addiction to cocaine ● **Anna Nicole Smith** is awarded a record settlement of $449 million from her late husband's $1.6 billion estate. Smith, who previously paid her rent as a topless dancer, was married to the octogenarian billionaire J Howard Marshall for 14 months ● According to *The Mirror*, the marriage of **David Arquette** and **Courteney Cox Arquette** is already on the rocks – after only 15 months.

## OCTOBER 2000

Prior to her first night on the London stage in *The Seven Year Itch*, **Darryl Hannah** suffers stage fright and seeks help from celebrity hypnotist **Paul McKenna** ● *Gone in 60 Seconds* grosses $100 million in the US ● After being diagnosed with terminal cancer, Oscar nominee **Richard Farnsworth** (*Comes a Horseman, The Straight Story*) shoots himself dead. The actor was 80 ● **Roger Moore** pays his wife of 27 years, Luisa, £10 million as part of his divorce settlement ● **Jean Rochefort**, starring as Don Quixote in **Terry Gilliam**'s *The Man Who Killed Don Quixote*, suffers a double disc hernia. Filming of the $32 million Franco-British-Spanish-German co-production is suspended indefinitely. Incidentally, co-star **Johnny Depp** faced a similar ignominy when, in July 1995, *Divine Rapture* – in which he was appearing alongside Marlon Brando, Debra Winger and John Hurt – was scrapped mid-shoot due to financial collapse ● **George Clooney** falls for Britain's **Lisa Snowdon**, the sexy host of MTV Europe. Apparently, the couple met on the set of an Italian commercial ● According to the *Daily Express*, **Leonardo DiCaprio** is about to marry his girlfriend, Brazilian supermodel **Gisele Bündchen**, for whom he has bought a $125,000 platinum and diamond engagement ring ● **Liza Minnelli**, who is suffering from the potentially fatal disease viral encephalitis, collapses at her Florida home. Doctors suspect that the star, who is paralysed down one side of her body, has had a stroke ● **Kate Winslet** and her husband, assistant director Jim Threapleton, are the proud parents of an 8lb 9oz baby girl, Mia ● **Macaulay Culkin** makes his theatrical debut in London's West End, starring opposite **Irene Jacob** in the erotic drama *Madame Melville* ● In spite of the disastrous box-performance of *Battlefield Earth* – dubbed 'the worst film of the century' by certain critics – **John Travolta** announces plans to make a sequel ● **Lauren Hutton** suffers concussion, a fractured leg and sternum, a broken wrist, severe burns and abundant cuts and bruises after being thrown from her motorbike in a celebrity 'cavalcade.' The event, which was also attended by **Jeremy Irons** and **Dennis Hopper**, was mounted to celebrate the opening of the Hermitage-Guggenheim museum in Las Vegas next year ● **Julie Andrews** confirms that, following her 1997 operation to remove non-cancerous nodules from her throat, she will never sing in public again ● *Meet the Parents* grosses $100 million at the US box-office in under four weeks.

## NOVEMBER 2000

**Harrison Ford** and his scenarist wife **Melissa Mathison** (*E.T. The Extra Terrestrial*) confirm that they are now living apart ● *Remember the Titans* grosses $100 million in the US ● Production on the $100 million *Lara Croft: Tomb Raider* grinds to a halt when star **Angelina Jolie** tears the ligaments in her ankle during a routine special effects shot. Production is suspended for a week, the delay set to cost the studio $1 million ● **Michael Douglas** and **Catherine Zeta-Jones** are married in a £1.2 million New York ceremony attended by **Ellen Barkin**, **Russell Crowe**, **Danny DeVito**, **Kirk Douglas**, **Goldie Hawn**, **Anthony Hopkins**, **Meg Ryan**, **Steven Spielberg**, **Oliver Stone** and **James Woods** ● **Patricia Arquette** files for divorce from **Nicolas Cage**, her husband of five years. Earlier this year Cage filed for divorce himself, but then changed his mind ● *Charlie's Angels* grosses $100 million in the US ● **Robert Downey Jr** is arrested in Palm Springs, California, for possession of cocaine. It is the fourth time he has been arrested for the same crime ● *The Grinch* grosses $100 million in the US – in under *ten days* ● *Mission: Impossible 2* grosses one billion dollars worldwide ● **Geena Davis** announces her engagement to the neurosurgeon Dr Reza Jarrahy, who is 15 years her junior. The actress has previously been married three times, to the restaurateur Richard Emmolo, the actor **Jeff Goldblum** and the Finnish director **Renny Harlin**.

## DECEMBER 2000

**Calista Flockhart** spends six hours in hospital undergoing treatment for dehydration and exhaustion. The actress claims that the reason for her collapse was due to the arrest of her *Ally McBeal* co-star **Robert Downey Jr** ● According to the *Daily Mail*, **Hugh Grant** is now in love with Caroline Stanbury, former girlfriend of **Prince Andrew** ● To the shock of Hollywood, **Jim Carrey** and **Renée Zellweger** call it a day ● **Elizabeth Hurley** is fined £70,000 for filming a commercial during strike action staged by the Screen Actor's Guild. Nevertheless, the actress-producer-model has already made a public apology and donated £17,000 to the strike fund ● *The Grinch* grosses $200 million in the US – in 29 days ● **Madonna** and director **Guy Ritchie** tie the knot at a quiet wedding ceremony in Scotland. **Gwyneth Paltrow** is the maid-of-honour ● *What Women Want* grosses $100 million in the US ● **Kate Hudson** weds **Chris Robinson**, lead singer of The Black Crowes ● On New Year's Eve, **Calista Flockhart** meets her son for the first time after seeing him born to a mother of four.

## JANUARY 2001

**Tom Courtenay** is bestowed with a knighthood in the New Year's Honours ● *Cast Away* grosses $100 million in the US ● After dalliances with **Bruce Willis** and **Harrison**

**Right:** *Elizabeth Hurley: a year of fines, donations, attacks and a possible romance (with Matthew Perry)*

Ford, actress **Lara Flynn Boyle** returns to the arms of former boyfriend **Jack Nicholson** ● Actor-writer-director **Ed Burns** (*She's the One*, *Saving Private Ryan*), ex-boyfriend of **Lauren Holly** and **Heather Graham**, plans to marry supermodel **Christy Turlington** in New York later this year (preferably June) ● Word has it that **Matthew Perry** has fallen head over heels for **Elizabeth Hurley**, his romantic co-star in *Servicing Sarah*. But what does *she* think of *him*? One observer reveals that 'They're drawn to each other like magnets' ● **Dennis Quaid** and **Andie MacDowell** are now reportedly a couple ● At the 58th Golden Globe awards, **Hugh Grant** announces **Renée Zellweger** as best comedy actress for her performance in *Nurse Betty*. However, Grant is left to improvise on stage as Ms Zellweger returns from the loo to make her acceptance speech ● **Jennifer Lopez** and her rapper boyfriend, **Sean 'Puff Daddy' Combs**, call it a day – just as he's facing charges of gun possession and bribery ● *Cast Away* grosses $200 million in the US ● After just three weeks of release, *Crouching Tiger, Hidden Dragon* becomes the most successful foreign-language film ever released in Britain ● Two weeks into filming **David Fincher**'s thriller *The Panic Room*, **Nicole Kidman** is forced to withdraw because of a knee injury. She is replaced by **Jodie Foster** who, four years earlier, had withdrawn from Fincher's thriller *The Game*.

## FEBRUARY 2001

Due to the mounting pressures of work commitments, **Tom Cruise** and **Nicole Kidman** announce that they are engineering an amicable separation. The couple have been married for nine years and eleven months ● Two days after announcing his separation from **Nicole Kidman**, **Tom Cruise** reveals that he is now seeking a divorce ● Having crawled up the American charts to fourth position, the Mandarin-language *Crouching Tiger, Hidden Dragon* becomes the most successful foreign-language film ever released in the US ● *Miss Congeniality* rakes in $100 million in the US – making it the highest grossing film ever to feature **Michael Caine** ● It's quite a week for **Ridley Scott**. Following the death of his mother, his new film, *Hannibal*, breaks records at the US box-office (accruing $58 million in one weekend) and then *Gladiator* collects 12 Oscar nominations, including a nod for best director ● *Hannibal* grosses $100 million at the US box-office in just ten days ● **Dennis Quaid** and **Andie**

**MacDowell** holiday together in Sicily ● Coca-Cola signs an exclusive £95 million deal with Warner Bros to market their product through the *Harry Potter* franchise ● **Harrison Ford** is to be paid a record $25 million for his part in the Twentieth Century Fox feature *K19: The Widowmaker*. The same sum was paid to **Mel Gibson** to star in *The Patriot*, but Harrison will get his $25m for just 20 days' work ● Having broken up with Rebecca Broussard, the mother of his two children, and his girlfriend **Lara Flynn Boyle**, **Jack Nicholson** moves in with his good friend and next-door neighbour **Marlon Brando**. Hollywood insiders are now calling them 'The Odd Couple' ● **Matthew Perry** enters rehab for an

*Left: Nicole Kidman and Tom Cruise before the divorce*

'unidentified addiction.' Perry was previously treated for an addiction to the painkiller Vicodin.

# MARCH 2001

While out socialising, **Elizabeth Hurley** is attacked by a fellow partygoer for wearing a fur coat. The enraged animal lover throws a glass of wine over the actress and calls her 'a murdering bitch' ● The FBI uncover a plot to kidnap **Russell Crowe**. The suspects, believed to be linked to a gang of South American revolutionaries, are apparently planning to cut off one of Russell's digits every hour until they receive their ransom demand of $15 million. ● A tabloid favourite at the moment, **Russell Crowe** is now said to be romantically linked with **Nicole Kidman** ● **Alec Baldwin**, 43, who is currently directing and starring in *The Devil & Daniel Webster*, is getting over his break-up with **Kim Basinger** by romancing his female lead,

**Jennifer Love Hewitt**, 22 ● **Lauren Holly**, ex-wife of **Jim Carrey**, marries investment banker Francis Greco ● **Nicole Kidman** miscarries the child she was carrying by her estranged husband **Tom Cruise** ● Word slips out that **Laura Dern** is engaged to the R&B singer **Ben Harper**, although the latter is still in the process of divorcing his wife of four years, Joanna. Dern has previously been involved with **Kyle MacLachlan**, **Peter Horton**, **Renny Harlin**, **Jeff Goldblum** and **Billy Bob Thornton** ● *Vertical Limit* grosses $200 million worldwide ● **Tobey Maguire** and **Kirsten Dunst**, currently filming *Spider-Man* together, are now an item ● **Elisabeth Shue** and her husband, director Davis Guggenheim, are the proud

parents of a bouncing baby girl, Stella * *What Women Want* grosses $300 million worldwide ● **Jane Fonda** donates $15 million to Harvard University to set up the college's 'Centre on Gender and Education' ● The affair between **Dennis Quaid** and **Andie MacDowell** already seems to be on the wane. Quaid is now reported to be romancing 'a mystery blonde' ● **Mike Myers** is in negotiations with New Line Cinema for a $25 million payday on *Austin Powers 3* ● *Crouching Tiger, Hidden Dragon* becomes the first foreign-language film in history to gross over $100 million at the US box-office. The previous record holder for a subtitled film was **Roberto Benigni**'s *Life is Beautiful*, which grossed $57.6 million.

# APRIL 2001

**Kevin Costner** is entertained by **Fidel Castro** in Havana, where the star and producer of *Thirteen Days* shows the president his film about the Cuban Missile Crisis ● *Billy Elliot* grosses $100 million

worldwide ● **Jane Fonda** files for divorce from her husband of ten years, **Ted Turner**, founder of CNN. Ms Fonda calls her marriage 'irretrievably broken', noting that her erstwhile husband 'needs

someone to be there 100 per cent of the time. He thinks that's love. That's not love. It's babysitting' ● Having cut a swathe through the affections of **Jodie Foster**, **Meg Ryan** and **Nicole Kidman**, Oscar-winner **Russell Crowe** is now homing in on current co-star **Jennifer Connelly**. They are filming **Ron Howard**'s *A Beautiful Mind* together but, according to insiders, Ms Connelly has repeatedly rebuffed Mr Crowe's advances ● **Robert Downey Jr** is arrested – yes, again – for being under the influence of, er, cocaine ● **James Cameron** and his actress

wife **Suzy Amis** are the proud parents of a baby girl ● **Jack Nicholson** and **Lara Flynn Boyle** split again, this time officially ● Insiders reveal that **Nicolas Cage** and **Lisa Marie Presley** are now dating. Cage has been a long-time Elvis fan, but nobody suspected that he would end up dating the King's daughter ● **Arnold Schwarzenegger** reveals that, in

order to concentrate on family life and the filming of *Terminator 3*, he is giving up plans to run for the Governorship of California. Damning stories in *Premiere* and the *National Enquirer* brand Schwarzenegger a womaniser and adulterer, leaving the star little option but to abandon his political hopes in favour of domestic renovation.

## MAY 2001

**Tom Cruise** launches a $100 million lawsuit against Chad Slater (aka Kyle Bradford), a gay porn star who claims that he and Cruise have been having an affair ● Bonny Lee Bakley, the wife of **Robert Blake**, is shot dead in the actor's car in Studio City, California. Bakley's family suspects that Blake, a former child star, is the culprit ● *Spy Kids* grosses $100 million in the US ● Also in the US, *The Mummy Returns* grosses a phenomenal $68,139,035 in one weekend, a box-office record for a non-holiday opening. A few days later the film passes the $100 million mark ● **Lara Flynn Boyle** and TV actor **Eric Dane** (*Gideon's Crossing*) are spotted holding hands and smooching on New York's Upper East Side. The actress was previously

involved with **Jack Nicholson** and has also been linked with **Bruce Willis** and **Harrison Ford** ● **James Woods** replaces **Marlon Brando** in *Scary Movie 2* after the latter (who was to be paid $2 million for four days' work) bows out due to ill health. ● In the US, *Shrek* grosses over $100 million in under ten days ● **Robert Downey Jr** is questioned by police concerning the unsolved murder of Alissa Sologubova. Sologubova, a Russian model, was the girlfriend of a friend of Downey's ● Having painted his castle in Roaringwater Bay, west Cork, 'a Mediterranean peach,' **Jeremy Irons** is forced to defend his choice of hue in the *Irish Times*. As neighbours express shock at the new colour scheme, the actor argues in

print that 'The colour had to work with the green of the fields, the blues of the bay, the greys and blues of the sky, the furnace of the sunset' ● **Anne Heche** and boyfriend Coley Laffoon are spotted browsing the bridal shop at Saks Fifth Avenue in Beverly Hills. Obviously, tongues are wagging ● Following the critical drubbing given *Pearl Harbor* on both sides of the Atlantic, the marketing people at Buena Vista promote their film with the slogan, 'Not since *Titanic* have the critics been so out of touch with their readers.' As most reviewers loved *Titanic*, this seems odd ● **Lisa Snowdon** gives **George Clooney** the elbow, complaining that he was more interested in partying than chilling. Or so we are told.

## JUNE 2001

**Right:** *Julia Roberts and Benjamin Bratt before the break-up*

*Bridget Jones's Diary* grosses $100m worldwide ● **Pierce Brosnan** announces that he is to wed his fiancée Keely Shaye-Smith this August (the 4th) ● **Brad Pitt** and

**Jennifer Aniston** reveal that they are expecting their first baby ● *Shrek* grosses $200 million in the US, making it the top-grossing 2001 release to date ● Following an 18-month treatment programme, **Andy Dick** (*Best Men, Road Trip*) is let off three drug-related charges ● **Lauren Holly** and her new husband Francis Greco adopt a five-week old son, Alexander Joseph ● **Jennifer Grey** announces that she and her screenwriter boyfriend, **Clark Gregg** (*What Lies Beneath*), are expecting a little one (their first) in December ● **Sharon Stone**'s husband, newspaper editor Phil Bronstein, is attacked by a

vicious Komodo dragon on a trip to the Los Angeles zoo ● **Harry Hamlin** and his actress wife **Lisa Rinna** (TV's *Melrose Place*) are the proud parents of a baby girl ● **Eileen Atkins** is made a dame in the Queen's birthday honours; **Christopher Lee**, meanwhile, becomes a CBE ● *Lara Croft: Tomb Raider* grosses $100 million in the US ● **Peter Schneider**, chairman of Walt Disney, resigns in the wake of the box-office disappointment of *Pearl Harbor* ● Amid growing rumours of her 'deepening friendship' with **George Clooney**, **Julia Roberts** breaks off her three-year relationship with actor **Benjamin Bratt**.

# Movie Quotations

'The only true currency in this bankrupt world is what you share with someone else when you're uncool.' Philip Seymour Hoffman in *Almost Famous*

Catchphrase of the world-weary Mrs Packard: 'We're all gonna die.' Florence Stanley, on the soundtrack of *Atlantis: The Lost Empire*

Dolores, as she shows an old friend into her apartment: 'Sorry about the mess. My maid died 14 years ago.' Elaine Stritch (to Richard Gere) in *Autumn in New York*

Good-time girl Mo Docherty, to three chaps down at the salsa club: 'You're right, I slept with all three of yer – and yer were all *fan*-tastic. Except one.' Jane Horrocks in *Born Romantic*

Abby Janello, on the true nature of courage: 'It's not brave if you're not scared.' Gwyneth Paltrow in *Bounce*

'Maybe laurels is a good place to rest.' Nathan West, questioning the import of a famous adage, in *Bring It On*

Benji, waking up in a hospital bed surrounded by his friends: 'I'm *so* Demi Moore in *St Elmo's Fire* right now.' Zach Braff in *The Broken Hearts Club*

Renegade Hollywood director Cecil B Demented, who has banned his crew from having sex until the completion of their film: 'We're horny – but the film comes first.' Stephen Dorff in *Cecil B. Demented*

'We're both sticking to our guns. The difference is that mine are loaded.' Gary Oldman to American president Jeff Bridges in *The Contender*

George Sand, explaining her son's upset to her friend, the poet Alfred de Musset: 'He had a nightmare.' De Musset: 'Good – it will make him a writer.' Juliette Binoche and Benoît Magimel in *Les Enfants du Siècle*

Avant-garde director Desmond Forrest-Oates: 'I follow the popular arts. To me, they're so *dope*.' Martin Short in *Get Over It*

Desmond Forrest-Oates: 'Just because God blesses you, it doesn't mean that another sneeze isn't coming.' Martin Short in *Get Over It*

Pamela Fitzgerald to her husband: 'Stay in your own little world, Henry. This one just confuses you.' Mimi Rogers in *Ginger Snaps*

Tiny Guzman, reassuring his sister that he'll be OK if she takes over his boxing classes: 'I'm a geek. I'll do something constructive with my time.' Ray Santiago in *Girlfight*

Rob Gordon to Laura: 'Liking both Marvin Gaye and Art Garfunkel is like supporting both the Israelis and the Palestinians.' Laura: 'No, it's really not, Rob. You know why? Because Marvin Gaye and Art Garfunkel make pop records.' John Cusack and Iben Hjejle in *High Fidelity*

Laura to Rob: 'Listen, Rob, would you have sex with me? Because I want to feel something else than this. It's either that, or I go home and put my hand in the fire. Unless you want to stub cigarettes out on my arm.' Rob Gordon: 'No. I only have a few left, I've been saving them for later.' Laura: 'Right.

It'll have to be sex, then.' Iben Hjejle and John Cusack in *High Fidelity*

MC Stan Fields to beauty contestant Miss Rhode Island: 'Describe your perfect date.' Miss Rhode Island: 'That's a hard one. I'd have to say April the 5th.' William Shatner and Heather Burns in *Miss Congeniality*

Outraged mother to her son's teacher, Eugene Simonet: 'You are really something.' Simonet: 'Thanks. I appreciate the euphemism.' Helen Hunt and Kevin Spacey in *Pay It Forward*

Michael 'Bugsy' Moran to Irene: 'Hey! Do you know what'll look good on you? Me!' John Hawkes to Rusty Schwimmer in *The Perfect Storm*

'The brave do not live forever, but the cautious do not live at all.' Words written in a letter to Mia Thermopolis by her father, in *The Princess Diaries*

'Conversation, like certain portions of the anatomy, always runs more smoothly when lubricated.' Geoffrey Rush as the Marquis De Sade, in *Quills*

A seemingly butch Ray to girlfriend: 'I'd sure like to get in your pants.' Girlfriend: 'Yeah?' Ray: 'Yep, what size are they?' Shawn Wayans in *Scary Movie*

Ray, to his wife Frenchy: 'What would you say if I told you you were married to a brilliant man?' Frenchy: 'I'd say I was a bigamist.' Woody Allen and Tracey Ullman in *Small Time Crooks*

Philosophical underachiever Dex: 'Doing stuff is overrated.' Donal Logue in *The Tao of Steve*

# of the Year

'Why is a hurricane like a woman? Because when they arrive they're all hot and wild, when they leave they take your house and your car.' Luis Guzman in *Traffic*

'A woman needs security like a man needs approval.' Scott Wilson (to Juliette Lewis) in *The Way of the Gun*

Joe Sarno: 'So, you the brains of this outfit, or is he?' Longbaugh: 'Tell ya the truth, I don't think this is a brains kind of operation.' James Caan and Benicio Del Toro in *The Way of the Gun*

'We're not talking about how long you're goin' to live, Hon, but how slow you're goin' to die.' Benicio Del Torro to his hostage, Juliette Lewis, in *The Way of the Gun*

'What's the difference between a job and a wife? After ten years a job still sucks.' Mel Gibson in *What Women Want*

Nurse Claire, threatening her criminal OAP patient Henry Manning: 'I may not call the cops, but that doesn't mean I won't sign you up for bingo.' Linda Fiorentino to Paul Newman in *Where the Money Is*

## Quotes, off-screen
(that is, notable lines not scripted)

'Is it just me, or am I an egomaniac?' Actor **Craig Bierko** (*The Long Kiss Goodnight, Sour Grapes*)

'It's like having a kind of Alzheimer's disease where everyone knows you and you don't know anyone.' **Tony Curtis**, on celebrity

'I work out so I can keep my ass high enough so it looks good, because I'm married to Antonio Banderas.' **Melanie Griffith**, on her exercise motivation

'I've never been fashionable. It's like I'm in a Brit Pack on me own: you know, "Young, interesting, handsome actors over here... and, well, he's in loads of films, you can't exactly ignore the bugger".' **Ian Hart**, star of *The Hours and Times, Backbeat, Clockwork Mice, Land of Freedom, The Closer You Get* and *Liam*

'I always play women I would date.' **Angelina Jolie** on why she decided to play the title role in *Lara Croft: Tomb Raider*

'I'm 40, I'm single and I work in musical theatre. You do the math.' **Nathan Lane** talking of his sexual orientation

'There are good films in Britain, but exhibitors won't let them into their cinemas.' **Ken Loach**

'Jerry Bruckheimer's movie is a piece of war pornography, weighed down with a sickening amount of historical self-importance ... No intelligent person could like this film.' **Andrew O'Hagan**, saying what he *really* thinks about *Pearl Harbor* (in the *Daily Telegraph*)

'He's one of the greatest gifts to American culture. You can't imagine what it's like at 6.00 am in some dis-

tant location and out of the car comes that face and says, "Morning boys".' Sean Penn on Jack Nicholson

'I saw a woman wearing a sweatshirt with "Guess" on it. I said, "Thyroid problem?"' **Arnold Schwarzenegger**

'Religion is for those trying to stay out of Hell, and spirituality is for those who have been through it.' Charlie Sheen

'Women might be able to fake orgasms. But men can fake whole relationships.' Sharon Stone

'To get angry on a movie set is as silly as getting angry in traffic.' Director **Billy Bob Thornton** (*Sling Blade, All the Pretty Horses*), who prefers an amicable working atmosphere

'I didn't even know there were such awards. I have people around me whose job it is to not tell me about such things.' **John Travolta**, after winning the Golden Raspberry Award for Worst Actor of the Year

'I am impressed with the way you play, Dudley. I have pianist envy.' Robin Williams, saluting Dudley Moore at the latter's 66th birthday benefit

'I can't stand showbiz stuff. I always know when it's time to go home and wash my knickers.' Kate Winslet

'Regarding Geoffrey Rush's comment that he thinks of himself as a "cuddly James Woods", please advise him that that makes two of us, since I've always thought that I was the cuddly James Woods.' **Cuddly James Woods**

# Film Soundtracks

If you're a fan of rap and/or hip-hop, then it's been a fantastic year for film music. If, however, you like a good symphonic wallow, then there were slim pickings indeed. But rather than repeat my gripes from last year, let's focus on the positive: some of the outstanding scores of the last 12 months – *All the Pretty Horses, Nurse Betty, Requiem For a Dream, Twin Falls Idaho* and *Crouching Tiger, Hidden Dragon* – were all from little-known composers, promising rich scores ahead. Indeed, **Tan Dun**'s diverse, Oscar-winning work for *Crouching Tiger* heralded a new interest in Eastern music, winning global recognition for a country (China) that is leading the world in film composition.

Notwithstanding, Britain, too, had something to be proud of, with **Clint Mansell** – founding member of the rock/hip hop band Pop Will Eat Itself – crafting a hypnotic, distinctive score for Darren Aronofsky's hallucinogenic *Requiem For a Dream*.

Meanwhile, **Stephen Warbeck** was shifting the goal posts by writing his superlative music for *Captain Corelli's Mandolin* before a foot of film had been shot, thus providing the aural inspiration for John Madden's unfolding narrative. **Rachel Portman**, too, was on good form with her irresistible melodies for *Chocolat*, securing her a third Academy Award nomination (she was short-listed for last year's *The Cider House Rules*), following her 1997 Oscar for *Emma*. However, Hollywood's big boys – **John Williams** (*A.I. Artificial Intelligence*) and **James Horner** (*The Grinch, Enemy at the Gates*) – had little to sing about, leaving the field wide open for **Hans Zimmer**'s appropriately epic work on *Pearl Harbor*.

As for the rest of the soundtracks, these were mainly compilations of songs, some good, some indescribable, the best of which are chronicled here along with the instrumental stuff.

## SOUNDTRACKS OF THE YEAR

### All the Pretty Horses
A sublime welter of Tex-Mex melodies played out on Spanish guitar, accordion, mandolin and viola, this is a fine evocation of the Old West with a seductive Latino edge. As credited to the singer-poet **Marty Stuart**, conductor-viola player **Kristin Wilkinson** and songwriter-bassist **Larry Paxton**, the score is a collaborative effort unlikely to be repeated.

### Almost Famous
Retro rock never had it so good, this hand-picked selection of Simon & Garfunkel, The Who, Yes, The Beach Boys, Rod Stewart, Lynyrd Skynyrd, Cat Stevens and David Bowie embraces both the artists' celebrated and less well-known work. And, for trivia buffs, there's even Led Zeppelin, the first time the heavy rock band has ever appeared on a soundtrack album.

### Amores Perros
Hard-hitting, uplifting and throbbing collection of Latin tracks that drive home the vibrancy of Mexico City. And, to catch one's breath between the electronic dementia of Control Machete and the head-spinning mantra of Illya Kuryaki and the Valderramas, there's the meditative guitar work of **Gustavo Santaolalla**, the film's composer.

### Born Romantic
Dubbed the 'salsa soundtrack of the year', this is actually considerably more. While Fania All Stars, Tito Puente and Elvis Crespo all strut their stuff with toe-stomping finesse, there's also classic work from Nat King Cole ('Love'), Dean Martin ('Sway'), a melodious lament from Morcheeba and a priceless duet between Jane Horrocks (in Judy Garland mode) and Mr Martin.

Add a couple of distinctive tracks from **Simon Boswell**'s incidental score – plus some choice lines of dialogue – and you have an irresistible cocktail.

### Bridget Jones's Diary
This is a treasure trove of classic acts (19 in all), both old and new, with Pretenders' 'Don't Get Me Wrong' and Diana Ross and Marvin Gaye's 'Stop, Look, Listen' pitted against newer gems from Gabrielle, Robbie Williams, Sheryl Crow, Shelby Lynne, Alisha's Attic and Rosey. Pure magic.

### Captain Corelli's Mandolin
An alternately lovely and haunting work from **Stephen Warbeck**, this ranks as one of the most consistently satisfying orchestral scores of the year. And it's not all dainty mandolin-plucking, either: there's some rousing brass, solo guitar, a handful of poignant vocals and a full orchestral sweep.

*Above left to right:* Crouching Tiger, Hidden Dragon, O Brother, Where Art Thou?, Pearl Harbor *and* Requiem For a Dream

## Charlie's Angels

Bumper selection of golden oldies and new cuts, including such highlights as Tavares' 'Heaven Must Be Missing an Angel', Destiny's Child's Number One hit 'Independent Woman', plus Leo Sayer, Spandau Ballet, Marvin Gaye, Aerosmith, Heart, Fatboy Slim and much more. Groovy fun.

## Chocolat

A vivid and lively soundtrack that doesn't fall back on the facile simplicity of many of her other scores, this is **Rachel Portman**'s densest, most distinctive and rewarding work since **Emma**. Even so, many of the composer's melodic standbys (bits of **Chocolat** sound indistinguishable from **The Closer You Get**) do still slip through the net.

## The Claim

Few composers can write music that becomes an essential colour in a film's emotional palette, as well as being a satisfying work in its own right. **Michael Nyman** can. And once again he has created a seductive, hypnotic score that serves the film and audience in equal measure. Positively more-ish.

## Crouching Tiger, Hidden Dragon

A work of many tones, this Oscar-winning score from **Tan Dun** works its plaintive magic from the cello of Yo-Yo Ma to the fiddle of Ma Xiao Hui. Equally, however, there is some wonderfully urgent percussion from David Cossin and a host of other sounds that build up to a distinctive, haunting soundtrack that grows in stature the more you listen to it.

## Dinosaur

A sweeping, dramatic, uplifting, Afro-centric score from **James Newton Howard**, this hits all the appropriate notes for what is truly an awesome piece of innovative cinema. Terrific film music.

## Duets

Real-life actors show off their vocal chords in this compilation of karaoke cuts, with Gwyneth Paltrow performing 'Bette Davis Eyes', Paul Giamatti ripping the gloss off 'Hello It's Me' and Mario Bello emptying her heart out on 'I Can't Make You Love Me' and 'Sweet Dreams'. Emotional stuff.

## Get Over It

Bouncy, polished and eccentric collection of tracks that reach the parts that other compilations... Fatboy Slim, Basement Jaxx, Elvis Costello, American Hi-Fi and Badly Drawn Boy provide the musical muscle, while Kirsten Dunst delivers a gentle refrain that will either enchant you or make you sick.

## Josie and the Pussycats

The greatest hard rock-chick act of the year. Or, to put it another way, a hard-driving, infectious collection in which Kay Hanley, lead singer of Letters to Cleo, sings her little socks off as Josie.

## Keeping the Faith

A marvellously soppy album with a robust, old-fashioned score from **Elmer Bernstein** and some toe-warming numbers from the likes of Tom Waits, Travis Pickle and the Beatle-esque Peter Salett. Bliss.

## Malena

Few composers have written so many outstanding scores for so many naff films as **Ennio Morricone**. Here, again, is another prime example of Morricone's squandered talent, this lush, elegiac and gushing work scraping by with an Oscar nomination. Incidentally, can this really be Morricone's 391st score?

## The Man Who Cried

It was music that kindled the creative spark for Sally Potter's lyrical if uneven drama. So it's rewarding to report that the soundtrack is considerably better than the film. With the Italian tenor Salvatore Licitra providing some passionate pieces of opera and some emotionally rich and melancholy gypsy music from the Kronos Quartet and the Taraf de Haïdouks, this is an affecting and quite haunting album.

## The Mexican

A deliciously playful score from **Alan Silvestri**, an entertaining package of homage, drama and upbeat tempos with strumming guitar, soaring trumpet solos, inspirational choirs, banjo plucking, idle whistling and general monkeying around. Great melodic fun.

## Moulin Rouge

Overwhelming, poignant CD to the dazzling film, with Nicole

Kidman, Ewan McGregor and Jim Broadbent giving new life to old standards, while the likes of Beck, Bono and Bowie provide their own interpretations. Oh, and there's the Number One 1 hit 'Lady Marmalade' as sung by Christina Aguilera, Lil' Kim, Mya and Pink. One of the must-have soundtracks of the year.

## Nurse Betty

One of the year's more surprising discoveries, an ostensibly delicious score from **Rolfe Kent** that's peppered with menace at the most unexpected moments. A perfect aural companion to a splendid film (in that it mirrors the dramatic tone), the album also includes Pink Martini's creepy rendition of 'Whatever Will Be, Will Be (Que Séra, Séra)', plus wholesomely upbeat tracks from Eddy Arnold and Della Reese.

## 101 Reykjavik

A typically idiosyncratic score from **Damon Albarn**, this time in collaboration with The Sugarcubes' **Einar Örn Benediktsson**. With much keyboard doodling, mouth organ, church organ and accordion, the pair rustle up a perfect aural backdrop to one of the year's most distinctive, original black comedies.

## O Brother, Where Art Thou?

The little soundtrack that could, this is an authentic collection of rustic Americana, a no-frills celebration of blues, gospel and hillbilly. And, in spite of such naked musical simplicity, the CD was a huge hit in the mainstream charts, shifting almost two million units – and spawning a sequel.

## Pearl Harbor

If you're going to have a cheesy, melodramatic epic, then you might as well have its emotive,

soaring score composed by **Hans Zimmer**. Utilising a full orchestra and an injection of Julia Migenes' soprano vocal chords, this could almost persuade you that *Pearl Harbor* was a better film. Almost.

## Play It To the Bone

Gritty, jazzy, muscular collection that towers over the movie it supports: an inspired version of 'Gonna Be a Lovely Day' from Kirk Franklin, a bluesy duet between B B King and Joe Cocker, a deliciously seductive anthem from Los Lobos, a rousing hymn from Gipsyland, some tingling gospel from Linda Jackson, John Lee Hooker's jamming 'Boom Boom', a soul-searching torch song from Jacintha ('There's no "yes" in yesterday...'), and more.

## Purely Belter

A lively combination of **Ian Broudie**'s throbbing, upbeat score punctuated by electric tracks from The Animalhouse, Bleachin' and Shed Seven, plus more conservative fare courtesy of Elvis Presley, John Lennon and Gabrielle. All rather rousing.

## Requiem For a Dream

Aided by the Kronos Quartet, Britain's **Clint Mansell** provides a Michael Nyman-esque electronic score of eerie dementia, with echoes of *Halloween* interspersed with cello-induced hysteria. Hypnotic and compelling.

## Snatch

A perfect aural companion to Guy Ritchie's funny and stylish film, mixing spicy dialogue with instrumentals and ear-catching tracks from Overseer, The Herbaliser and the Johnston Brothers. And there's some great back-catalogue stuff here, too, including The Specials, The Stranglers and even Mrs Ritchie herself.

## Twin Falls Idaho

Appropriately weird, haunting and moody companion piece to the Polish Brothers' surreal and haunting contemplation on alienation and intimacy. Besides the contemplative, occasionally Morricone-esque instrumentals from **Stuart Matthewman**, there are choice vocals, too, from Fong Naan (disturbing), Lisa Ekdahl (heart-massaging) and Marc Anthony Thompson (smoky).

## Very Annie Mary

A glorious mix of operatic arias and Welsh ballads, this is soul-stirring stuff with top talent, including Russell Watson, José Carreras, Renee Fleming, Cerys Matthews, plus a magical duet from Anne Sofie Von Otter and Elvis Costello. **Stephen Warbeck** supplies the lyrical incidental score.

## Where the Heart Is

The chick flick album of the year, every bit as sweet to the ears and soul as last year's *Anywhere But Here*. Class acts include Beth Nielsen Chapman, Martina McBride, The Corrs, Lyle Lovett and Lonestar.

## Top 20 Film Soundtracks in the UK

*courtesy of CIN*
(compilations excluded)

1) *Gladiator*; 2) *Captain Corelli's Mandolin*; 3) *Crouching Tiger, Hidden Dragon*; 4) *Hannibal*; 5) *More Music from Gladiator*; 6) *Pearl Harbor*; 7) *Brassed Off*; 8) *Titanic*; 9) *Braveheart*; 10) *The Piano*; 11) *Chocolat*; 12) *Star Wars Episode 1: The Phantom Menace*; 13) *Back to Titanic*; 14) *X-Men*; 15) *The Perfect Storm*; 16) *Schindler's List*; 17) *More Music from Braveheart*; 18) *Star Wars Episode IV: A New Hope*; 19) *Star Wars Episode V: The Empire Strikes Back*; 20) *Requiem for a Dream*.

# Bookshelf

## A round-up of the year's best film books

● **Alien: A Complete Illustrated Screenplay**, by Paul M Sammon; Orion; £17.99.

● **The Apocalypse Now Book**, by Peter Cowie; Faber and Faber; £14.99. Informed, incredibly detailed study of Coppola's masterpiece.

● **The Art of The Matrix**; Titan Books; £49.99. Consummate gift companion to the movie, complete with amazing visuals, sketches, cartoons, shooting script and infinite trivia.

● **BFI Film and Television Handbook 2001**; £20.00. For such an established reference, covering box-office data, analysis of TV trends, film courses, various film and TV facilities, PR companies, video labels and websites, this stalwart manual is surprisingly out of date. For instance, Jonathan Ross, not Simon Rose, is film critic for the *Mirror* (and has been since January 1999). However, like all fact-crammed books, there are plenty of gems to be found: ie, the most productive year in the history of British film was 1936, when no less than 192 films were made – 92 more than in 1999.

● **The Big Picture**, by William Goldman; Applause; £16.99. Collection of opinionated essays written for *New York Magazine* in which the author of *Adventures in the Screen Trade* shares more outrageous secrets about Tinseltown.

● **Blade Runner: The Inside Story**, by Don Shay; Titan; £16.99.

● **Brazil**, by Terry Gilliam, Charles Alverson and Bob McCabe; Prion; £12.99. Detailed document of Gilliam's troubled masterpiece, complete with the original script and the director's sketches.

● **A British Picture**, by Ken Russell; Mandarin; £4.99. Reissue of the *enfant terrible*'s diverting 1989 autobiography (compare *Directing Film*, qv).

● **Buster Keaton Remembered**, by Eleanor Keaton and Jeffrey Vance; Abrams; £28. Glowing biography of the silent giant written by his late wife in collaboration with film historian Vance. And, besides the biographical anecdotage (particularly revealing about Keaton's later life), there are 225 handsomely reproduced (and rare) stills.

● **Cassell's Movie Quotations**, by Nigel Rees; Cassell; £20.00. Rees' 432-page 'labour of love' is described as 'the first major dictionary of movie quotes,' a plug that is an insult to *Halliwell's Filmgoer's Book of Quotes* and Harry Haun's even more comprehensive *The Movie Quote Book*. Printed on high-gloss paper and punctuated with a handful of large stills and lots of white space, Cassell's companion at least has the advantage of quotes uttered off-screen as well as on, including Marlon Brando's observation that Montgomery Clift 'acts like he's got a Mixmaster up his ass.' This, of course, makes the book a useful reference, although why it includes dialogue from the Robin Williams turkey *The Cadillac Man* and the lame Leslie Phillips comedy *Doctor in Clover* ('You sexy beast!') is a mystery. Incomplete, to say the least, but not without its pleasures.

● **Christopher Lee: The Authorised Screen History**, by Jonathan Rigby; Reynolds & Hearn; £15.95. Invaluable chronicle of the film and TV career of the Crown Prince of Terror.

● **The Coen Brothers: The Life of the Mind**, by James Mottram; Batsford;

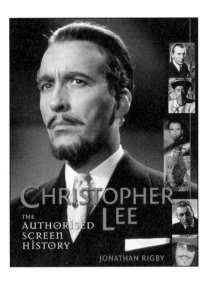

£15.99. Mottram gives us the detailed lowdown, focusing on the Coens' work, inspirations and collaborators; and while some may find the book deeply pretentious, it definitely has its insights.

● **The Complete Frankie Howerd**, by Robert Ross; Reynolds & Hearn; £15.95. Definitive, exhaustive and affectionate chronicle of the great comic's career.

● **The Complete Spielberg**, by Ian Freer; Virgin; £15.99. Exhaustive, enticing examination of the world's greatest filmmaker, stretching from the maestro's early amateur doodlings and the TV years right up to *Minority Report*. Accessible and readable, the book arranges Spielberg's career into bite-sized vignettes, supplying credits, cast lists, plot breakdowns, back story, box-office performance, classic lines, cut scenes, in-jokes, critical analysis, awards and tons of trivia. Irresistible.

● **The Complete Lynch**, by David Hughes; Virgin; £15.99. Like the above, this is an astonishing capsule of the career of a consummate filmmaker. The trivia is mind-boggling: did you know that the house occupied by Bill Pullman and Patricia Arquette in *Lost Highway* actually belonged to Lynch? 'The house got destroyed, so the *Lost Highway* house doesn't really exist any more,' the director notes, without apparent regret. There's also a ton of stuff about films that didn't even see the light of day. Indispensable.

● **Contemporary North American Directors**, edited by Yoram Allon, Del Cullen and Hannah Patterson; Wallflower; £17.99. A guide to over 500 US filmmakers, this book's embrace is commendable. However, it is let down by rather lifeless, prosaic writing (much of it the work of lecturers, professors and postgraduate students) and devotes more attention to the films themselves than their 'authors'. Still, any tome that has something serious to say about Bob Clark, Dennis Dugan and Burt Reynolds is worth a look, if only for novelty's sake.

● **Crouching Tiger, Hidden Dragon**, Faber and Faber; £14.99. Handsome, enlightening companion to the film with screenplay, stills, trivia and a study of Wuxia Pian.

● **Cybill Disobedience: My Autobiography**, by Cybill Shepherd; Ebury Press; £14.99. Enjoyable, bitchy inside look at fame and hormones.

● **Directing Film**, by Ken Russell; Batsford; £15.99. Engaging autobiography (his third) of the erstwhile *enfant terrible* of British cinema. See *A British Picture* (qv).

● **Directors A-Z: A Concise Guide to the Art of 250 Great Film-Makers**, by Geoff Andrew; Prion; £15. Adopting the format of the popular *Art Book* published by Phaidon, this distil-

lation of the essence of global cinema explores the style and *modus operandi* of 250 'great' filmmakers by taking one representative film and analysing it. Part of the fun is seeing which work Geoff Andrews chooses to exemplify his subject and to marvel at the juxtaposition of stills, such as an enigmatic shot from Ingmar Bergman's *Persona* positioned opposite a vulgar wedding cake of dancers from Busby Berkeley's *Footlight Parade*. The volume, much like *The Art Book*, is to be commended for its range (Souleymane Cissé, Max Fleischer, D A Pennebaker, Walter Salles, Todd Solondz, John Waters), eschewing the popular for the visually innovative. Thus, there's no Ron Howard, Michael Bay, Tony Scott or Coline Serreau, but celluloid artists who really do count in the wider canvas of artistic cinema. A choice companion piece, then, to David Quinlan's more conventional and considerably more comprehensive *Film Directors*.

● **Film Facts**, by Patrick Robertson; Aurum; £14.99. Which British film received the most Oscars? How many cinemas are there in Afghanistan? Which country produced the last silent film? While most film buffs may easily identify *Gandhi* as the most Oscar-laden British feature, they may be surprised to learn that Afghanistan has no cinemas at all (all picture houses being closed by the Taliban in 1996), and that Thailand, due to financial constraints, was producing films without sound up until 1965. Patrick Robertson's treasure trove, previously published under the title *The Guinness Book of Film Facts & Feats*, is a cinéaste's dream, a compendium of data that puts to rest all those after-dinner arguments. Yet it's the little incidental asides that make it such a good browse, while the exhaustive tabulations of data (bloopers, box-office stars, US presidents played on screen,

etc, etc) make it an essential companion to the *Radio Times Guide* (qv) and *Quinlan's Film Stars* (qv). Unfortunately, the book is riddled with typos (including one on the back cover), but this is a small price to pay for such riches.

● **The FilmFour Book of Film Quotes**; FilmFour Books; £4.99. Thin, over-produced bog reading.

● **Film Posters of the 50s: The Essential Movies of the Decade**, by Tony Nourmand and Graham Marsh; Aurum Press; £14.95.

● **Gary Cooper – American Hero**, by Jeffrey Meyers; Hale; £25. Exhaustive, well-balanced and absorbing biography of the Quiet American.

● **The Gorehound's Guide to Splatter Films of the 1960s and 1970s**, by Scott Aaron Stine; McFarland & Co; £28.45. The title says it all, although the breadth of the subject is well covered. Definitely a fan's manual.

● **Halliwell's Film & Video Guide 2001**, edited by John Walker; HarperCollins; £19.99. The 16th edition of the granddaddy of film guides can't compete with such new impostors as *Radio Times* (qv) or *VideoHounds* (qv), but it still has its uses. This update includes publicity taglines, critics' quotes, soundtrack availability, notable songs, 'points of interest', Oscar nominations, and even some memorable movie quotes. Its breadth is remarkable, yet it somehow remains frustratingly patchy.

● **The Hannibal Files**, by Daniel O'Brien; Reynolds & Hearn; £14.95. Well-written, thoroughly researched look at the phenomenon of Hannibal Lecter, the charismatic villain of *Manhunter*, *The Silence of the Lambs* and *Hannibal*.

● **Hollywood Portraits: Classic Shots and How To Take Them**, by Roger Hicks and Christopher Nisperos; Collins & Brown; £17.99.

● **In or Out: Stars on Sexuality**, Boze Hadleigh; Fusion Press; £9.99. Moreish collection of celebrity quotes on the raw stuff.

● **In Search of The Third Man**, by Charles Drazin; Methuen; £9.99. Consummate chronicle of the Carol Reed classic.

● **John Cassavetes: Lifeworks**, by Tom Charity; Omnibus Press; £10.95. Intelligent, incisive portrait of the filmmaker.

● **Kubrick**, by Michael Herr; Picador; £10.00. Discriminating and perceptive (if rather thin) evaluation of the late, great Stanley.

● **Lara Croft: Tomb Raider**, by Alan Jones; Carlton; £9.99. Lively and level-headed companion to the terrible movie.

● **The Million Dollar Mermaid**, by Esther Williams and Digby Diehl; Pocket Books; £7.99. Candid, affectionate inside take on Hollywood by the stellar swimmer.

● **My Time With Antonioni**, by Wim Wenders; Faber and Faber; £14.99. Enlightening look at the troubled making of Wenders' and Antonioni's *Beyond the Clouds*.

● **On Set**, by Greg Williams; £23. Eye-opening collection of photographs chronicling the informal battlefield of the movie set.

● **On Sunset Boulevard: The Life and Times of Billy Wilder**, by Ed Sikhov; Hyperion Press; £12.99.

● **On Writing**, by Stephen King; Hodder & Stoughton; £16.99. Colourful autobiography and writer's instruction manual from the master of suspense.

● **Oscar Fever: The History and Politics of the Academy Awards**, by Emmanuel Levy; Continuum; £19.99.

● **Pearl Harbor: The Movie and the Moment**, Boxtree; £14.99. So, if you loved the movie...

● **A Positively Final Appearance**, by Alec Guinness; Penguin; £7.99. Pungent ragbag of anecdotes, marking the gentle knight's third volume of autobiography.

● **Print the Legend: The Life and Times of John Ford**, by Scott Eyman; Simon & Schuster; £25.00. Definitive biography of one of the all-time greats.

● **Projections 11: New York Film-Makers On New York Film-Making**, edited by Tod Lippy; Faber and Faber; £14.99. Collection of illuminating interviews with New York-based personnel, including Lumet, Spike Lee, David O Russell, Tim Robbins etc.

● **Quinlan's Film Stars**, by David Quinlan; Batsford; £25.00. This is the fifth edition of the best book on the market devoted solely to film stars. Covering over 2000 names with as many pictures, the volume boasts the most comprehensive filmographies that you will find anywhere (including uncredited appearances and cameos), along with useful thumbnail sketches (incorporating Oscar nominations, marriages, hair colour) on each entry. This time, Quinlan's reach runs the gamut from such silent stars as Betty Balfour and Mae Marsh right up to Wes Bentley, Elodie Bouchez, Rachael Leigh Cook, Craig Ferguson and Douglas Henshall. A handsome and essential component of any film buff's library.

● **Radio Times Guide to Films**, edited by Kilmeny Fane-Saunders; BBC Worldwide Limited; £19.99. With the market flooded by outstanding film guides (*Maltin's, VideoHound, Time Out*), I never thought I would come across a compendium that would top the lot. But this really is the most comprehensive, all-inclusive companion you could hope to own. Not only does it feature over 20,000 films, it is merciless in its coverage, including a healthy dose of TV movies and foreign language titles alongside direct-to-video and mainstream fare. It also includes character names and breakdowns of adult content (swearing, violence, nudity). This alone would merit the book a place on the top of my TV set. But there's more. Just as the last review (*Zulu Dawn*) concludes on page 1625, 273 more pages unfold to reveal exhaustive filmographies of every director featured in the book, followed by a whopping index of every actor as well. Inevitably with a tome this size there are some intriguing anomalies. *Loser Takes All* and *Strike It Rich* are provided with separate entries, although they are the same film. Astonishing value.

• **Scriptwriting for the Screen**, by Charlie Moritz; Routledge; £8.99. Everything you always wanted to know about transforming words into celluloid.

• **Sean Connery**, by Bob McCabe; Pavilion; £19.99. Reverential, well-researched biography of the actor, icon and man.

• **See No Evil: Banned Films and Video Controversy**, by David Kerekes and David Slater; Head Press; £15.95.

• **SF: UK**, by Daniel O'Brien; Reynolds & Hearn; £12.95. Attractively packaged, illuminating and empathic look at British sci-fi in all its many forms, including the written word, on stage, on radio, in films, comics and even albums.

• **Shakespeare On Screen**, by Daniel Rosenthal; Hamlyn; £20. A glossy, lavishly illustrated coffee-table book that devotes chapters to the Bard's most oft-filmed plays (as well as movies *about* Shakespeare and TV adaptations), this really merits an A for effort. As Our Ken has taught us, Shakespeare need not be the inaccessible terrain of Oxonian nerdmeisters alone.

• **Sharp**, Nigel Parry; PowerHouse Books; £35. Superlative collection of black-and-white stills of the Hollywood elite and other celebrities, beautifully presented, complete with quotes.

• **Smoking in Bed: Conversations with Bruce Robinson**, edited by Alistair Owen; Bloomsbury; £12.99. Stimulating insight into the pear-shaped world of the director-writer-actor.

• **So You Want To Be in Pictures?**, by Val Guest; Reynolds & Hearn; £14.95. Informal, chatty autobiography from the director of *The Day the*

*Earth Caught Fire* and *Confessions of a Window Cleaner*.

• **Steven Spielberg Interviews**, edited by Lester D. Friedman and Brent Notbohm; University Press of Mississippi; £16.99.

• **This is Spinal Tap: The Official Companion**, by Karl French; Bloomsbury; £16.99.

• **The Ultimate DVD Guide**; Titan Books; £8.99. Compilation of DVD reviews plucked from *DVD Review* magazine, but by no means an 'ultimate' guide.

• **The Ultimate Film Festival Survival Guide**, by Chris Gore; Gazelle; £17.50. Perceptive compendium to the growing world of the film festival. A must for aspiring filmmakers.

• **VideoHound's DVD Guide**, edited by Mike Mayo and Jim Olenski; Visible Ink; £17.99. With 3000 films covered and exhaustive attendant lists of actors, directors, DPs, composers, themes, etc, this really is the ultimate DVD directory. And unlike other guides, this really does give the lowdown on each disc (picture and sound quality, extra features, interviews, biographies, trailers, etc), not just the film. There's even tons of additional DVD credits, such as stereo details, catalogue number, contents of extras and the like. Awesome.

• **VideoHound's Golden Movie Retriever 2001**, edited by Jim Craddock; Visible Ink; £19.99. While Leonard Maltin's annual and the *Radio Times* guide grab the lion's share of publicity, the VideoHound collection seems to remain a tightly guarded secret. At 1812 pages, this tenth imprint not only covers 24,000 films, videos and made-for-TV movies, but includes exhaustive

indexes. Thus, you will find filmographies of the great (Audrey Hepburn, Katharine Hepburn) and the not-so-great (Shannon Tweed, Terry Tweed), be they actors, directors, scenarists, cinematographers or composers. The fun part is the tome's irreverent but passionate style and the comprehensive lists of films divided into thematic categories running the gamut from 'I Love Detroit' (*Bird On a Wire*, *RoboCop*) to 'Wedding Hell' (*The Blood Spattered Bride*, *The Newlydeads*), as well as the usual tables of top-grossing films, Oscars, Sundance winners and screen adaptations of Barbara Cartland and Leo Tolstoy. It's fun, it's helpful and it's essential reference.

• **The Virgin Book of Film Records**, by Phil Swern and Toby Rowan; Virgin; £12.99. This is what's known as a browser or a loo book; something to dip into when you've got nothing better to do.

• **What They Don't Teach You at Film School**, by Camille Landau and Tiare White; Hyperion/Turnaround; £10.99. Invaluable collection of tips for the aspiring director.

• **Who's Who On Television**, Boxtree; £12.99. The latest *TV Times* guide to the faces of the small screen now includes American stars but has ditched the photographs. Inconsistent, patchy and uninspiring.

• **The Worldwide Guide to Movie Locations**, by Tony Reeves; Titan Books; £16.99. Exhaustive, to say the least.

• **The Zombie Movie Encyclopedia**, by Peter Dendle; Shelwing/McFarland; £33.25. A thorough, twinkle-eyed examination of those movies that celebrate the walking dead – albeit just 200 from 16 countries.

# Internet

by Josephine Botting

**Above:** *Hugh Grant ponders spending an evening in with the Bridget Jones website*

With Hollywood studios continuing to view the Internet as a key marketing tool for their product, most official movie sites are becoming more sophisticated and offering more than just cast, crew and production information. Along with the usual trailers, stills galleries and reviews, there's a move towards more complex design and greater interactivity, with games and competitions featured on many of them.

The *Bridget Jones's Diary* website, at www.miramax.com/bridgetjonesdiary, visually captures the lifestyle of the 30-something single woman and contains a personality quiz where visitors can find out which of her two beaux is most suitable for them. Similarly, the *Charlie's Angels* site (www.spe.sony.com/movies/charliesangels) allows you to test your compatibility with the three lovely crimefighters, although you may be put off a liaison with any of them after you've read Bosley's secret files, which reveal some of their less appealing personal habits. At www.crouchingtiger.com, the site for *Crouching Tiger, Hidden Dragon*, whooshing sword sound effects usher in the different characters and, for the creative, there's an opportunity to edit your own trailer for the film.

For the information addict, useless facts to impress your friends with are still available in abundance. At www.grinched.com, the website for *The Grinch*, one

such titbit is that two million linear feet of styrofoam was used to build the film's sets. www.captain-corellis-mandolin.com has a more serious educational angle, with articles on the role that Greece played in World War II and the history of war and romance in the movies. All worthwhile reading if you can bear to listen to the tinny music playing on a loop in the background.

British sites may not be quite as elaborate or eye-catching as the big-budget Hollywood ones but what they lack in spectacle they often make up for in humour. At www.virgin.net/purelybelter visitors are greeted with a 'ha'way' (according to the site's Geordie glossary, 'a purposeless but obligatory word used at the start of every sentence') and have the chance to win £1000, collecting points by clicking on pop-up images. At the www.essexboysthemovie.com site, visitors are taught the Essex Boy golden rules – never mess with your best mate's girlfriend; reserve your charm for the ladies – and can play a game in which they have to guide Gary through a night out in Southend without getting into trouble.

The rest of the world has produced some stylish promotional sites this year too. www.wkw-inthemood-forlove.com is navigated via a rolling montage depicting the claustrophobic flats in which the protagonists' chaste romance begins. Each room gives access to a different page: in the kitchen are menus for Maggie's meals and

the Mahjong room appropriately houses the chatroom. The beautifully animated official site for Mexican drama *Amores perros* at multimedia.elfoco.com/elfoco/amores-perros has excellent music and effects, while Australia also competes well with *The Dish* site at www.thedish-movie.warnerbros.com, entered via an animated page of a field full of televisions broadcasting images of the moon landing surrounded by sheep. The site for French film *Crimson Rivers* (www.rivieres-pourpres.com) contains information on the film accompanied by spooky, atmospheric images and sounds. Unfortunately, but not surprisingly, it's entirely in French…

As well as being a promotional device for the studios, the Internet has also become a threat to them. Surfers can pick up trailers and even whole movies before their official release, along with confidential production material such as scripts and contracts, and security experts reckon that somewhere in the region of 400,000 bootlegged films are exchanged on the Internet every day. In response to this, studios are employing hackers to identify the holes in their security, although these measures cannot prevent attacks from the inside. To render the black market redundant, five of the major studios are looking into an Internet video on-demand service, charging around $5 per film. While the broadband Internet access needed to view an entire feature is not yet widespread enough to make the service profitable, the technology will eventually catch up.

The short film is a more manageable cinematic form for the Internet and the web is the perfect platform for bite-sized mini-movies. Here the art of the short film – the ability to get a point across in a just few minutes – has become an even tighter discipline and many of the films last two minutes or less. Animated and live action shorts by both amateurs and professionals are available at sites like www.atomfilms.com, www.trailervision.com and www.hypnotic.com, where viewers can submit reviews and ratings for the films.

Trailervision shows trailers for 'movies that don't exist', mainly comic twists on current blockbusters such as *American Booty* and *Sexmen*. Their shorts have been shown on Channel 5 in the UK and are also being compiled into an hour-long programme for theatrical release in North America. But the creators of this Canadian site have gone a step further. They have taken their mission to challenge Hollywood dominance and phoniness beyond the relative obscurity of the net, managing to get fake stars into premieres at the Toronto Film Festival by hiring limos for them and planting paparazzi to shout out their names as they step out.

ifilm.com features online shorts in its 'streaming cinema' section while hypnotic.com exhibits the winners of the Coca-Cola Refreshing Filmmaker's Award, an excellent selection of 60-second movies by up-and-coming directors. The creators of www.thrillpill.com are more interested in 'developing digital subcultures', an aim demonstrated by the site's content of mainly experimental animated snippets, some interactive, rather than the narrative short.

While many of these films exhibit a high level of originality and creativity, here as well there is room for improvement in the technology available for showing them. Video streaming currently delivers matchbox-sized, pixelated images which are jerky due to their reliance on download speeds. Downloading the films first and then playing them provides more satisfactory viewing; software such as flash allows the picture to be any size by treating images in vector format rather than as pixels. The Internet in its current state is most suited to the delivery of animation. At the moment, the downloading of video images leaves a lot to be desired but it's only a matter of time until the technology develops sufficiently to allow frustration-free movie viewing.

*Left, top to bottom:* The Dish, Charlie's Angels, Crouching Tiger, Hidden Dragon *and* The Grinch

# Awards and Festivals

The 73rd American Academy of Motion Picture Arts and Sciences Awards ('The Oscars') and Nominations for 2000, Los Angeles, 25 March 2001

● **Best Film:** *Gladiator*. Nominations: *Chocolat*; *Crouching Tiger, Hidden Dragon*; *Erin Brockovich*; *Traffic*.
● **Best Director:** Steven Soderbergh, for *Traffic*. Nominations: Stephen Daldry, for *Billy Elliot*; Ang Lee, for *Crouching Tiger, Hidden Dragon*; Ridley Scott, for *Gladiator*; Steven Soderbergh, for *Erin Brockovich*.
● **Best Actor:** Russell Crowe, for *Gladiator*. Nominations: Javier Bardem, for *Before Night Falls*; Tom Hanks, for *Cast Away*; Ed Harris, for *Pollock*; Geoffrey Rush, for *Quills*.

● **Best Actress:** Julia Roberts, for *Erin Brockovich*. Nominations: Joan Allen, for *The Contender*; Juliette Binoche, for *Chocolat*; Ellen Burstyn, for *Requiem For a Dream*; Laura Linney, for *You Can Count On Me*.
● **Best Supporting Actor:** Benicio Del Toro, for *Traffic*. Jeff Bridges, for *The Contender*; Willem Dafoe, for *Shadow of the Vampire*; Albert Finney, for *Erin Brockovich*; Joaquin Phoenix, for *Gladiator*.
● **Best Supporting Actress:** Marcia Gay Harden, for *Pollock*. Nominations: Judi Dench, for *Chocolat*; Kate Hudson, for *Almost Famous*; Frances McDormand, for *Almost Famous*; Julie Walters, for *Billy Elliot*.
● **Best Original Screenplay:** Cameron Crowe, for *Almost Famous*. Nominations: Lee Hall, for *Billy Elliot*; Susannah Grant, for *Erin Brockovich*; David Franzoni, John Logan and William Nicholson, for *Gladiator*; Kenneth Lonergan, for *You Can Count On Me*.
● **Best Screenplay Adaptation:** Stephen Gaghan, for *Traffic*. Nominations: Robert Nelson Jacobs, for *Chocolat*; Wang Hui Ling, James Schamus and Tsai Kuo Jung, for *Crouching Tiger, Hidden Dragon*; Ethan Coen and Joel Coen, for *O Brother, Where Art Thou?*; Steven Kloves, for *Wonder Boys*.
● **Best Cinematography:** Peter Pau, for *Crouching Tiger, Hidden Dragon*. Nominations: Roger Deakins, for *O Brother, Where Art Thou?*; Caleb Deschanel, for *The Patriot*; Lajos Koltai, for *Malèna*; John Mathieson, for *Gladiator*.
● **Best Editing:** Stephen Mirrione, for *Traffic*. Nominations: Joe Hutshing and Saar Klein, for *Almost Famous*; Tim Squyeres, for *Crouching Tiger, Hidden Dragon*; Pietro Scalia, for *Gladiator*; Dede Allen, for *Wonder Boys*.
● **Best Original Score:** Tan Dun, for *Crouching Tiger, Hidden Dragon*. Nominations: Ennio Morricone, for *Malèna*; Rachel Portman, for *Chocolat*; John Williams, for *The Patriot*; Hans Zimmer, for *Gladiator*.
● **Best Original Song:** 'Things Have Changed' by Bob Dylan, from *Wonder Boys*. Nominations: 'A Love before Time,' music by Jorge Calandrelli and Tan Dun, lyrics by James Schamus, from *Crouching Tiger, Hidden Dragon*; 'I've Seen It All', music by Björk, lyrics by Lars von Trier and Sjon Sigurdsson, from *Dancer in the Dark*; 'My Funny Friend and Me,' music by Sting and David Hartley, lyrics by Sting, from *The Emperor's New Groove*; 'A Fool in Love' by Randy Newman, from *Meet the Parents*
● **Best Art Direction:** Tim Yip, for *Crouching Tiger, Hidden Dragon*. Nominations: Martin Childs (art direction) and Jill Quertier (set decoration),

for *Quills*; Michael Corenblith (art) and Merideth Boswell (set), for *The Grinch*; Arthur Max (art) and Crispian Sallis (set), for *Gladiator*; Jean Rabasse (art) and Françoise Benoit-Fresco (set), for *Vatel*.
● **Best Costume Design:** Janty Yates, for *Gladiator*. Nominations: Anthony Powell, for *102 Dalmatians*; Rita Ryack, for *The Grinch*; Jacqueline West, for *Quills*; Tim Yip, for *Crouching Tiger, Hidden Dragon*.
● **Best Sound:** Scott Millan, Bob Beemer and Ken Weston, for *Gladiator*. Nominations: Steve Maslow, Gregg Landaker, Rick Kline and Ivan Sharrock, for *U-571*; Kevin O'Connell, Greg P Russell and Lee Orloff, for *The Patriot*; John Reitz, Gregg Rudloff, David Campbell and Keith A. Wester, for *The Perfect Storm*; Randy Thom, Tom Johnson, Dennis Sands and William B. Kaplan, for *Cast away*.
● **Best Sound Effects Editing:** Jon Johnson, for *U-571*. Nominations: Alan Robert Murray and Bub Asman, for *Space Cowboys*.
● **Best Make-Up:** Rick Baker and Gail Ryan, for *The Grinch*. Nominations: Ann Buchanan and Amber Sibley, for *Shadow of the Vampire*; Michele Burke and Edouard Henriques, for *The Cell*.
● **Best Visual Effects:** John Nelson, Neil Corbould, Tim Burke and Rob Harvey, for *Gladiator*. Nominations: Scott E. Anderson, Craig Hayes, Scott Stokdyk and Stan Parks, for *Hollow Man*; Stefen Fangmeier, Habib Zargarpour, John Frazier and Walt Conti, for *The Perfect Storm*.
● **Best Animated Short Film:** *Father and Daughter*. Nominations: *The Periwig-Maker*; *Rejected*.
● **Best Live Action Short Film:** *Quiero Ser (I Want to Be...)*. Nominations: *By Courier*; *One Day Crossing*; *Seraglio*; *A Soccer Story (Una Historia de Futebol)*.
● **Best Documentary Feature:** *Into the Arms of Strangers: Stories of the Kindertransport*, by Mark Jonathan Harris. Nominations: *Legacy*; *Long Night's Journey Into Day*; *Scottsboro: An American Tragedy*; *Sound and Fury*.
● **Best Documentary Short:** *Big Mama*. Nominations: *Curtain Call*; *Dolphins*; *The Man on Lincoln's Nose*; *On Tiptoe: Gentle Steps to Freedom*.
● **Best Foreign-Language Film:** *Crouching Tiger, Hidden Dragon* (Hong

Kong/Taiwan/USA). Nominations: *Amores Perros* (Mexico); *Divided We Fall* (Czech Republic); *Everybody Famous!* (Belgium); *The Taste of Others* (France).
- **Irving G. Thalberg Award:** Dino De Laurentiis.
- **Honorary Award:** Ernest Lehman, veteran screenwriter.
- **Lifetime Achievement Award:** Jack Cardiff, cinematographer.

### The 42nd Australian Film Institute Awards, 18 November 2000

- **Best Film:** *Looking For Alibrandi*.
- **Best Actor:** Eric Bana, for *Chopper*.
- **Best Actress:** Pia Miranda, for *Looking For Alibrandi*.
- **Best Supporting Actor:** Simon Lyndon, for *Chopper*.
- **Best Supporting Actress:** Greta Scacchi, for *Looking For Alibrandi*.
- **Best Director:** Andrew Dominik, for *Chopper*.
- **Best Original Screenplay:** Stavros Kazantzidis and Allanah Zitserman, for *Russian Doll*.
- **Best Screenplay Adaptation:** Melina Marchetta, for *Looking For Alibrandi*.
- **Best Cinematography:** Steve Mason, for *Bootmen*.
- **Best Editing:** Martin Connor, for *Looking For Alibrandi*.
- **Best Music:** Cezary Skubiszewski, for *Bootmen*.
- **Best Young Actor:** Kane McNay, for *Mallboy*.
- **Best Foreign Film:** *American Beauty*, by Sam Mendes (USA).

### The 51st Berlin International Film Festival, 18 February 2001

- **Golden Bear for Best Film:** *Intimacy* (France/Italy).
- **Silver Bear, Grand Jury Prize:** *Beijing Bicycle* (Taiwan/France).
- **Silver Bear for Best Director:** Lin Cheng-sheng, for *Betelnut Beauty* (Taiwan/France).
- **Silver Bear, Best Actor:** Benicio Del Toro, for *Traffic*.
- **Silver Bear, Best Actress:** Kerry Fox, for *Intimacy*.
- **Silver Bear for Outstanding Single Achievement:** Cinematographer Raul Perez Cubro, for *You're the One* (Spain).
- **Blue Angel Prize:** Patrice Chereau, for

*Intimacy*.
- **Alfred Bauer Prize:** *The Swamp* (Argentina).
- **Golden Bear for Best Short Film:** *Black Soul* (Canada).
- **Silver Bear for Best Short Film:** *Jungle Jazz: Public Enemy #1* (USA).
- **Ecumenical Jury Prize:** *Italian for Beginners* (Denmark).
- **Special Prize:** *Wit* (USA).
- **FIPRESCI Prizes** (International Film Critics' Association):
- **Best Film:** *Italian for Beginners*. Panorama: *Maelström* (Canada). International Forum: *It Should Have Been Nice After That* (Germany).
- **Wolfgang Staudte Prize:** *Love/Juice* (Japan).
- **CICAE** (international confederation of art cinemas):
  Panorama: *Late Night Shopping* (UK). Forum: *Love/Juice*.
- **German Arthouse Cinemas Guild:** *Finding Forrester* (USA).
- **Gay Teddy Bear Award, Best Feature:** *Hedwig and the Angry Inch* (USA).
- **Peace Film Prize:** *Living Afterwards: Words of Women* (France).
- **Panorama Audience Award:** *Berlin Is in Germany* (Germany).
- **Piper Heidsieck New Talent Awards:** Angelica Lee Sinje, for her performance in *Betelnut Beauty*; and Cui Lin and Li Bin, for their performances in *Beijing Bicycle*.

*Jury president: Bill Mechanic.*

### The 21st Canadian Film Awards ('Genies'), Toronto, Ontario, 29 January 2001

- **Best Film:** *Maelström*.
- **Best Director:** *Maelström*.
- **Best Actor:** Tony Nardi, for *My Father's Angel*.
- **Best Actress:** Marie-Josée Croze, for *Maelström*.
- **Best Supporting Actor:** Martin Cummins, for *Love Come Down*.
- **Best Supporting Actress:** Helen Shaver, for *We All Fall Down*.
- **Best Screenplay:** Denis Villeneuve, for *Maelström*.
- **Best Cinematography:** André Turpin, for *Maelström*.
- **Best Editing:** Susan Shipton, for *Possible Worlds*.
- **Best Art Direction:** François Séguin

and Daniéle Rouleau, for *Possible Worlds*.
- **Best Music:** Pat Caird, for *Here's to Life!*
- **Best Original Song:** François Dompierre. for 'Dumb Ol' Heart,' from *Here's to Life!*
- **Best Costumes:** Michel Robidas, for *Stardom*.
- **Best Sound** Editing: David McCallum, Fred Brennan, Susan Conley, Steve Hammond, Garrett Kerr, Jane Tattersall and Robert Warchol, for *Love Come Down*.
- **Best Overall Sound:** Daniel Pellerin, Paul Adlaf, Peter Kelly, Brad Thornton and, for Brad Zoern *Love Come Down*.
- **Claude Jutra Award for Best First Feature:** *La Moitie gauche du frigo*, by Philippe Falardeau.
- **Best Feature-length Documentary:** *Grass*, by Ron Mann.
- **Best Animated Short:** *Village of Idiots*, by Michael Scott, Eugene Fedorenko, Rose Newlove and David Verrall.
- **Best Live-Action Short:** *Petit varius*, by André Théberge and Alain Jacques.
- **The Golden Reel Award for Box-Office Performance:** *The Art of War*.

### The 54th Cannes Film Festival Awards, 9-20 May 2001

- **Palme d'Or for Best Film:** *The Son's Room* (Italy/France), by Nanni Moretti.
- **Grand Prix du Jury:** *The Piano Teacher* (Austria/France), by Michael Haneke.
- **Best Actor:** Benoît Magimel, for *The Piano Teacher*.
- **Best Actress:** Isabelle Huppert, for *The Piano Teacher*.
- **Best Director:** Joel Coen, for *The Man Who Wasn't There* (USA); and David Lynch, for *Mulholland Drive* (USA/France).
- **Best Screenplay:** Danis Tanovic, for *No Man's Land* (France/Italy/Belgium/UK/Slovenia).
- **Technical Prize:** Tu Duu-chih, for the sound on *Millennium Mambo* (Taiwan/France) and *What Time Is It There?* (Taiwan/France).
- **Palme d'Or for Best Short:** *Bean Cake* (USA), by David Greenspan.
- **Prix du Jury (Fiction):** *Daddy's Girl* (UK), by Irvine Allan.
- **Prix du Jury (Animation):** *Pizza Passionata* (Finland), by Kari Juusonen.
- **Camera d'Or** (for first feature): *Atanarjuat the Fast Runner* (Canada), by Zacharias Kunuk.
- **Cinefondation:**
  First Prize: *Portrait* (Russia), by Sergei

Luchishin.

**Second Prize:** *Reparation* (Sweden), by Jens Jonsson.

**Third Prize** (shared): *Run Away* (China), by Yang Chao); and *Crow Stone* (UK), by Alicia Duffy.

● **Fipresci International Critics' Award:** *The Son's Room.*

**Un Certain Regard:** *Pulse* (Japan), by Kiyoshi Kurosawa.

**Parallel Sections:** *Martha... Martha* (France), by Sandrine Veysset; and *The Pornographer* (France), by Bertrand Bonello.

● **Ecumenical Prizes:**

**Best Film:** *Kandahar* (Iran), by Mohsen Makhmalbaf.

**Future Talent:** Manda Kunitoshi, for *Unloved* (Japan).

● **Critics' Week Awards:**

**Grand Prix:** *Under the Moonlight* (Iran), by Reza Mir-Karimi.

**Best Short:** *Eat* (USA), by Bill Plympton.

*Jury: Liv Ullmann (president), director Mimmo Calopresti, Charlotte Gainsbourg, Terry Gilliam, Mathieu Kassovitz, Sandrine Kiberlain, writer Philippe Labro, Julia Ormond, director Moufisda Tlatli, Edward Yang*

## The 26th Deauville Festival of American Cinema, 1-10 September 2000

● **Grand Prix for Best Film:** *Girlfight*, by Karyn Kusama.

● **Jury Prize:** *Boiler Room* by Ben Younger; and *Memento*, by Christopher Nolan.

● **Grand Prix for Best Short:** *Seraglio*, by Gail Lerner and Colin Campbell.

● **Jury Prize for Best Short:** *Zen and the Art of Landscaping*, by David Kartch.

● **Honourees:** Clint Eastwood, Susan Sarandon, Chow Yun-Fat, Samuel L. Jackson.

*Jury president: Neil Jordan*

## The 13th European Film Awards ('The Felixes'), Palais de Chaillot, Paris, 2 December 2000

● **Best European Film:** *Dancer in the Dark* (Denmark/Sweden/France), by Lars von Trier.

● **Best Actor:** Sergi Lopez, for *Harry, He's Here To Help.*

● **Best Actress:** Björk, for *Dancer in the Dark.*

● **Best Screenplay:** Agnès Jaoui and Jean-Pierre Bacri, for *It Takes All Kinds* (France).

● **Best Cinematography:** Vittorio Storaro, for *Goya in Bordeaux* (Spain/Italy).

● **Best Short Film:** *Our Stork* (Hungary), by Livia Gyarmathy.

● **Discovery of the Year** (Fassbinder Award): Laurent Cantet, director of *Ressources humaines* (*Human Resources*).

● **Best Documentary** (Prix Arte): *The Gleaners and I* (France), by Agnès Varda.

● **People's Awards:**

**Best Actor:** Ingvar E. Sigurdsson, for *Angels of the Universe* (Iceland).

**Best Actress:** Björk, for *Dancer in the Dark.*

**Best Director:** Lars von Trier, for *Dancer in the Dark.*

● **Best Non-European Film:** *In the Mood For Love* (Hong Kong), by Wong Kar-wei.

● **Achievement in World Cinema:** Jean Reno.

● **FIPRESCI Award** (Critics' Prize): *Clouds of May* (Turkey), by Nuri Bilge Ceylan.

● **Lifetime Achievement Award:** Richard Harris.

## The 26th French Academy ('Cesar') Awards, Champs Elysees Théâtre, Paris, 24 February 2001

● **Best Film:** *The Taste of Others.*

● **Best Director:** Dominik Moll, for *Harry, He's Here to Help.*

● **Best Actor:** Sergi Lopez, for *Harry, He's Here To Help.*

● **Best Actress:** Dominique Blanc, for *Stand-By.*

● **Best Supporting Actor:** Gerard Lanvin, for *The Taste of Others.*

● **Best Supporting Actress:** Anne Alvaro, for *The Taste of Others.*

● **Most Promising Young Actor:** Jalil Lespert, for *Human Resources.*

● **Most Promising Young Actress:** Sylvie Testud, for *Murderous Maids.*

● **Best First Film:** *Human Resources*, by Laurent Cantet.

● **Best Screenplay:** Agnes Jaoui and Jean-Pierre Bacri, for *The Taste of Others.*

● **Best cinematography:** Agnes Godard, for *Good Work.*

● **Best Production Design:** Jean Rabasse, for *Vatel.*

● **Best Editing:** Yannick Kergoat, for *Harry, He's Here To Help.*

● **Best Music:** Tomatito, Sheikh Ahmad Al Tuni, La Caita and Tony Gatlif, for *Vengo.*

● **Best Costumes:** Edith Versperini and Jean-Daniel Vuillermoz, for *St Cyr.*

● **Best Sound:** François Maurel and Gerard Lamps, for *Harry, He's Here To Help.*

● **Best Short:** *Salam*, by Souad El Bouhati; and *Un petit air de dete*, by Eric Guirado.

● **Best Foreign Film:** *In the Mood For Love* (Hong Kong), by Wong Kar-wei.

● **Honorary Cesars:** Charlotte Rampling, Agnes Varda and veteran actor Darryl Cowl.

*Host: Daniel Auteuil*

## Golden Raspberries ('The Razzies'), 24 March 2001

● **Worst Film:** *Battlefield Earth.*

● **Worst Actor:** John Travolta, for *Battlefield Earth* and *Lucky Numbers.*

● **Worst Actress:** Madonna, for *The Next Best Thing.*

● **Worst Screen Couple:** John Travolta and *anyone* in *Battlefield Earth.*

● **Worst Supporting Actress:** Kelly Preston, for *Battlefield Earth.*

● **Worst Supporting Actor:** Barry Pepper, for *Battlefield Earth.*

● **Worst Director:** Roger Christian, for *Battlefield Earth.*

● **Worst Screenplay:** Corey Mandell and J D Shapiro, for *Battlefield Earth.*

● **Worst Remake or Sequel:** *Book of Shadows: Blair Witch 2.*

## The 58th Hollywood Foreign Press Association ('Golden Globes') Awards, 21 January 2001

● **Best Picture – Drama:** *Gladiator.*

● **Best Picture – Musical or Comedy:** *Almost Famous.*

● **Best Actor – Drama:** Tom Hanks, for *Cast Away*.

● **Best Actress – Drama:** Julia Roberts, for *Erin Brockovich*.
● **Best Actor – Musical or Comedy:** George Clooney, for *O Brother, Where Art Thou?*
● **Best Actress – Musical or Comedy:** Renée Zellweger, for *Nurse Betty*.
● **Best Supporting Actress:** Kate Hudson, for *Almost Famous*.
● **Best Supporting Actor:** Benicio Del Toro, for *Traffic*.
● **Best Director:** Ang Lee, for *Crouching Tiger, Hidden Dragon*.
● **Best Screenplay:** Stephen Gaghan, for *Traffic*.
● **Best Original Score:** Hans Zimmer and Lisa Gerrard, for *Gladiator*.
● **Best Original Song:** 'Things Have Changed,' from *Wonder Boys*, by Bob Dylan.
● **Best Foreign Language Film:** *Crouching Tiger, Hidden Dragon* (Hong Kong/Taiwan/USA), by Ang Lee.
● **Best TV Film or miniseries:** *Dirty Pictures*.

**The 21st London Film Critics' Circle Awards, The Savoy, London, 15 February 2001**

● **Best Film:** *Being John Malkovich*.
● **Best Actor:** Russell Crowe, for *Gladiator* and *The Insider*.
● **Best Actress:** Julia Roberts, for *Erin Brockovich*.
● **Best Director:** Spike Jonze, for *Being John Malkovich*.
● **Best Screenwriter:** Charlie Kaufman, for *Being John Malkovich*.
● **Best British Film:** *Billy Elliot*.
● **Best British Producer:** Greg Brenman and Jonathan Finn, for *Billy Elliot*.

● **Best British Director:** Stephen Daldry, for *Billy Elliot*.
● **Best British Screenwriter:** Christopher Nolan, for *Memento*.
● **Best British Actor:** Jim Broadbent, for *Topsy-Turvy*.
● **Best British Actress:** Julie Walters, for *Billy Elliot*.
● **Best British Supporting Actor:** Albert Finney, for *Erin Brockovich*.
● **Best British Supporting Actress:** Samantha Morton, for *Sweet and Lowdown*.
● **Best British Newcomer:** Jamie Bell, for *Billy Elliot*.
● **Best Foreign Language Film:** *Crouching Tiger, Hidden Dragon*.
● **Dilys Powell Award:** Richard Harris.

*Presenters: John Marriott, Mariella Frostrup, Carol Allen, James Cameron-Wilson, Dee Carey, Quentin Falk, Paul Gambaccini, Marianne Gray, Karen Krizanovich, Wendy Lloyd, George Perry, Simon Rose, Jason Solomons and Christopher Tookey*

**The Los Angeles Film Critics' Association Awards, December 2000**

● **Best Picture:** *Crouching Tiger, Hidden Dragon*.
● **Best Actor:** Michael Douglas, for *Wonder Boys*.
● **Best Actress:** Julia Roberts, for *Erin Brockovich*.
● **Best Supporting Actor:** Willem Dafoe, for *Shadow of the Vampire*.
● **Best Supporting Actress:** Frances McDormand, for *Almost Famous* and *Wonder Boys*.
● **Best Director:** Steven Soderbergh, for *Erin Brockovich* and *Traffic*.
● **Best Screenplay:** Kenneth Lonergan, for *You Can Count on Me*.
● **Best Foreign-Language Film :** *Yi Yi* (Taiwan).
● **Best Cinematography:** Peter Pau, for *Crouching Tiger, Hidden Dragon*.
● **Best Music:** Tan Dun, for *Crouching Tiger, Hidden Dragon*.
● **Best Production Design:** Tim Yip, for *Crouching Tiger, Hidden Dragon*.
● **New Generation Award:** Mark Ruffalo, for *You Can Count on Me*.
● **Best Animation:** *Chicken Run*, by Nick Park and Peter Lord
● **Best Documentary:** *Dark Days*, by Marc Singer.

**The 92nd National Board of Review of Motion Picture Awards, New York, 6 December 2000**

● **Best Film:** *Quills*.
● **Best Actor:** Javier Bardem, for *Before Night Falls*.
● **Best Actress:** Julia Roberts, for *Erin Brockovich*.
● **Best Supporting Actor:** Joaquin Phoenix, for *Gladiator*, *Quills* and *The Yards*.
● **Best Supporting Actress:** Lupe Ontiveros, for *Chuck and Buck*.
● **Best Musical Performance:** Björk, for *Dancer in the Dark*.
● **Best Director:** Steven Soderbergh, for *Erin Brockovich* and *Traffic*.
● **Best Screenplay:** Ted Tally, for *All the Pretty Horses*.
● **Best Production Design/art direction:** *Gladiator*.
● **Best Ensemble Cast:** *State and Main*.
● **Best Foreign Film:** *Crouching Tiger, Hidden Tiger* (Hong Kong/Taiwan/USA).
● **Best animated film:** *Chicken Run*.
● **Breakthrough Performance:** Michelle Rodriguez, for *Girlfight*.
● **Outstanding young actor:** Jamie Bell, for *Billy Elliot*.
● **Special Achievement in Filmmaking Award:** Kenneth Lonergan, for *You Can Count On Me*.
● **Special Achievement in Foreign film:** Krzysztof's *Decalogue* series.
● **Career achievement:** Ellen Burstyn, Ennio Morricone.

**The 35th National Society of Film Critics' Awards, New York, 6 January 2001**

● **Best Film:** *Yi Yi* (Taiwan).
● **Best Actor:** Javier Bardem, for *Before Night Falls*.

● **Best Actress:** Laura Linney, for *You Can Count On Me*.
● **Best Director:** Steven Soderbergh, for *Traffic*.
● **Best Supporting Actor:** Benicio Del Toro, for *Traffic*.
● **Best Supporting Actress:** Elaine May, for *Small Time Crooks*.
● **Best Screenplay:** Ken Lonergan, for *You Can Count On Me*.
● **Best Cinematography:** Agnès Godard, for *Beau Travail*.
● **Best Documentary:** *The Life and Times of Hank Greenberg*.
● **Best Experimental Film:** *The Heart of the World*, by Guy Maddin.
● **Special Citation:** Michelangelo Antonioni, for the exemplary intelligence, creativity and integrity of his half-century-long career.
● **Special award:** National Film Preservation Foundation.

### The 66th New York Film Critics' Circle Awards, December 2000

● **Best Film:** *Traffic*.
● **Best Actor:** Tom Hanks, for *Cast Away*.
● **Best Actress:** Laura Linney, for *You Can Count On Me*.
● **Best Supporting Actor:** Benicio Del Toro, for *Traffic*.
● **Best Supporting Actress:** Marcia Gay Harden, for *Pollock*.
● **Best Director:** Steven Soderbergh, for *Erin Brockovich* and *Traffic*.
● **Best Screenplay:** Kenneth Lonergan, for *You Can Count On Me*.
● **Best Cinematography:** Peter Pau, for *Crouching Tiger, Hidden Tiger*.
● **Best Foreign Film:** *Yi-Yi* (Taiwan).
● **Best Non-Fiction Film:** *The Life and Times of Hank Greenberg*.
● **Best animated film:** *Chicken Run*.
● **Best First Film:** *George Washington*.

### The 2000 Orange British Academy of Film and Television Arts Awards ('BAFTAs'), Odeon Leicester Square, London, 25 February 2001

● **Best Film:** *Gladiator*.
● **David Lean Award for Best Direction:** Ang Lee, for *Crouching Tiger, Hidden Dragon*.
● **Best Original Screenplay:** Cameron Crowe, for *Almost Famous*.

● **Best Adapted Screenplay:** Stephen Gaghan, for *Traffic*.
● **Best Actor:** Jamie Bell, for *Billy Elliot*.
● **Best Actress:** Julia Roberts, for *Erin Brockovich*.
● **Best Supporting Actor:** Benicio Del Toro, for *Traffic*.
● **Best Supporting Actress:** Julie Walters, for *Billy Elliot*.
● **Best Cinematography:** John Mathieson, for *Gladiator*.
● **Best Production Design:** Arthur Max, for *Gladiator*.
● **Best Editing:** Pietro Scalia, for *Gladiator*.
● **The Anthony Asquith Award for Best Music:** Tan Dun, for *Crouching Tiger, Hidden Dragon*.
● **Best Costumes:** Tim Yip, for *Crouching Tiger, Hidden Dragon*.
● **Best Sound:** Jeff Wexler, D.M. Hemphill, Rick Kline, Paul Massey and Mike Wilhoit, for *Almost Famous*.
● **Best Special Visual Effects:** Stefen Fangmeier, John Frazier, Habib Zargarpour, Walt Conti and Tim Alexander, for *The Perfect Storm*.
● **Best Make-up/hair:** Rick Baker, Kazuhiro Tsuji and Toni G, for *The Grinch*.
● **Alexander Korda Award for Best British Film:** *Billy Elliot*.
● **Best Foreign Language Film:** for *Crouching Tiger, Hidden Dragon*.
● **Best Short Film:** *Shadowscan*.
● **Best Animated Short:** *Father and Daughter*.
● **Carl Foreman Award for British Newcomer:** Pawel Pawlikowski, for *Last Resort*.
● **BAFTA Fellowship:** Albert Finney.

*Host: Stephen Fry*

### The 17th Sundance Film Festival, Park City, Utah, 18-28 January 2001

● **The Grand Jury Prize (best feature):** *The Believer*, by Henry Bean.
● **The Grand Jury Prize (Best Documentary):** *Southern Comfort*, by Kate Davis.
● **Best Performance:** Tom Wilkinson and Sissy Spacek, for *In the Bedroom*.
● **Best Direction:** John Cameron Mitchell, for *Hedwig and the Angry Inch*.
● **Best Direction (documentary):** Stacy Peralta, for *Dogtown and Z-Boys*.

● **Best Cinematography:** Giles Nuttgens, for *The Deep End*.
● **Best Cinematography (documentary):** Albert Maysles, for *Lalee's Kin: The Legacy of Cotton*.
● **Audience Award (best feature):** *Hedwig and the Angry Inch* by John Cameron Mitchell.
● **Audience Award (Best Documentary):** *Dogtown and Z-Boys*, by Stacy Peralta; and *Scout's Honor*, by Tom Shepard.
● **World Cinema Audience Award:** *The Road Home*, by Zhang Yimou.
● **Short Filmmaking Award:** *Gina, an Actress, Age 29*, by Paul Harrill.
● **Waldo Salt Screenwriting Award:** Christopher Nolan, for *Memento*.
● **Freedom of Expression Award:** *Scout's Honor*.
● **Special Jury Award (documentary):** *Children Underground*, by Edet Belzberg.
● **Latin American Cinema Award:** *Possible Loves*, by Sandra Werneck; and *Without a Trace*, by Maria Navaro.

*Jury: Darren Aronofsky, Elpidia Carrillo, Joan Chen, Kasi Lemmons, Bingham Ray, Gavin Smith, Guinevere Turner, etc.*

### The 57th Venice International Film Festival Awards, 30 August 2000

● **Golden Lion for Best Film:** *The Circle* (Iran/Italy), by Jafar Panahi.
● **Special Jury Grand Prix:** *Before Night Falls* (USA), by Julian Schnabel.
● **Best Actor:** Javier Bardem, for *Before Night Falls*.
● **Best Actress:** Rose Byrne, for *The Goddess of 1967* (Australia).
● **Marcello Mastroianni Award for Emerging Actor:** Megan Burns, for *Liam* (UK/Germany/Italy).
● **Fipresci International Critics' Award:** *The Circle*.
● **Venezia Opera Prima Luigi De Laurentiis Award for Best First Feature:** *La faute a Voltaire* (Tunisia), by Abdel Kechiche.
● **Special Prize For Direction:** Buddhadeb Dasgupta, for *The Wrestlers* (India).

*Jury: Milos Forman (president), actress Jennifer Jason Leigh, director Samira Makhmalbaf, director Giuseppe Bertolucci, director Claude Chabrol, writer Tahar Ben-Jelloun and film critic Andreas Kilb*

# In Memoriam

## JOHN A ALONZO

**Born:** 12 June 1934 in Dallas, Texas.
**Died:** 13 March 2001 in Beverly Hills, California, of natural causes.

● Cinematographer. **Main films:** *Bloody Mama* (1970), *Vanishing Point, Harold and Maude* (both 1971), *Sounder, Lady Sings the Blues, Pete 'n' Tillie* (all 1972), *Conrack* (1974), *Farewell My Lovely, The Fortune* (both 1975), *The Bad News Bears* (1976), *Black Sunday* (1977), *The Cheap Detective* (1978), *Tom Horn, Norma Rae* (both 1979), *Blue Thunder, Scarface, Cross Creek* (all 1983), *Nothing in Common* (1986), *Overboard* (1987), *Steel Magnolias* (1989), *Internal Affairs* (1990), *HouseSitter* (1992), *Star Trek: Generations* (1994), *The Grass Harp* (1995), *Letters From a Killer* (1998), *Deuces Wild* (2001).

A former actor (he was in *The Magnificent Seven* and played Manuel in the 1964 *Invitation to a Gunfighter*), John Alonzo was nominated for an Oscar for his photography of *Chinatown* (1974) and went on to direct the musical drama *FM* (1977).

## JEAN ANDERSON

**Born:** 12 December 1907 in Eastbourne, Sussex. **Died:** 1 April 2001.
**Real name:** Mary Jean Heriot Anderson.

● Benign character actress. **Main films:** *The Mark of Cain* (1946), *The Romantic Age* (aka *Naughty Arlette*), *Elizabeth of Ladymead* (both 1949), *White Corridors* (1951), *Time Bomb* (aka *Terror On a Train*) (1952), *Street Corner* (1955), *A Town Like Alice* (1956), *Robbery Under Arms, Lucky Jim, The Barretts of Wimpole Street* (all 1957), *Solomon and Sheba, SOS Pacific* (both 1959), *Half a Sixpence* (1967), *Country Dance* (aka *Brotherly Love*) (1969), *The Night Digger* (1971), *The Lady Vanishes* (1979), *Leon the Pig Farmer* (1992).

In her later years, she became best known for her TV roles, particularly as the matriarch of Hammond Transport Services in the BBC's *The Brothers* (1972-76) and as Lady Jocelyn Holbrook in the Beeb's POW drama *Tenko* (1981-84).

## LEWIS ARQUETTE

**Born:** 14 December 1935 in Chicago.
**Died:** 10 February 2001 of congestive heart failure in Los Angeles.

● Actor-comedian. **Main films:** *The China Syndrome* (1979), *Nobody's Fool* (1986), *Big Business* (1988), *Tango & Cash* (1989), *Book of Love* (1991), *The Linguini Incident* (1992), *Attack of the 50ft Woman* (1993), *Sleep With Me* (1994), *Waiting For Guffman* (1996), *Scream 2* (1997), *Twilight* (1998), *Little Nicky, Ready to Rumble, Best in Show* (all 2000).

Lewis Arquette was the father of actors Rosanna, Richmond, Patricia, Alexis and David Arquette.

## JEAN-PIERRE AUMONT

**Born:** 5 January 1909 in Paris. **Died:** 30 January 2001 at his home in St Tropez on the French Riviera.
**Real name:** Jean-Pierre Salomons.

● French romantic leading man and playwright. **Main film appearances:** *Jean de la lune* (1931), *Marie Chapdelaine* (1934), *Drôle de Drame* (1936), *Hôtel du Nord, La Belle Etoile* (both 1938), *Assignment to Brittany, The Cross of Lorraine* (both 1943), *Heartbeat* (1946), as Rimski-Korsakov in *Song of Scheherazade* (1947), *Siren of Atlantis* (1948), *Lili* (1953), *Royal Affairs in Versailles* (1954), *Hilda Crane* (1956), *John Paul Jones* (1959), *The Devil at 4 o'clock* (1961), *Castle Keep* (1969), *Day for Night* (1973), *The Happy Hooker, Mahogany* (both 1975), *Le sang des autres, Nana* (both 1983), *Becoming Collette* (1991), *Jefferson in Paris* (1995).

He was married to the actress Maria Montez from 1943 until her death in 1951. Their daughter, Tina Aumont, later became a successful actress in her own right. His autobiography, *Sun and Shadow*, appeared in 1977.

## BILLY BARTY

**Born:** 25 October 1924 in Millsboro, Pennsylvania. **Died:** 23 December 2000.
**Real name:** William John Bertanzetti.

● Actor. **Main films:** *Daddy Long Legs* (1931), *Gold Diggers of 1933, Roman Scandals, Footlight Parade, Alice in Wonderland* (all 1933), *A Midsummer Night's Dream, Bride of Frankenstein* (both 1935), *Hollywood Hotel* (1937), *Pigmy Island* (1950), *The Clown* (1952), *The Undead* (1957), *Harem Holiday* (1965), *Pufnstuf* (1970), *The Day of the Locust* (1974), *Foul Play* (1978), *Under the Rainbow* (1981), *Legend* (1985), *Masters of the Universe, Rumpelstiltskin* (both 1987), *Willow* (1988), *Life Stinks* (1991), *Wishful Thinking* (1992).

Barty, who suffered from Cartilage Hair Syndrome Hypoplasia, capitalised on his diminutive stature, playing infants in Warner Bros musicals of the 1930s and Mickey Rooney's younger brother in many *Mickey McGuire* comedy shorts (1927-34). When maturity did, inevitably, catch up with him, he continued playing wily short people until the end of his life.

## RALF D BODE

**Born:** 31 March 1941 in Berlin, Germany. **Died:** 27 February 2001 of lung cancer at his home in Santa Monica, California.

● Cinematographer. **Main films:** *Saturday Night Fever* (1977), *Somebody Killed Her Husband, Rich Kids, Coal Miner's Daughter, Dressed to Kill, Gorky Park, Distant Thunder, The Accused, Uncle Buck, Cousins, Love Field, Made in America, Bad Girls, Safe Passage, Boys and Girls* (2000) etc.

Bode received an Oscar nomination for his work on *Coal Miner's Daughter* and an Emmy for his photography of the TV productions *A Streetcar Named Desire* (1995) and *Annie* (1999).

## JEAN CHAMPION

**Born:** 9 March 1914 in Chalon-sur-Saône, France. **Died:** 23 May 2001 at his home in Chalon-sur-Saône, France.

● Character actor. **Main films:** *Cleo From 5 to 7* (1961), *Muriel* (1963), *The Umbrellas of Cherbourg* (1964), *Day for Night* (1973), *The Phantom of Liberty*

(1974), *Monsieur Klein* (1976), *Clean Slate* (1981), *Life and Nothing But* (1989).

## PAUL DANEMAN

**Born:** 26 October 1925 in London. **Died:** April 2001.

● Stage and TV actor whose few film credits included *Time Without Pity* (1957), *The Clue of the New Pin* (1961), *Zulu* (1964), *How I Won the War* (1967) and *Oh! What a Lovely War* (1968).

## ROSEMARY DeCAMP

**Born:** 14 November 1911 in Prescott, Arizona. **Died:** 20 February 2001 of pneumonia in Torrance, California.

● Character actress. **Main films:** *Cheers for Miss Bishop*, *Hold Back the Dawn* (both 1941), *Yankee Doodle Dandy*, *Jungle Book* (both 1942), *This is the Army* (1943), in which she played Ronald Reagan's mother, *Rhapsody in Blue* (1945), *On Moonlight Bay* (1950), *Strategic Air Command* (1955), *13 Ghosts* (1960), and *Saturday the 14th* (1981).

She was also a familiar face on television, playing the wife of Jackie Gleason in *The Life of Riley*, the matronly Margaret MacDonald in *Love That Bob* (with Bob Cummings) and the mother of Marlo Thomas in *That Girl*. In 1962 she wrote a children's novel and in 1991 produced her autobiography, *Tales From Hollywood*, as an audio book.

## DAVID DUKES

**Born:** 6 June 1945 in San Francisco. **Died:** 9 October 2000 after collapsing in Spanaway, Washington, from a heart attack brought on by cardiovascular disease.

● Actor. **Main films:** *A Little Romance* (1979), *The First Deadly Sin* (1980), *Only When I Laugh* (1981), *Without a Trace* (1983), *The Men's Club* (1986), *See You In the Morning* (1989), *And the Band Played On* (1993), *Gods and Monsters* (1998), and his last film, *Sex and a Girl* (2000), with Robert Hays.

In spite of his 30-odd film appearances and TV work (*The Mommies, Sisters*, etc), Dukes' first love was the theatre. He is survived by his second wife, the writer Carol Muske-Dukes, and was filming the Stephen King miniseries *Rose Red* when he died.

## ROBERT ENRICO

**Born:** 13 April 1931 in Liévin, France. **Died:** 23 February 2001 of cancer in Paris.

● Film director. **Main films:** *La Belle Vie* (1963), *Wise Guys* (1965), *The Last Adventure* (1966), *Rum Runners* (1971), *The Old Gun* (1975), *Coup de Foudre* (1977), *Fait d'Hiver* (1999).

Few directors could boast of winning an Oscar for their first film, but Enrico did just that when his short, *Incident at Owl Creek* (1962) – which had already won the Palme d'Or at Cannes – went on to snap up the Academy Award two years later. A commercial filmmaker renowned for his versatility, Enrico directed some of the biggest stars in France, including Brigitte Bardot, Alain Delon, Catherine Deneuve, Philippe Noiret and Lino Ventura.

## JULIUS J EPSTEIN

**Born:** 22 August 1909 in the Lower East Side of New York City. **Died:** 30 December 2000 in Los Angeles.

● Screenwriter. **Main films:** *The Man Who Came To Dinner* (1941), *Arsenic and Old Lace* (1942), *Casablanca* (1942), *Mrs Skeffington* (1944), *Romance of the High Seas* (1948), *My Foolish Heart* (1949), *The Tender Trap* (1955), *Pete 'n' Tillie* (1972), *Cross of Iron* (1977), *House Calls* (1978), *Reuben, Reuben* (1982).

Epstein wrote his Oscar-winning screenplay for *Casablanca* with his twin brother Philip who, on his death in 1952, Julius insisted on referring to as if he were still alive. Julius himself started out as a film critic for *Billboard*.

## DALE EVANS

**Born:** 31 October 1912 in Uvalde, Texas. **Died:** 7 February 2001 of congestive heart failure at her home in Apple Valley, east of Los Angeles. **Real name:** Frances Octavia Smith.

● Singer, writer and actress. **Main films:** *Orchestra Wives* (1942), *Swing Your Partner* (1943), *The Yellow Rose of Texas* (1944), *Utah* (1945), *Don't Fence Me In* (1945), *My Pal Trigger* (1946), *Apache Rose* (1947), *Pals of the Golden West* (1951).

The wife of singing cowboy star Roy Rogers, Dale was dubbed 'Queen of the West' to his 'King of the West.' The couple married in 1947, starred in several films together, formed their own production company and then appeared in such TV shows as *The Roy Rogers and Dale Evans Show* (1962) and *Happy Trails Theatre* (1986-89). They also recorded more than 400 songs together. Dale herself wrote the gospel standard 'The Bible Tells Me So', was extremely active in Christian evangelism and penned more than 20 'inspirational' books, including the autobiographical *Angel Unaware*, a best-seller about the couple's only daughter, Robin, a victim of Down's Syndrome. In 1967 Dale was voted California Mother of the Year.

## RICHARD FARNSWORTH

**Born:** 1 September 1920 in Los Angeles. **Died:** 6 October 2000 from self-inflicted gun-shot wounds, in New Mexico.

● Stunt man and character actor. **Main films as actor:** *A Day at the Races* (1937), *Red River* (1948), *The Wild One* (1953), *The Tin Star* (1957), *Spartacus* (1960), *Monte Walsh* (1970), *The Cowboys*, *Pocket Money* (both 1971), *Another Man, Another Woman* (1977), *Tom Horn*, *Resurrection* (both 1980), *Waltz Across Texas*, *The Grey Fox* (both 1982), *The Natural* (1984), *Misery*, *The Two Jakes*, *Havana* (all 1990), *The Getaway* and *Lassie* (both 1994).

He was nominated for an Oscar twice, in the Best Supporting Actor category for *Comes a Horseman* (1978) and as Best Actor for David Lynch's masterpiece *The Straight Story* (1999). A performer of

enormous presence, Farnsworth's greatest
gift was to convey so much with so little.

## SHELAGH FRASER

**Born:** 25 November 1922, Purley.
**Died:** 13 September 2000, London.
● Actress. **Main films:** *Master of Bankdam*
(1947), *Esther Waters* (1948), *Trio* (1950),
*Raising a Riot* (1955), *The Witches* (1966),
*Till Death Us Do Part* (1968), *Staircase*
(1969), *Doomwatch* (1972), *Nothing But
the Night* (1972), *Star Wars*, in which she
played Luke Skywalker's aunt (1977),
*Hope and Glory* (1987).

In an acting career kick-started by playwright Terence Rattigan, Fraser not only
made numerous film appearances but was
also a leading player in the award-winning Granada serial, *A Family at War*
(1970-72).

## DAVID GRAF

**Born:** April 1950 in Lancaster, Ohio.
**Died:** 7 April 2001 of a heart attack,
in Arizona.
● An actor and activist for the Screen
Actors Guild, Graf was best known for his
recurring role as Eugene Tackleberry in
the *Police Academy* comedies. Other films
include *Guarding Tess* (1994), *The Brady
Bunch Movie* (1995), *Citizen Ruth* (1996)
and *Rules of Engagement* (2000).

## ALEC GUINNESS

**Born:** 2 April 1914 in London. **Died:** 5
August 2000 of liver cancer, in Sussex.
**Real name:** Alec Guinness de Cuffe.
● Actor. **Main film appearances:** *Evensong*
(1934), Herbert Pocket in *Great
Expectations* (1947), Fagin in *Oliver Twist*
(1948), *Kind Hearts and Coronets*, *A Run
for Your Money* (both 1949), *Last Holiday*,
*The Mudlark* (both 1950), *The Man in
the White Suit*, *The Lavender Hill Mob*
(both 1951), *The Card* (1952), *The
Captain's Paradise* (1953), *Father Brown*
(1954), *The Ladykillers* (1955), *The Swan*
(1956), *The Bridge On the River Kwai*
(1957), *The Horse's Mouth* (1958), *The
Scapegoat*, *Our Man in Havana* (both

1959), *Tunes of Glory* (1960), *A Majority
of One* (1961), *HMS Defiant* (aka *Damn
the Defiant!*), Prince Feisal in *Lawrence of
Arabia* (both 1962), Marcus Aurelius in
*The Fall of the Roman Empire* (1964),
*Doctor Zhivago* (1965), *The Quiller
Memorandum* (1966), *The Comedians*
(1967), King Charles I in *Cromwell*
(1970), the title role in *Hitler: The Last
Ten Days*, Pope Innocent III in *Brother
Sun, Sister Moon* (both 1973), *Murder by
Death* (1976), Obi-Wan Kenobi in *Star
Wars* (1977), *A Passage to India* (1984), *A
Handful of Dust* (1988) and Steven
Soderbergh's *Kafka* (1991). His very last
appearance was a brief cameo (as 'The
Reaper') in the Anglo-Russian *Mute Witness*
(1995), his footage having been shot sever-
al years before the rest of the film.

Besides receiving the best actor
Academy Award for *The Bridge On the
River Kwai* (for a role originally offered to
Charles Laughton) and an Honorary
Award 'for advancing the art of screen
acting through a host of memorable and
distinguished performances,' Guinness
was Oscar-nominated for *The Lavender
Hill Mob*, *Star Wars* and *Little Dorritt* as
well as for his screenplay for *The Horse's
Mouth*. He was knighted in 1959 and
published his autobiography, *Blessings in
Disguise*, in 1985. In typically self-effac-
ing mood, he once said of his talent that
'I gave my best performances, perhaps,

during the war, trying to be an officer and
a gentleman.'

## LIANE HAID

**Born:** 16 August 1895 in Vienna,
Austria. **Died:** 28 November 2000 in
Bern, Switzerland, aged 105.
● Actress and pin-up. **Main films:** *Lady
Hamilton* (1921), *Lukrezia Borgia* (1926),
*Old Vienna* (1928), *Whom the Gods Love*
(1936), *The Five Karnickels* (1953) etc.

Austria's first movie star (a Viennese
alley was named after her), Frau Haid
appeared in some 90 German films.

## JACK HALEY JR

**Born:** 25 October 1933 in Los Angeles.
**Died:** 21 April 2001 in Los Angeles.
● Director, producer, writer, executive. As
director, Haley made *Norwood* (1969)
and *The Love Machine* (1971), but is best
known for his wonderful compilation of
highlights from MGM's musical treasure-
trove, *That's Entertainment!* (1974). He
also directed a number of award-winning
documentaries and was married to Liza
Minnelli (1974-79). His father was the
actor Jack Haley, who played the Tin Man
in *The Wizard of Oz* (1939).

## WILLIAM HANNA

**Born:** 14 July 1910 in Melrose, New
Mexico. **Died:** 22 March 2001 at his
home in North Hollywood, California.
● William Hanna was an animator and
production executive who, with Joseph
Barbera, set up Hanna-Barbera in 1957 to
produce such legendary cartoon characters as Huckleberry Hound, Yogi Bear,
Top Cat, The Flintstones, The Jetsons, *ad
infinitum*. Earlier, in collaboration with
Fred Quimby, Hanna and Barbera created
Tom & Jerry at MGM. In all, Hanna
received seven Oscars and eight Emmys.

## JAMES HILL

**Born:** 1 August 1915 in Jeffersonville,
Indiana. **Died:** 11 January 2001 in Santa
Monica, California, from complications
with Alzheimer's disease.

● Producer. **Main films:** *Vera Cruz* (1953), *The Kentuckian*, *Marty* (both 1955), *Trapeze* (1956), *The Sweet Smell of Success* (1957). Forming his own production company (Hecht, Hill and Lancaster) in collaboration with Burt Lancaster, James Hill was largely responsible for the collapse of the old studio system. He was also famous for his promiscuity, an inclination that hardly helped sustain his short-lived marriage to Rita Hayworth (1958-61).

## KEN HUGHES

**Born:** 19 January 1922 in Liverpool. England. **Died:** 28 April 2001 in Panorama City, California, from complications with Alzheimer's disease.

● Director. **Main films:** *Wide Boys* (1952), *The Brain Machine* (1954), *Joe Macbeth* (1955), *The Trials of Oscar Wilde* (1960), *The Small World of Sammy Lee* (1963), *Of Human Bondage* (1964), *Casino Royale* (1967), *Chitty Chitty, Bang Bang* (1968), *Cromwell* (1970), *Alfie Darling* (aka *Oh, Alfie*) (1975), *Sextette* (1978), *Night School* (aka *Terror Eyes*) (1981).

After a string of flops in his later years, Hughes found some success writing episodes of *The Incredible Hulk* for American TV. In 1982 he remarried his first wife, Charlotte Epstein.

## BURT KENNEDY

**Born:** 3 September 1922 in Muskegon, Michigan. **Died:** 15 February 2001 of cancer at his home in Sherman Oaks, California.

● Director. **Main films:** *The War Wagon* (1967) with John Wayne and Kirk Douglas, *The Good Guys and the Bad Guys* (1969) with Robert Mitchum, *Support Your Local Sheriff!* (1969) with James Garner, *Dirty Dingus McGee* (1970) with Frank Sinatra, *The Deserter* (1971), *Hannie Caulder* (1971) with Raquel Welch, *Support Your Local Gunfighter* (1971) with Garner, and *The Train Robbers* (1973) with Wayne and Ann-Margret.

Kennedy also directed a lot for television, including episodes of *The Lawman*,

*The Virginian* and *Magnum P.I* and in 1990 he co-scripted Clint Eastwood's *White Hunter, Black Heart*. In 1996 he was honoured with a star on Palm Springs' Walk of Fame.

## HOWARD W KOCH

**Born:** 11 April 1916 in New York City. **Died:** 16 February 2001 'of natural causes' at his home in Beverly Hills.

● Executive producer and former president of production at Paramount. Main films (as producer): *The Manchurian Candidate* (1962), *None But the Brave* (1965), *The Odd Couple* (1968), *On a Clear Day You Can See Forever* (1970) *Airplane!* (1980) and *Ghost* (1990). In 1989 he was bestowed with the Jean Hersholt Humanitarian Award.

## STANLEY KRAMER

**Born:** 23 September 1913 in New York City. **Died:** 19 February 2001 of pneumonia in Woodland Hills, California.

● Producer and director. **Main films** (as director): *Not as a Stranger* (1955), *The Pride and the Passion* (1957), *The Defiant Ones* (1958), *On the Beach* (1959), *Inherit the Wind* (1960), *Judgment at Nuremberg* (1961), *It's a Mad, Mad, Mad, Mad World* (1963), *Ship of Fools* (1965), *Guess Who's Coming to Dinner* (1967), *The Secret of Santa Vittoria* (1969), *RPM* (1970), *Bless the Beasts and Children* (1971), *Oklahoma Crude* (1973), *The Domino Principle* (1977), *The Runner Stumbles* (1979).

In his later years Kramer tried to mount two major projects, *Beirut* and *Chernobyl*, but failed to find the financing.

## RING LARDNER JR

**Born:** 19 August 1915 in Chicago. **Died:** 31 October 2000.

● Scriptwriter. **Main films:** *A Star is Born* (1937; uncredited), *Woman of the Year* (1942), *Laura* (1944; uncredited), *Cloak and Dagger* (1946), *Forever Amber* (1947), *The Big Night* (1951; uncredited), *A Breath of Scandal* (1960; uncredited), *The Cardinal* (1963; uncredited), *The*

*Cincinnati Kid* (1965), *M\*A\*S\*H* (1970), *The Deadly Trap* (1972, uncredited), *The Greatest* (1977).

A member of the Hollywood Ten, Lardner was, in 1948, sentenced to prison for contempt of Congress for refusing to name names for the House Un-American Activities Committee. It wasn't until the mid-1960s that, for the Steve McQueen vehicle *The Cincinnati Kid*, he finally received his own credit. But it wasn't just Joe McCarthy and his Commie-bashing gang that had a bone to pick with Lardner. According to Robert Altman, 'I never forgave Ring Lardner Jr, the writer of *M\*A\*S\*H*, which I made in 1969. He lost his temper with me because he said I hadn't used a word of his screenplay – which was true. But then he won the Oscar for that screenplay and – this is the dreadful part – accepted it and made a speech, which didn't mention me at all. It was years before I spoke to him again.'

## JACK LEMMON

**Born:** 8 February 1925 in Boston, Massachusetts. **Died:** 28 July 2001, of cancer.

● Actor, director, pianist. A much loved performer equally at home in comedy and drama, Lemmon liked to think of himself as a character actor. In 1955 he won the Oscar for his comic role as Ensign Pulver in

*Mister Roberts* and achieved real stardom in Billy Wilder's *Some Like it Hot* (1959), in a performance that he modelled on his mother. Incidentally, he almost didn't get the part, even though it was written for him, when the studio decided to cast Frank Sinatra instead. He proved his knack for gut-wrenching drama as the alcoholic Joe Clay in *Days of Wine and Roses* (1962) and embarked on a marvellous working relationship with Walter Matthau in *The Fortune Cookie* (1966) and *The Odd Couple* (1968), with whom he worked on a total of 11 films, including *Kotch* (1970), which Lemmon directed. Born in a lift, Lemmon won his second Oscar for the role of the disillusioned businessman Harry Stoner in *Save the Tiger* (1973). The actor continued to take chances in his later career, accepting supporting roles in film, working on Broadway, doing TV movies and even tackling Shakespeare (Marcellus in Branagh's *Hamlet*, 1996). He is survived by the actress Felicia Farr, whom he married in 1962, with Billy Wilder serving as best man.

**The other main films:** 1954: *It Should Happen To You!* (debut; with Judy Holliday). 1955: *My Sister Eileen.* 1957: *Fire Down Below.* 1958: *Bell, Book and Candle.* 1960: *The Apartment* (as C C Baxter, for which he was nominated for an Oscar). 1963: *Irma La Douce.* 1965: *The Great Race.* 1970: *The Out-of-Towners.* 1972: *Avanti!* 1974: *The Front Page* (with Matthau). 1979: *The China Syndrome* (Oscar nomination). 1980: *Tribute* (Oscar nomination). 1981: *Buddy Buddy* (with Matthau). 1982: *Missing* (Oscar nomination). 1986: *That's Life.* 1991: *JFK* (with Matthau). 1992: *The Player* (in which he played the piano); *Glengarry Glen Ross.* 1993: *Short Cuts.* 1993: *Grumpy Old Men* (with Matthau). 1995: *The Grass Harp* (as Dr Morris Ritz; with Matthau). 1996: *Grumpier Old Men* (with Matthau). 1997: *Out to Sea* (with Matthau). 1998: *Neil Simon's The Odd Couple II* (with Matthau). 2000: *The Legend of Bagger Vance* (uncredited; as Old Hardy Greaves).

## JOSEPH H LEWIS

**Born:** 6 April 1900 in New York City.
**Died:** 30 August 2000.
● Director. **Main films:** *Boys of the City* (1940), *That Gang of Mine* (1940), *Pride of the Bowery* (1941), *Invisible Ghost* (1941), *The Mad Doctor of Market Street* (1942), *The Falcon in San Francisco* (1945), *My Name is Julia Ross* (1945), *So Dark the Night* (1946), *The Return of October* (1948), *Gun Crazy, The Undercover Man* (both 1949), *A Lady Without Passport* (1950), *Desperate Search, Retreat, Hell!* (both 1952), *Cry of the Hunted* (1953), *The Big Combo, A Lawless Street* (both 1955), *Seventh Cavalry* (1956), *The Halliday Brand* (1957), *Terror in a Texas Town* (1958).

## JULIE LONDON

**Born:** 26 September 1926 in Santa Clara, California. **Died:** 18 October 2000 in Encino, California, of a stroke.
**Real name:** Julie Peck
Actress, singer. **Main films:** *Nabonga* (aka *The Girl and the Gorilla*) (1944), *The Red House* (1947), *Task Force* (1949), *The Great Man* (1956), *Drango* (1957), *Man of the West, Saddle the Wind, Voice in the Mirror* (all 1958), *The Wonderful Country* (1959), *The Third Voice* (1960), *The George Raft Story* (1961), *Emergency!* (TV) (1970).

## LEO MARKS

**Born:** 24 September 1920 in London.
**Died:** 15 January 2001.
● Scriptwriter. **Main films:** *Cloudburst* (1951), *Peeping Tom* (1960), *Twisted Nerve* (1968), *Sebastian* (1968; story only).

In spite of his fame as the writer of Michael Powell's notorious chiller *Peeping Tom*, Leo Marks was even better established as a cryptographer. He began his career at the age of eight, working in his father's second-hand bookshop, Marks & Co, which later became the subject of Helen Hanff's memoir *84 Charing Cross Road* and the 1987 film thereof. Then, in his early twenties, Marks revolutionised

the security and construction of the ciphers used by the Special Operations Executive and during the Second World War was the department's chief man. He wrote his autobiography, *Between Silk and Cyanide*, in 1998, and divorced his wife of 34 years the year before he died, aged 80.

## CHRISTIAN MARQUAND

**Born:** 15 March 1927 in Marseilles, France. **Died:** 22 November 2000 from complications of Alzheimer's disease, in Paris.
● Actor, director. **Main films as actor:** *Lucretia Borgia* (1953), *Senso* (1954), *And God Created Woman* (1956), *The Longest Day* (1962), *Behold a Pale Horse* (1964), *Victory at Entebbe* (TV), *The Other Side of Midnight* (1977), *Je vous aime* (1980), *Choice of Arms* (1981). **As director:** *Candy* (1968).

## WALTER MATTHAU

**Born:** 1 October 1920 in New York City. **Died:** 1 July 2000 in Santa Monica, California, from a heart attack.
**Real name:** Walter Matuschanskavasky.
● Actor, director. **Main films:** *The Kentuckian* (1955), *Bigger Than Life* (1956), *A Face in the Crowd, Slaughter On Tenth Avenue* (both 1957), *Kid Creole, Onionhead* (both 1958), *Gangster Story* (which he also directed, 1960), *Lonely Are the Brave* (1962),

*Charade* (1963), *Ensign Pulver, Fail-Safe, Goodbye Charlie* (all 1964), *The Mirage* (1965), *The Fortune* (1966), *A Guide For the Married Man* (1967), *The Odd Couple* (1968), *Cactus Flower, Hello, Dolly!* (both 1969), *A New Leaf* (1970), *Kotch, Plaza Suite* (both 1971), *Charley Varrick* (1973), *Earthquake* (billed as Walter Matuschan-skavasky), *The Front Page, The Laughing Policeman, The Taking of Pelham 1-2-3* (all 1974), *The Sunshine Boys* (1975), *The Bad News Bears* (1976), *California Suite, House Calls* (both 1978), *Hopscotch, Little Miss Marker* (both 1980), *Buddy Buddy, First Monday in October* (both 1981), *Pirates* (1986), *The Couch Trip* (1988), *JFK* (1991), *Dennis the Menace, Grumpy Old Men* (both 1993), *IQ* (1994), *The Grass Harp* (1995), *Neil Simon's The Odd Couple 2*(1998), *Hanging Up* (2000).

At his best playing a loveable rogue, Matthau was a master of the sarcastic aside, a talent he turned into a career. Still, he complained that 'A lot of parts I want they give to Robert Redford.' He won the Oscar for *The Fortune Cookie* (as best supporting actor) and received further nominations for *Kotch* and *The Sunshine Boys*. His son is the actor-director Charles Matthau.

## JASON MILLER

**Born:** 22 April 1939 in Long Island City, New York. **Died:** 13 May 2001 in his hometown of Scranton, Pennsylvania, of heart failure.
● Actor, playwright. **Main films as actor**: *The Exorcist* (1973), *The Devil's Advocate* (1977), *The Ninth Configuration* (1979), *Marilyn – The Untold Story* (1980), *The Best Little Girl in the World* (1981), *Monsignor* (1982), *Toy Soldiers* (1984), *Light of Day* (1987), *The Exorcist III* (1990), *Rudy* (1993).

As a playwright, Miller won the Pulitzer Prize and Tony Award for *That Championship Season*; as an actor, he was nominated for an Oscar for his performance as Father Karras in *The Exorcist*. His son is the actor Jason Patric.

## GEORGE MONTGOMERY

**Born:** 29 August 1916 in Brady, Montana. **Died:** 12 December 2000 of heart failure in Rancho Mirage, California.
**Real name:** George Letz.
● Actor and director. **Main films:** *The Cisco Kid and the Lady* (1939), *Riders of the Purple Sage* (1941), *China Girl, Orchestra Wives, Roxie Hart, Ten Gentlemen From West Point* (all 1942), *Bomber's Moon, Coney Island* (both 1943), *Three Little Girls in Blue* (1946), *Belle Starr's Daughter, Lulu Belle* (both 1948), *The Sword of Monte Cristo, Indian Uprising* (both 1951), *Last of the Badmen, Gun Duel in Durango* (both 1957), *The Steel Claw* (1961; also directed), *Samar* (1962; also directed), *From Hell to Borneo* (1964; also directed), *Battle of the Bulge, Satan's Harvest* (both 1965), *Hostile Guns, Bomb at 10:10* (both 1967).

A good friend of the Reagans and the husband of Dinah Shore for 17 years (1943-60), George Montgomery was a virile leading man whose speciality was action films and Westerns. On TV, he starred as cattleman Matt Rockford in NBC's *Cimarron City* (1958-59).

## RICHARD MULLIGAN

**Born:** 13 November 1932 in New York City. **Died:** 26 September 2000 of cancer at his home in Hollywood.
● Comic character actor. **Main films:** *Love With the Proper Stranger* (1963), *One Potato, Two Potato (1964), The Group (1966), The Undefeated (1969), Little Big Man* – as General George Armstrong Custer (1970), *Visit To a Chief's Son* (1974), *The Big Bus* (1976), *Scavenger Hunt* (1979), *SOB* (1981), *Trail of the Pink Panther* – as Clouseau Sr (1982), *Micki + Maude, Teachers* (both 1984), *A Fine Mess* (1986*), Neil Simon's London Suite* (1996; for TV). On television, he became enormously popular as Burt Campbell in the controversial comedy serial *Soap*.

## JACK NITZSCHE

**Born:** 22 April 1937 in Chicago.

**Died:** 25 August 2000.
**Real name:** Bernard Nitzsche.
● Composer. **Main films:** *Village of the Giants* (1965), *Performance* (1970), *The Exorcist* (1973), *One Flew Over the Cuckoo's Nest* (1975), *Blue Collar* (1978), *Hardcore* (1979), *Cruising* (1980), *Cutter's Way* (1981), *An Officer and a Gentleman* (1982), *Starman* (1984), *The Jewel of the Nile* (1985), *Stand by Me, 9_ Weeks* (both 1986), *The Seventh Sign* (1988), *Revenge, Mermaids* (both 1990), *The Crossing Guard* (1994).

Besides his work as a film composer, Nitzsche served as an arranger and pianist for The Rolling Stones, toured with Neil Young, collaborated with Sonny Bono on a number of records (they co-wrote The Searchers' hit 'Needles and Pins') and prospered as a songwriter. He was also a major presence behind the likes of Doris Day, Frankie Laine, The Monkees, Bobby Darin and Marianne Faithfull.

## VIRGINIA O'BRIEN

**Born:** 18 April 1919 in Los Angeles. **Died:** 18 January 2001 at the Motion Picture & Television Hospital in Woodland Hills, California.
● Singer-comedienne. **Main films:** *Hullaballoo* (1940), *The Big Store* (1941; in which she sang 'Rockabye Baby' to the Marx Brothers); *Thousands Cheer* (1943), *Dubarry Was a Lady* (1944), *The Harvey Girls* (1946), *Ziegfeld Follies* (1946), *Francis in the Navy* (1955).

Such was O'Brien's deadpan delivery in musicals of the 1940s that Ms O'Brien acquired the nickname Miss Frozen Face. She was married to the actor Kirk Alyn (1942-55) and retired from the cinema after her divorce. However, she made a brief comeback in the 1976 Disney comedy *Gus*.

## CARROLL O'CONNOR

**Born:** 25 August 1925 in the Bronx, New York City. **Died:** 21 June 2001 of a heart attack (brought on by complications with diabetes), in Culver

City, California.

● Actor. **Main films:** *A Fever in the Blood* (1961), *Lonely Are the Brave* (1962), *Cleopatra* (1963), *In Harm's Way* (1965), *Hawaii, Not With My Wife, You Don't!* (both 1966), *Point Blank, Waterhole #3* (both 1967), *Death of a Gunfighter, Marlowe* (both 1969), *Kelly's Heroes, Doctors' Wives* (both 1970), *Return to Me* (2000).

His film work notwithstanding, O'Connor will be best remembered for his role on TV as the outspoken bigot Archie Bunker (modelled on Warren Mitchell's Alf Garnett) in CBS TV's *All in the Family* (1971-79) and *Archie Bunker's Place* (1979-83). He also had some success as Bill Gillespie, the Mississippi Chief of Police in the TV crime show *In the Heat of the Night* (1988-94). Later TV work included *Mad About You* (as the father of Helen Hunt) and *Party of Five*.

## JOSEPH O'CONOR

**Born:** 14 February 1916 in Dublin.
**Died:** 21 January 2001 in London, England.

● **Main films:** *Gorgo* (1960*)*, *Crooks in Cloisters* (1963), *The Gorgon* (1964), *Oliver!* (1968), *Doomwatch* (1972), *Penny Gold* (1973), *The Black Windmill* (1974).

Joseph O'Conor was predominantly a much-loved stage actor, with a dignified, benevolent presence, given his big break by Donald Wolfit, who cast him as Hamlet. O'Conor also wrote six plays, directed a number of successful repertory and festival productions and was a popular figure on television as Old Jolyon in the BBC's *The Forsyte Saga* (1967).

## GARY OLSEN

**Born:** 3 November 1957 in London.
**Died:** 13 September 2000 in Australia.

● Actor. **Main films:** *Party Party* (1982), *The Cook, The Thief, His Wife and Her Lover* (1989), *Up 'n' Under* (1997), *24 Hours in London* (1999).

In spite of forays into theatre and film, Olsen was best known for his role as Ben Porter, the layabout plumber in the British sitcom *2 Point 4 Children*.

## JEAN PETERS

**Born:** 15 October 1926 in Canton, Ohio. **Died:** 13 October 2000 in Carlsbad, California, of leukaemia.
**Real name:** Elizabeth Jean Peters.

● Actress. **Main films:** *Captain From Castille* (1947), *Deep Waters* (1948), *Love That Brute* (1950), *As Young As You Feel* (1951), *Viva Zapata!, O Henry's Full House* (both 1952), *Niagara, Pickup On South Street, Blueprint For Murder* (all 1953), *Three Coins in the Fountain, Apache, Broken Lance* (all 1954), *A Man Called Peter* (1955), *Winesburg, Ohio* (TV movie) (1973), *Peter and Paul* (TV movie) (1981).

Despite her standing as an actress and a fair number of film credits, Peters remains best known for her marriage to Howard Hughes, whom she secretly wed in 1957 prior to retiring from the screen. After their divorce in 1971, she resumed her career, appearing mainly in TV.

## JUSTIN PIERCE

**Born:** 21 March 1975 in London, England. **Died:** 10 July 2000, by hanging himself in a room at the Bellagio Hotel, Las Vegas.

● Actor. **Main films:** *A Brother's Kiss* (1997), *Wild Horses* (1998), *The Big Tease* (1999), *Next Friday, BlackMale* (both 2000).

Pierce's main to claim to fame was as the star of Larry Clark's controversial *Kids* (1995) and as the ex-boyfriend of Chloë Sevigny. His last film was *Pigeonholed* with Chris Noth and Rosanna Arquette.

## NYREE DAWN PORTER

**Born:** 22 January 1936 in Napier, New Zealand. **Died:** 10 April 2001 in London from unreported causes.
**Real name:** Ngaire (meaning 'little white star-shaped flower').

● Actress. **Main films:** *Part-Time Wife* (1961), *Live Now – Pay Later* (1962), *The Cracksman, Two Left Feet* (both 1963), *Jane Eyre* (1970), *The House That Dripped Blood* (1971), *From Beyond the Grave* (1973).

In Britain, Porter was forever associated with the part of the glacial Irene Forsyte, which she played in the BBC's phenomenally popular *The Forsyte Saga* (1967).

## ANTHONY QUINN

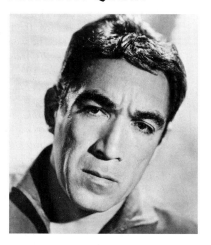

**Born:** 21 April 1915 in Chihuahua, Mexico. **Died:** 3 June 2001 of respiratory failure, in Boston, Massachusetts.
**Real name:** Antonio Quiñones.

● Actor. **Complete filmography:** *Parole* (bit-part), *The Plainsman, The Milky Way, Sworn Enemy, Night Waitress* (all 1936), *Swing High, Swing Low, Waikiki Wedding, Daughter of Shanghai* (UK: *Daughter of the Orient*), *Last Train from Madrid, Partners in Crime* (all 1937), *The Buccaneer, Tip Off Girls, Dangerous To Know, Bulldog Drummond in Africa, Hunted Men, King of Alcatraz* (UK: *King of the Alcatraz*) (all 1938), *Island of Lost Men, King of Chinatown, Union Pacific, Television Spy* (all 1939), *Road to Singapore, Parole Fixer, Emergency Squad, City for Conquest, The Ghost Breakers* (all 1940), *Thieves Fall Out, Knockout, Texas Rangers Ride Again, Blood and Sand, Bullets for O'Hara, They Died With Their Boots On, The Perfect Snob* (all 1941), *The Black Swan, Road to Morocco, The Ox-Bow Incident* (UK: *Strange Incident*),

*Larceny Inc* (all 1942), *Guadalcanal Diary* (1943), *Buffalo Bill, Roger Touhy, Gangster* (UK: *The Last Gangster*), *Ladies of Washington, Irish Eyes Are Smiling* (all 1944), *Where Do We Go From Here?, China Sky, Back to Bataan* (all 1945). *California, The Imperfect Lady* (UK: *Mrs Loring's Secret*) (both 1946), *Sinbad the Sailor, Black Gold, Tycoon* (all 1947), *The Brave Bulls, Mask of the Avenger* (both 1951), *Viva Zapata!* (for which he won his first Oscar), *The World In His Arms, The Brigand, Against All Flags* (all 1952), *City Beneath the Sea, Seminole, Ride, Vaquero!, East of Sumatra, Blowing Wild, Ulysses, Donne proibite* (UK: *Forbidden Women*, US: *Angels of Darkness*), *Cavalleria Rusticana* (all 1953), *Attila, La Strada, The Long Wait, Il piu comico spettacolo del mondo* (all 1954), *The Magnificent Matador* (UK: *The Brave and the Beautiful*), *The Naked Street, Seven Cities of Gold* (all 1955), *The Man from Del Rio, Lust For Life* (for which he won his second Oscar), *The Wild Party* (all 1956), *The River's Edge, The Ride Back, The Hunchback of Notre Dame, Wild is the Wind* (Oscar nomination) (all 1957), *The Buccaneer* (directed only), *Hot Spell* (both 1958), *The Black Orchid, Last Train From Gun Hill, Warlock, The Savage Innocents* (all 1959), *Heller In Pink Tights, Portrait in Black* (both 1960), *The Guns of Navarone* (1961), *Barabbas, Requiem for a Heavyweight* (UK: *Blood Money*), *Lawrence of Arabia* (all 1962), *The Fabulous Adventures of Marco Polo* (UK: *Marco the Magnificent*), *Behold a Pale Horse, The Visit, Zorba the Greek* (Oscar nomination) (all 1964), *A High Wind in Jamaica* (1965), *Lost Command* (1966), *The Rover, The 25th Hour, The Happening* (all 1967), *Guns for San Sebastian, The Shoes of the Fisherman, The Magus* (all 1968), *The Secret of Santa Vittoria, A Dream of Kings, A Walk in the Spring Rain* (all 1969), *R.P.M., Flap* (UK: *The Last Warrior*) (both 1970), *The City* (TV), *Forbidden Knowledge* (TV) (both 1971), *Across*

*110th Street, The Voice of La Raza* (both 1972), *Los amigos* (UK/US: *Deaf Smith and Johnny Ears*), *The Don is Dead* (all 1973), *The Marseilles Contract* (US: *The Destructors*) (1974), *Bluff, L'eredita Ferramonti* (UK: *The Inheritance*) (both 1975), *Tigers Don't Cry, The Message* (both 1976), *The Greek Tycoon, Caravans, The Children of Sanchez, The Passage* (all 1978), *Lion of the Desert* (aka *Omar Mukhtar – Lion of the Desert*), *The Contender* (both 1980), *High Risk, The Salamander, Bon Appetit, The Dream of Tangier* (all 1981), *Roma Regina, Valentina* (both 1982), *1919 – cronica del Alba* (1983), *The Last Days of Pompeii* (1984), *Isola del tesoro* (1986), *Stradivarius, Tough Guys in Marseilles, A Man of Passion* (all 1988), *Revenge* (1989), *The Old Man and the Sea* (TV), *Ghosts Can't Do It, The Actor* (all 1990), *Jungle Fever, Mobsters, Only the Lonely* (1991), *Last Action Hero, Il mago* (both 1993), *This Can't Be Love* (TV), with Katharine Hepburn, *Somebody to Love* (both 1994), *A Walk in the Clouds, Hercules and the Amazon Woman* (both 1995), *Seven Servants, Il sindaco* (aka *The Mayor*, *Gotti* (TV) (all 1996), *For Love and State, Oriundi* (both 1999), *Avenging Angelo* (2001).

Adept at playing blustering Arabs, cold-blooded Mexicans and warm-hearted peasants, Quinn was a larger-than-life character actor with star charisma to spare. Best known for his immortal performance as *Zorba the Greek*, he won his two Oscars in supporting roles, as Marlon Brando's revolutionary brother Eufemio in *Viva Zapata!* and as Gauguin to Kirk Douglas' Van Gogh in *Lust for Life*. The son of a half-Irish father and Mexican mother (of Aztec descent), he became an actor after overcoming a speech impediment and had his first speaking part on film in Cecil B de Mille's *The Plainsman*. A year later, he married the director's daughter, Katherine. The couple remained together for 28 years, when Quinn wed Iolanda

Addolori, a costume designer he had met on the set of *Barabbas*. Then, in March 1995, Iolanda filed for separation when the actor refused to keep his affair with his secretary, Kathy Bevin, secret. By the latter, who became his third wife in 1997, he sired his eleventh child, Patricia. He wrote two autobiographies, *The Original Sin* and *Suddenly Sunset*, and devoted most of his last years to painting and sculpture. It was Quinn who once noted that 'In Europe an actor is an artist; in Hollywood, if he isn't working, he's a bum.'

## BEAH RICHARDS

**Born:** 12 July 1920 in Vicksburg, Mississippi. **Died:** 14 September 2000 of emphysema in Vicksburg, Mississippi.
● Character actress. **Main films:** *The Mugger* (1958), *The Miracle Worker* (1962), *Gone Are the Days* (1963), *Guess Who's Coming to Dinner, Hurry Sundown, In the Heat of the Night* (all 1967), *The Biscuit Eater* (1972), *Mahogany* (1975), *As Summers Die* (1986), *Drugstore Cowboy, Homer and Eddie* (both 1989), *Out of Darkness* (TV; 1994), *Beloved* (1998).

## MICHAEL RITCHIE

**Born:** 28 November 1938 in Waukesha, Wisconsin. **Died:** 16 April 2001 in New York from complications with prostate cancer.
● Director. **Main films:** *Downhill Racer* (1969), *The Candidate* (1972), both with Robert Redford, *Prime Cut* (1972), *Smile* (1975), *The Bad News Bears* (1976), *Semi-Tough* (1977), *An Almost Perfect Affair* (1979), *Divine Madness* (1980), *The Island* (1980), *Fletch, Wildcats* (both 1985), *The Golden Child* (1986), *Diggstown* (aka *Midnight Sting*),(1992), *The Positively True Adventures of the Alleged Texas Cheerleader-Murdering Mom* (1993, for TV), *A Simple Wish* (1997).

In his later years, Ritchie concentrated on more interesting fare for TV and was working on a documentary about Albert Einstein when he died.

## JASON ROBARDS

**Born:** 26 July 1922 in Chicago.
**Died:** 26 December 2000 at Bridgeport Hospital in Fairfield, Connecticut.
● Actor. **Main film appearances:** *The Journey* (1959), *By Love Possessed* (1961), Dick Diver in *Tender is the Night*, Jamie Tyrone in *Long Day's Journey Into Night* (both 1962), George S Kaufman in *Act One* (1963), *A Thousand Clowns* (1965), Al Capone in *The St Valentine's Day Massacre*, Doc Holliday in *Hour of the Gun* (both 1967), *Divorce American Style* (1967), *The Night They Raided Minsky's*, *Once Upon a Time in the West* (both 1968), General Walter C Short in *Tora! Tora! Tora!*, *The Ballad of Cable Hogue*, Brutus in *Julius Caesar* (all 1970), Lew Wallace in *Pat Garrett and Billy the Kid* (1973), *All the President's Men* (1976), *Julia* (1976), *Raise the Titanic!*, Howard Hughes in *Melvin and Howard* (both 1980), *Something Wicked This Way Comes*, *The Day After* for TV (both 1983), *Square Dance* (1987), *The Good Mother* (1988), *Black Rainbow*, *Reunion*, *Parenthood* (all 1989), *Quick Change* (1990), *Philadelphia* (1993), *The Paper* (1994), *Crimson Tide* (1995), *A Thousand Acres* (1997), *Enemy of the State*, *Beloved* (both 1998).

In 1976 Robards won the Oscar for Best Supporting Actor in *All the President's Men* (as Ben Bradlee, editor of *The Washington Post*), followed a year later by a second Academy Award in the same category for *Julia* (in which he played the novelist and short-story writer Dashiell Hammett). His very last film was Paul Thomas Anderson's outstanding *Magnolia*, in which he played a TV tycoon dying of cancer. Robards was also a distinguished stage actor who, in 1956, made a huge impact with two Eugene O'Neill productions on Broadway, *The Iceman Cometh* and *Long Day's Journey Into Night*.

## CLAUDE SAUTET

**Born:** Montrouge, Paris.
**Died:** 22 July 2000 of liver cancer.
● Film director. **Main films:** *The Big Risk* (1960), *The Things of Life* (1969), *César and Rosalie* (1972), *Vincent, François, Paul and the Others* (1974), *Mado* (1976), *Une Histoire simple* (1978), *Un Coeur en hiver* (1992), *Les Enfants de Lumière* (1995), *Nelly & Monsieur Arnaud* (1995).

## HARRY SECOMBE

**Born:** 8 September 1921 in Swansea, South Wales. **Died:** 11 April 2001 of prostate cancer in Guildford, Surrey.
● Actor, comedian, Goon, singer, tireless charity worker. **Main films:** *Hocus Pocus* (1948), *Down Among the Z-Men* (1952), *Forces' Sweetheart* (1953), *Svengali* (1954), *Jet Storm* (1959), *Oliver!* (1968), *The Bed Sitting Room* (1969), *Doctor in Trouble*, *Song of Norway* (both 1970), *Sunstruck* (1972).

## JOAN SIMS

**Born:** 9 May 1930 in Laindon, Essex.
**Died:** 28 June 2001.
**Real name:** Irene Joan Marion Sims.
● Character actress, comedienne. **Main films:** *Colonel March Investigates*, *The Square Ring*, *Trouble in Store*, *Will Any Gentleman?* (all 1953), *The Young Lovers* (1954), *As Long As They're Happy* (1955), *Dry Rot* (1956), *Carry On Admiral* (1957), then, starting with *Carry On Sergeant* in 1958, she appeared in a total of 24 of the official *Carry On* films, culminating with *Carry On Emmanuelle* in 1978. Paid £2500 for the first film, she never received a rise in 21 years.

Sims' autobiography, *High Spirits*, was published in 2000 and revealed a number of startling facts, not least that the homosexual Kenneth Williams proposed marriage to her and that she enjoyed a prolonged but chaste affair with Tyrone Power.

## PIOTR SOBOCINSKI

**Born:** 3 February 1958 in Lodz, Poland.
**Died:** 26 March 2001 of a heart attack in Vancouver.
● Cinematographer. **Main films:** *Decalogue*, *Three Colours Red*, *Marvin's Room*, *Ransom* (all 1996), *Twilight*. Sobocinski was shooting Luis Mandoki's *Angel Eyes*, with Jennifer Lopez, when he died. He was the son of cinematographer Witold Sobocinski.

## ANN SOTHERN

**Born:** 22 January 1909 in Valley City, North Dakota. **Died:** 15 March 2001 of heart failure at her home in Ketchum, Idaho.
**Real name:** Harriette Lake.
● Actress. **Main films:** *Let's Fall in Love*, *The Party's Over*, *Kid Millions* (all 1934), *Folies Bergère* (1935), *Super Sleuth* (1937), *Maisie* (1939), *Congo Maisie* (1940), *Undercover Maisie* (1947), *Lady Be Good* (1941), *Panama Hattie* (1942), *Cry Havoc* (1943), *A Letter to Three Wives* (1949), *Lady in a Cage*, *The Best Man* (both 1964), *Crazy Mama* (1975), *The Manitou* (1978). Her last film was Lindsay Anderson's *The Whales of August* (1987) for which she received an Oscar nomination.

Sothern also had some success on TV, starring in the sitcoms *Private Secretary* (1953-57) and *The Ann Sothern Show* (1958-61). She was married to the actor Robert Sterling (1943-49). Their daughter, Tisha Sterling, is also an actress and played her mother as a younger woman in *The Whales of August*.

## ANTHONY STEEL

**Born:** 21 March 1919 in London.
**Died:** 21 March 2001.

● Actor. **Main films:** *Saraband for Dead Lovers* (1948), *The Mudlark, The Wooden Horse* (both 1950), *Laughter in Paradise, Where No Vultures Fly, Another Man's Poison* (all 1951), *The Planter's Wife, Emergency Call* (both 1952), *Albert RN, The Malta Story, The Master of Ballantrae* (all 1953), *Out of the Clouds, The Sea Shall Not Have Them, West of Zanzibar* (all 1954), *Passage Home, Storm over the Nile* (both 1955), *The Black Tent, Checkpoint* (both 1956), *Valerie* (1957), *Honeymoon* (1959), *Tiger of the Seven Seas* (1962), *Anzio* (1968), *Story of O* (1975), *Hardcore, Let's Get Laid* (both 1977), *The World is Full of Married Men* (1979), *The Mirror Crack'd, The Monster Club* (both 1980).

For a time in the 1950s, Steel was up there with Dirk Bogarde as the Rank Organisation's most highly paid heart-throb. His career seemed to take a turn for the worse, however, after his tempestuous marriage to blonde bombshell Anita Ekberg (1956-59).

## BEATRICE STRAIGHT

**Born:** 2 August 1916 in Old Westbury, New York. **Died:** 7 April 2001 in Los Angeles.

● Actress. **Main films:** *Patterns* (1956), *The Silken Affair* (1957), *The Nun's Story* (1959), *The Young Lovers* (1964), *Network* (1976), *The Face of a Stranger* (1978), *Sidney Sheldon's Bloodline, The Promise* (both 1979), *The Formula* (1980), *Endless Love* (1981), *Poltergeist* (1982), *Two of a Kind* (1983), *Chiller* (1985), *Power* (1986), *Deceived* (1991).

Beatrice Straight was the cousin of Gloria Vanderbilt, the former wife of the director Sidney Lumet. When Lumet cast the actress as William Holden's cuckolded wife in *Network*, Ms Straight sniffed, 'It's a very short part – if you blink, you miss it.' Nevertheless, it landed her the Oscar for Best Supporting Actress.

## HIROSHI TESHIGAWARA

**Born**: 28 January 1927 in Tokyo, Japan.
**Died**: 14 April 2001 of lymphatic leukaemia, in Tokyo.

● Teshigawara was an acclaimed director whose poignant, visually audacious *Woman of the Dunes* (1964) won the jury prize at Cannes and whose *Rikyu* (1989) received the artistic prize at the Montreal Film Festival. He directed his last film, *Basara, the Princess Goh,* in 1992. Teshigawara was also a celebrated flower arranger and potter.

## RALPH THOMAS

**Born**: 10 August 1915 in Hull, Yorkshire. **Died**: 17 March 2001 in London after a long illness.

● Director. **Main films:** *The Clouded Yellow* (1950), *Appointment With Venus* (1951), *Doctor in the House* (1954), *Above Us the Waves* (1955), *The Iron Petticoat* (1956), *Campbell's Kingdom* (1957), *A Tale of Two Cities, The Wind Cannot Read* (both 1958), *Hot Enough For June* (1964) and *Percy* (1971).

## GWEN VERDON

**Born**: 13 January 1926 in Culver City, California. **Died**: 18 October 2000 of natural causes in Woodstock, Vermont.

● Legendary dancer, singer and actress, best known for her reign on Broadway; married to the director-choreographer Bob Fosse.

**Main films:** *On the Riviera, David and Bathsheba* (both 1951), *The Merry Widow* (1952), *The Farmer Takes a Wife* (1953), *Damn Yankees* (1958), *Legs* (TV) (1983), *The Cotton Club* (1984), *Cocoon* (1985), *Nadine* (1987), *Cocoon: The Return* (1988), *Alice* (1990), *Marvin's Room* (1996), *Best Friends for Life* (1998), *Walking Across Egypt* (1999).

## SACHA VIERNY

**Born:** 10 August 1919 in Bois-le-roi, outside Paris, France.
**Died:** 15 May 2001.

● Cinematographer. **Main films:** *Hiroshima, Mon Amour* (1959), *Last Year at Marienbad* (1961), *Muriel* (1963), *Belle de Jour* (1966), *Stavisky* (1974), *Mon Oncle d'Amerique* (1980), *The Draughtsman's Contract* (1982), *Drowning by Numbers* (1988), *The Cook, The Thief, His Wife and Her Lover* (1989), *Prospero's Books* (1991), *The Baby of Macon* (1993), *The Pillow Book* (1996), *The Man Who Cried* (2000).

## RAY WALSTON

**Born:** 22 November 1917 in New Orleans. **Died:** 1 January 2001 of natural causes at his home in Beverly Hills, California.

● Character actor. **Main films:** *Kiss Them For Me* (1957), *Damn Yankees, South Pacific* (both 1958), *Say One For Me* (1959), *The Apartment* (1960), *Who's Minding the Store?* (1963), *Kiss Me Stupid* (1964), *Caprice* (1967), *Paint Your Wagon* (1969) as Mad Jack Duncan, *The Sting* (1973), *Silver Streak* (1976), *Popeye* (1980) as Poopdeck Pappy, *Of Mice and Men, The Player* (both 1992).

Walston, who was a hit on TV as an extraterrestrial visitor in *My Favorite Martian* (a role he reprised for the 1999 film version), won an Emmy for playing Judge Bone in CBS TV's *Picket Fences*. He also took home a Tony for playing the Devil in the 1955 musical *Damn Yankees*.

## AL WAXMAN

**Born:** 2 March 1935 in Toronto, Canada. **Died:** 18 January 2001 in Toronto, following complications after heart surgery.

● Character actor. **Main films:** *Sunday in the Country* (1975), *Atlantic City* (1980), *Class of 1984* (1982), *Switching Channels* (1987), *I Still Dream of Jeannie* (1991), *Bogus* (1996), *The Hurricane* (1999).

Outside the cinema, Waxman was best known as Lieutenant Bert Samuels, the tough-talking boss on TV's *Cagney & Lacey*. In 1997 he was honoured with the Order of Canada and two years later penned his autobiography, *That's What I Am.*

## KEN WESTON

**Born:** 30 May 1947. **Died:** 13 April 2001 from cancer.

● Sound editor. **Main films:** *Jack and Sarah* (1995), *Evita* (for which he received an Oscar nomination), *The Parent Trap*, *Angela's Ashes*, *Up at the Villa*, *Shiner*.

Only the third British sound man to win an Oscar, Weston was too ill to receive his award for *Gladiator*. He married his second wife, Janice Warnes, just three months before his death.

## SAM WIESENTHAL

**Born:** 26 January 1909 in New York City. **Died:** 11 February 2001 at the Motion Picture & Television Hospital in Woodland Hills, California.

● Producer and studio executive. Wiesenthal worked in the Manhattan offices of Universal Pictures while still at school and went on to become production manager of the studio in Hollywood. It was there that, with vice president Carl Laemmle Jr, he helped launch such pictures as *All Quiet On the Western Front* (1930), *Dracula* and *Frankenstein* (both 1931). Later, he took on top positions at Goldwyn and RKO.

## MICHAEL WILLIAMS

**Born:** 9 July 1935 in Manchester. **Died:** 12 January 2001 of cancer.

● Character actor. **Main films:** *Marat/Sade* (1966), *Dead Cert* (1974), *Educating Rita* (1982), *Enigma* (1982), *Henry V* (1990), *Tea With Mussolini* (1999).

In Britain, Williams was recognised as a particularly fine stage actor and gained even greater popularity on the small screen as a deft comic actor, notching up such TV credits as *Elizabeth R, The Comedy of Errors, Love in a Cold Climate, September Song, Conjugal Rights* and *A Dance To the Music of Time*. Perhaps best of all, he was known as the husband of Judi Dench, with whom he appeared in the enormously successful sitcom *A Fine Romance* (1980-82).

## TOBY WING

**Born:** 14 July 1915 near Richmond, Virginia. **Died:** 22 March 2001 at home in Mathews, Virginia.

**Real name:** Martha Virginia Wing.

● Actress. **Main films:** *Palmy Days* (1931), *The Kid from Spain* (1932), *Gold Diggers of 1933*, *42nd Street* (both 1933), *Kiss and Make Up*, *Search for Beauty*, *School for Girls*, *Come On Marines*, *Murder at the Vanities* (all 1934), *Rhythm on the Roof* (1935), *Rhythmitis* (1936), *Women Men Marry* (1937), *Mr Boggs Steps Out* (1938), *The Marines Come Thru* (1943).

The original Goldwyn Girl and a protégée of Busby Berkeley, Toby Wing was the archetypal platinum blonde bombshell of the 1930s. She was touted by Paramount as receiving more fan mail than either Marlene Dietrich or Claudette Colbert, was romanced by Maurice Chevalier and more or less retired on her marriage to aviator Dick Merrill in 1938.

## LORETTA YOUNG

**Born:** 6 January 1912 in Salt Lake City, Utah. **Died:** 12 August 2000 in Los Angeles, from ovarian cancer.

**Real name:** Gretchen Michaela Young.

● Actress. **Main films:** *Sweet Kitty Bellairs* (1916), *The Only Way* (1917), *Naughty But Nice* (1927), *Laugh, Clown,*

*Laugh* (1928), *The Show of Shows* (1929), *The Devil to Pay* (1930), *Platinum Blonde* (1931), *Taxi!* (1932), *A Man's Castle*, *Zoo in Budapest* (both 1933), *Call of the Wild*, *The Crusades* (both 1935), *Ramona* (1936), *Four Men and a Prayer*, *Suez* (both 1938), *The Story of Alexander Graham Bell* (1939), *A Night to Remember* (1942), *China* (1943), *The Stranger* (1946), *The Farmer's Daughter* (1947), *The Accused* (1948), *Come to the Stable* (1949), *It Happens Every Thursday* (1953), *The Immaculate Road* (1960).

One of four daughters who sporadically appeared in small bits in silents, 'Gretchen' nipped off for a convent education before returning to the silver screen with a vengeance in 1927, replacing her sister Polly Ann Young in *Naughty But Nice*. She won an Oscar for her role as a Swedish woman running for Congress in H C Potter's *The Farmer's Daughter*, and was nominated for *Come to the Stable*. She was also extremely successful on TV, starring in *The Loretta Young Show* for nine years (1954-63), winning herself three Emmys into the bargain. Following marriages to the actor Grant Withers and producer Tom Lewis, she wed the Oscar-winning costume designer Jean-Louis in 1993; he died four years later. Her autobiography, *The Things I Had to Learn*, was published in 1962.

# Index

Names of films, videos and books appear in the index in *italics*. Page references for illustrations appear in **BOLD**. The last separate word of an individual's name is used as the index entry. Thus Robert De Niro appears within 'N' as Niro, Robert De